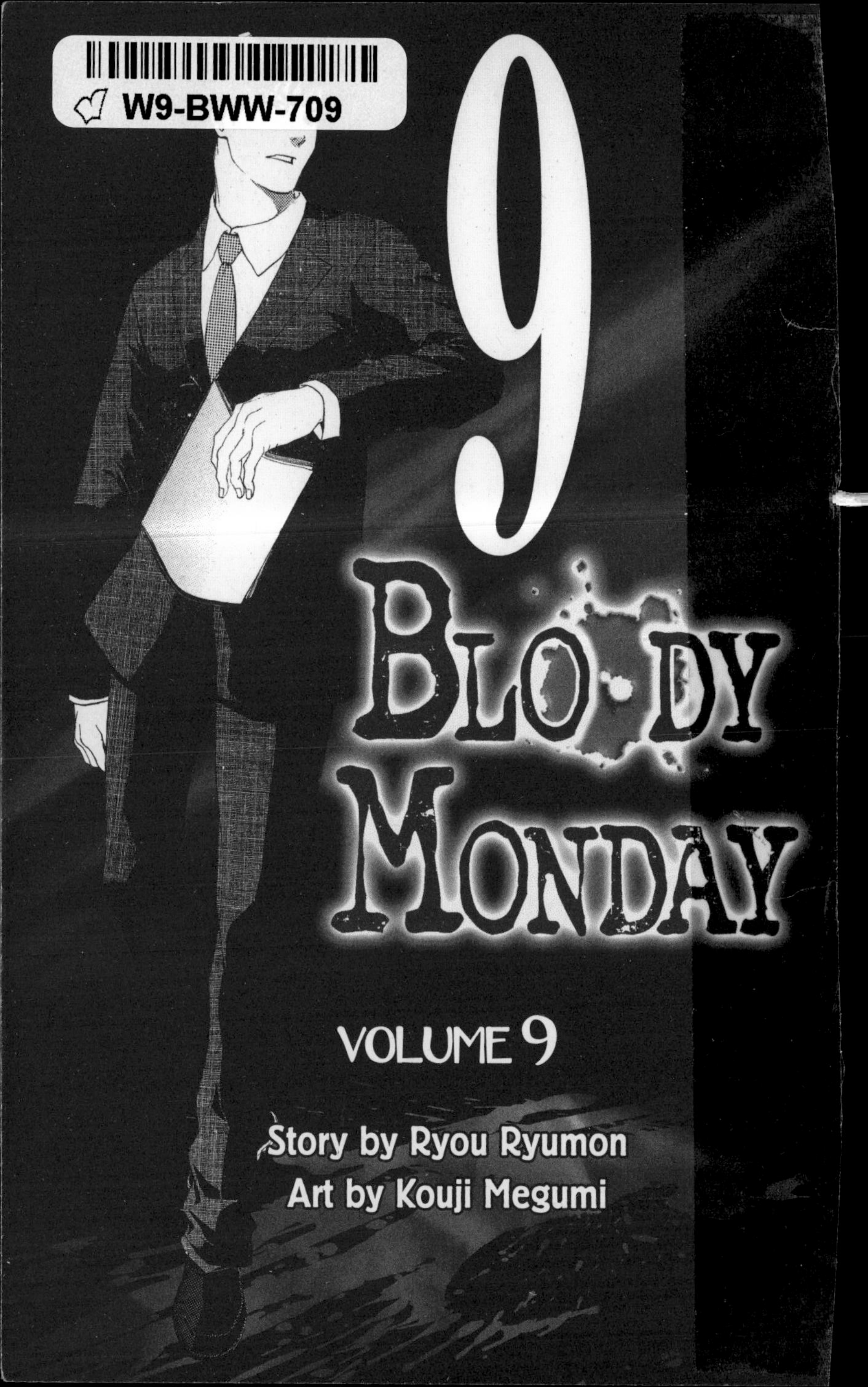
9
BLOODY MONDAY
VOLUME 9
Story by Ryou Ryumon
Art by Kouji Megumi

BLOODY MONDAY

Character Introductions

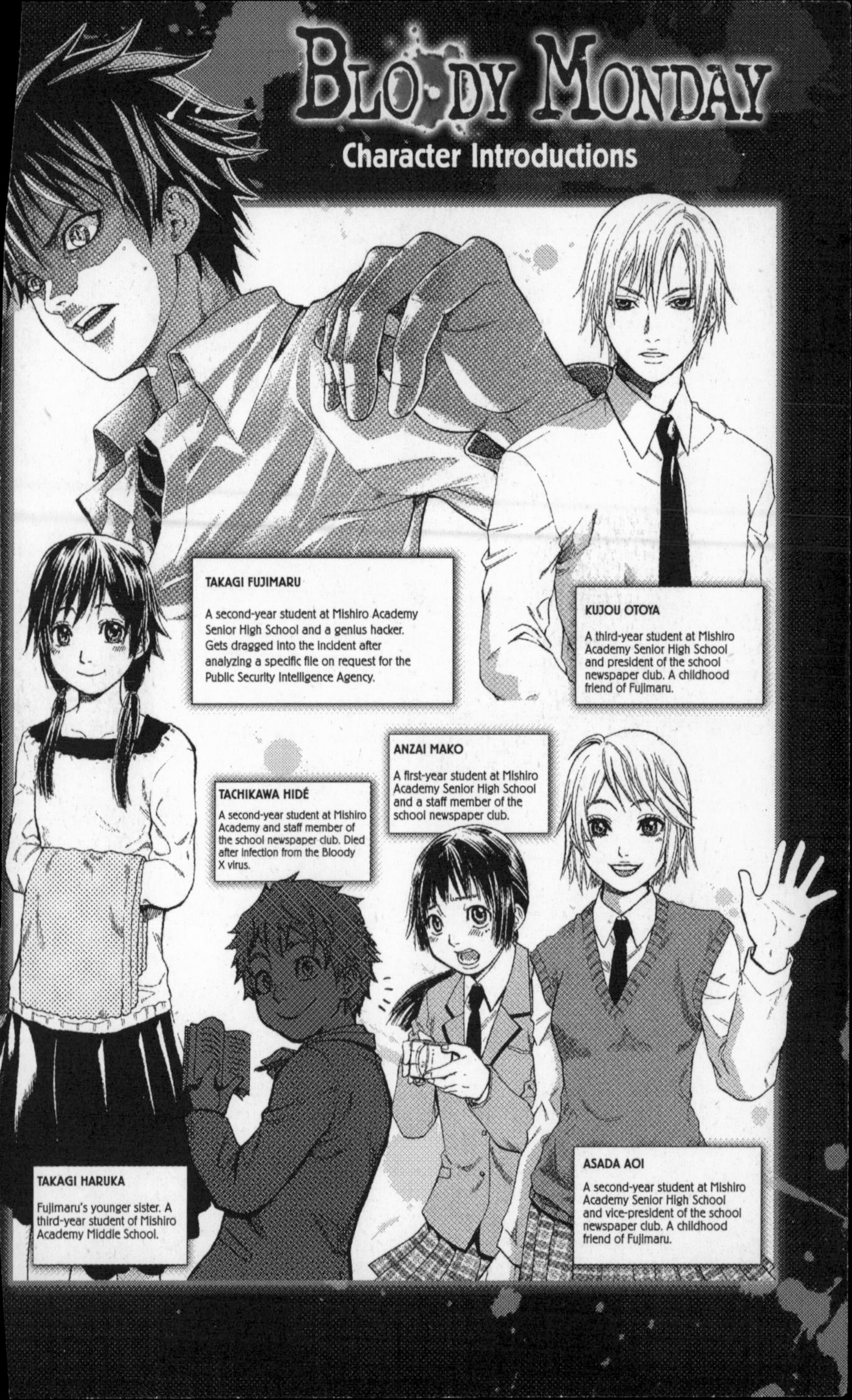

TAKAGI FUJIMARU

A second-year student at Mishiro Academy Senior High School and a genius hacker. Gets dragged into the incident after analyzing a specific file on request for the Public Security Intelligence Agency.

KUJOU OTOYA

A third-year student at Mishiro Academy Senior High School and president of the school newspaper club. A childhood friend of Fujimaru.

ANZAI MAKO

A first-year student at Mishiro Academy Senior High School and a staff member of the school newspaper club.

TACHIKAWA HIDÉ

A second-year student at Mishiro Academy and staff member of the school newspaper club. Died after infection from the Bloody X virus.

TAKAGI HARUKA

Fujimaru's younger sister. A third-year student of Mishiro Academy Middle School.

ASADA AOI

A second-year student at Mishiro Academy Senior High School and vice-president of the school newspaper club. A childhood friend of Fujimaru.

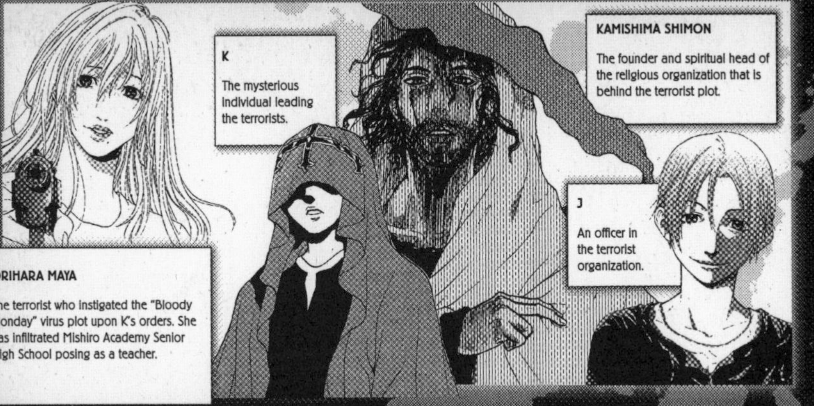
KAMISHIMA SHIMON
The founder and spiritual head of the religious organization that is behind the terrorist plot.
K
The mysterious individual leading the terrorists.
J
An officer in the terrorist organization.
ORIHARA MAYA
The terrorist who instigated the "Bloody Monday" virus plot upon K's orders. She has infiltrated Mishiro Academy Senior High School posing as a teacher.

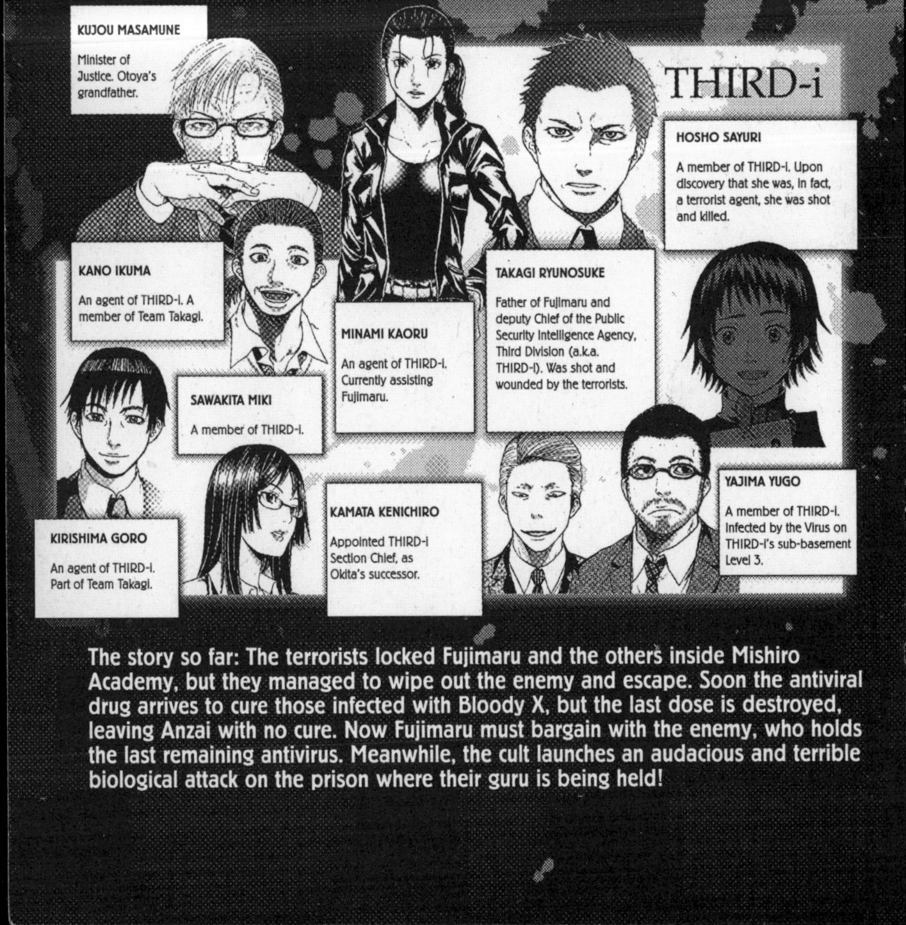
THIRD-i
KUJOU MASAMUNE
Minister of Justice. Otoya's grandfather.
HOSHO SAYURI
A member of THIRD-i. Upon discovery that she was, in fact, a terrorist agent, she was shot and killed.
TAKAGI RYUNOSUKE
Father of Fujimaru and deputy Chief of the Public Security Intelligence Agency, Third Division (a.k.a. THIRD-i). Was shot and wounded by the terrorists.
MINAMI KAORU
An agent of THIRD-i. Currently assisting Fujimaru.
KANO IKUMA
An agent of THIRD-i. A member of Team Takagi.
SAWAKITA MIKI
A member of THIRD-i.
YAJIMA YUGO
A member of THIRD-i. Infected by the Virus on THIRD-i's sub-basement Level 3.
KAMATA KENICHIRO
Appointed THIRD-i Section Chief, as Okita's successor.
KIRISHIMA GORO
An agent of THIRD-i. Part of Team Takagi.

The story so far: The terrorists locked Fujimaru and the others inside Mishiro Academy, but they managed to wipe out the enemy and escape. Soon the antiviral drug arrives to cure those infected with Bloody X, but the last dose is destroyed, leaving Anzai with no cure. Now Fujimaru must bargain with the enemy, who holds the last remaining antivirus. Meanwhile, the cult launches an audacious and terrible biological attack on the prison where their guru is being held!

Contents

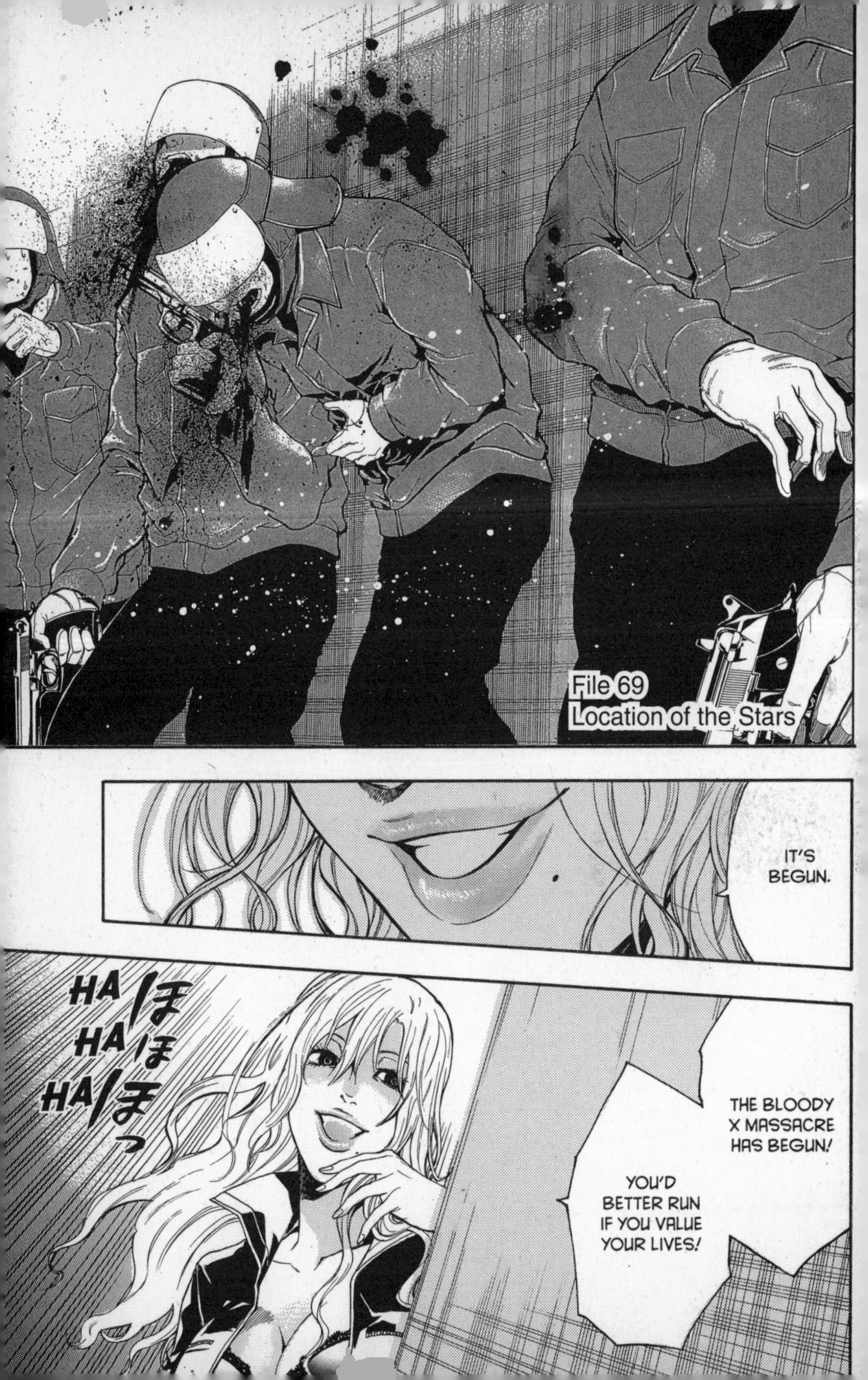
File 69
Location of the Stars
IT'S BEGUN.
THE BLOODY X MASSACRE HAS BEGUN!
YOU'D BETTER RUN IF YOU VALUE YOUR LIVES!
HA HA HA
ほほほっ

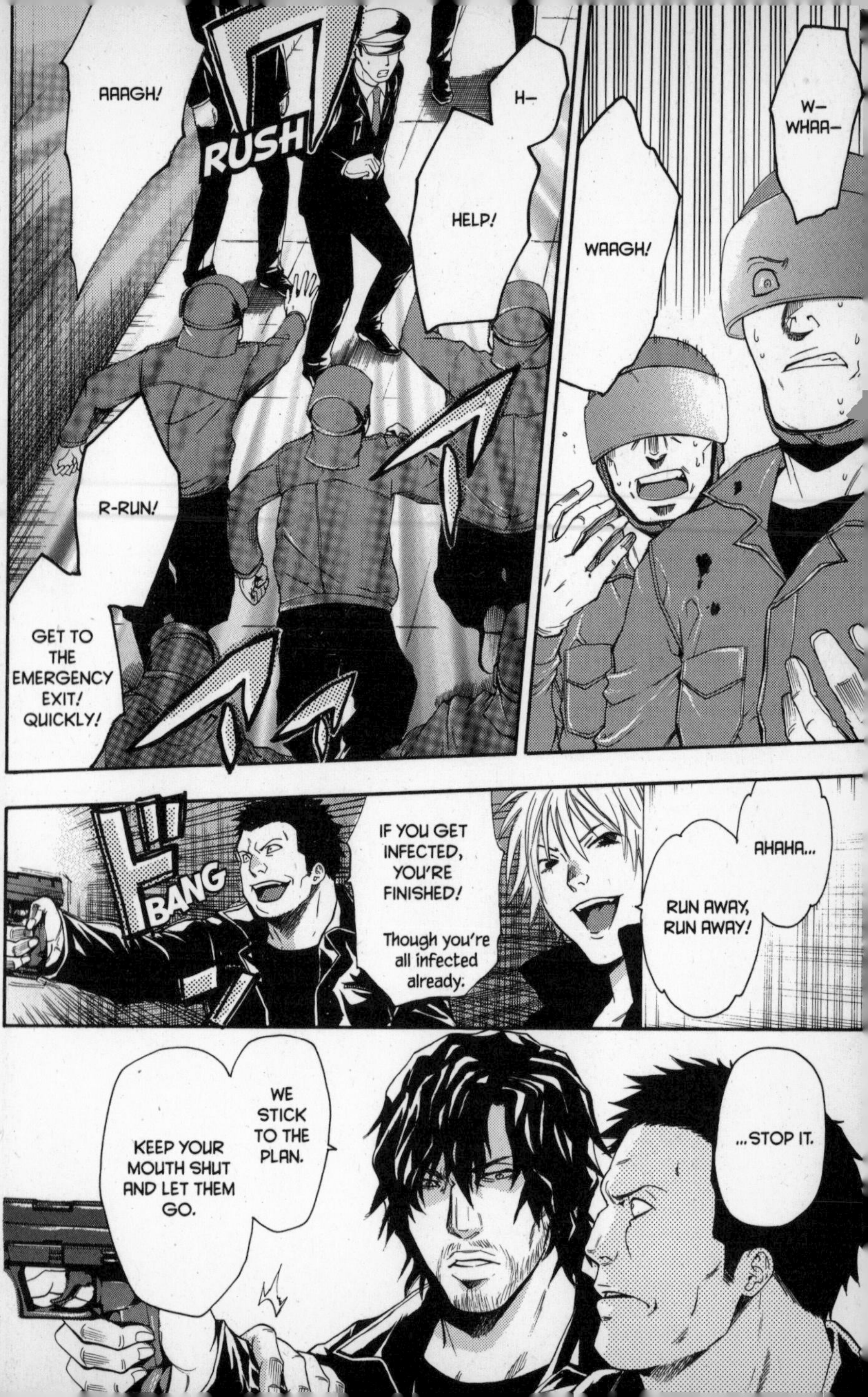
W— WHAA—
WAAGH!
H—
AAAGH!
RUSH
HELP!
R-RUN!
GET TO THE EMERGENCY EXIT! QUICKLY!
AHAHA...
RUN AWAY, RUN AWAY!
IF YOU GET INFECTED, YOU'RE FINISHED!
Though you're all infected already.
BANG
...STOP IT.
WE STICK TO THE PLAN.
KEEP YOUR MOUTH SHUT AND LET THEM GO.

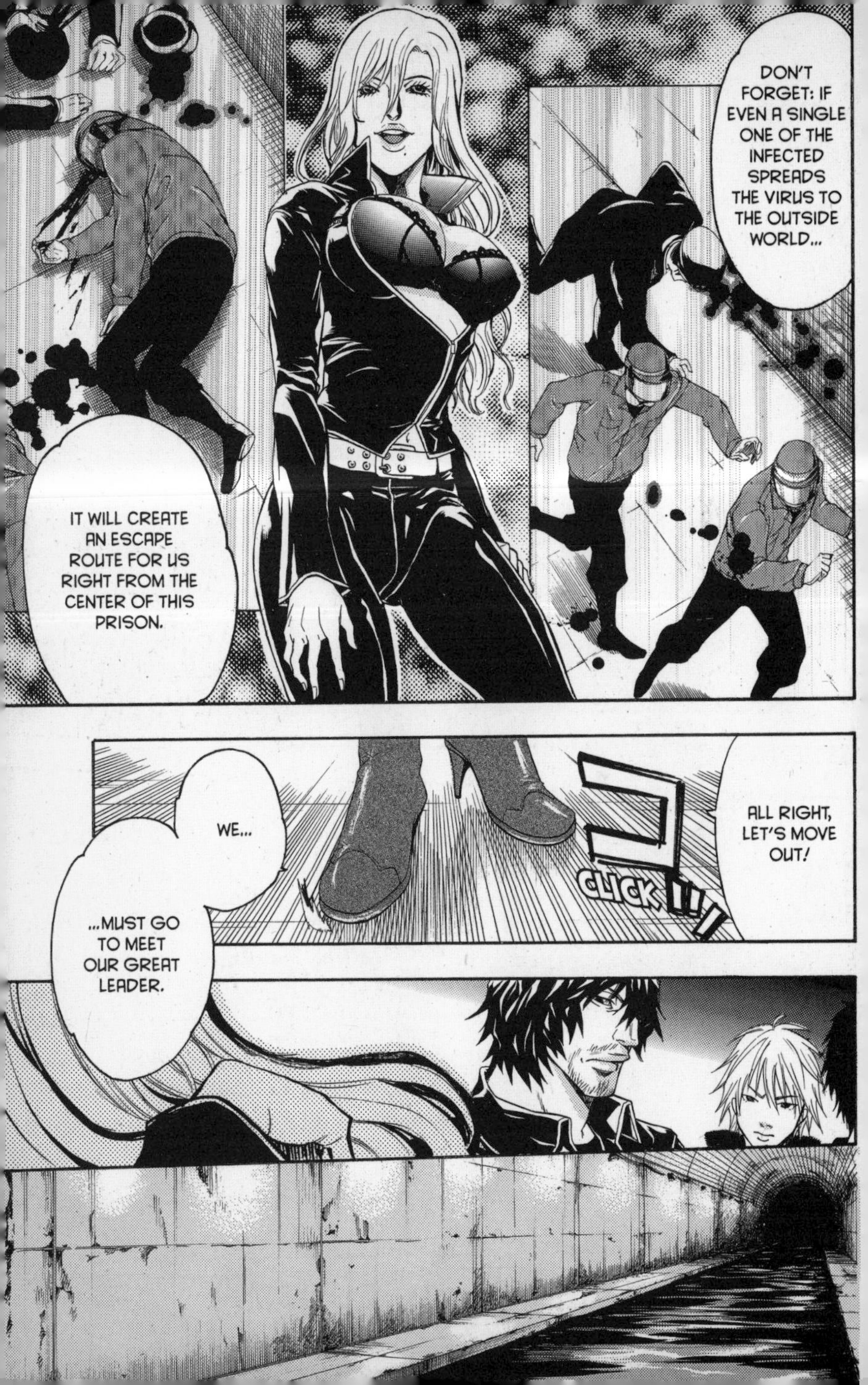
DON'T FORGET: IF EVEN A SINGLE ONE OF THE INFECTED SPREADS THE VIRUS TO THE OUTSIDE WORLD...
IT WILL CREATE AN ESCAPE ROUTE FOR US RIGHT FROM THE CENTER OF THIS PRISON.
ALL RIGHT, LET'S MOVE OUT!
CLICK
WE...
...MUST GO TO MEET OUR GREAT LEADER.

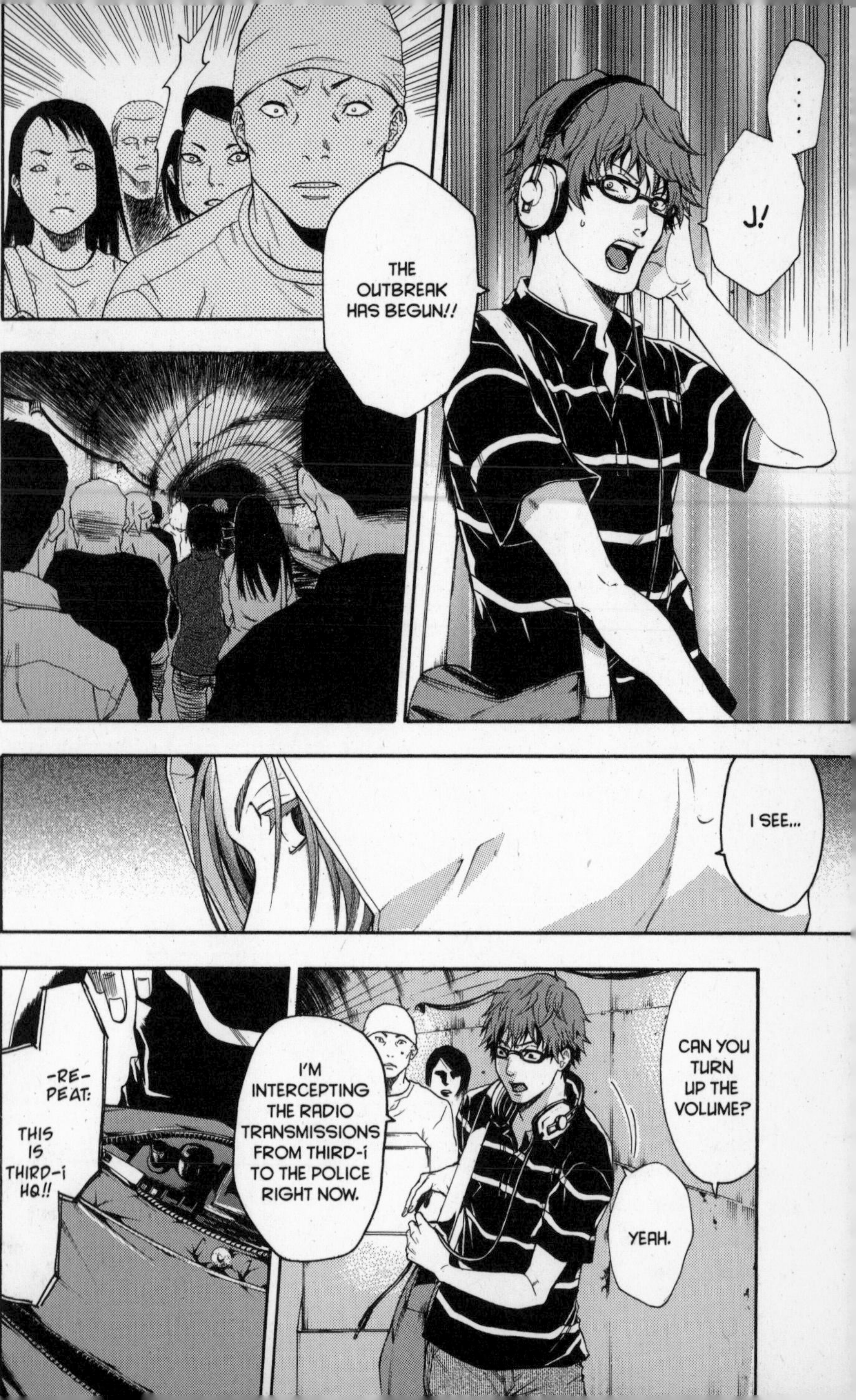
......
J!
THE OUTBREAK HAS BEGUN!!
I SEE...
CAN YOU TURN UP THE VOLUME?
YEAH.
I'M INTERCEPTING THE RADIO TRANSMISSIONS FROM THIRD-i TO THE POLICE RIGHT NOW.
-RE-PEAT:
THIS IS THIRD-i HQ!!

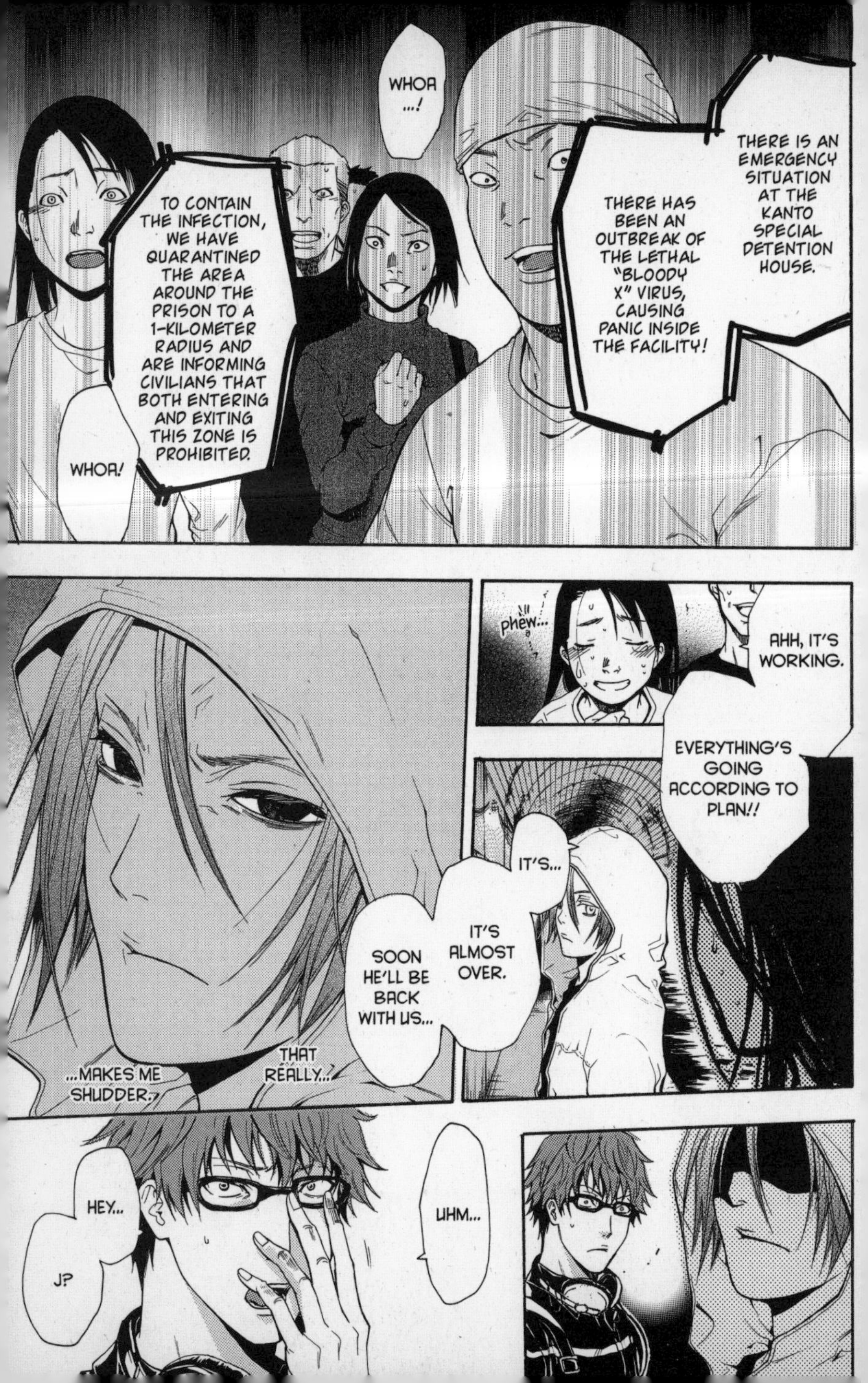
THERE IS AN EMERGENCY SITUATION AT THE KANTO SPECIAL DETENTION HOUSE.
THERE HAS BEEN AN OUTBREAK OF THE LETHAL "BLOODY X" VIRUS, CAUSING PANIC INSIDE THE FACILITY!
WHOA ...!
TO CONTAIN THE INFECTION, WE HAVE QUARANTINED THE AREA AROUND THE PRISON TO A 1-KILOMETER RADIUS AND ARE INFORMING CIVILIANS THAT BOTH ENTERING AND EXITING THIS ZONE IS PROHIBITED.
WHOA!
phew...
AHH, IT'S WORKING.
EVERYTHING'S GOING ACCORDING TO PLAN!!
IT'S...
IT'S ALMOST OVER.
SOON HE'LL BE BACK WITH US...
THAT REALLY...
...MAKES ME SHUDDER.
UHM...
HEY...
J?

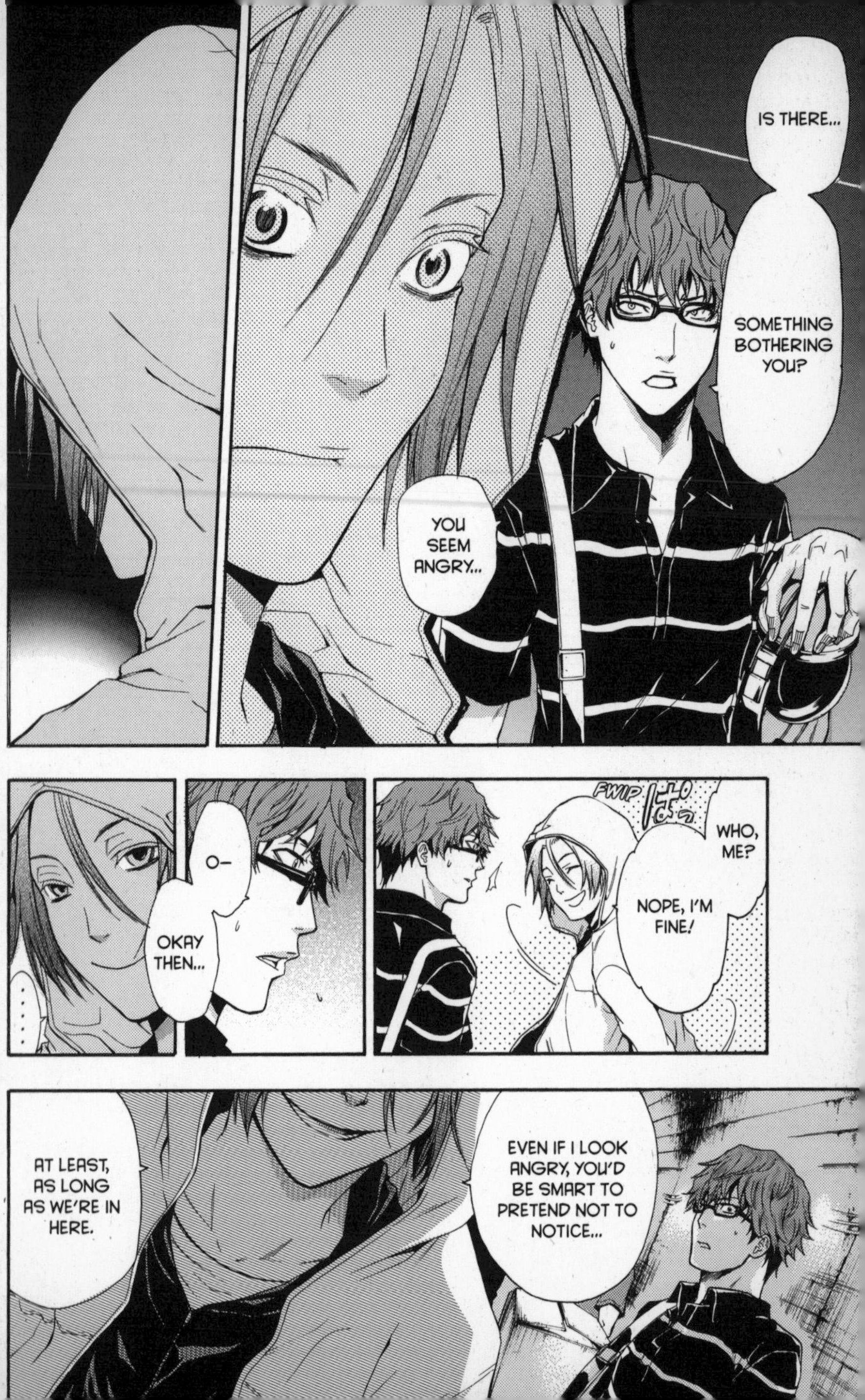
IS THERE...
SOMETHING BOTHERING YOU?
YOU SEEM ANGRY...
FWIP
ぱっ
WHO, ME?
NOPE, I'M FINE!
O—
OKAY THEN...
EVEN IF I LOOK ANGRY, YOU'D BE SMART TO PRETEND NOT TO NOTICE...
AT LEAST, AS LONG AS WE'RE IN HERE.

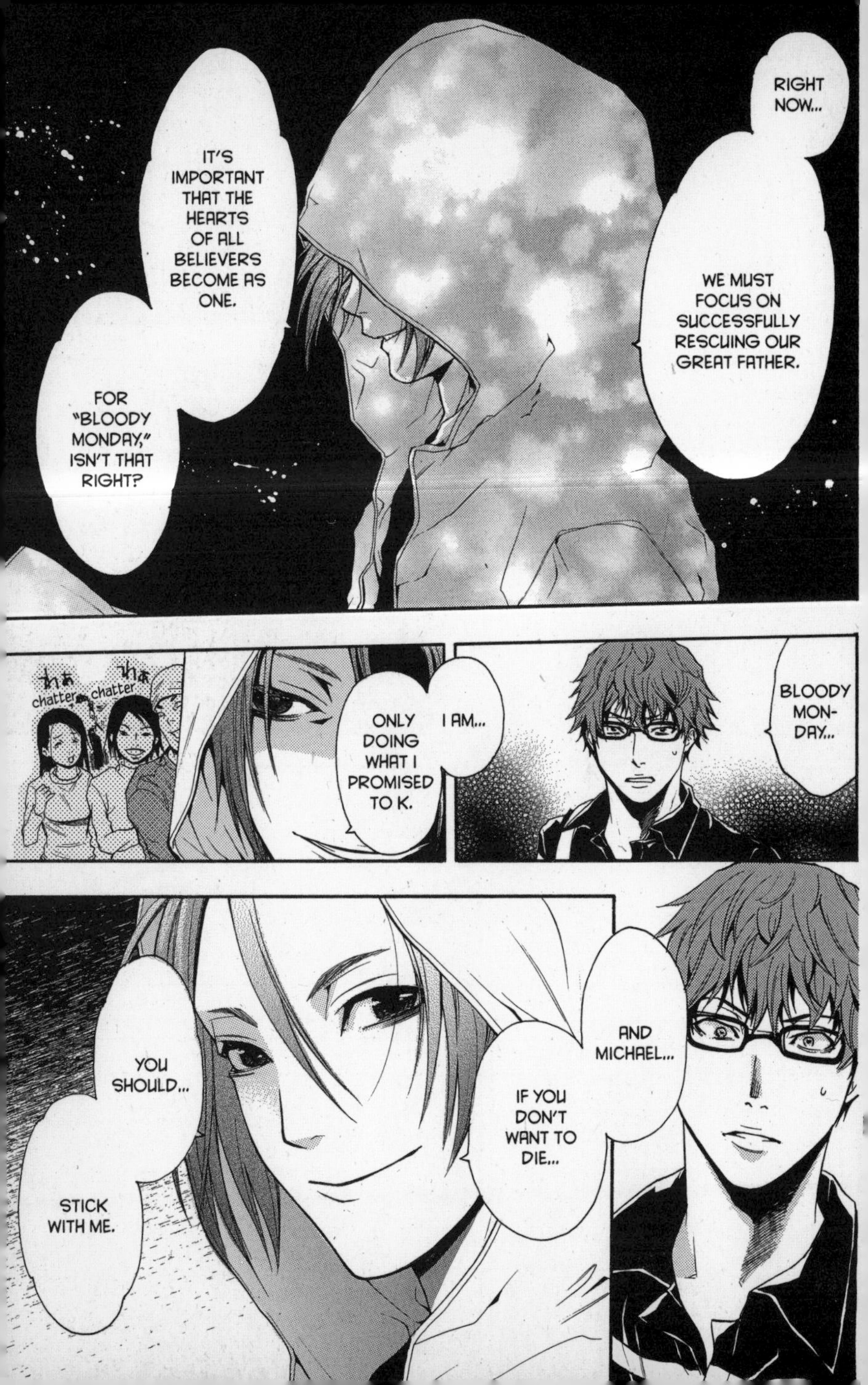
RIGHT NOW...
WE MUST FOCUS ON SUCCESSFULLY RESCUING OUR GREAT FATHER.
IT'S IMPORTANT THAT THE HEARTS OF ALL BELIEVERS BECOME AS ONE.
FOR "BLOODY MONDAY," ISN'T THAT RIGHT?
BLOODY MON-DAY...
I AM...
ONLY DOING WHAT I PROMISED TO K.
chatter
chatter
AND MICHAEL...
IF YOU DON'T WANT TO DIE...
YOU SHOULD...
STICK WITH ME.

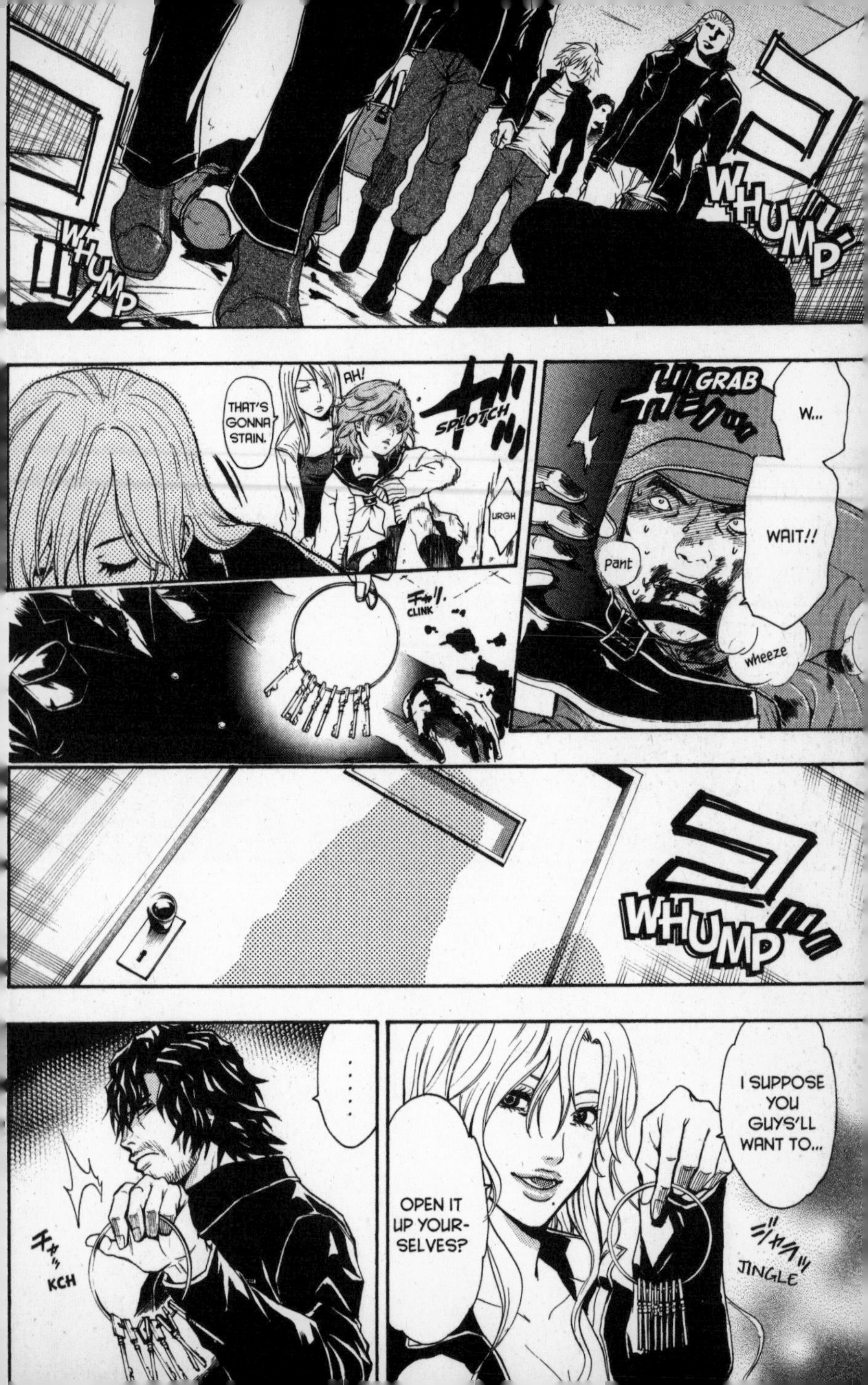
WHUMP
WHUMP
GRAB
W...
WAIT!!
pant
wheeze
SPLOTCH
AH!
THAT'S GONNA STAIN.
URGH
CLINK
WHUMP
I SUPPOSE YOU GUYS'LL WANT TO...
OPEN IT UP YOUR-SELVES?
JINGLE
....
KCH

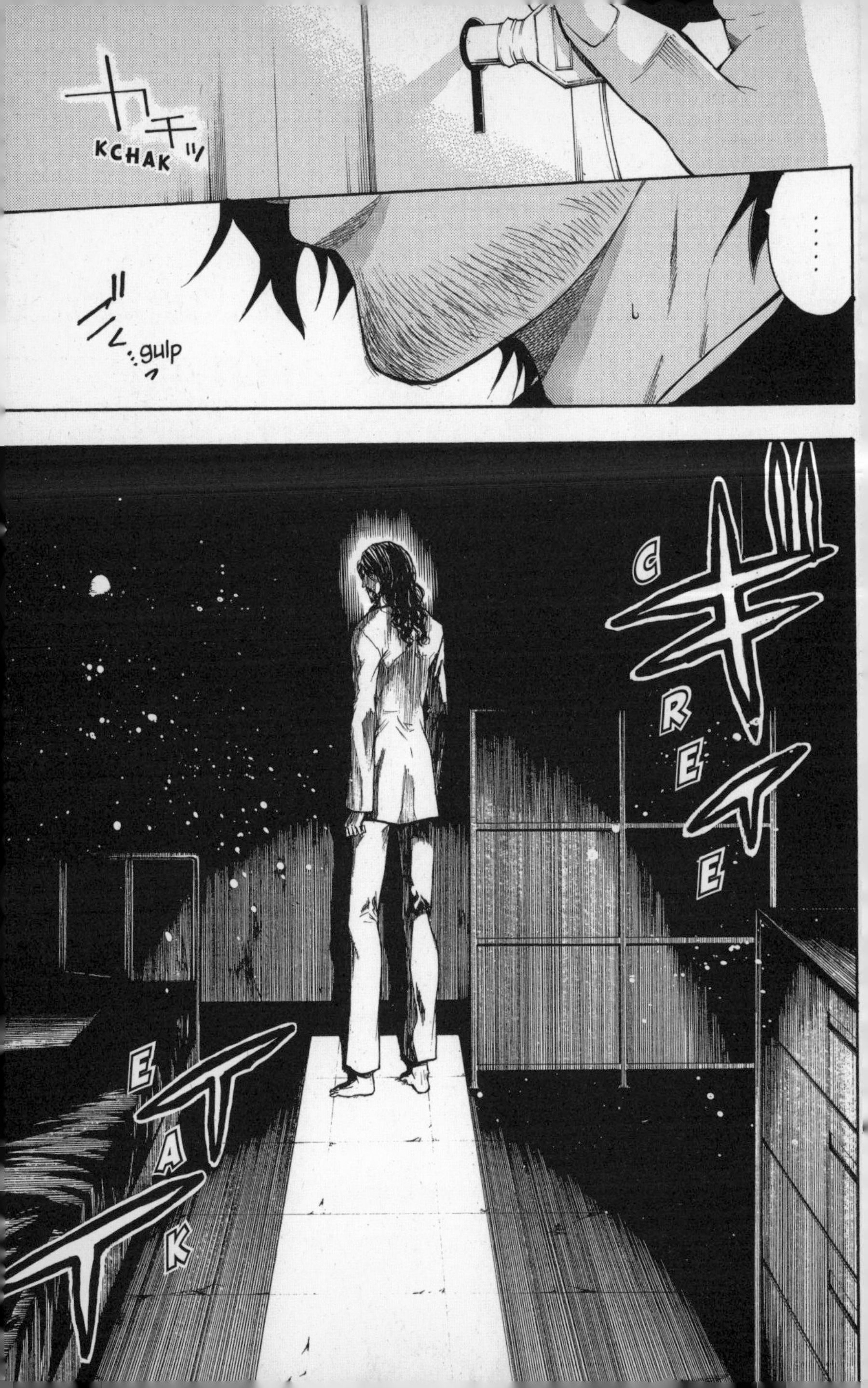
KCHAK
......
gulp
CREE
EAK

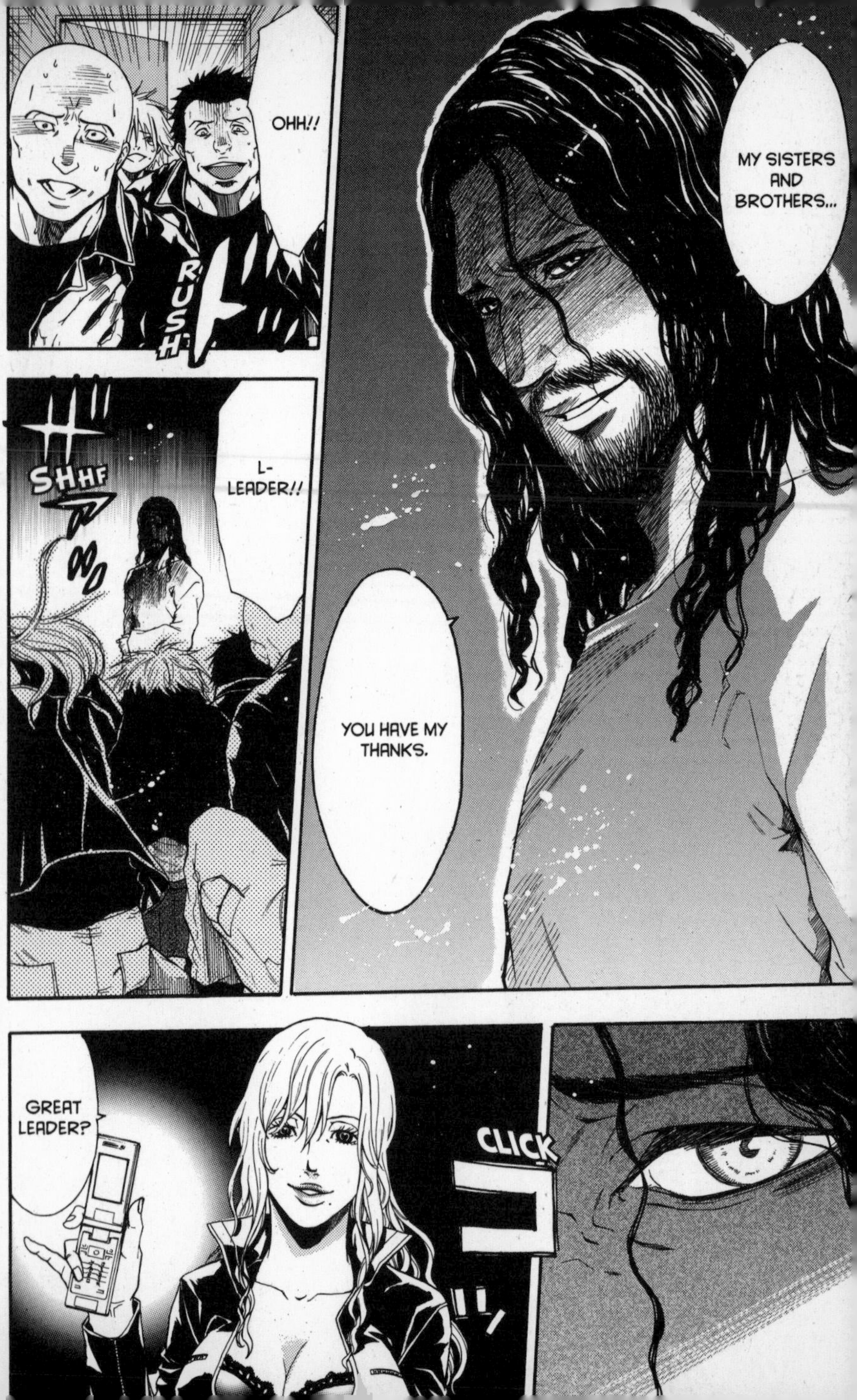
MY SISTERS AND BROTHERS...
YOU HAVE MY THANKS.
OHH!!
RUSH
L-LEADER!!
SHHF
CLICK
GREAT LEADER?

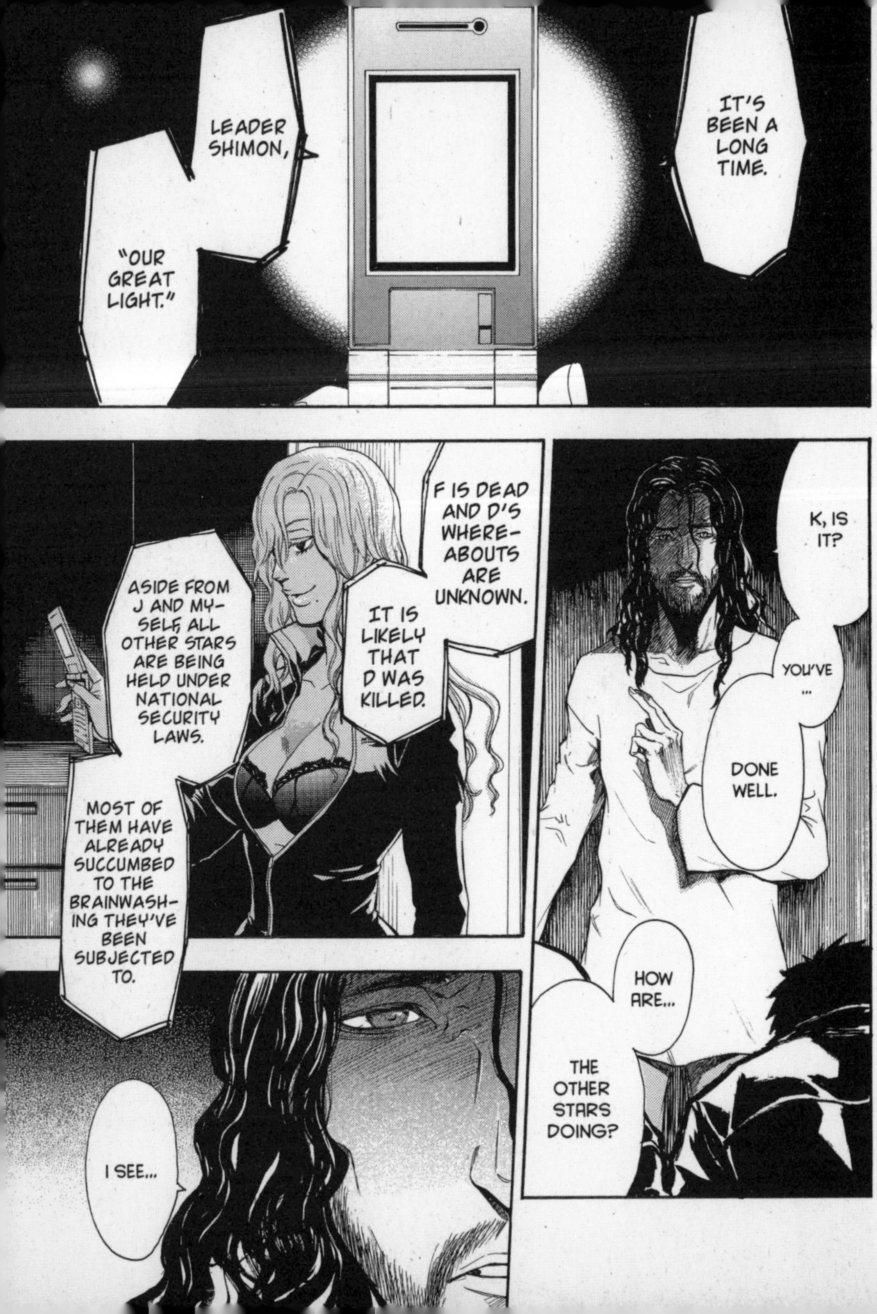
IT'S BEEN A LONG TIME.
LEADER SHIMON,
"OUR GREAT LIGHT."
K, IS IT?
YOU'VE ...
DONE WELL.
HOW ARE...
THE OTHER STARS DOING?
F IS DEAD AND D'S WHERE-ABOUTS ARE UNKNOWN.
IT IS LIKELY THAT D WAS KILLED.
ASIDE FROM J AND MY-SELF, ALL OTHER STARS ARE BEING HELD UNDER NATIONAL SECURITY LAWS.
MOST OF THEM HAVE ALREADY SUCCUMBED TO THE BRAINWASH-ING THEY'VE BEEN SUBJECTED TO.
I SEE...

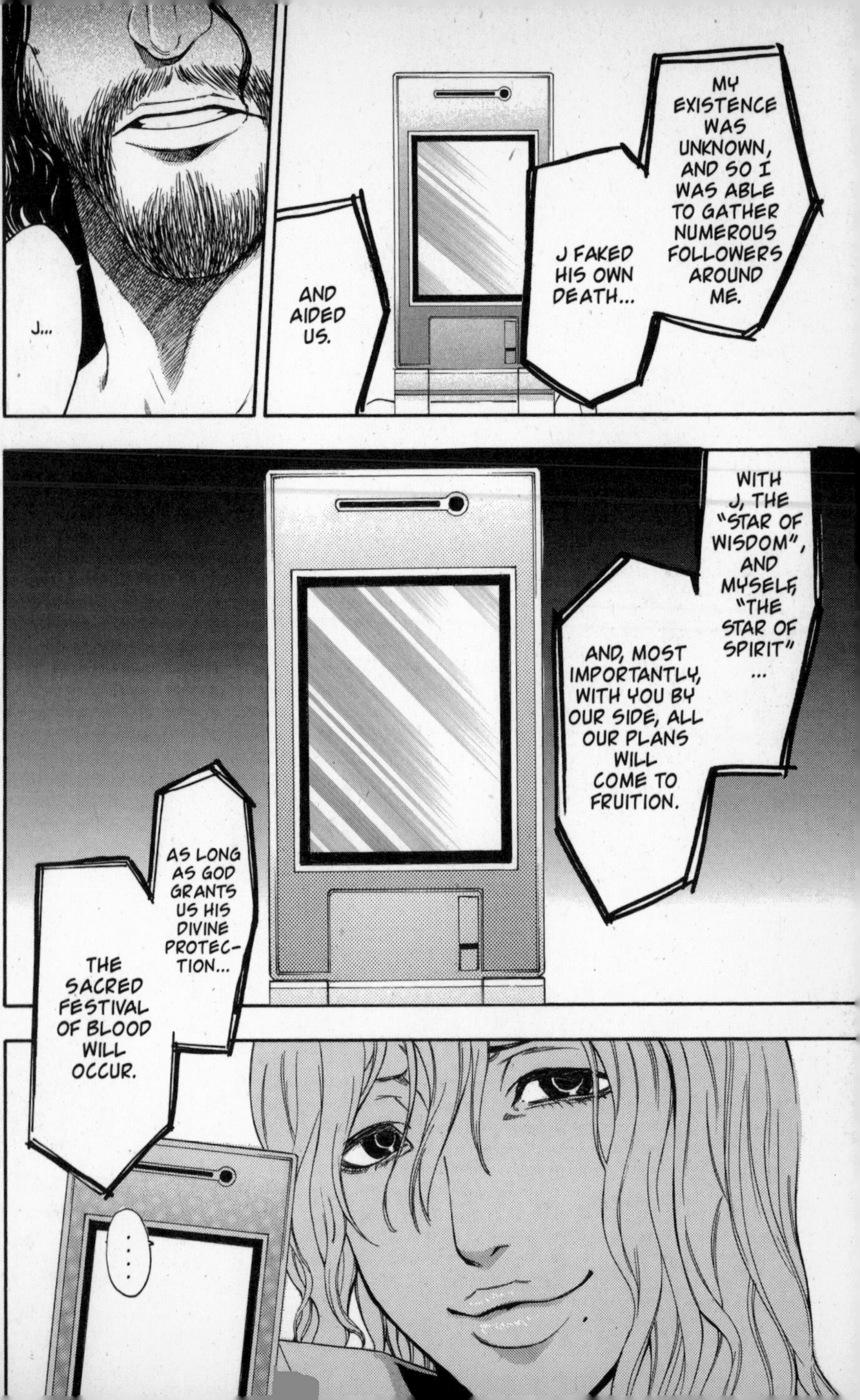
MY EXISTENCE WAS UNKNOWN, AND SO I WAS ABLE TO GATHER NUMEROUS FOLLOWERS AROUND ME.
J FAKED HIS OWN DEATH...
AND AIDED US.
J...
WITH J, THE "STAR OF WISDOM", AND MYSELF, "THE STAR OF SPIRIT"...
AND, MOST IMPORTANTLY, WITH YOU BY OUR SIDE, ALL OUR PLANS WILL COME TO FRUITION.
AS LONG AS GOD GRANTS US HIS DIVINE PROTECTION...
THE SACRED FESTIVAL OF BLOOD WILL OCCUR.
....

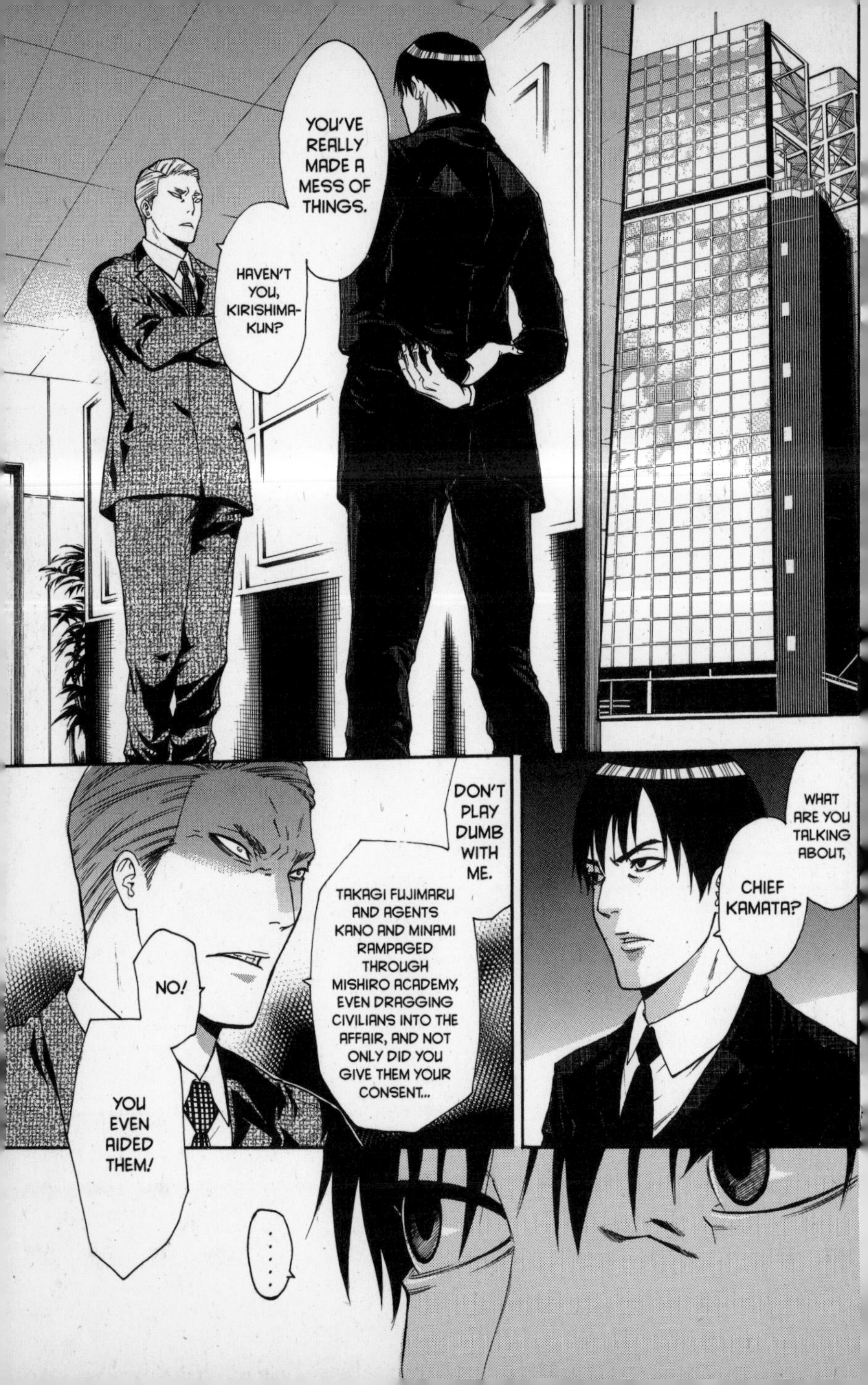
YOU'VE REALLY MADE A MESS OF THINGS.
HAVEN'T YOU, KIRISHIMA-KUN?
WHAT ARE YOU TALKING ABOUT,
CHIEF KAMATA?
DON'T PLAY DUMB WITH ME.
TAKAGI FUJIMARU AND AGENTS KANO AND MINAMI RAMPAGED THROUGH MISHIRO ACADEMY, EVEN DRAGGING CIVILIANS INTO THE AFFAIR, AND NOT ONLY DID YOU GIVE THEM YOUR CONSENT...
NO!
YOU EVEN AIDED THEM!
......

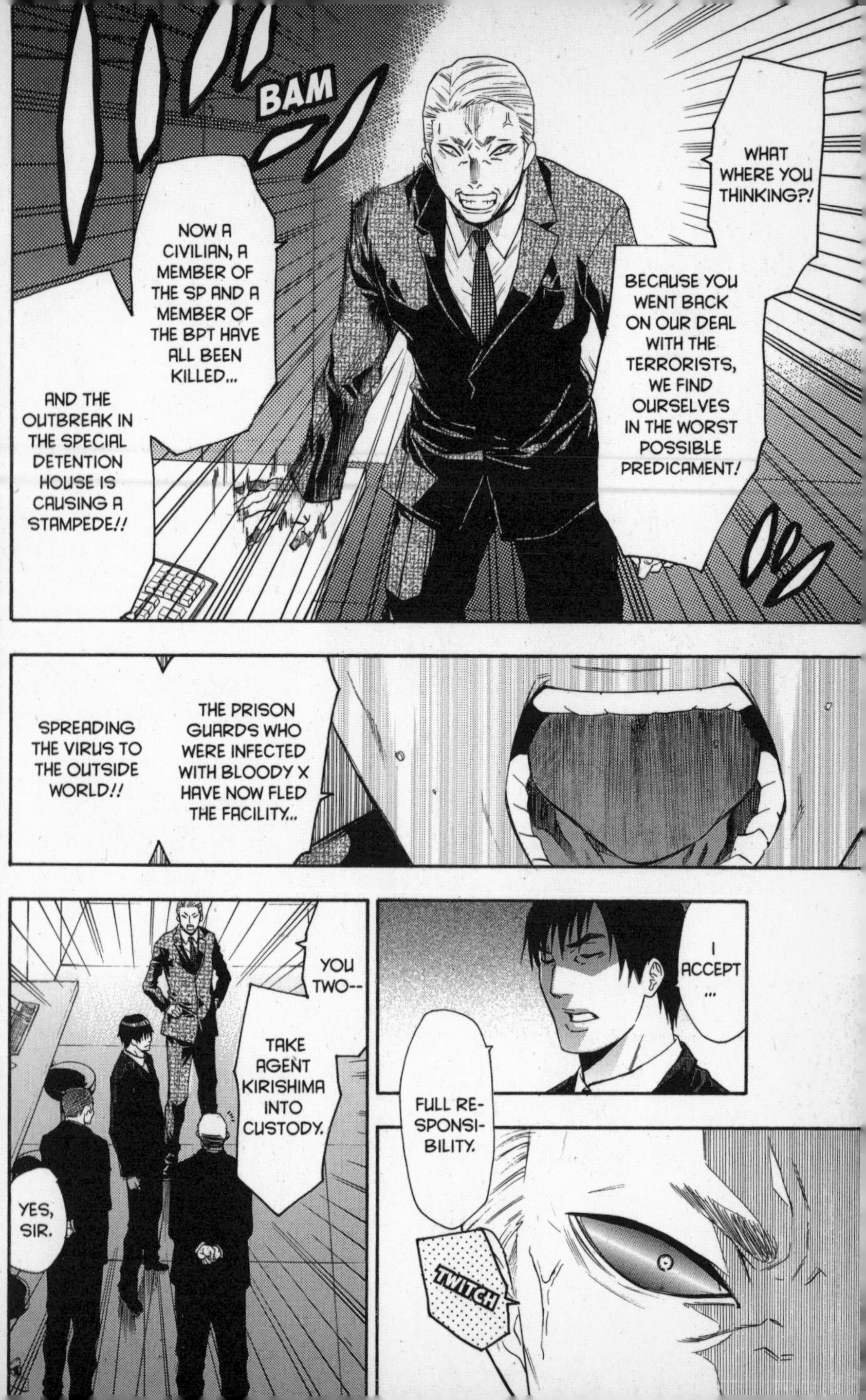
WHAT WHERE YOU THINKING?!
BAM
BECAUSE YOU WENT BACK ON OUR DEAL WITH THE TERRORISTS, WE FIND OURSELVES IN THE WORST POSSIBLE PREDICAMENT!
NOW A CIVILIAN, A MEMBER OF THE SP AND A MEMBER OF THE BPT HAVE ALL BEEN KILLED...
AND THE OUTBREAK IN THE SPECIAL DETENTION HOUSE IS CAUSING A STAMPEDE!!
THE PRISON GUARDS WHO WERE INFECTED WITH BLOODY X HAVE NOW FLED THE FACILITY...
SPREADING THE VIRUS TO THE OUTSIDE WORLD!!
I ACCEPT ...
FULL RE-SPONSI-BILITY.
TWITCH
YOU TWO--
TAKE AGENT KIRISHIMA INTO CUSTODY.
YES, SIR.

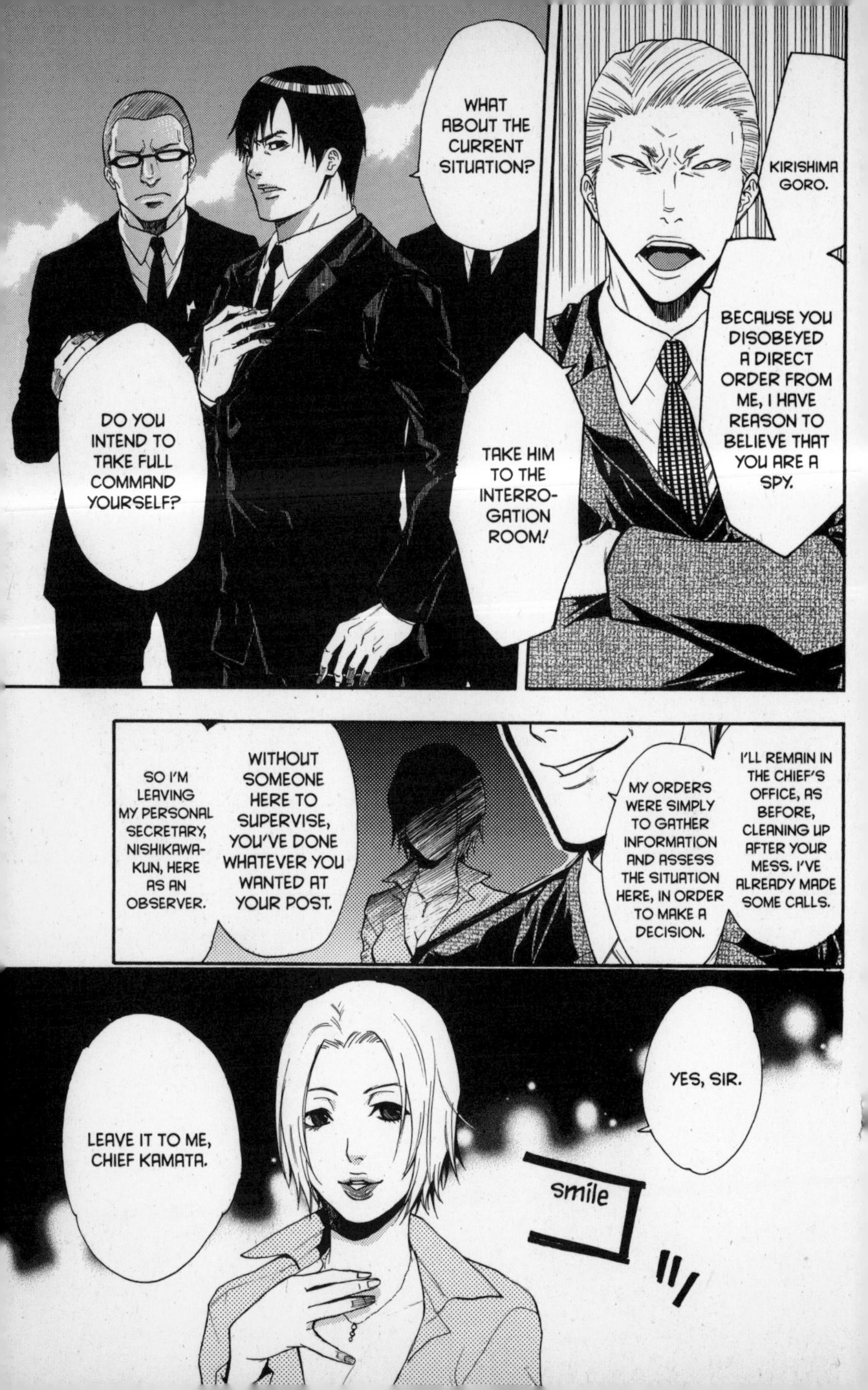
KIRISHIMA GORO.
BECAUSE YOU DISOBEYED A DIRECT ORDER FROM ME, I HAVE REASON TO BELIEVE THAT YOU ARE A SPY.
TAKE HIM TO THE INTERRO-GATION ROOM!
WHAT ABOUT THE CURRENT SITUATION?
DO YOU INTEND TO TAKE FULL COMMAND YOURSELF?
I'LL REMAIN IN THE CHIEF'S OFFICE, AS BEFORE, CLEANING UP AFTER YOUR MESS. I'VE ALREADY MADE SOME CALLS.
MY ORDERS WERE SIMPLY TO GATHER INFORMATION AND ASSESS THE SITUATION HERE, IN ORDER TO MAKE A DECISION.
WITHOUT SOMEONE HERE TO SUPERVISE, YOU'VE DONE WHATEVER YOU WANTED AT YOUR POST.
SO I'M LEAVING MY PERSONAL SECRETARY, NISHIKAWA-KUN, HERE AS AN OBSERVER.
YES, SIR.
smile
LEAVE IT TO ME, CHIEF KAMATA.

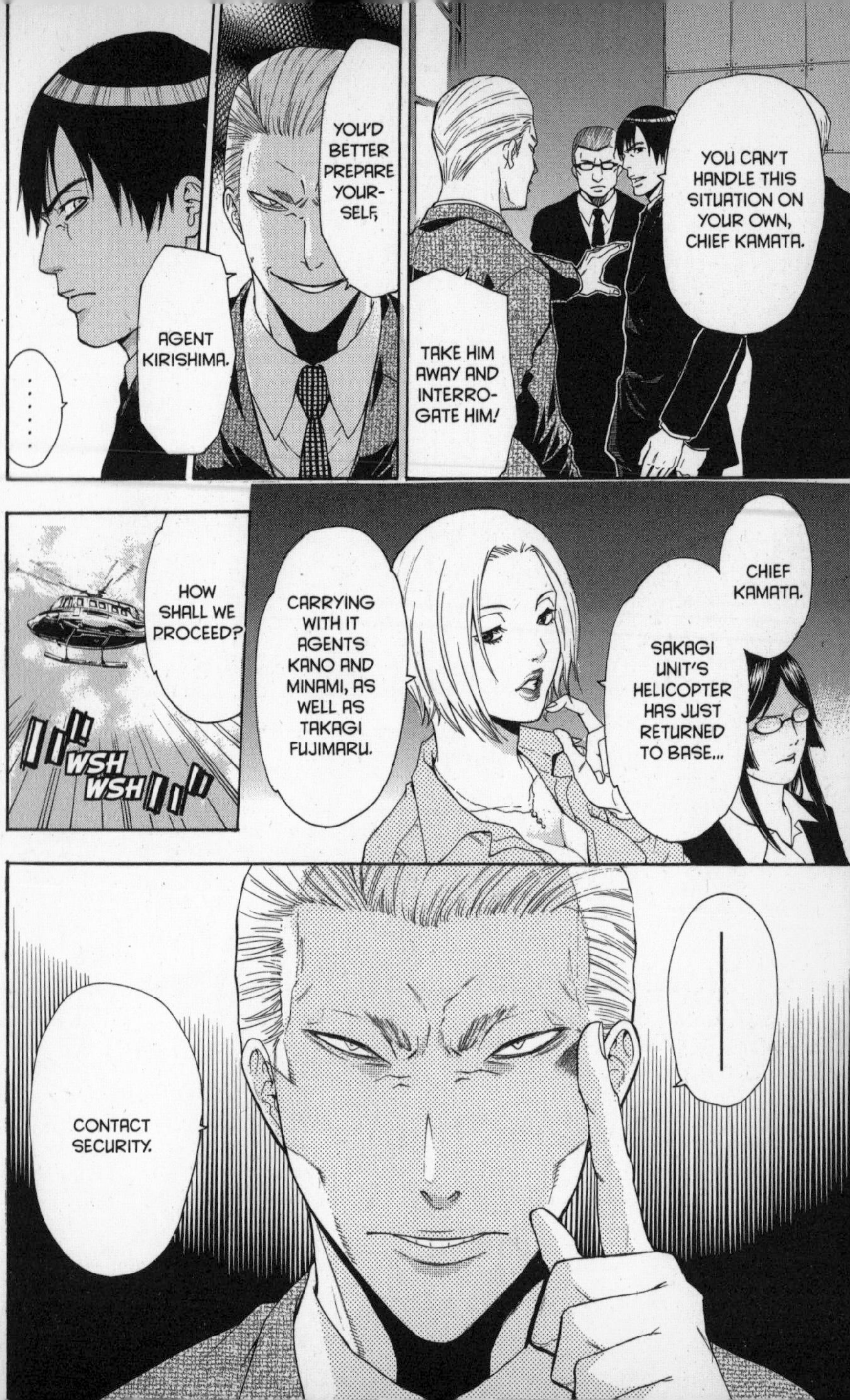
YOU CAN'T HANDLE THIS SITUATION ON YOUR OWN, CHIEF KAMATA.
TAKE HIM AWAY AND INTERRO-GATE HIM!
YOU'D BETTER PREPARE YOUR-SELF,
AGENT KIRISHIMA.
......
CHIEF KAMATA.
SAKAGI UNIT'S HELICOPTER HAS JUST RETURNED TO BASE...
CARRYING WITH IT AGENTS KANO AND MINAMI, AS WELL AS TAKAGI FUJIMARU.
HOW SHALL WE PROCEED?
WSH WSH
—
CONTACT SECURITY.

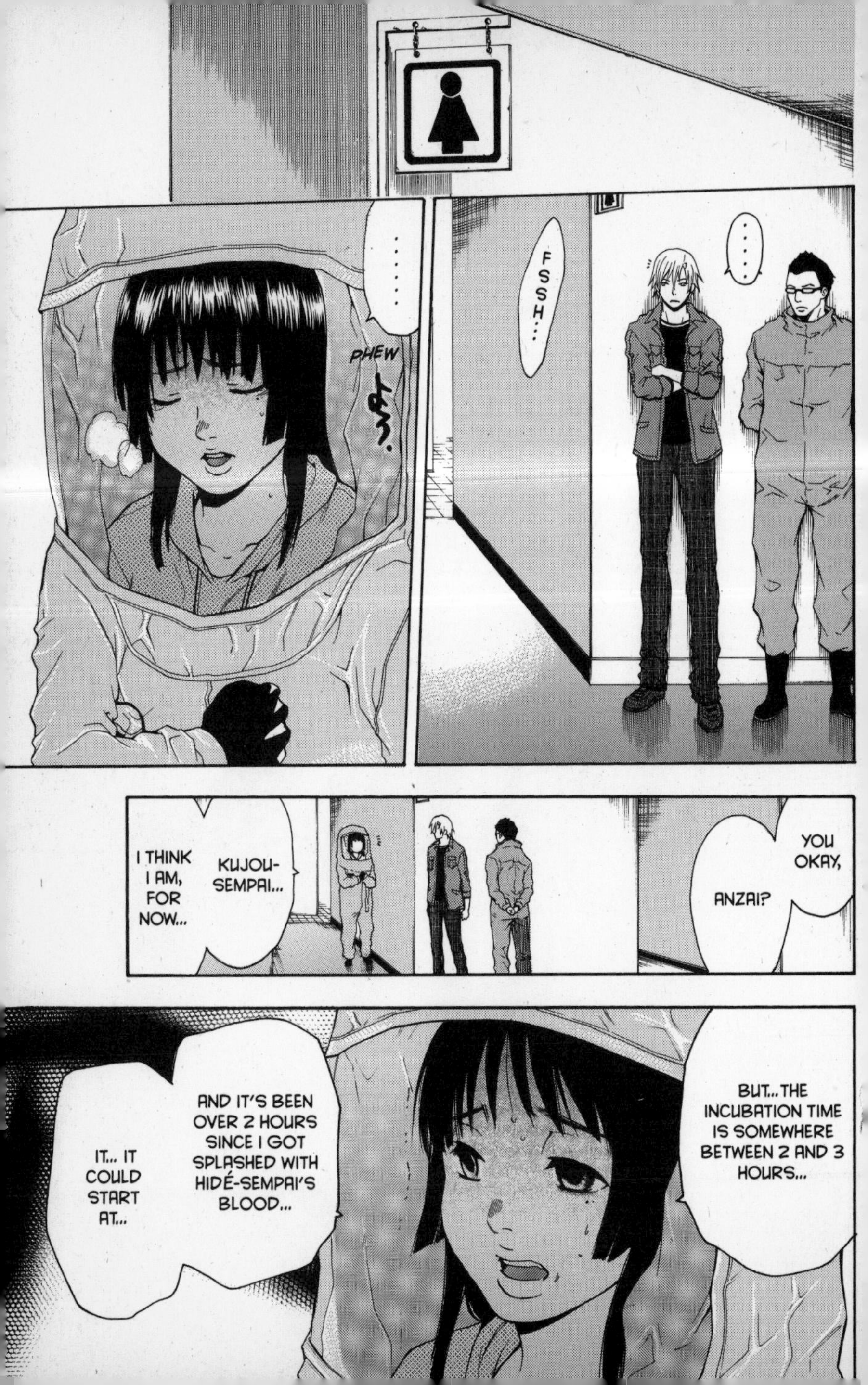
.....
FSSH...
......
PHEW
YOU OKAY, ANZAI?
KUJOU-SEMPAI...
I THINK I AM, FOR NOW...
BUT... THE INCUBATION TIME IS SOMEWHERE BETWEEN 2 AND 3 HOURS...
AND IT'S BEEN OVER 2 HOURS SINCE I GOT SPLASHED WITH HIDÉ-SEMPAI'S BLOOD...
IT... IT COULD START AT...

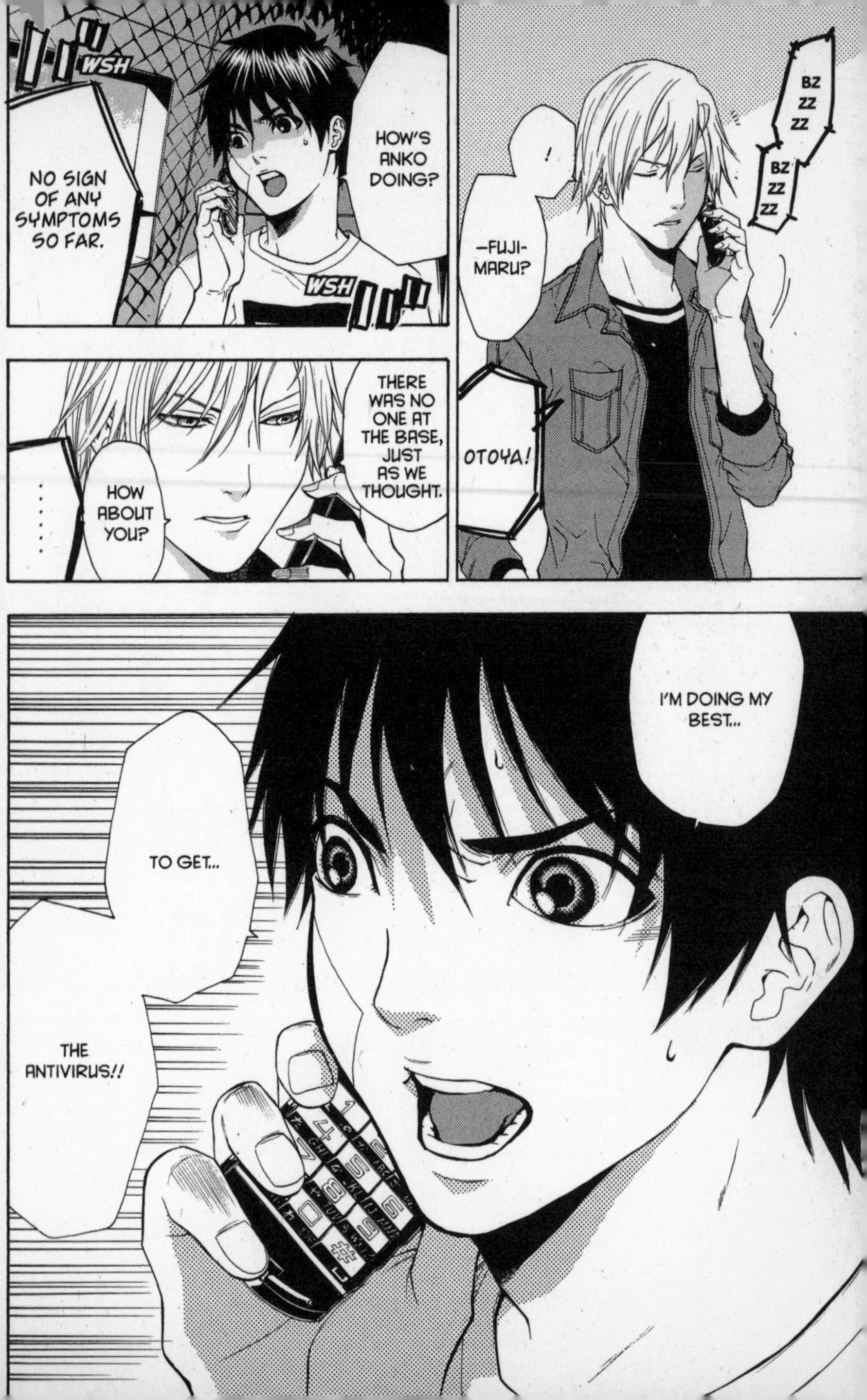
BZ ZZ ZZ
BZ ZZ ZZ
!
—FUJI-MARU?
OTOYA!
WSH
HOW'S ANKO DOING?
WSH
NO SIGN OF ANY SYMPTOMS SO FAR.
THERE WAS NO ONE AT THE BASE, JUST AS WE THOUGHT.
HOW ABOUT YOU?
......
I'M DOING MY BEST...
TO GET...
THE ANTIVIRUS!!

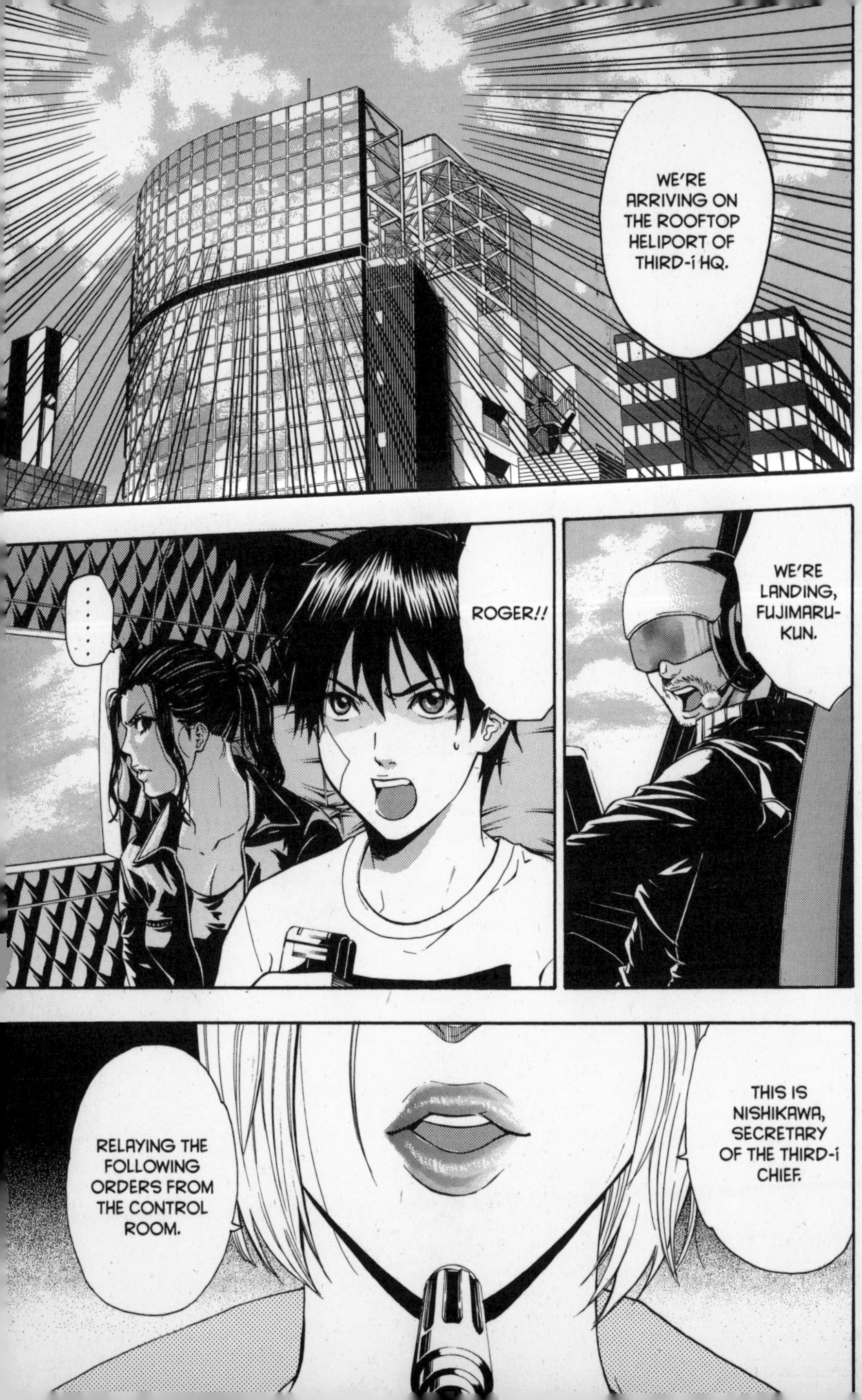
WE'RE ARRIVING ON THE ROOFTOP HELIPORT OF THIRD-i HQ.
WE'RE LANDING, FUJIMARU-KUN.
ROGER!!
......
THIS IS NISHIKAWA, SECRETARY OF THE THIRD-i CHIEF.
RELAYING THE FOLLOWING ORDERS FROM THE CONTROL ROOM.

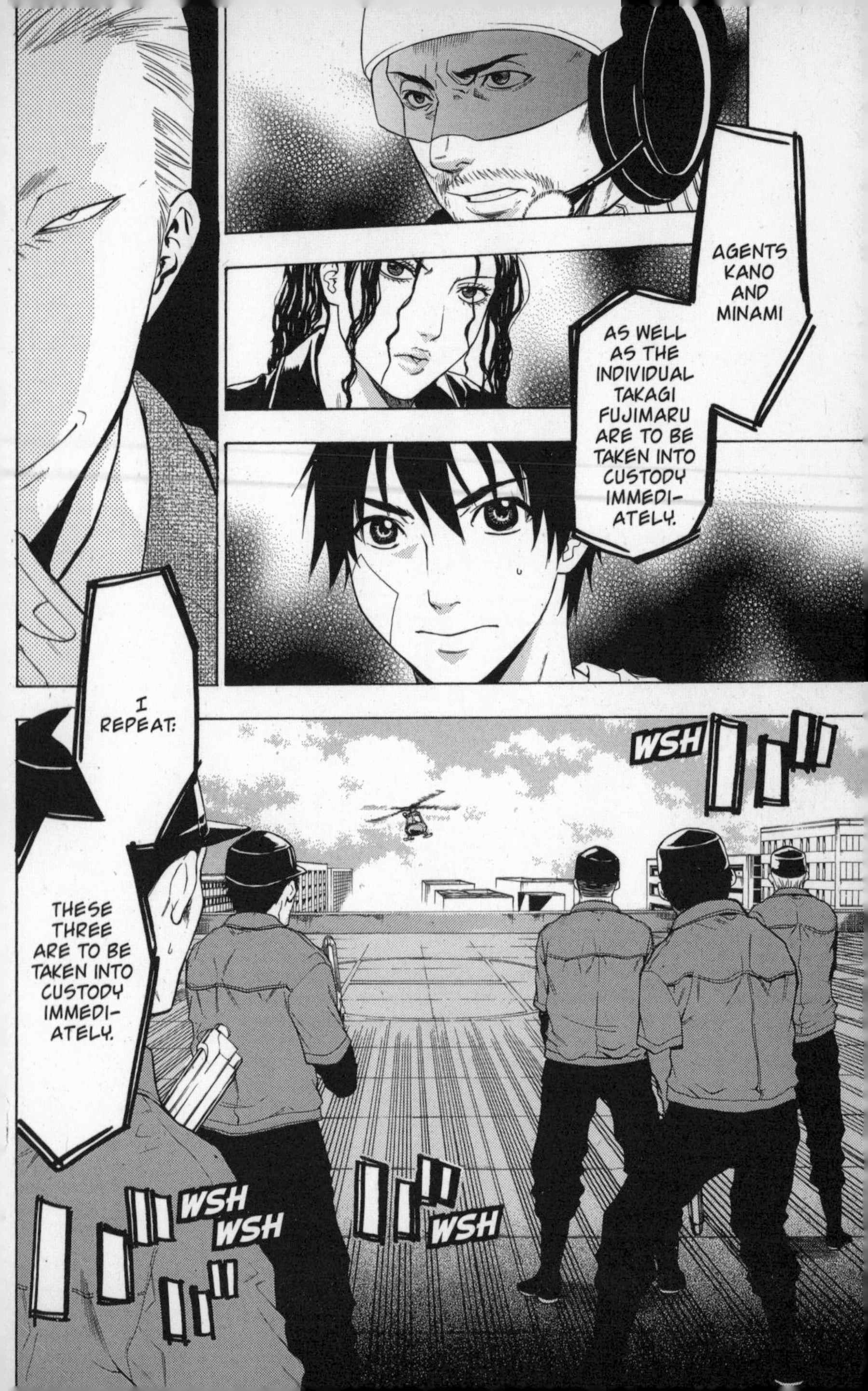
AGENTS KANO AND MINAMI
AS WELL AS THE INDIVIDUAL TAKAGI FUJIMARU ARE TO BE TAKEN INTO CUSTODY IMMEDI-ATELY.
I REPEAT:
THESE THREE ARE TO BE TAKEN INTO CUSTODY IMMEDI-ATELY.
WSH
WSH
WSH
WSH

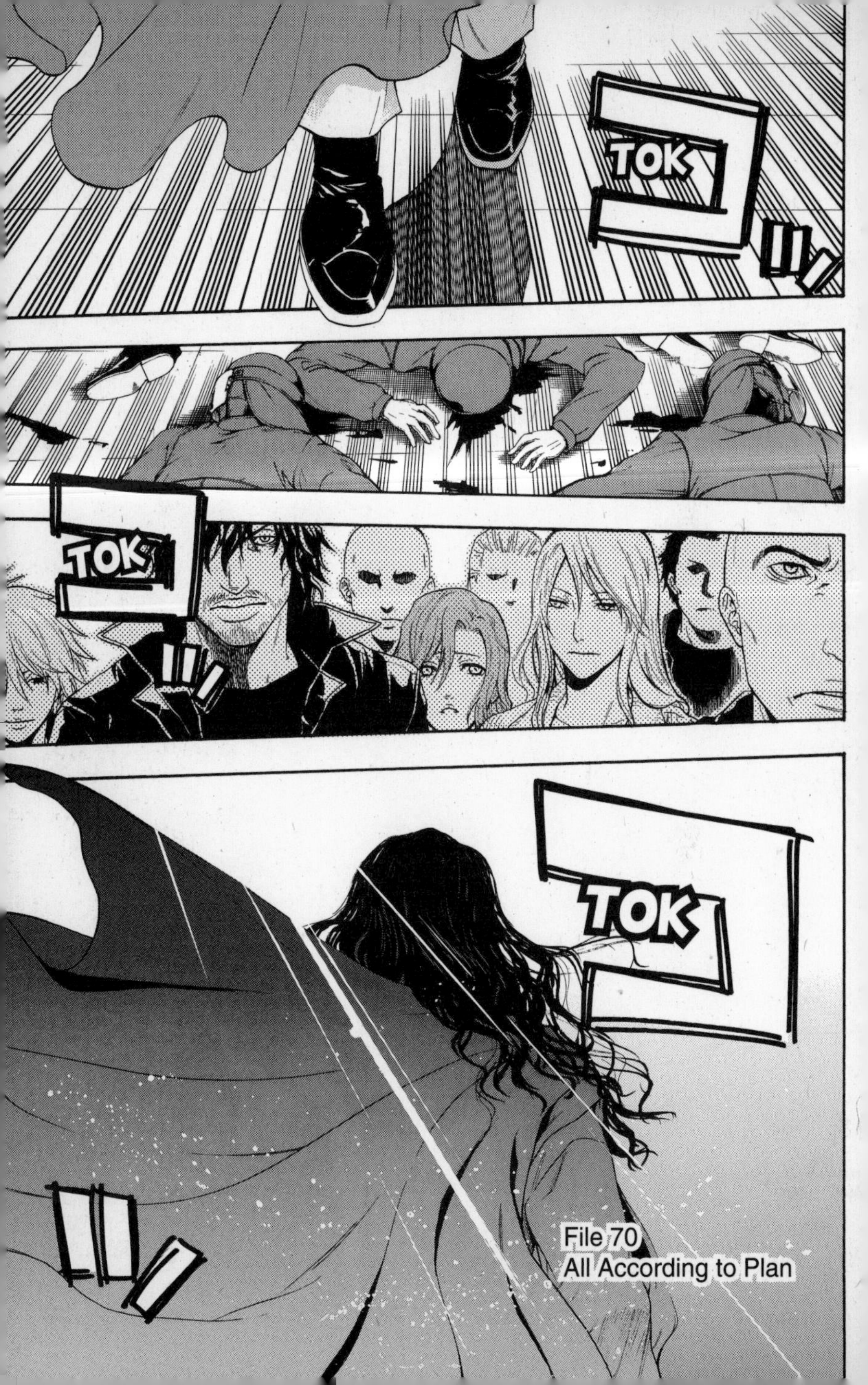
TOK
TOK
TOK
File 70
All According to Plan

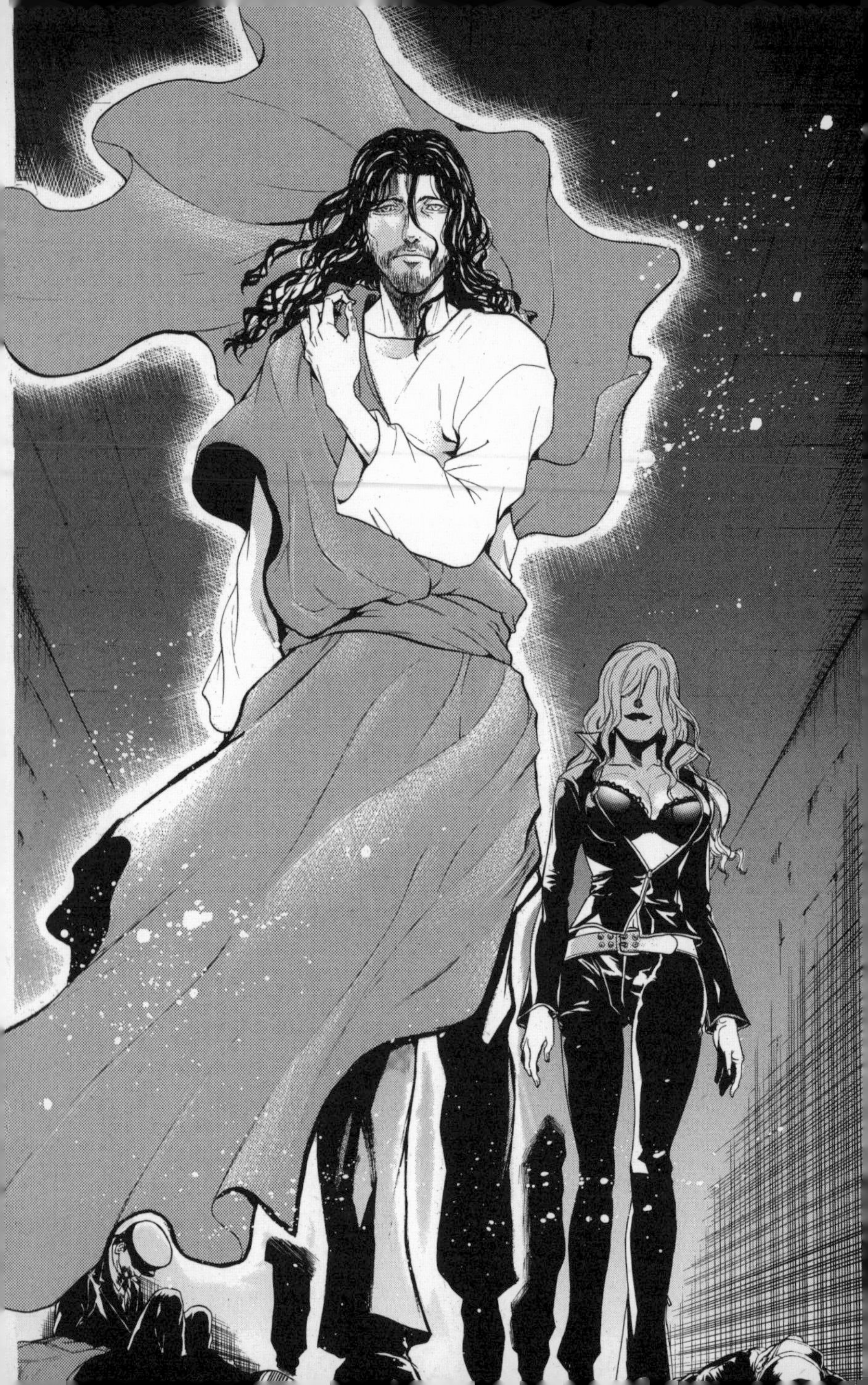

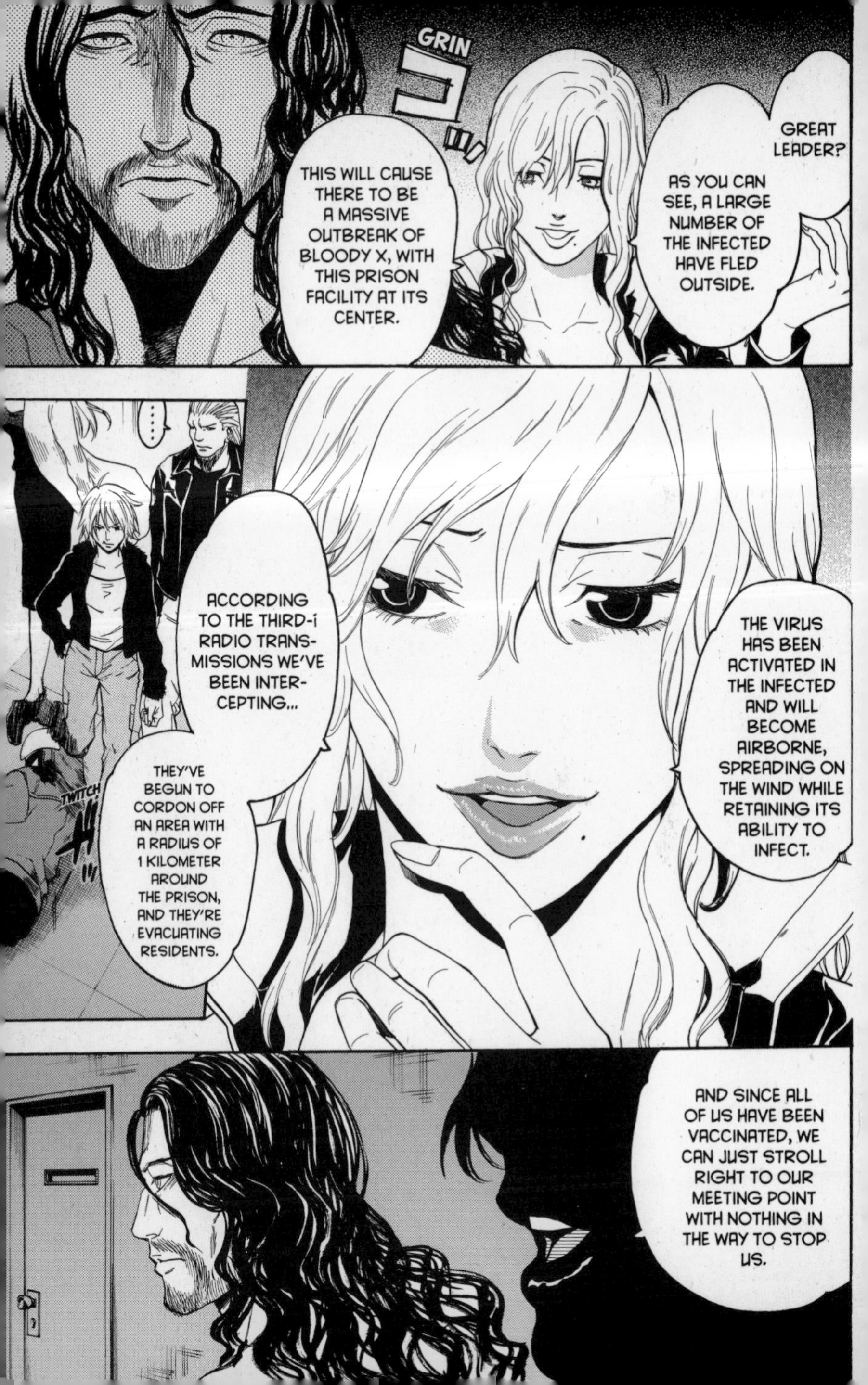
GREAT LEADER?
AS YOU CAN SEE, A LARGE NUMBER OF THE INFECTED HAVE FLED OUTSIDE.
GRIN
THIS WILL CAUSE THERE TO BE A MASSIVE OUTBREAK OF BLOODY X, WITH THIS PRISON FACILITY AT ITS CENTER.
THE VIRUS HAS BEEN ACTIVATED IN THE INFECTED AND WILL BECOME AIRBORNE, SPREADING ON THE WIND WHILE RETAINING ITS ABILITY TO INFECT.
ACCORDING TO THE THIRD-i RADIO TRANSMISSIONS WE'VE BEEN INTERCEPTING...
THEY'VE BEGUN TO CORDON OFF AN AREA WITH A RADIUS OF 1 KILOMETER AROUND THE PRISON, AND THEY'RE EVACUATING RESIDENTS.
.....
TWITCH
AND SINCE ALL OF US HAVE BEEN VACCINATED, WE CAN JUST STROLL RIGHT TO OUR MEETING POINT WITH NOTHING IN THE WAY TO STOP US.

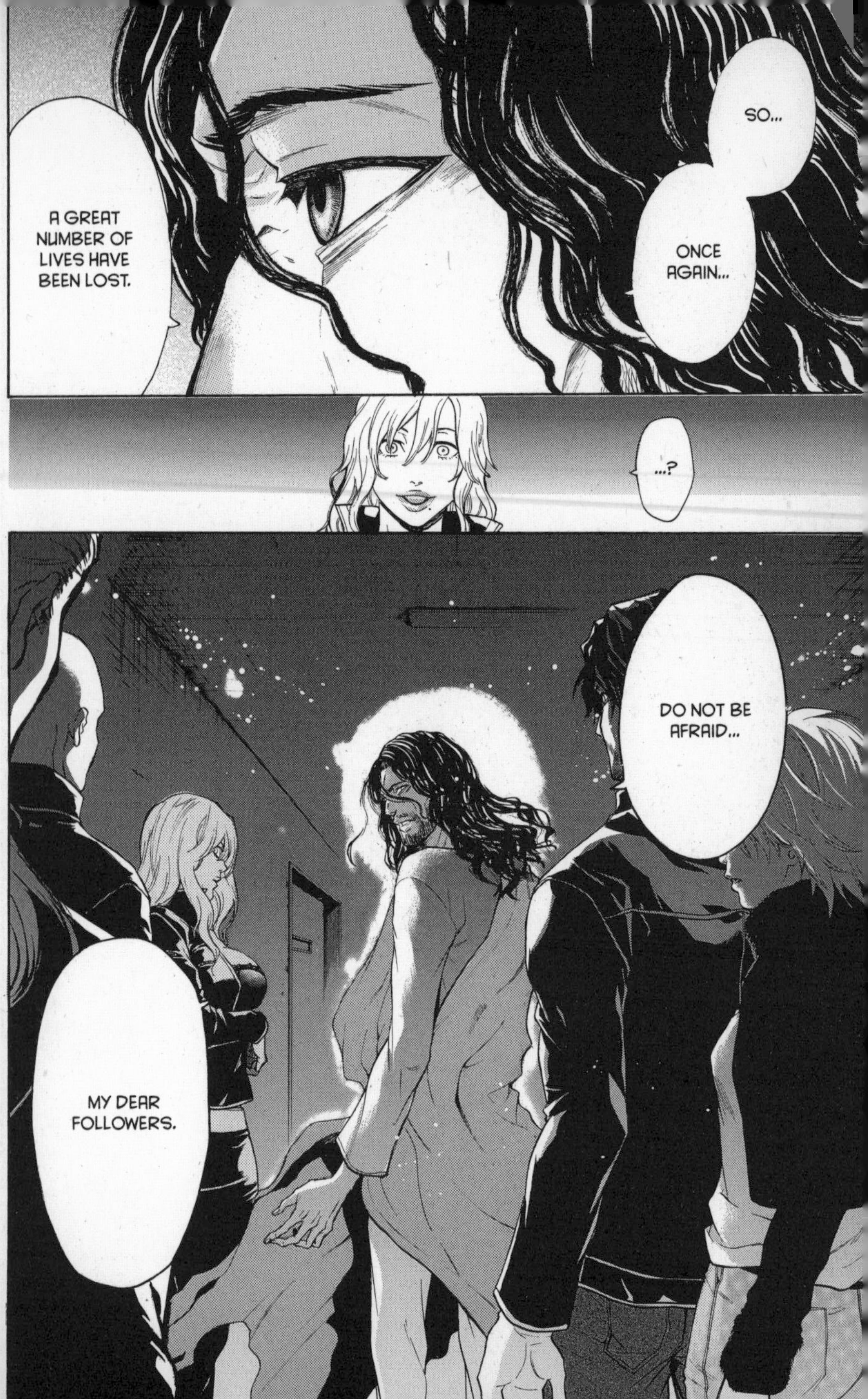
SO...
ONCE AGAIN...
A GREAT NUMBER OF LIVES HAVE BEEN LOST.
...?
DO NOT BE AFRAID...
MY DEAR FOLLOWERS.

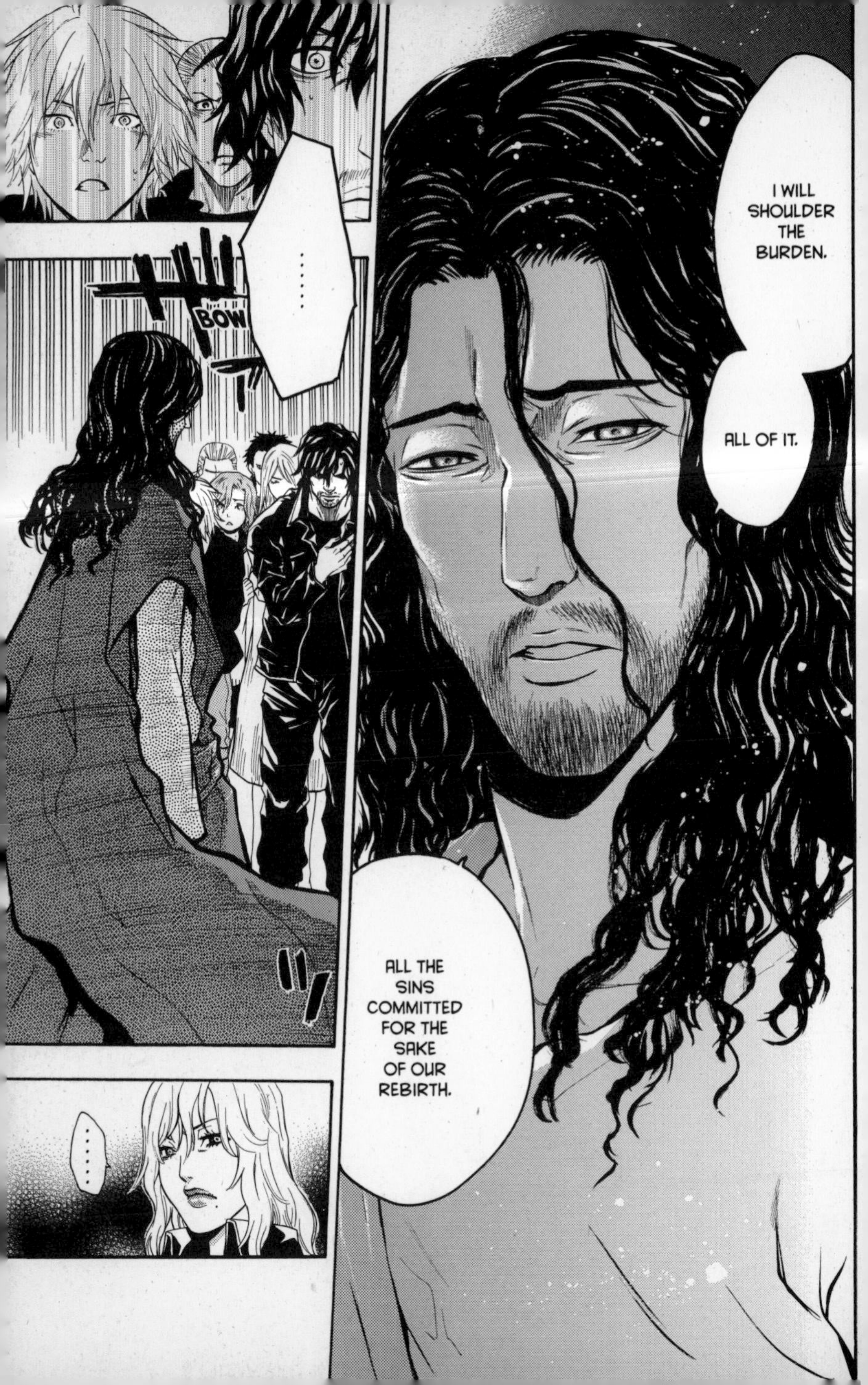
I WILL SHOULDER THE BURDEN.
ALL OF IT.
ALL THE SINS COMMITTED FOR THE SAKE OF OUR REBIRTH.
......
BOW
......

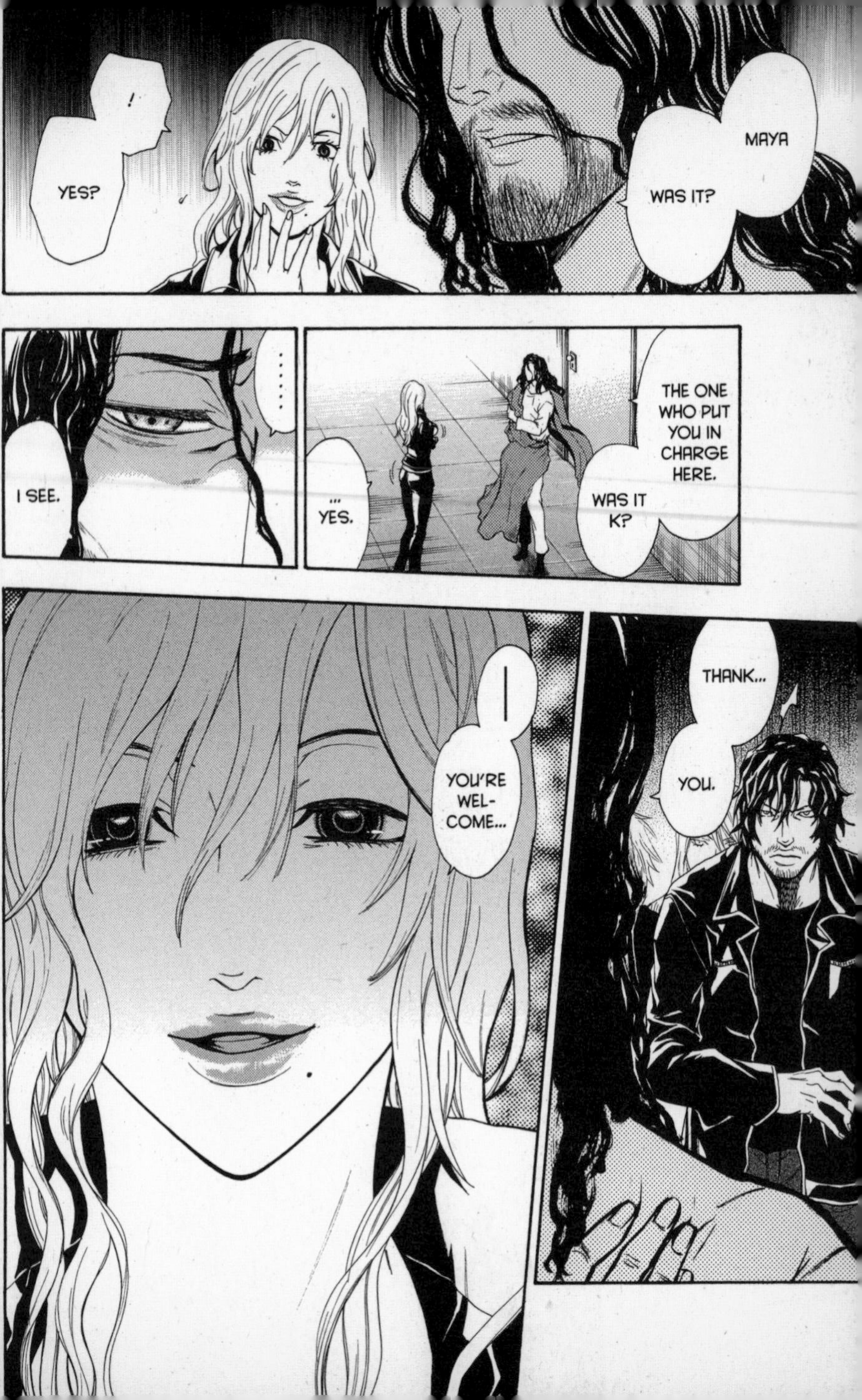
MAYA
WAS IT?
!
YES?
THE ONE WHO PUT YOU IN CHARGE HERE.
WAS IT K?
... YES.
......
I SEE.
THANK...
YOU.
—
YOU'RE WEL-COME...

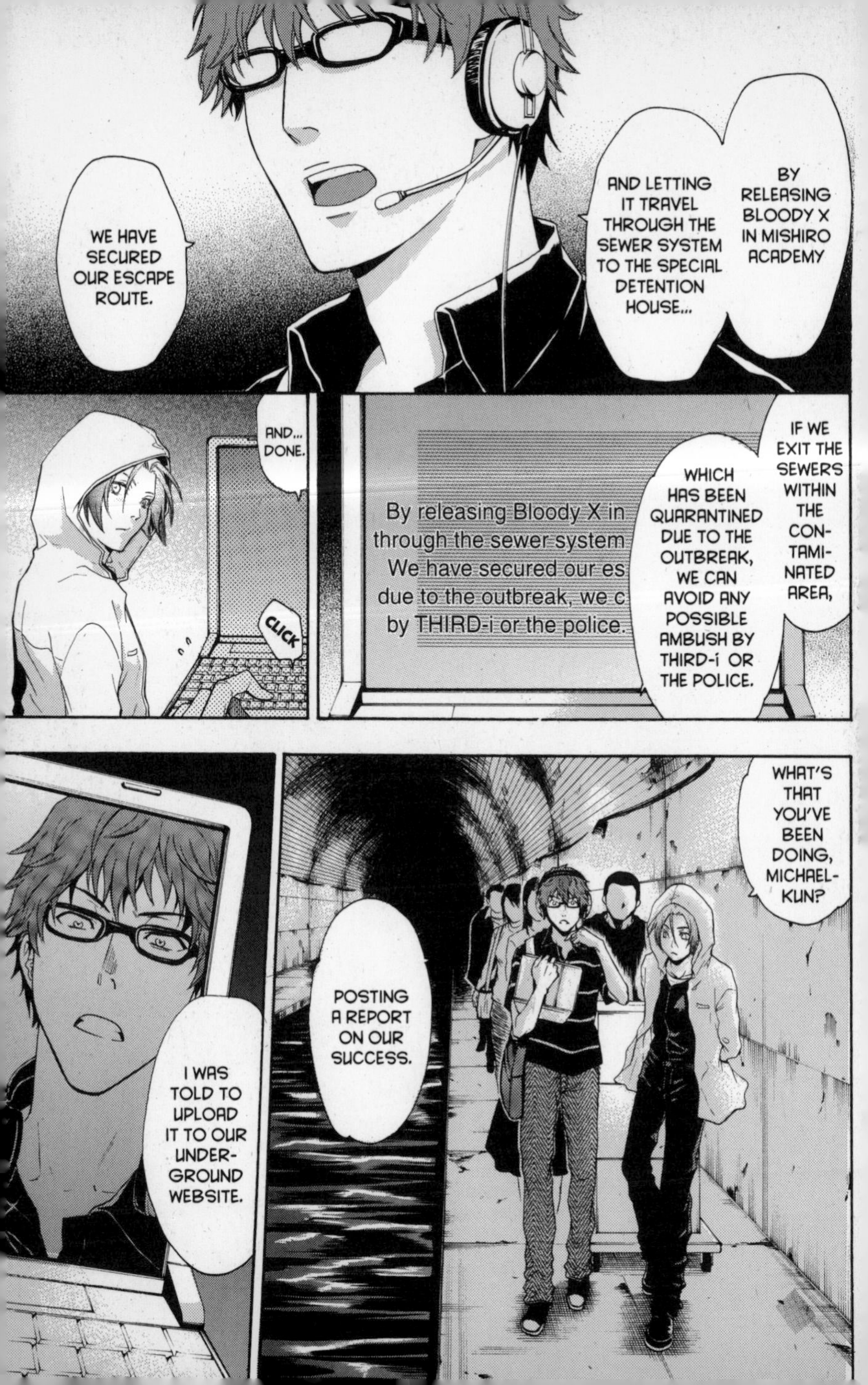
BY RELEASING BLOODY X IN MISHIRO ACADEMY
AND LETTING IT TRAVEL THROUGH THE SEWER SYSTEM TO THE SPECIAL DETENTION HOUSE...
WE HAVE SECURED OUR ESCAPE ROUTE.
By releasing Bloody X in
through the sewer system
We have secured our es
due to the outbreak, we c
by THIRD-i or the police.
IF WE EXIT THE SEWERS WITHIN THE CONTAMINATED AREA,
WHICH HAS BEEN QUARANTINED DUE TO THE OUTBREAK, WE CAN AVOID ANY POSSIBLE AMBUSH BY THIRD-i OR THE POLICE.
AND... DONE.
CLICK
WHAT'S THAT YOU'VE BEEN DOING, MICHAEL-KUN?
POSTING A REPORT ON OUR SUCCESS.
I WAS TOLD TO UPLOAD IT TO OUR UNDERGROUND WEBSITE.

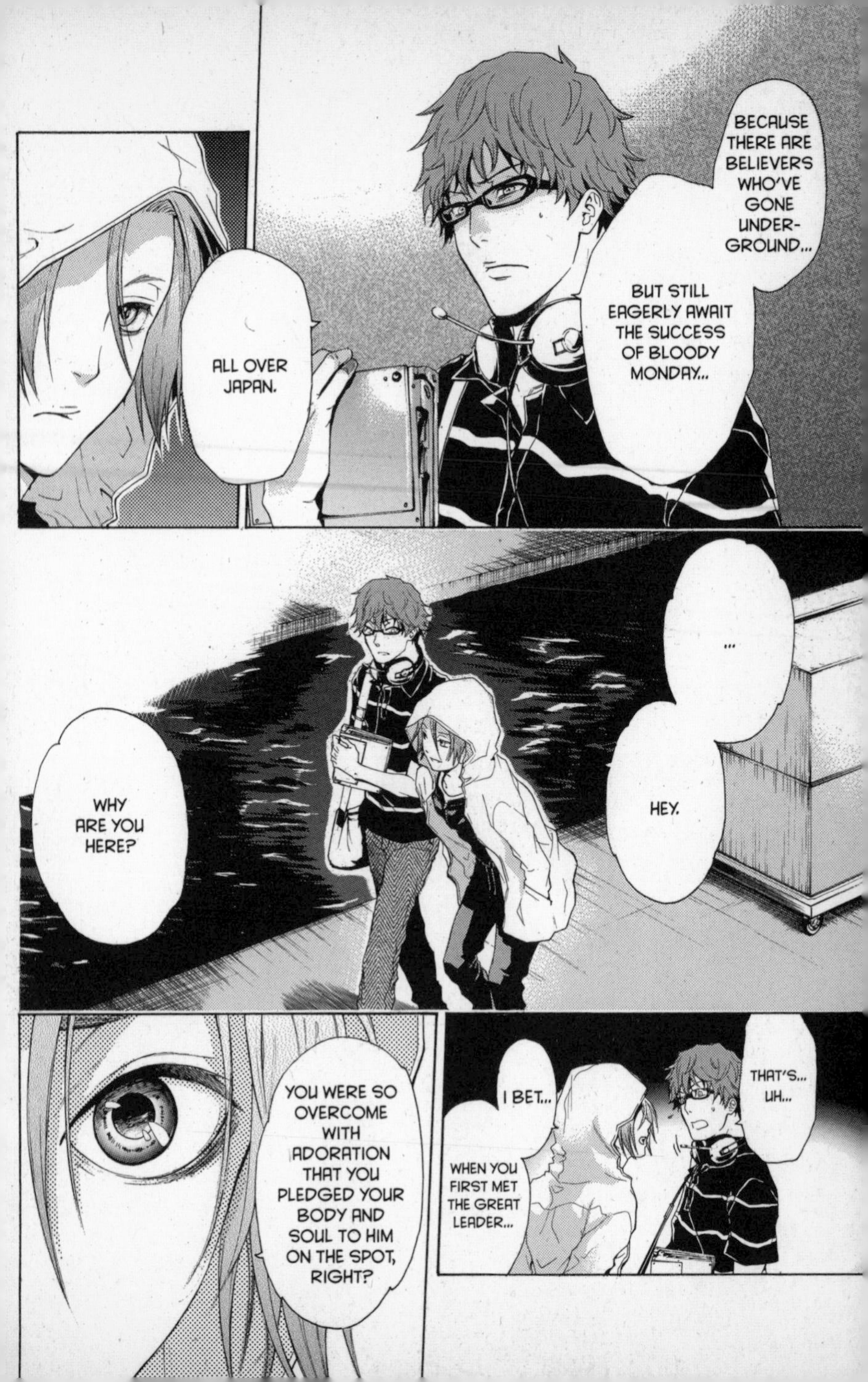
BECAUSE THERE ARE BELIEVERS WHO'VE GONE UNDER-GROUND...
BUT STILL EAGERLY AWAIT THE SUCCESS OF BLOODY MONDAY...
ALL OVER JAPAN.
...
HEY.
WHY ARE YOU HERE?
THAT'S... UH...
I BET...
WHEN YOU FIRST MET THE GREAT LEADER...
YOU WERE SO OVERCOME WITH ADORATION THAT YOU PLEDGED YOUR BODY AND SOUL TO HIM ON THE SPOT, RIGHT?

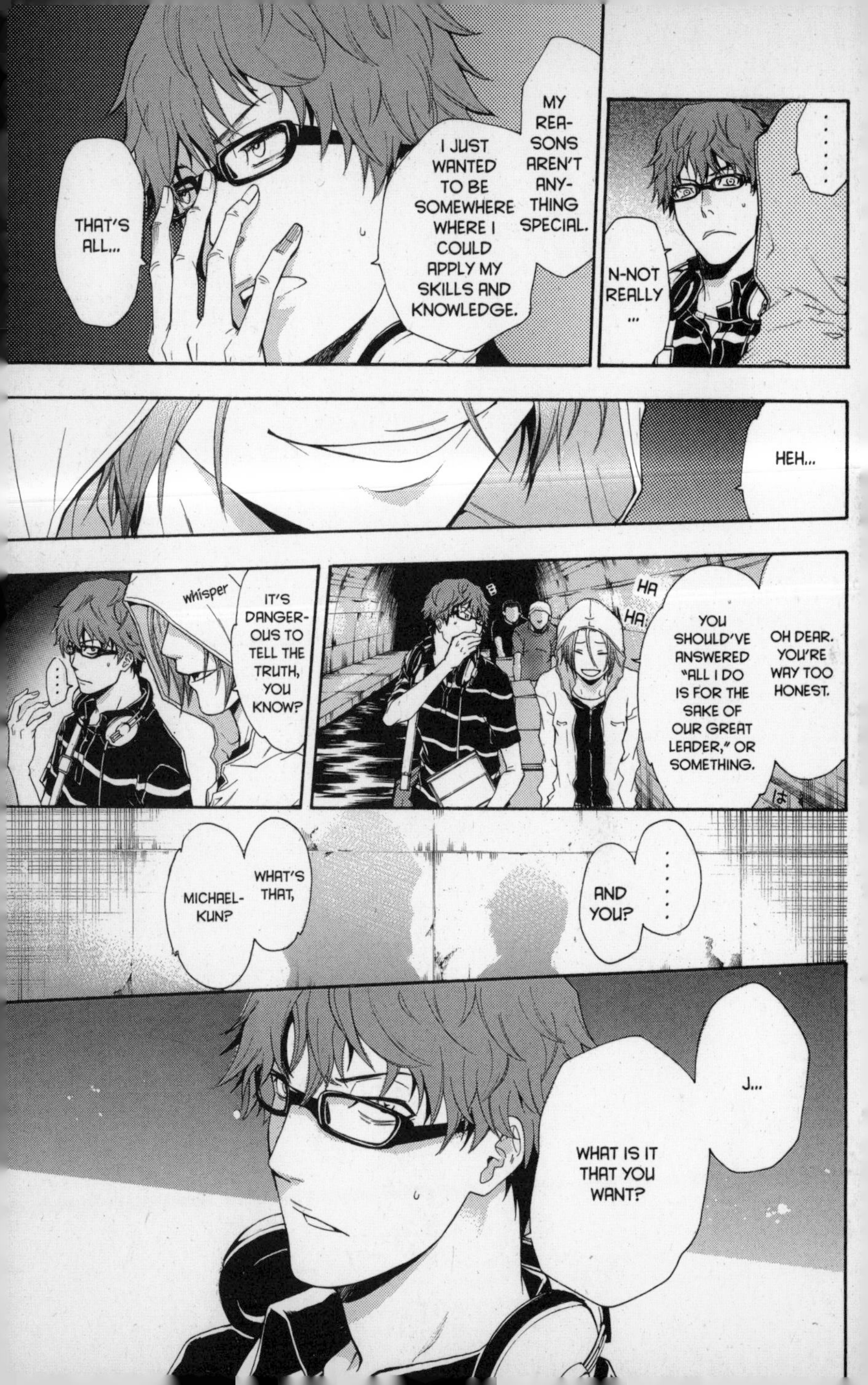
……
N-NOT REALLY …
MY REA-SONS AREN'T ANY-THING SPECIAL.
I JUST WANTED TO BE SOMEWHERE WHERE I COULD APPLY MY SKILLS AND KNOWLEDGE.
THAT'S ALL…
HEH…
OH DEAR. YOU'RE WAY TOO HONEST.
HA HA
YOU SHOULD'VE ANSWERED "ALL I DO IS FOR THE SAKE OF OUR GREAT LEADER," OR SOMETHING.
whisper
IT'S DANGER-OUS TO TELL THE TRUTH, YOU KNOW?
……
……
AND YOU?
WHAT'S THAT, MICHAEL-KUN?
J…
WHAT IS IT THAT YOU WANT?

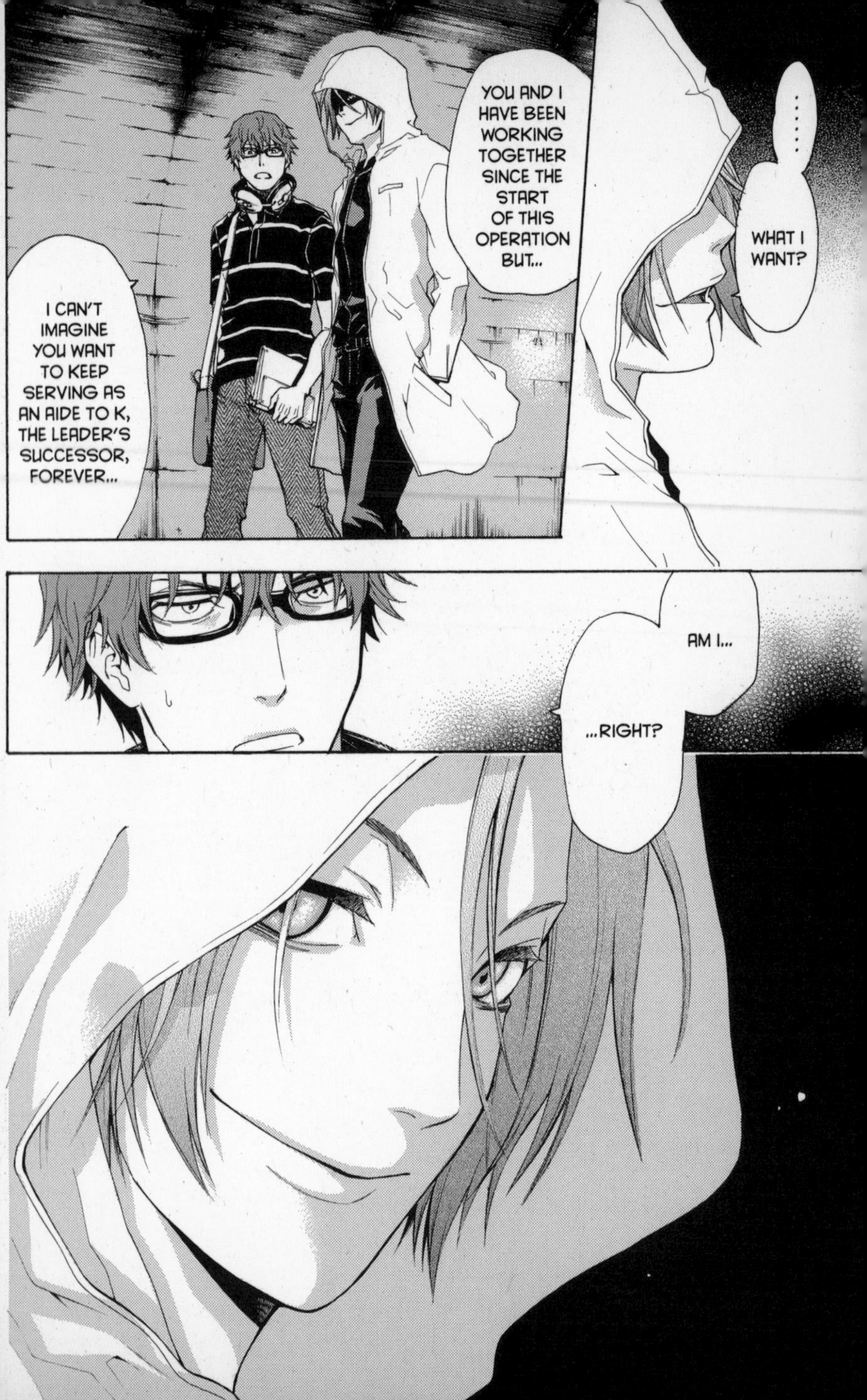
......
WHAT I WANT?
YOU AND I HAVE BEEN WORKING TOGETHER SINCE THE START OF THIS OPERATION BUT...
I CAN'T IMAGINE YOU WANT TO KEEP SERVING AS AN AIDE TO K, THE LEADER'S SUCCESSOR, FOREVER...
AM I...
...RIGHT?

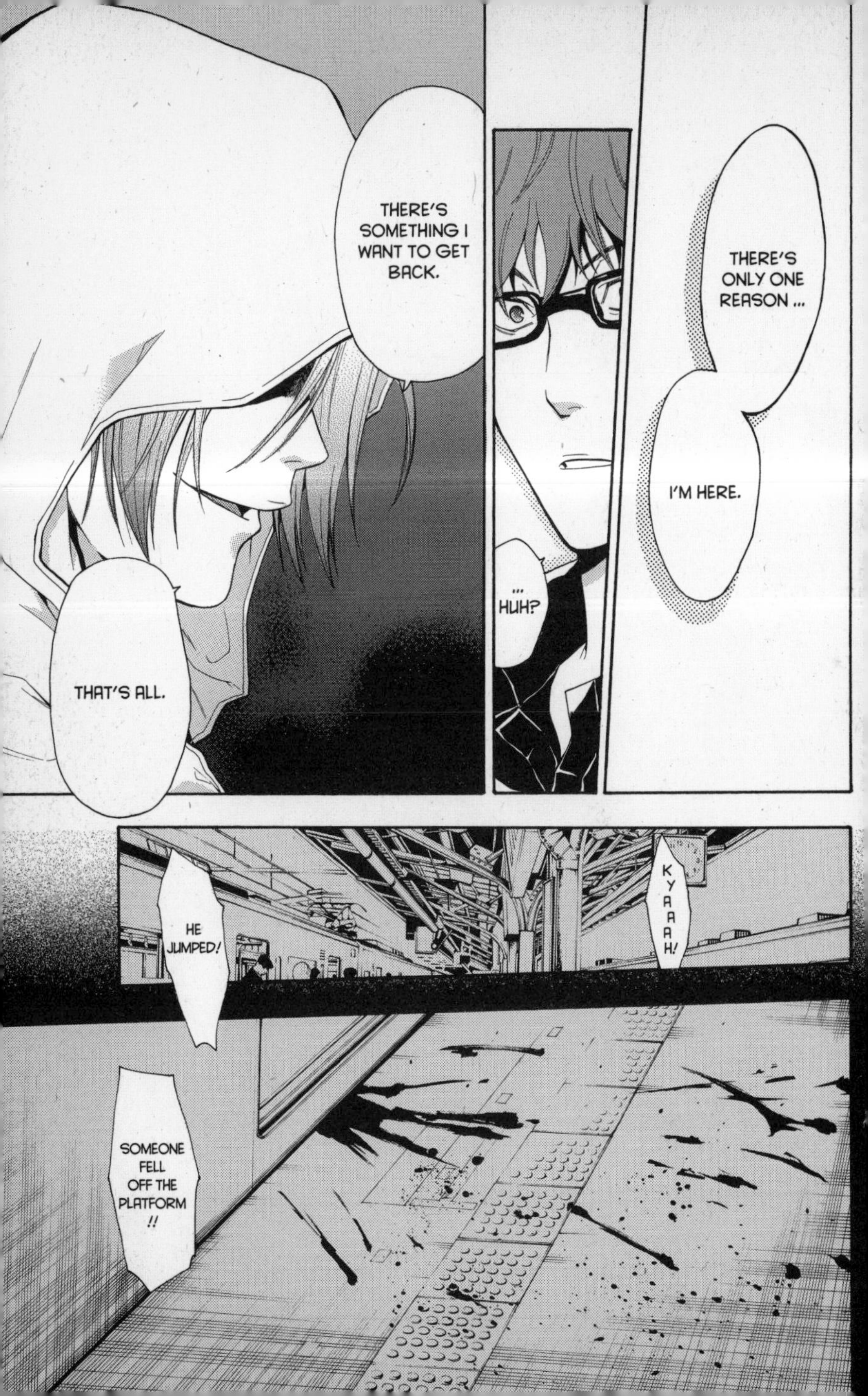
THERE'S ONLY ONE REASON ...
I'M HERE.
... HUH?
THERE'S SOMETHING I WANT TO GET BACK.
THAT'S ALL.
KYAAAH!
HE JUMPED!
SOMEONE FELL OFF THE PLATFORM !!

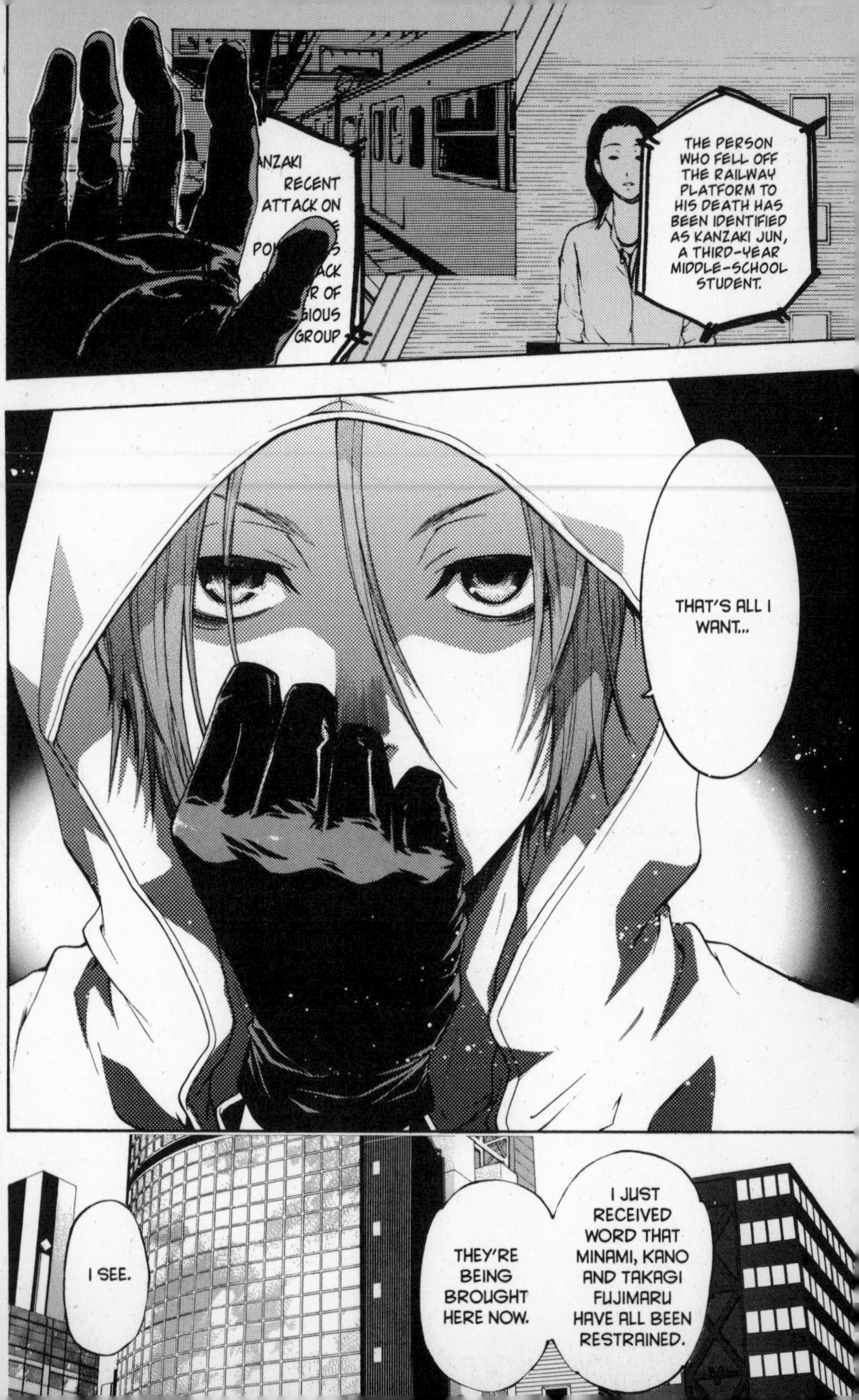
THE PERSON WHO FELL OFF THE RAILWAY PLATFORM TO HIS DEATH HAS BEEN IDENTIFIED AS KANZAKI JUN, A THIRD-YEAR MIDDLE-SCHOOL STUDENT.
RECENT
ATTACK ON
GROUP
THAT'S ALL I WANT...
I JUST RECEIVED WORD THAT MINAMI, KANO AND TAKAGI FUJIMARU HAVE ALL BEEN RESTRAINED.
THEY'RE BEING BROUGHT HERE NOW.
I SEE.

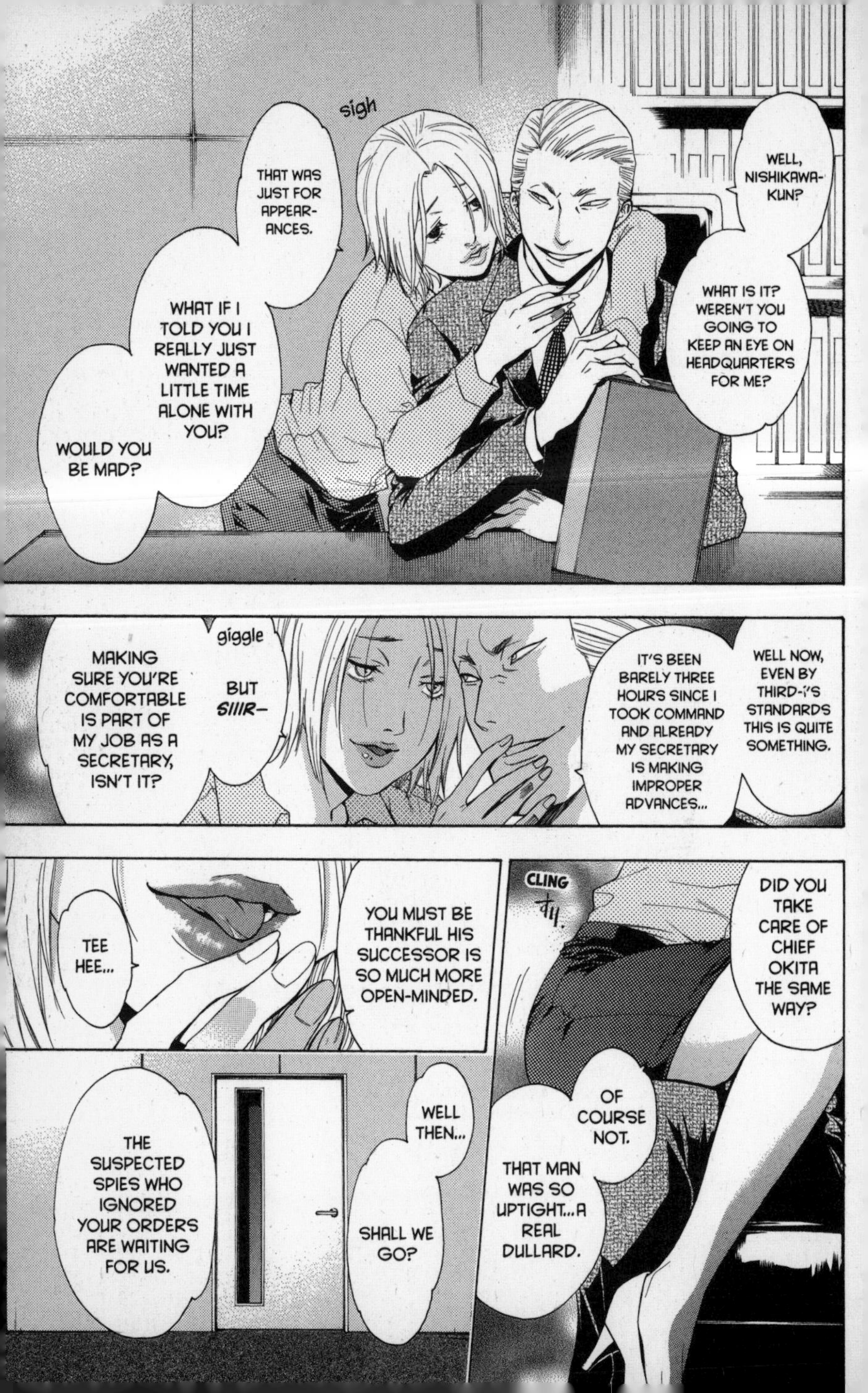
WELL, NISHIKAWA-KUN?
WHAT IS IT? WEREN'T YOU GOING TO KEEP AN EYE ON HEADQUARTERS FOR ME?
sigh
THAT WAS JUST FOR APPEAR-ANCES.
WHAT IF I TOLD YOU I REALLY JUST WANTED A LITTLE TIME ALONE WITH YOU?
WOULD YOU BE MAD?
WELL NOW, EVEN BY THIRD-i'S STANDARDS THIS IS QUITE SOMETHING.
IT'S BEEN BARELY THREE HOURS SINCE I TOOK COMMAND AND ALREADY MY SECRETARY IS MAKING IMPROPER ADVANCES...
giggle
BUT SIIIR–
MAKING SURE YOU'RE COMFORTABLE IS PART OF MY JOB AS A SECRETARY, ISN'T IT?
CLING
DID YOU TAKE CARE OF CHIEF OKITA THE SAME WAY?
OF COURSE NOT.
THAT MAN WAS SO UPTIGHT...A REAL DULLARD.
YOU MUST BE THANKFUL HIS SUCCESSOR IS SO MUCH MORE OPEN-MINDED.
TEE HEE...
WELL THEN...
SHALL WE GO?
THE SUSPECTED SPIES WHO IGNORED YOUR ORDERS ARE WAITING FOR US.

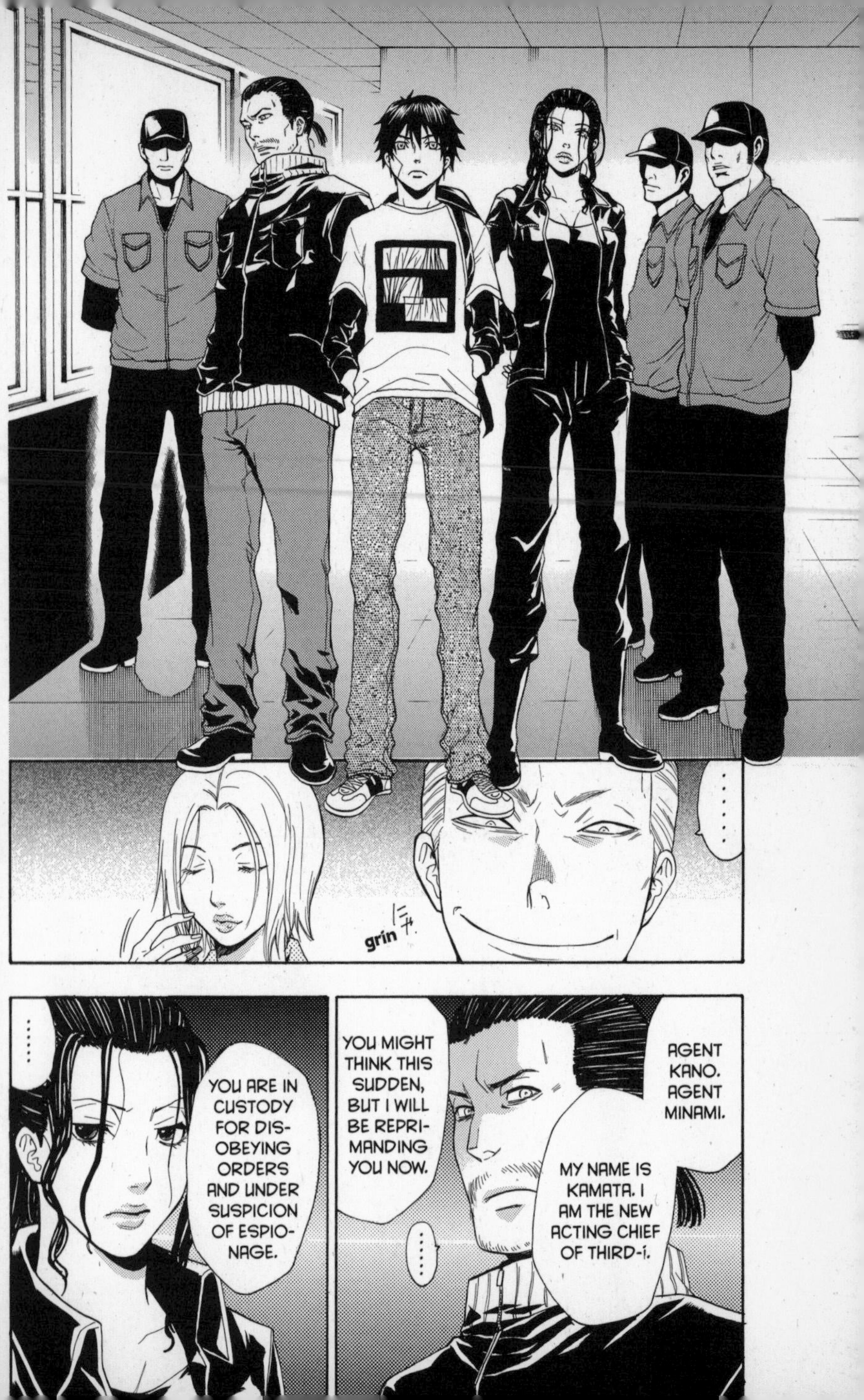
......
ニヤ
grin
AGENT KANO. AGENT MINAMI.
MY NAME IS KAMATA. I AM THE NEW ACTING CHIEF OF THIRD-i.
YOU MIGHT THINK THIS SUDDEN, BUT I WILL BE REPRIMANDING YOU NOW.
......
......
YOU ARE IN CUSTODY FOR DIS-OBEYING ORDERS AND UNDER SUSPICION OF ESPIO-NAGE.

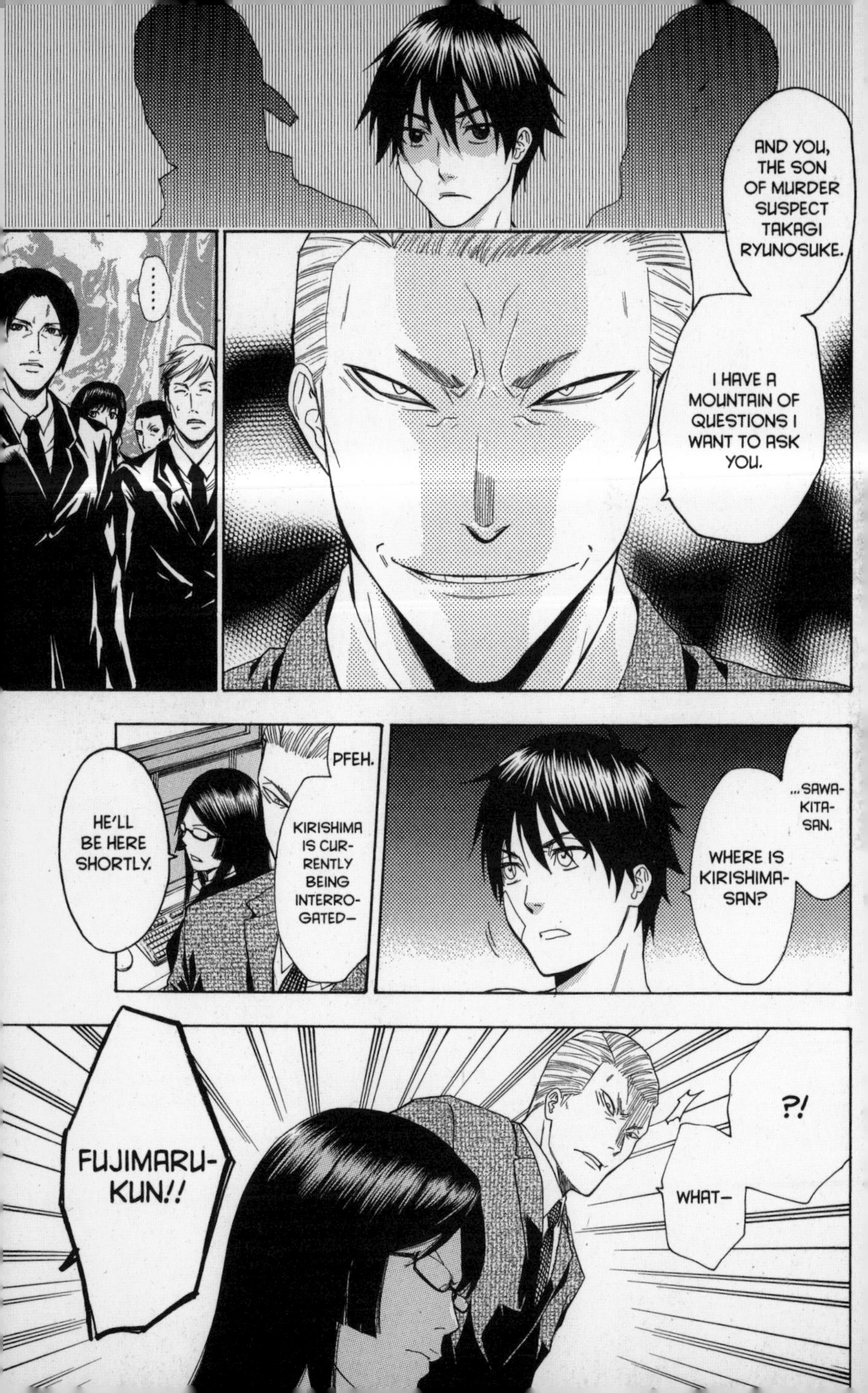
AND YOU, THE SON OF MURDER SUSPECT TAKAGI RYUNOSUKE.
I HAVE A MOUNTAIN OF QUESTIONS I WANT TO ASK YOU.
......
...SAWA-KITA-SAN.
WHERE IS KIRISHIMA-SAN?
PFEH.
KIRISHIMA IS CUR-RENTLY BEING INTERRO-GATED—
HE'LL BE HERE SHORTLY.
?!
WHAT—
FUJIMARU-KUN!!

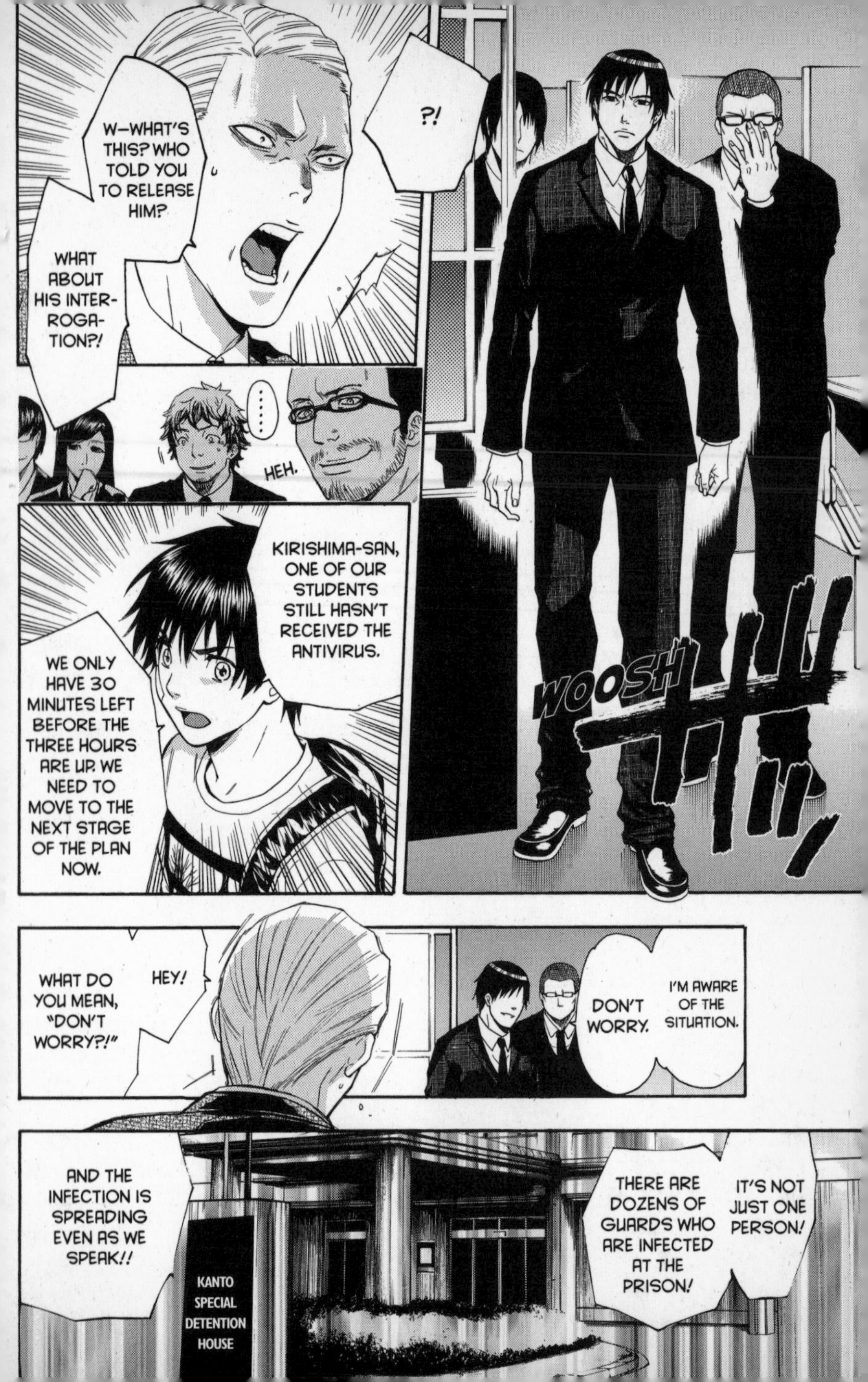
?!
WOOSH
W-WHAT'S THIS? WHO TOLD YOU TO RELEASE HIM?
WHAT ABOUT HIS INTER-ROGA-TION?!
......
HEH.
KIRISHIMA-SAN, ONE OF OUR STUDENTS STILL HASN'T RECEIVED THE ANTIVIRUS.
WE ONLY HAVE 30 MINUTES LEFT BEFORE THE THREE HOURS ARE UP. WE NEED TO MOVE TO THE NEXT STAGE OF THE PLAN NOW.
I'M AWARE OF THE SITUATION.
DON'T WORRY.
HEY!
WHAT DO YOU MEAN, "DON'T WORRY?!"
IT'S NOT JUST ONE PERSON!
THERE ARE DOZENS OF GUARDS WHO ARE INFECTED AT THE PRISON!
KANTO SPECIAL DETENTION HOUSE
AND THE INFECTION IS SPREADING EVEN AS WE SPEAK!!

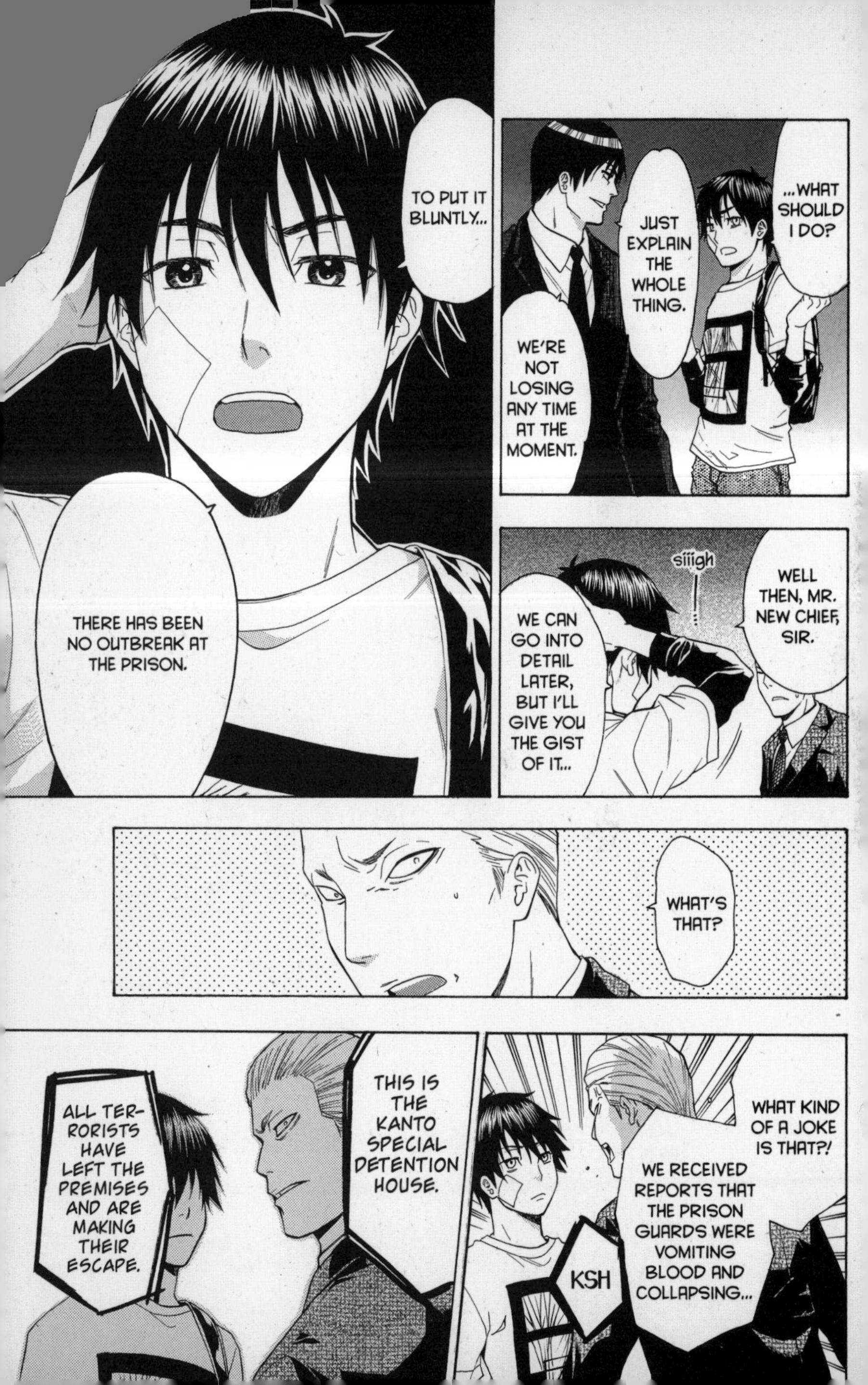
...WHAT SHOULD I DO?
JUST EXPLAIN THE WHOLE THING.
WE'RE NOT LOSING ANY TIME AT THE MOMENT.
WELL THEN, MR. NEW CHIEF, SIR.
siiigh
WE CAN GO INTO DETAIL LATER, BUT I'LL GIVE YOU THE GIST OF IT...
TO PUT IT BLUNTLY...
THERE HAS BEEN NO OUTBREAK AT THE PRISON.
WHAT'S THAT?
WHAT KIND OF A JOKE IS THAT?!
WE RECEIVED REPORTS THAT THE PRISON GUARDS WERE VOMITING BLOOD AND COLLAPSING...
KSH
THIS IS THE KANTO SPECIAL DETENTION HOUSE.
ALL TERRORISTS HAVE LEFT THE PREMISES AND ARE MAKING THEIR ESCAPE.

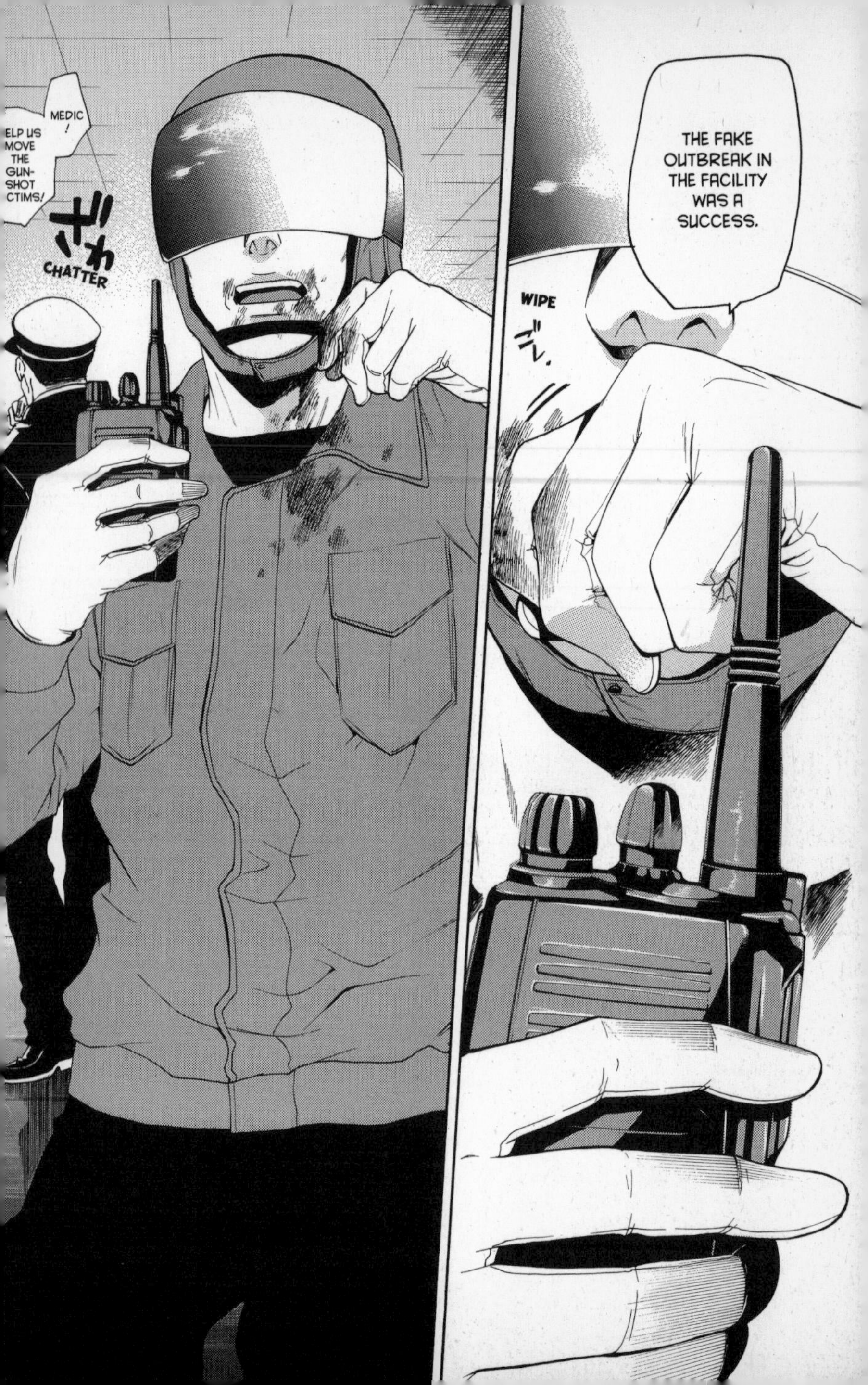
THE FAKE OUTBREAK IN THE FACILITY WAS A SUCCESS.
WIPE
MEDIC!
ELP US MOVE THE GUN-SHOT CTIMS!
CHATTER

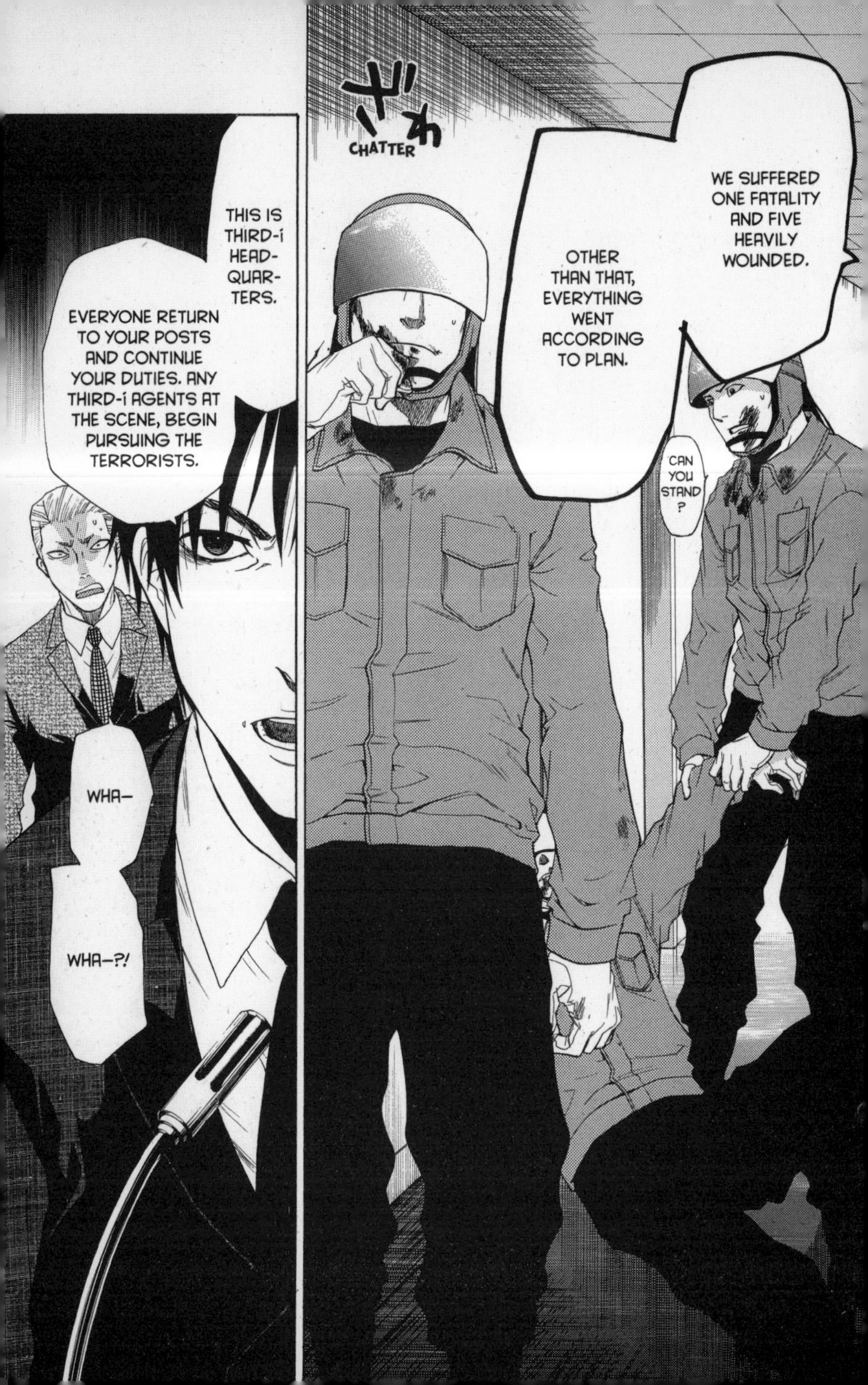
ざわ
CHATTER
WE SUFFERED ONE FATALITY AND FIVE HEAVILY WOUNDED.
OTHER THAN THAT, EVERYTHING WENT ACCORDING TO PLAN.
CAN YOU STAND?
THIS IS THIRD-i HEAD-QUARTERS.
EVERYONE RETURN TO YOUR POSTS AND CONTINUE YOUR DUTIES. ANY THIRD-i AGENTS AT THE SCENE, BEGIN PURSUING THE TERRORISTS.
WHA-
WHA-?!

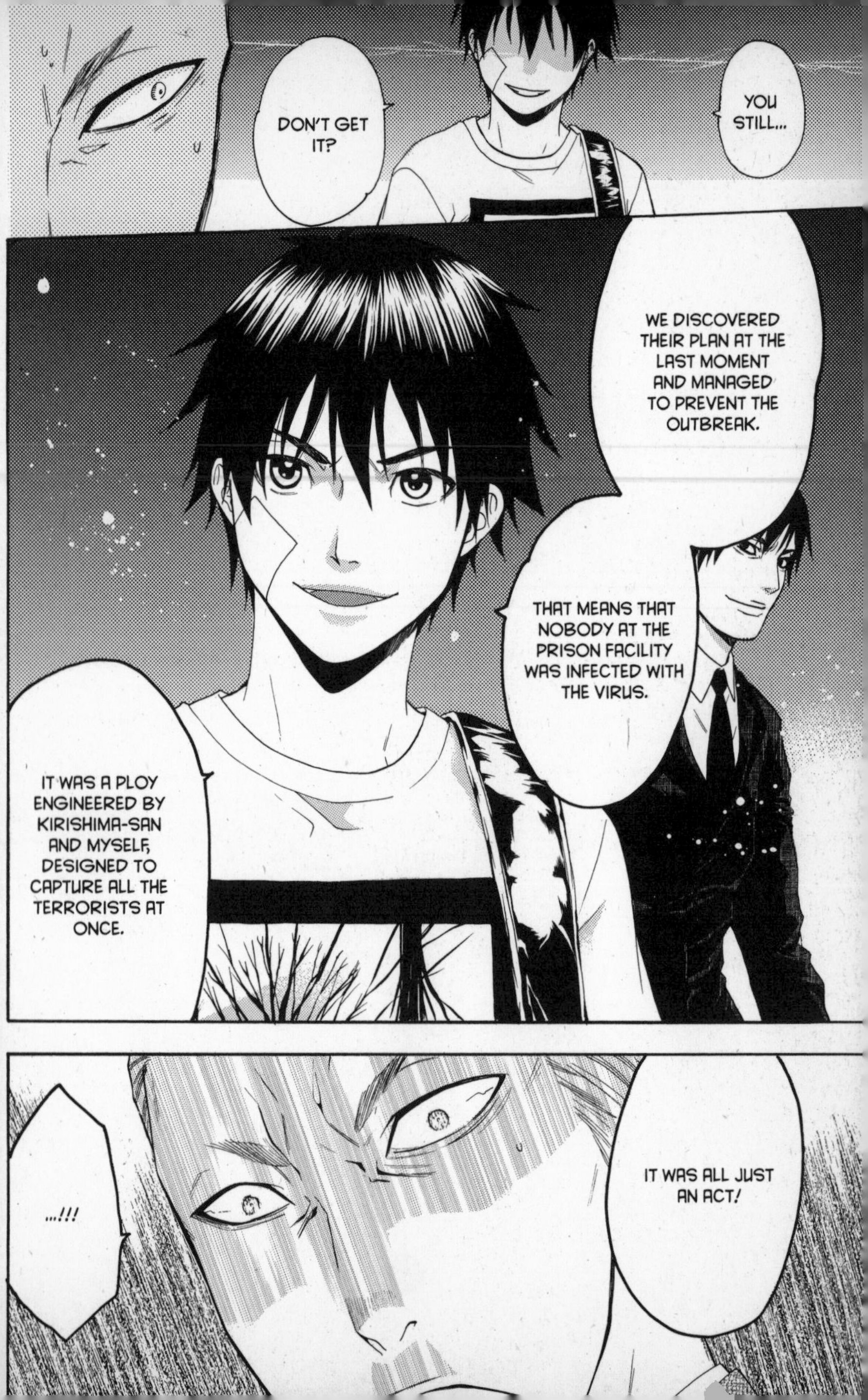
YOU STILL...
DON'T GET IT?
WE DISCOVERED THEIR PLAN AT THE LAST MOMENT AND MANAGED TO PREVENT THE OUTBREAK.
THAT MEANS THAT NOBODY AT THE PRISON FACILITY WAS INFECTED WITH THE VIRUS.
IT WAS A PLOY ENGINEERED BY KIRISHIMA-SAN AND MYSELF, DESIGNED TO CAPTURE ALL THE TERRORISTS AT ONCE.
IT WAS ALL JUST AN ACT!
...!!!

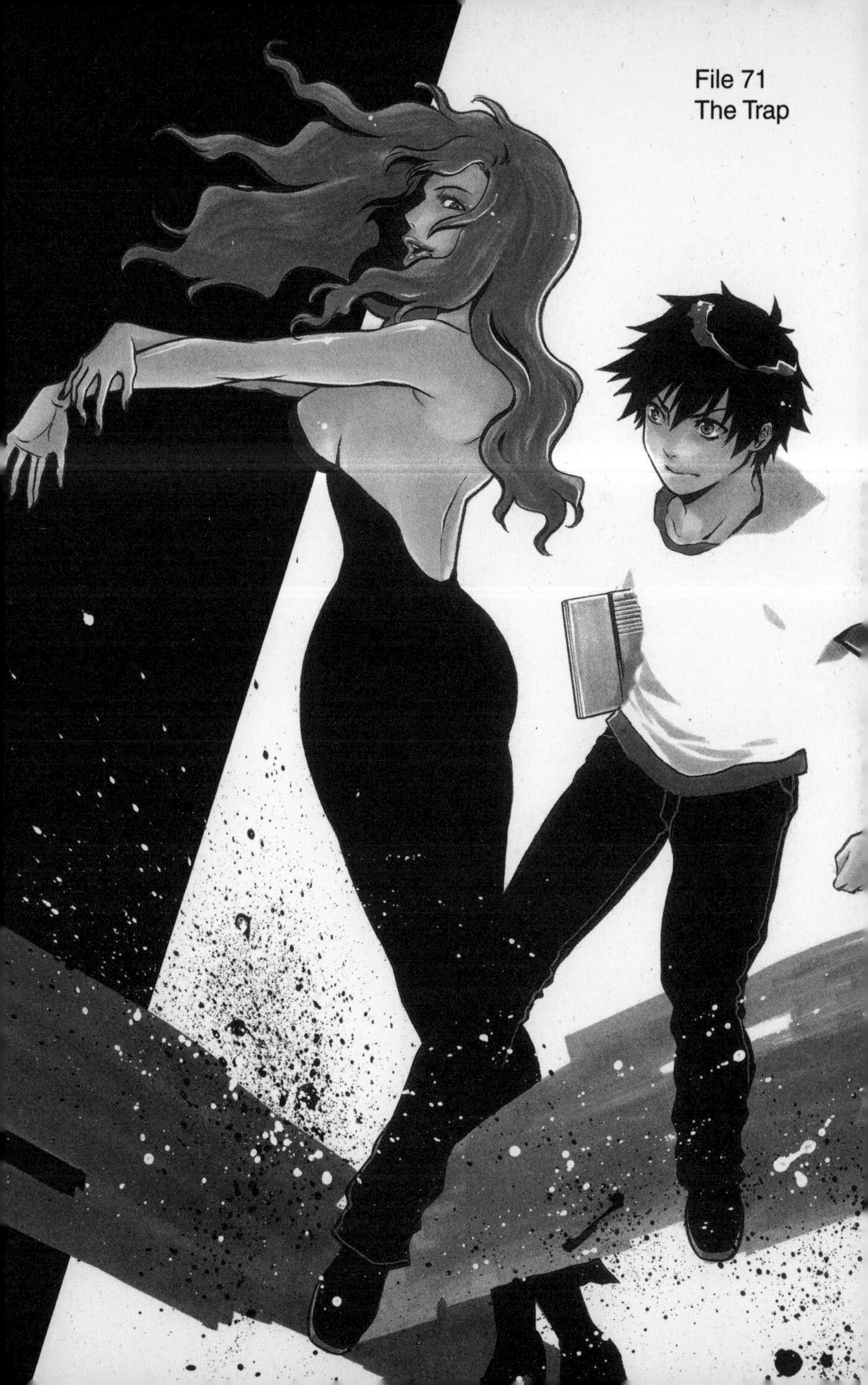
File 71
The Trap

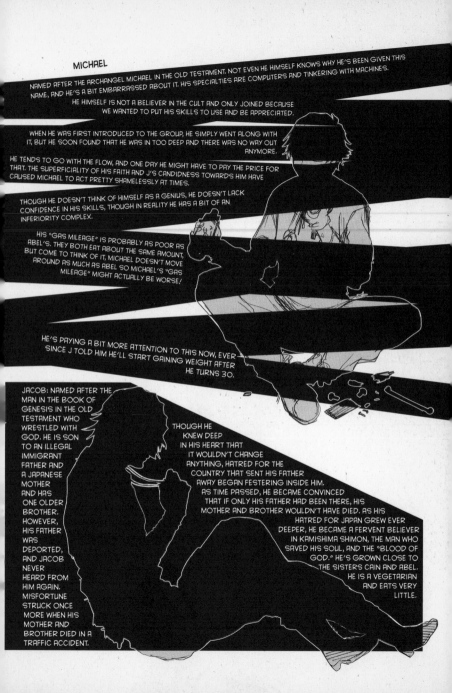

MICHAEL

NAMED AFTER THE ARCHANGEL MICHAEL IN THE OLD TESTAMENT. NOT EVEN HE HIMSELF KNOWS WHY HE'S BEEN GIVEN THIS NAME, AND HE'S A BIT EMBARRASSED ABOUT IT. HIS SPECIALTIES ARE COMPUTERS AND TINKERING WITH MACHINES.

HE HIMSELF IS NOT A BELIEVER IN THE CULT AND ONLY JOINED BECAUSE WE WANTED TO PUT HIS SKILLS TO USE AND BE APPRECIATED.

WHEN HE WAS FIRST INTRODUCED TO THE GROUP, HE SIMPLY WENT ALONG WITH IT, BUT HE SOON FOUND THAT HE WAS IN TOO DEEP AND THERE WAS NO WAY OUT ANYMORE.

HE TENDS TO GO WITH THE FLOW, AND ONE DAY HE MIGHT HAVE TO PAY THE PRICE FOR THAT. THE SUPERFICIALITY OF HIS FAITH AND J'S CANDIDNESS TOWARDS HIM HAVE CAUSED MICHAEL TO ACT PRETTY SHAMELESSLY AT TIMES.

THOUGH HE DOESN'T THINK OF HIMSELF AS A GENIUS, HE DOESN'T LACK CONFIDENCE IN HIS SKILLS, THOUGH IN REALITY HE HAS A BIT OF AN INFERIORITY COMPLEX.

HIS "GAS MILEAGE" IS PROBABLY AS POOR AS ABEL'S. THEY BOTH EAT ABOUT THE SAME AMOUNT, BUT COME TO THINK OF IT, MICHAEL DOESN'T MOVE AROUND AS MUCH AS ABEL SO MICHAEL'S "GAS MILEAGE" MIGHT ACTUALLY BE WORSE!

HE'S PAYING A BIT MORE ATTENTION TO THIS NOW, EVER SINCE J TOLD HIM HE'LL START GAINING WEIGHT AFTER HE TURNS 30.

JACOB: NAMED AFTER THE MAN IN THE BOOK OF GENESIS IN THE OLD TESTAMENT WHO WRESTLED WITH GOD. HE IS SON TO AN ILLEGAL IMMIGRANT FATHER AND A JAPANESE MOTHER AND HAS ONE OLDER BROTHER. HOWEVER, HIS FATHER WAS DEPORTED, AND JACOB NEVER HEARD FROM HIM AGAIN. MISFORTUNE STRUCK ONCE MORE WHEN HIS MOTHER AND BROTHER DIED IN A TRAFFIC ACCIDENT.

THOUGH HE KNEW DEEP IN HIS HEART THAT IT WOULDN'T CHANGE ANYTHING, HATRED FOR THE COUNTRY THAT SENT HIS FATHER AWAY BEGAN FESTERING INSIDE HIM. AS TIME PASSED, HE BECAME CONVINCED THAT IF ONLY HIS FATHER HAD BEEN THERE, HIS MOTHER AND BROTHER WOULDN'T HAVE DIED. AS HIS HATRED FOR JAPAN GREW EVER DEEPER, HE BECAME A FERVENT BELIEVER IN KAMISHIMA SHIMON, THE MAN WHO SAVED HIS SOUL, AND THE "BLOOD OF GOD." HE'S GROWN CLOSE TO THE SISTERS CAIN AND ABEL. HE IS A VEGETARIAN AND EATS VERY LITTLE.

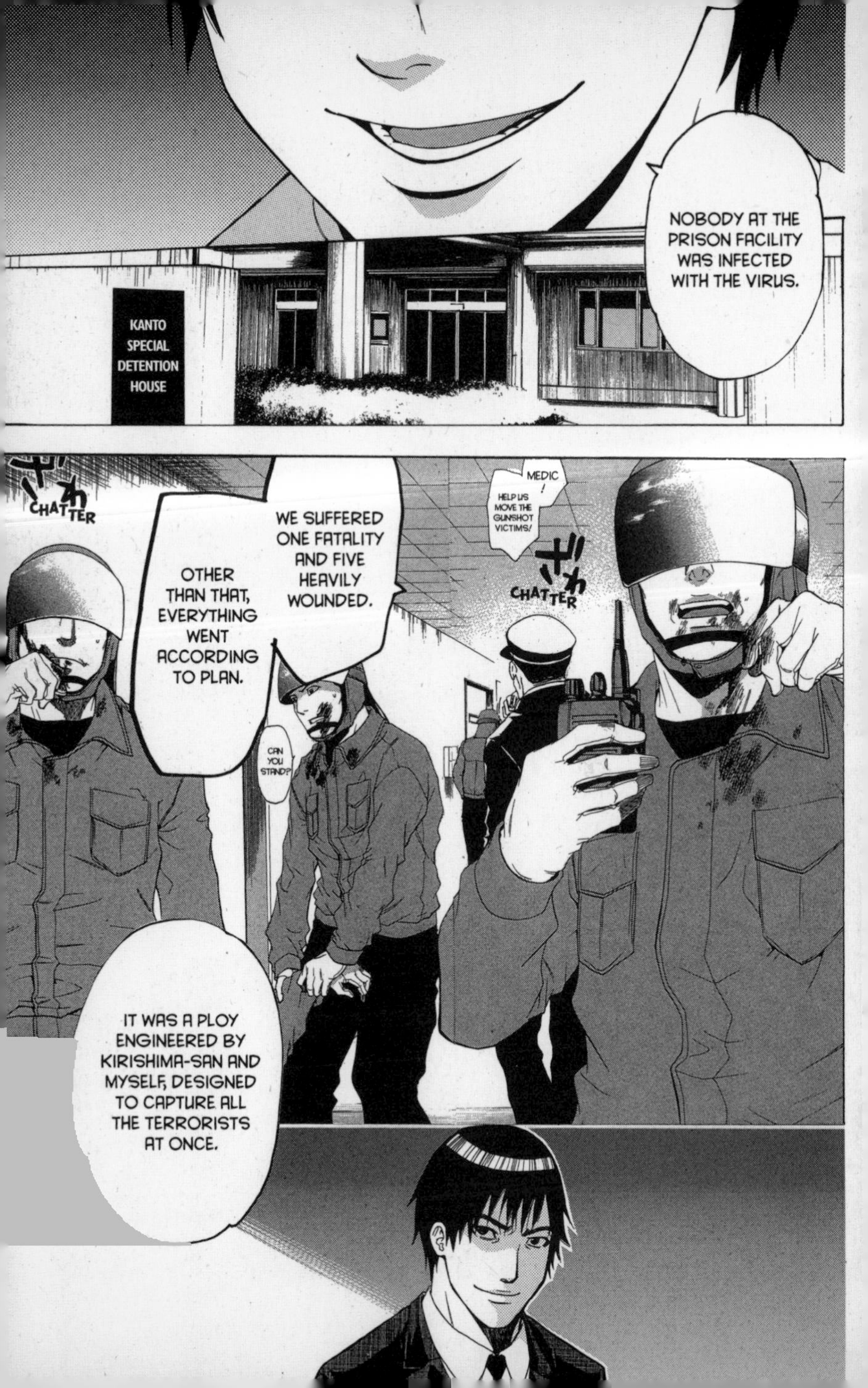
NOBODY AT THE PRISON FACILITY WAS INFECTED WITH THE VIRUS.
KANTO SPECIAL DETENTION HOUSE
MEDIC!
HELP US MOVE THE GUNSHOT VICTIMS!
CHATTER
WE SUFFERED ONE FATALITY AND FIVE HEAVILY WOUNDED.
OTHER THAN THAT, EVERYTHING WENT ACCORDING TO PLAN.
CHATTER
CAN YOU STAND?
IT WAS A PLOY ENGINEERED BY KIRISHIMA-SAN AND MYSELF, DESIGNED TO CAPTURE ALL THE TERRORISTS AT ONCE.

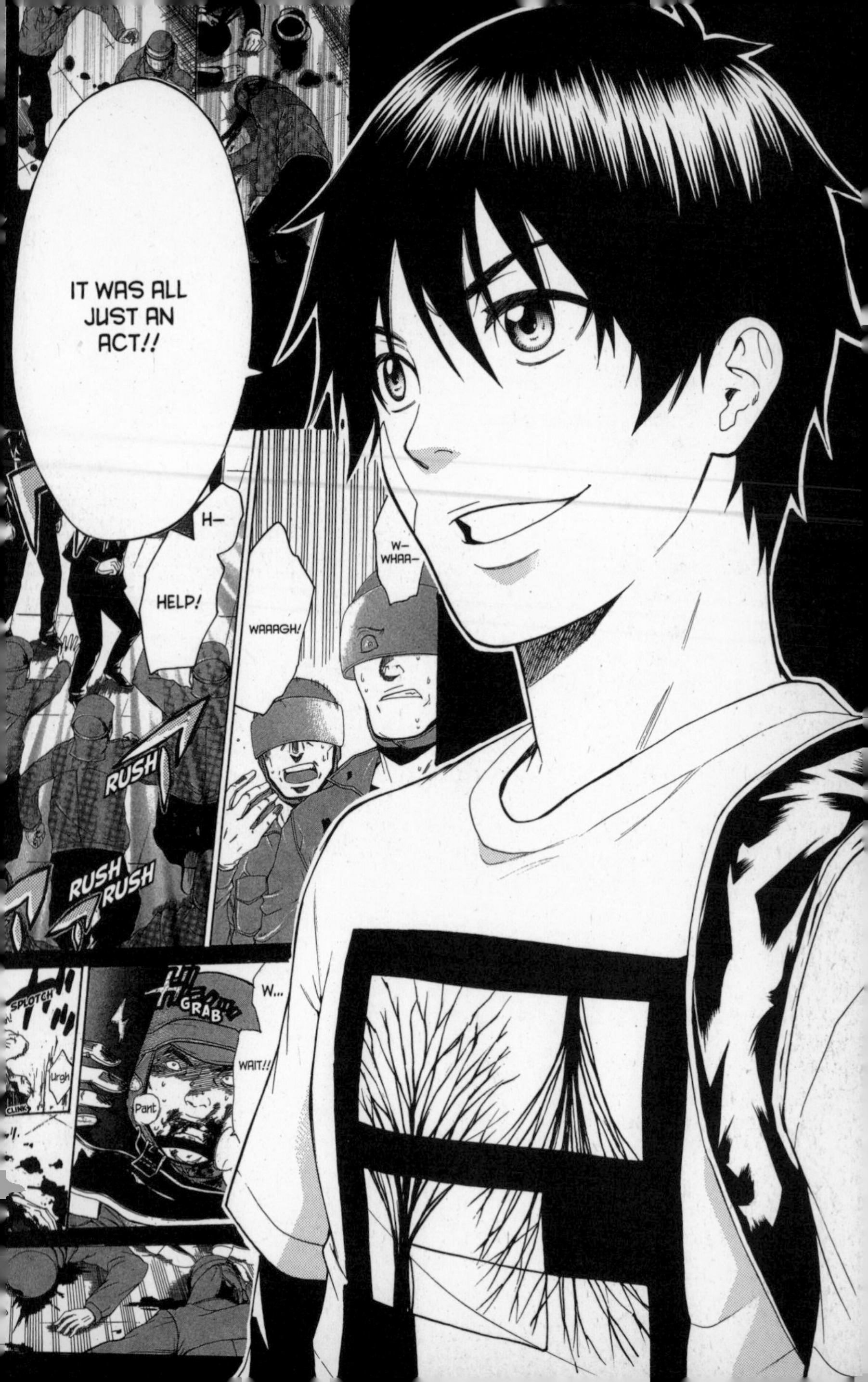
IT WAS ALL JUST AN ACT!!
W— WHAA—
WAAAGH!
H—
HELP!
RUSH
RUSH RUSH
W...
WAIT!!
GRAB
Pant
Urgh
SPLOTCH
CLINK

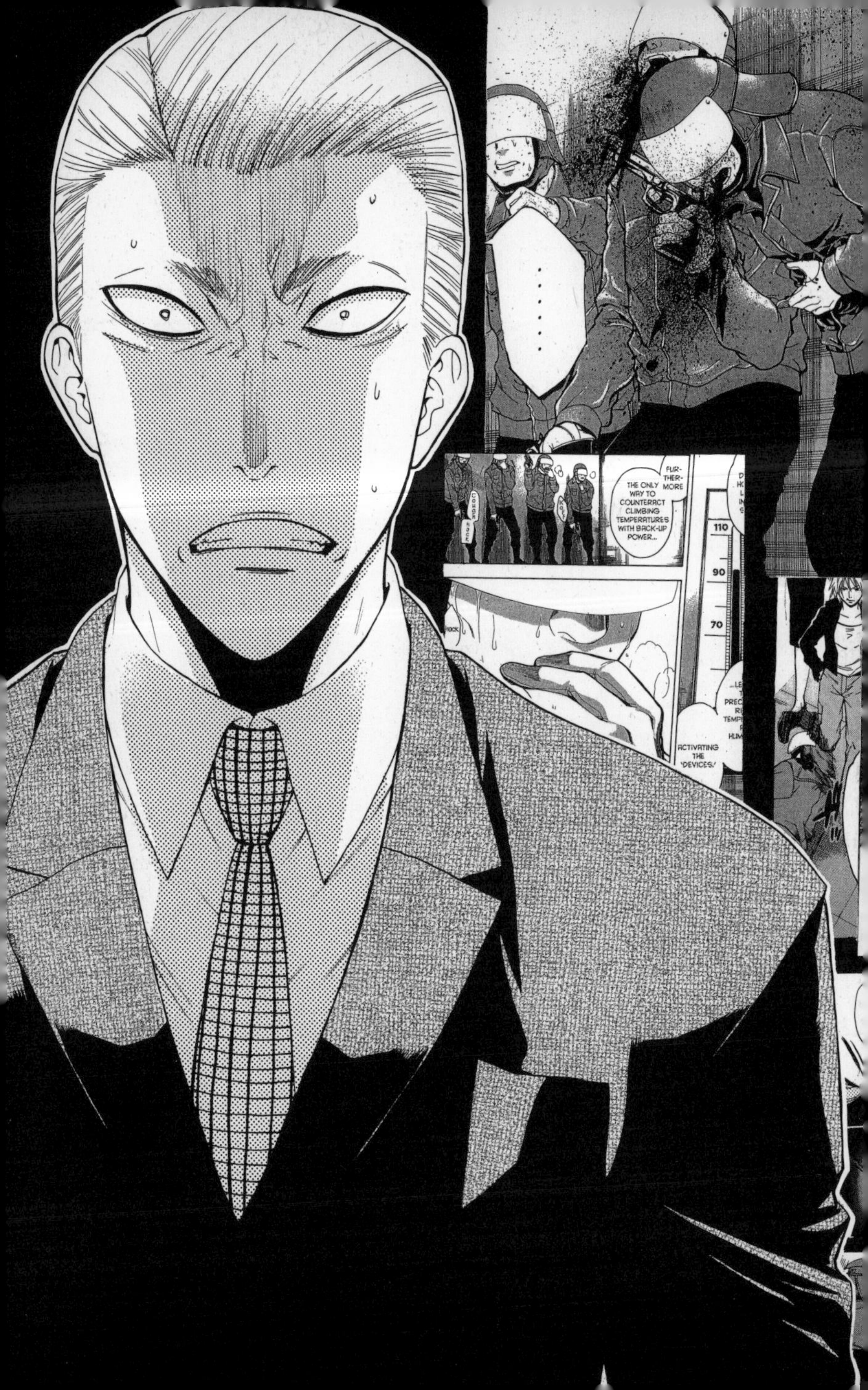
110
90
70
FURTHERMORE THE ONLY WAY TO COUNTERACT CLIMBING TEMPERATURES WITH BACK-UP POWER...
KOFF
COUGH HACK
ACTIVATING THE 'DEVICES!'
HACK

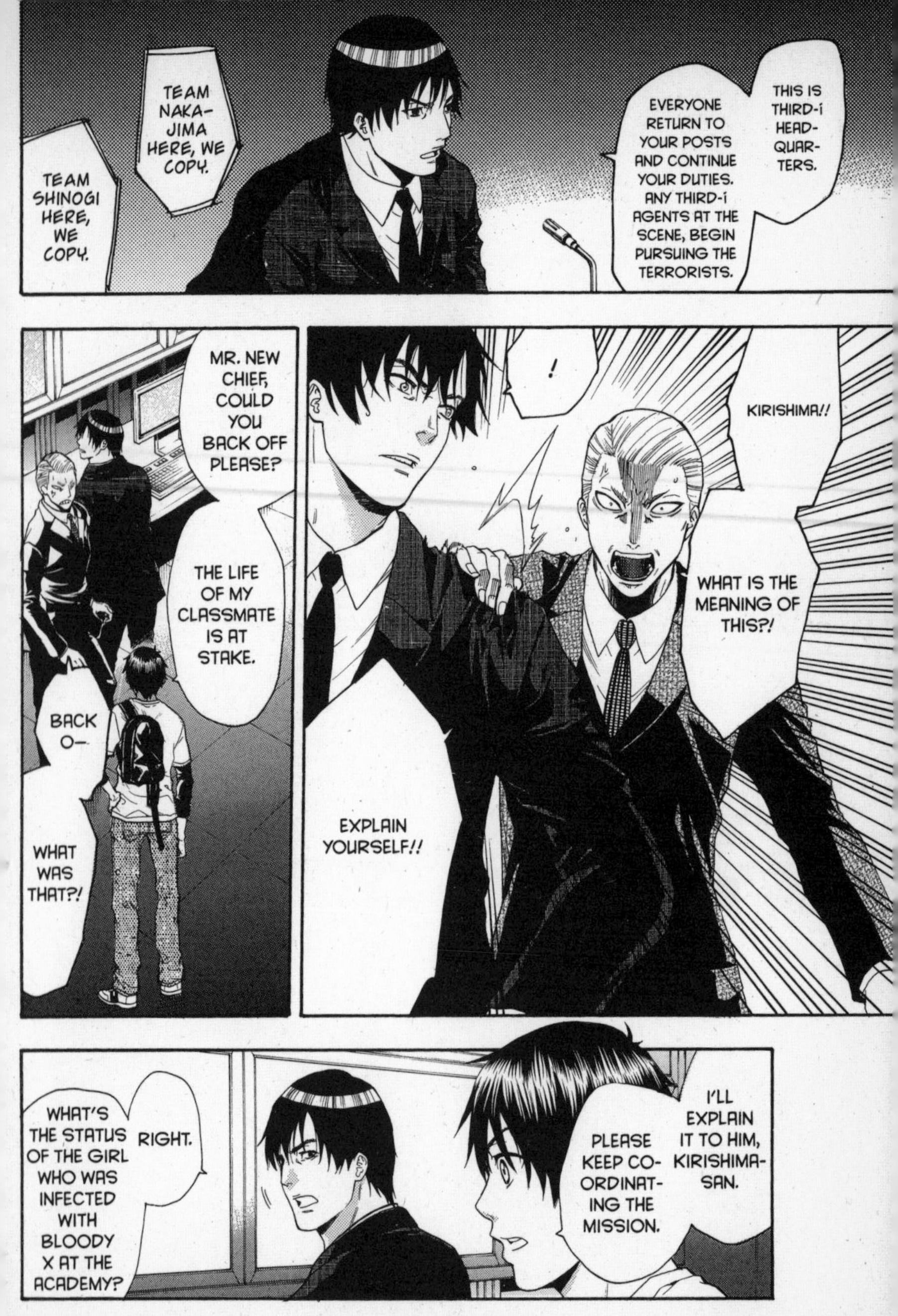
THIS IS THIRD-i HEADQUARTERS.
EVERYONE RETURN TO YOUR POSTS AND CONTINUE YOUR DUTIES. ANY THIRD-i AGENTS AT THE SCENE, BEGIN PURSUING THE TERRORISTS.
TEAM NAKAJIMA HERE, WE COPY.
TEAM SHINOGI HERE, WE COPY.
!
KIRISHIMA!!
WHAT IS THE MEANING OF THIS?!
EXPLAIN YOURSELF!!
MR. NEW CHIEF, COULD YOU BACK OFF PLEASE?
THE LIFE OF MY CLASSMATE IS AT STAKE.
BACK O—
WHAT WAS THAT?!
I'LL EXPLAIN IT TO HIM, KIRISHIMA-SAN.
PLEASE KEEP CO-ORDINATING THE MISSION.
RIGHT.
WHAT'S THE STATUS OF THE GIRL WHO WAS INFECTED WITH BLOODY X AT THE ACADEMY?

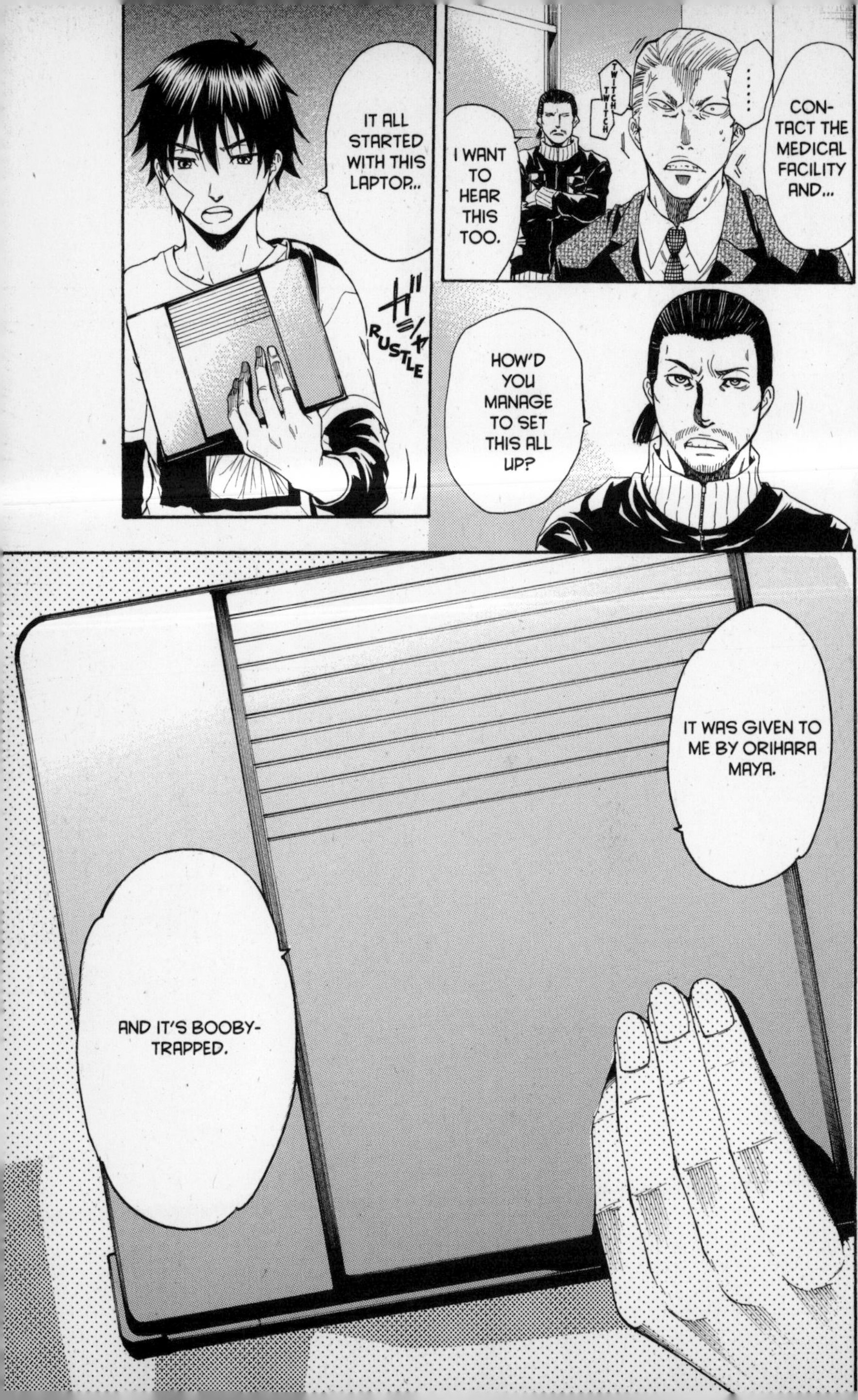
CON-TACT THE MEDICAL FACILITY AND...
......
TWITCH TWITCH
I WANT TO HEAR THIS TOO.
HOW'D YOU MANAGE TO SET THIS ALL UP?
IT ALL STARTED WITH THIS LAPTOP...
RUSTLE
IT WAS GIVEN TO ME BY ORIHARA MAYA.
AND IT'S BOOBY-TRAPPED.

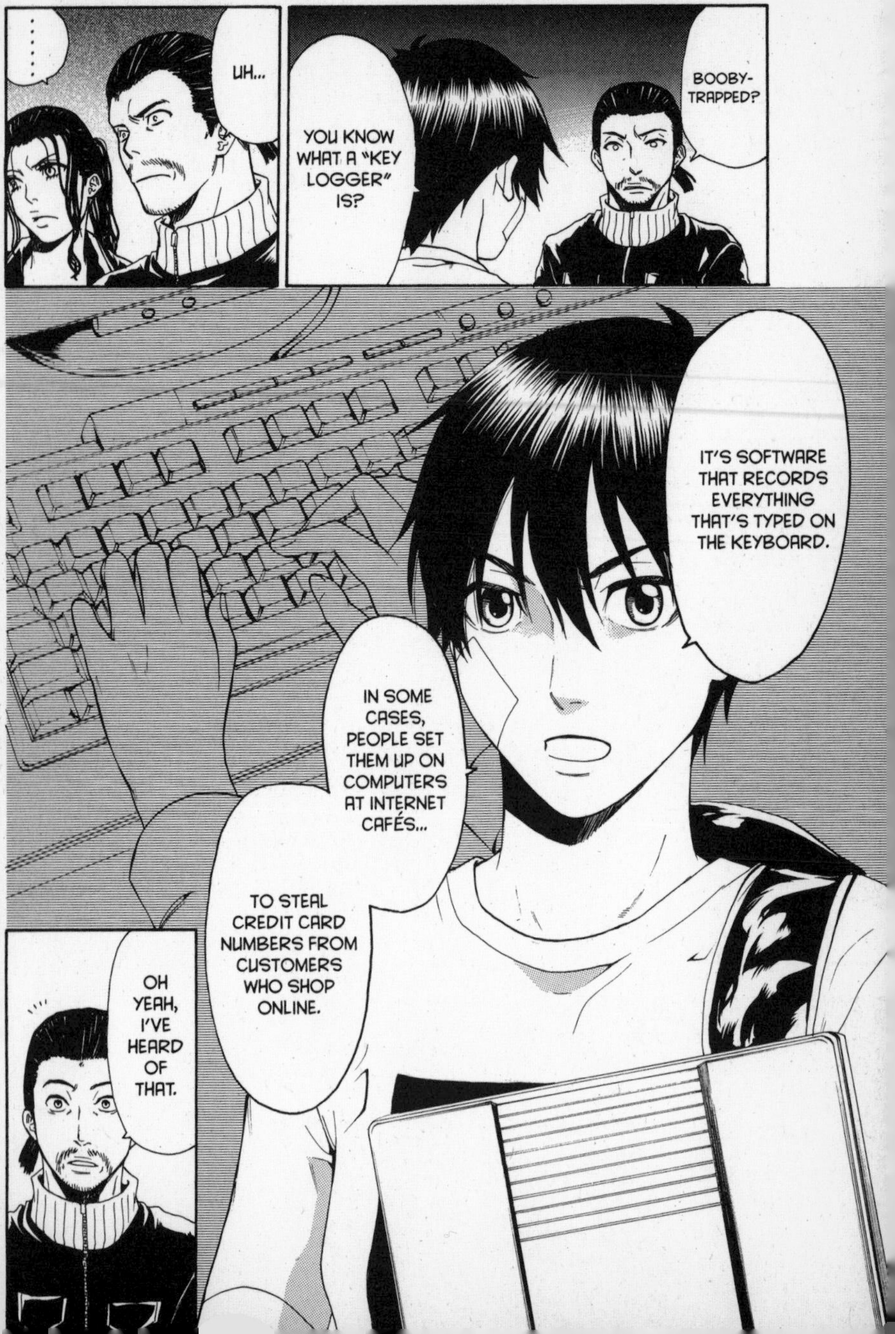
BOOBY-TRAPPED?
YOU KNOW WHAT A "KEY LOGGER" IS?
UH...
......
IT'S SOFTWARE THAT RECORDS EVERYTHING THAT'S TYPED ON THE KEYBOARD.
IN SOME CASES, PEOPLE SET THEM UP ON COMPUTERS AT INTERNET CAFÉS...
TO STEAL CREDIT CARD NUMBERS FROM CUSTOMERS WHO SHOP ONLINE.
OH YEAH, I'VE HEARD OF THAT.

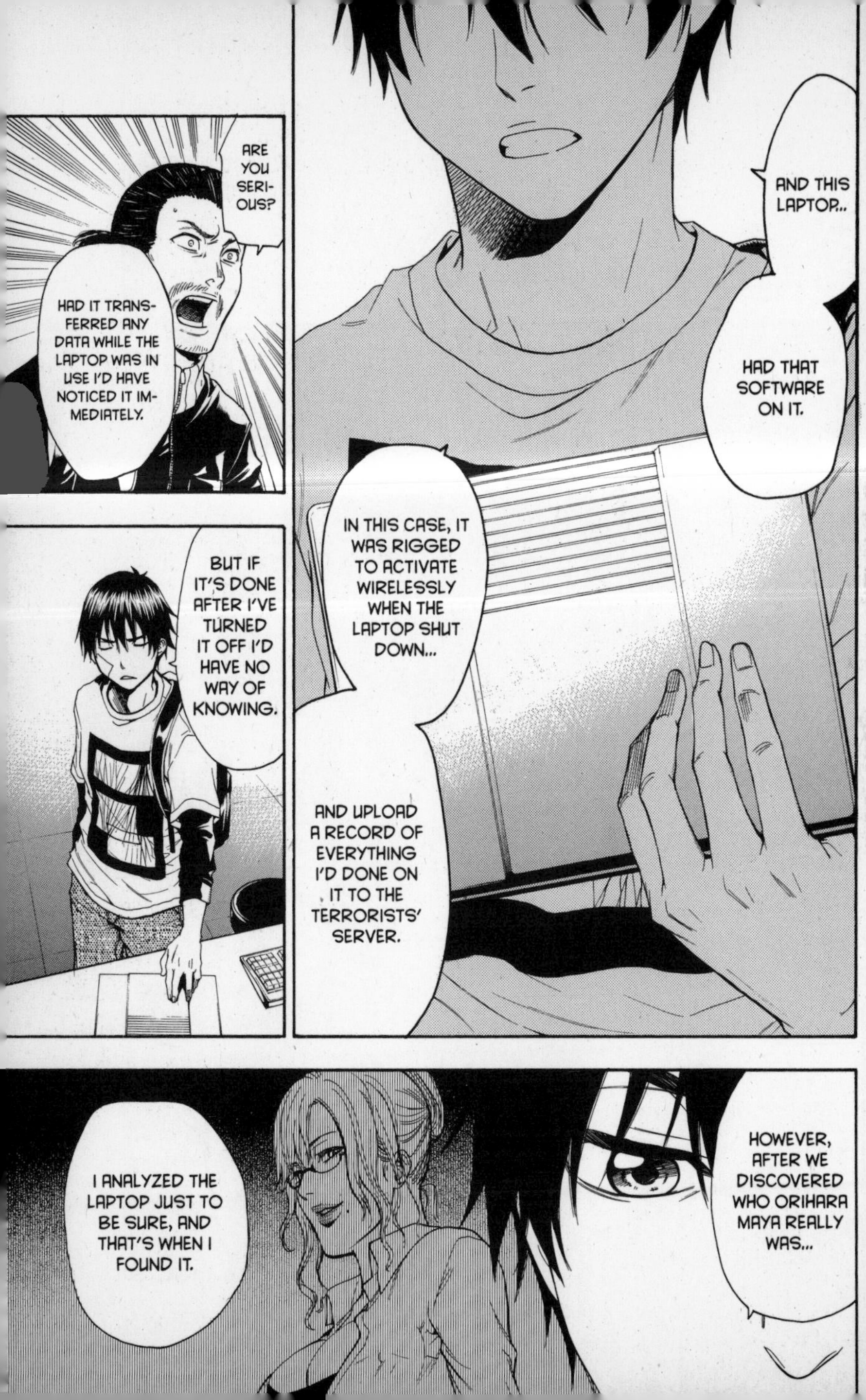
AND THIS LAPTOP..
HAD THAT SOFTWARE ON IT.
IN THIS CASE, IT WAS RIGGED TO ACTIVATE WIRELESSLY WHEN THE LAPTOP SHUT DOWN...
AND UPLOAD A RECORD OF EVERYTHING I'D DONE ON IT TO THE TERRORISTS' SERVER.
ARE YOU SERI-OUS?
HAD IT TRANS-FERRED ANY DATA WHILE THE LAPTOP WAS IN USE I'D HAVE NOTICED IT IM-MEDIATELY.
BUT IF IT'S DONE AFTER I'VE TURNED IT OFF I'D HAVE NO WAY OF KNOWING.
HOWEVER, AFTER WE DISCOVERED WHO ORIHARA MAYA REALLY WAS...
I ANALYZED THE LAPTOP JUST TO BE SURE, AND THAT'S WHEN I FOUND IT.

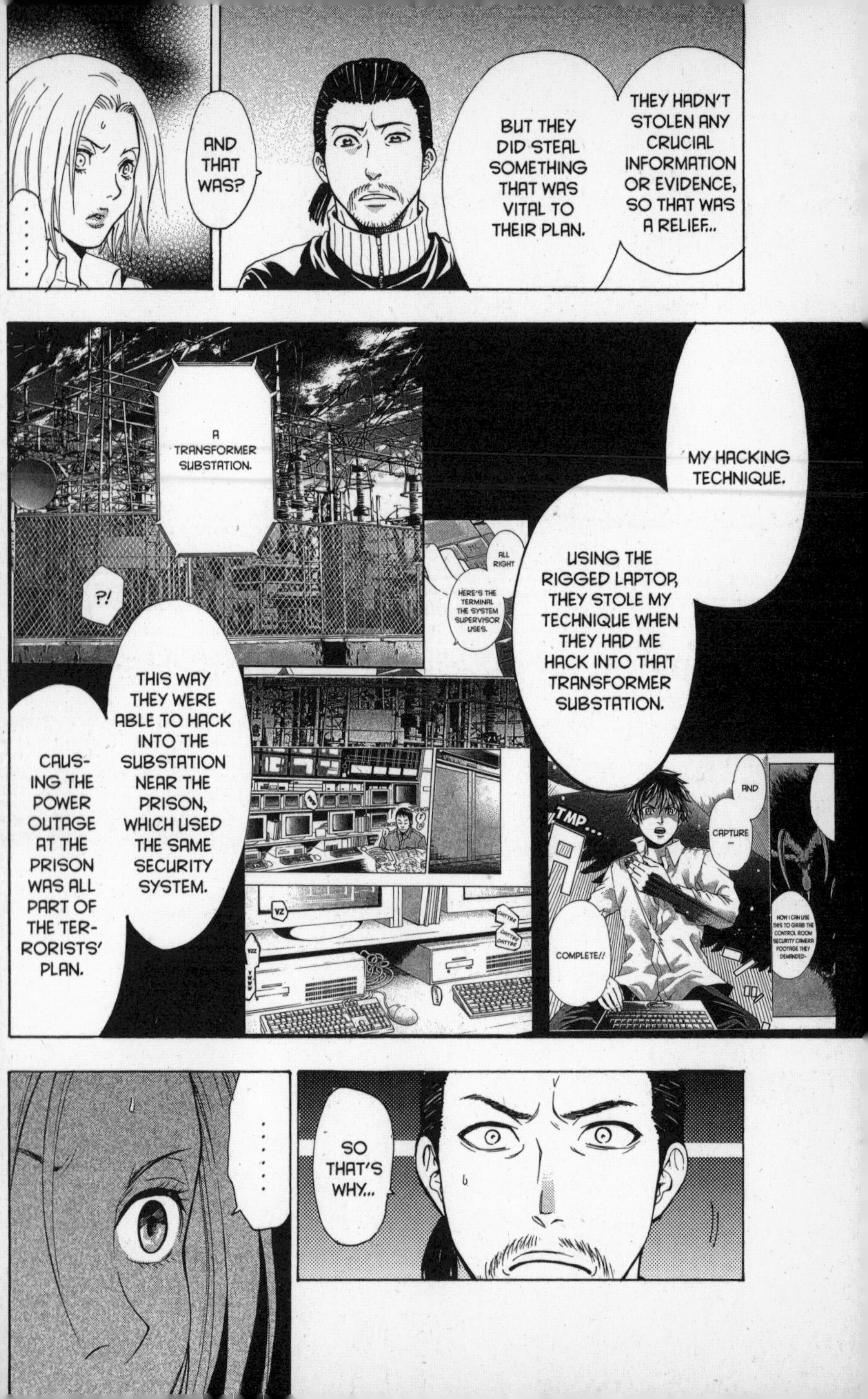
THEY HADN'T STOLEN ANY CRUCIAL INFORMATION OR EVIDENCE, SO THAT WAS A RELIEF...
BUT THEY DID STEAL SOMETHING THAT WAS VITAL TO THEIR PLAN.
AND THAT WAS?
MY HACKING TECHNIQUE.
USING THE RIGGED LAPTOP, THEY STOLE MY TECHNIQUE WHEN THEY HAD ME HACK INTO THAT TRANSFORMER SUBSTATION.
NOW I CAN USE THIS TO GRAB THE CONTROL ROOM SECURITY CAMERA FOOTAGE THEY DEMANDED-
AND
CAPTURE...
TMP...
COMPLETE!!
ALL RIGHT
HERE'S THE TERMINAL THE SYSTEM SUPERVISOR USES.
A TRANSFORMER SUBSTATION.
?!
THIS WAY THEY WERE ABLE TO HACK INTO THE SUBSTATION NEAR THE PRISON, WHICH USED THE SAME SECURITY SYSTEM.
CHAKA
CHAKA
CHITTER
CHITTER CHITTER
VZ
VZZ
CAUSING THE POWER OUTAGE AT THE PRISON WAS ALL PART OF THE TERRORISTS' PLAN.
SO THAT'S WHY...

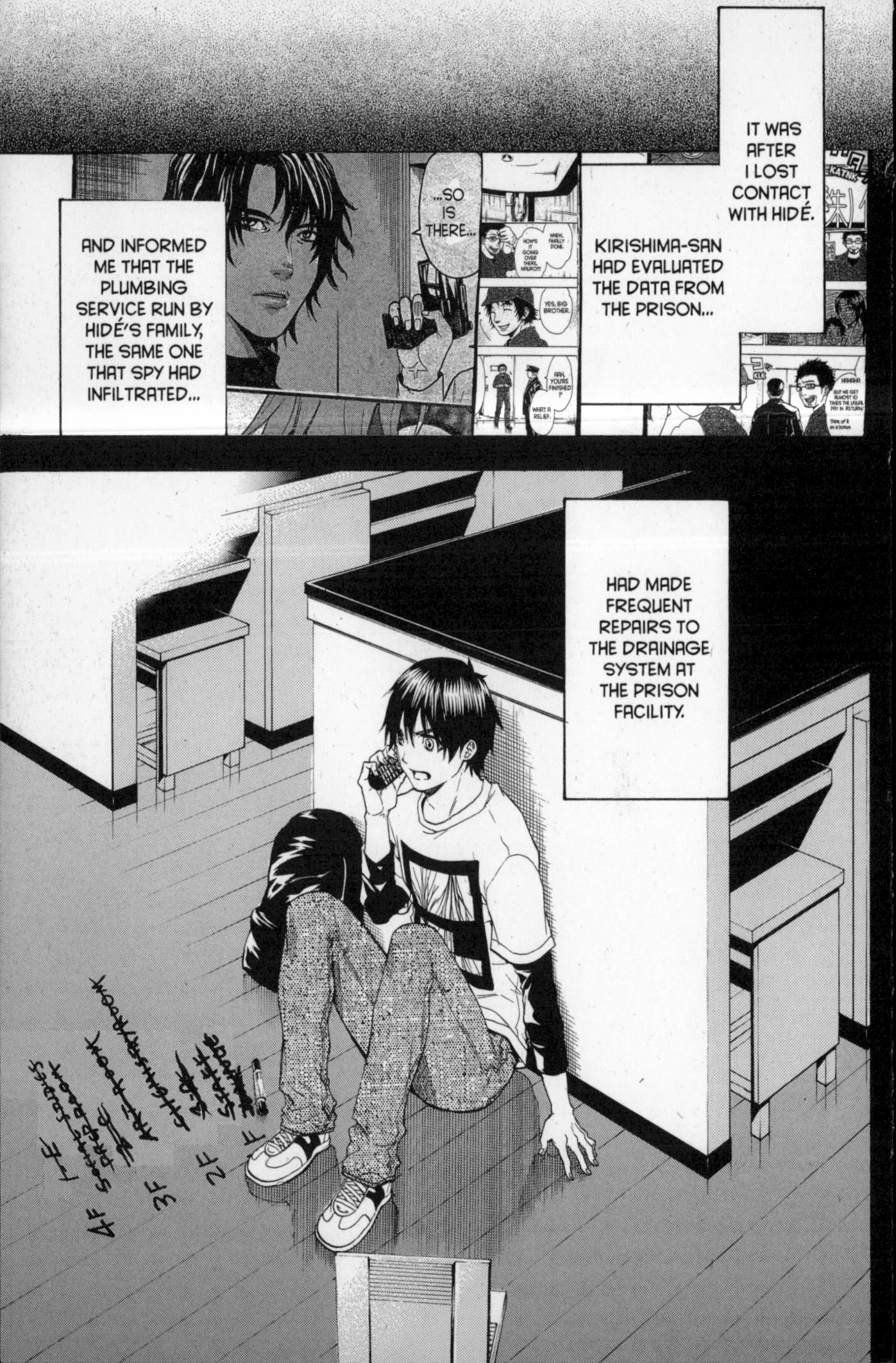
IT WAS AFTER I LOST CONTACT WITH HIDÉ.
KIRISHIMA-SAN HAD EVALUATED THE DATA FROM THE PRISON...
HAHAHA
BUT WE GET ALMOST 10 TIMES THE USUAL PAY IN RETURN!
Think of it as a bonus
WHEW, FINALLY DONE.
YES, BIG BROTHER.
AAH, YOU'RE FINISHED?
WHAT A RELIEF.
...SO IS THERE...
AND INFORMED ME THAT THE PLUMBING SERVICE RUN BY HIDÉ'S FAMILY, THE SAME ONE THAT SPY HAD INFILTRATED...
HAD MADE FREQUENT REPAIRS TO THE DRAINAGE SYSTEM AT THE PRISON FACILITY.

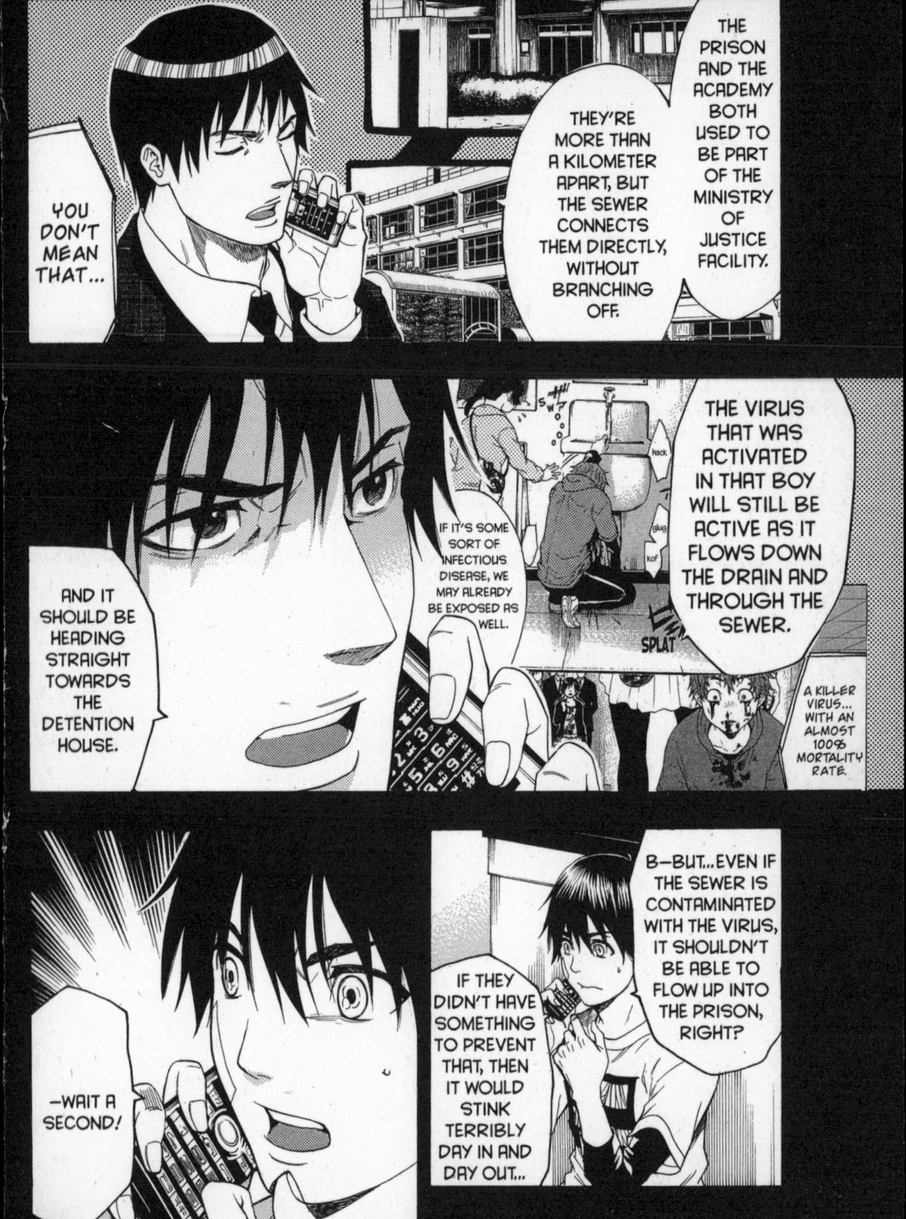
THE PRISON AND THE ACADEMY BOTH USED TO BE PART OF THE MINISTRY OF JUSTICE FACILITY.
THEY'RE MORE THAN A KILOMETER APART, BUT THE SEWER CONNECTS THEM DIRECTLY, WITHOUT BRANCHING OFF.
YOU DON'T MEAN THAT...
THE VIRUS THAT WAS ACTIVATED IN THAT BOY WILL STILL BE ACTIVE AS IT FLOWS DOWN THE DRAIN AND THROUGH THE SEWER.
hack
glug
kof
SPLAT
IF IT'S SOME SORT OF INFECTIOUS DISEASE, WE MAY ALREADY BE EXPOSED AS WELL.
A KILLER VIRUS... WITH AN ALMOST 100% MORTALITY RATE.
AND IT SHOULD BE HEADING STRAIGHT TOWARDS THE DETENTION HOUSE.
B—BUT...EVEN IF THE SEWER IS CONTAMINATED WITH THE VIRUS, IT SHOULDN'T BE ABLE TO FLOW UP INTO THE PRISON, RIGHT?
IF THEY DIDN'T HAVE SOMETHING TO PREVENT THAT, THEN IT WOULD STINK TERRIBLY DAY IN AND DAY OUT...
—WAIT A SECOND!

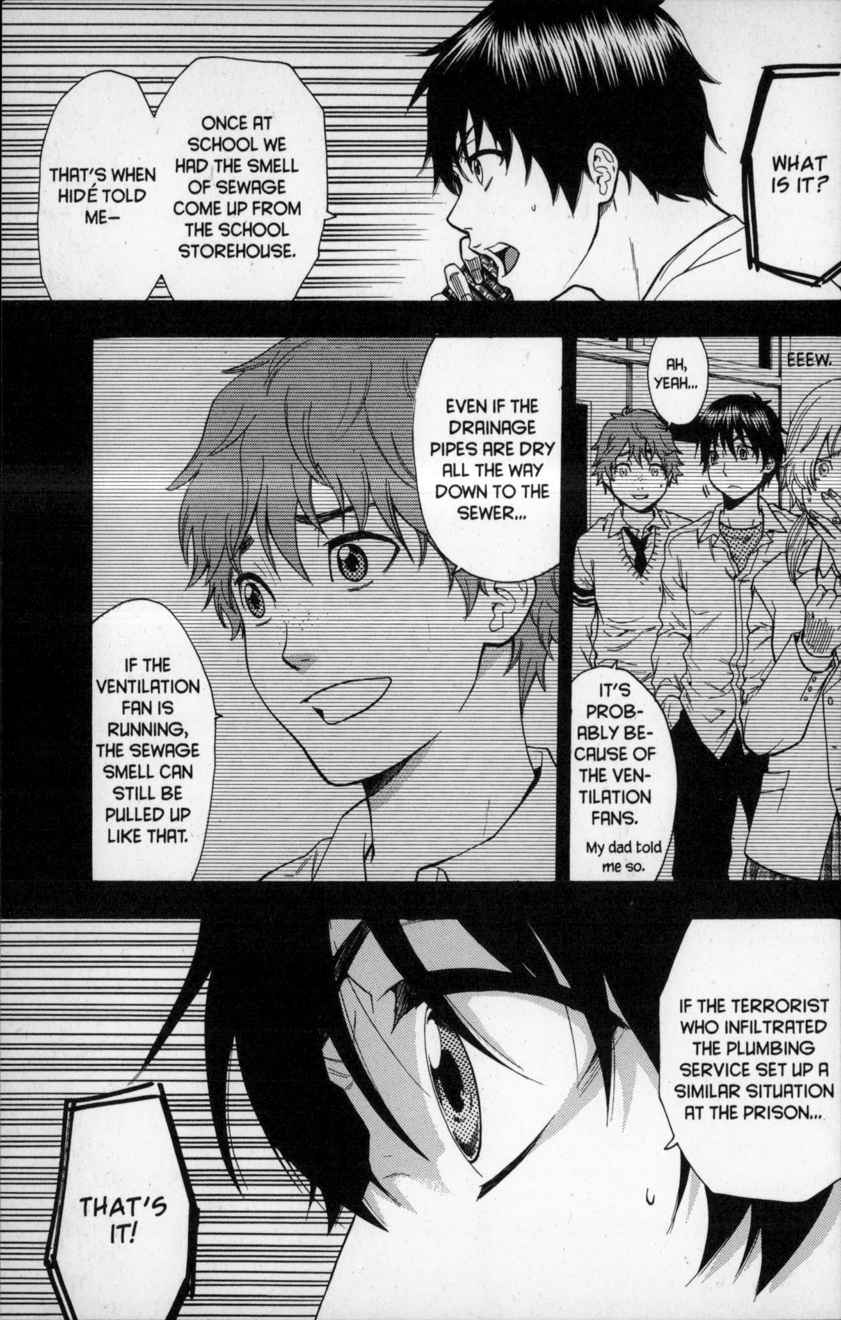
WHAT IS IT?
ONCE AT SCHOOL WE HAD THE SMELL OF SEWAGE COME UP FROM THE SCHOOL STOREHOUSE.
THAT'S WHEN HIDÉ TOLD ME—
EEEW.
AH, YEAH...
IT'S PROB-ABLY BE-CAUSE OF THE VEN-TILATION FANS.
My dad told me so.
EVEN IF THE DRAINAGE PIPES ARE DRY ALL THE WAY DOWN TO THE SEWER...
IF THE VENTILATION FAN IS RUNNING, THE SEWAGE SMELL CAN STILL BE PULLED UP LIKE THAT.
IF THE TERRORIST WHO INFILTRATED THE PLUMBING SERVICE SET UP A SIMILAR SITUATION AT THE PRISON...
THAT'S IT!

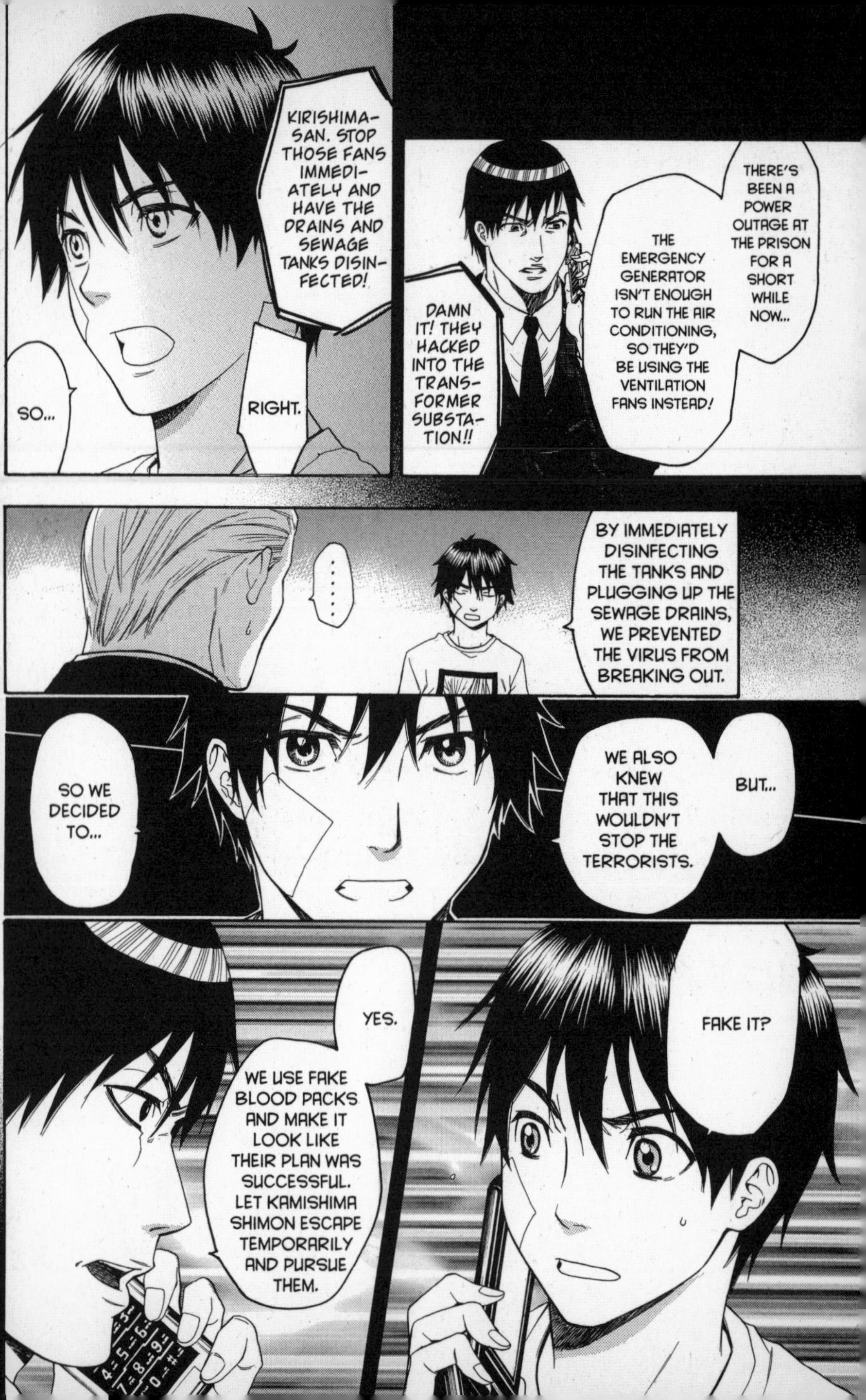
THERE'S BEEN A POWER OUTAGE AT THE PRISON FOR A SHORT WHILE NOW...
THE EMERGENCY GENERATOR ISN'T ENOUGH TO RUN THE AIR CONDITIONING, SO THEY'D BE USING THE VENTILATION FANS INSTEAD!
DAMN IT! THEY HACKED INTO THE TRANSFORMER SUBSTATION!!
KIRISHIMA-SAN. STOP THOSE FANS IMMEDIATELY AND HAVE THE DRAINS AND SEWAGE TANKS DISINFECTED!
RIGHT.
SO...
BY IMMEDIATELY DISINFECTING THE TANKS AND PLUGGING UP THE SEWAGE DRAINS, WE PREVENTED THE VIRUS FROM BREAKING OUT.
......
BUT...
WE ALSO KNEW THAT THIS WOULDN'T STOP THE TERRORISTS.
SO WE DECIDED TO...
FAKE IT?
YES.
WE USE FAKE BLOOD PACKS AND MAKE IT LOOK LIKE THEIR PLAN WAS SUCCESSFUL. LET KAMISHIMA SHIMON ESCAPE TEMPORARILY AND PURSUE THEM.

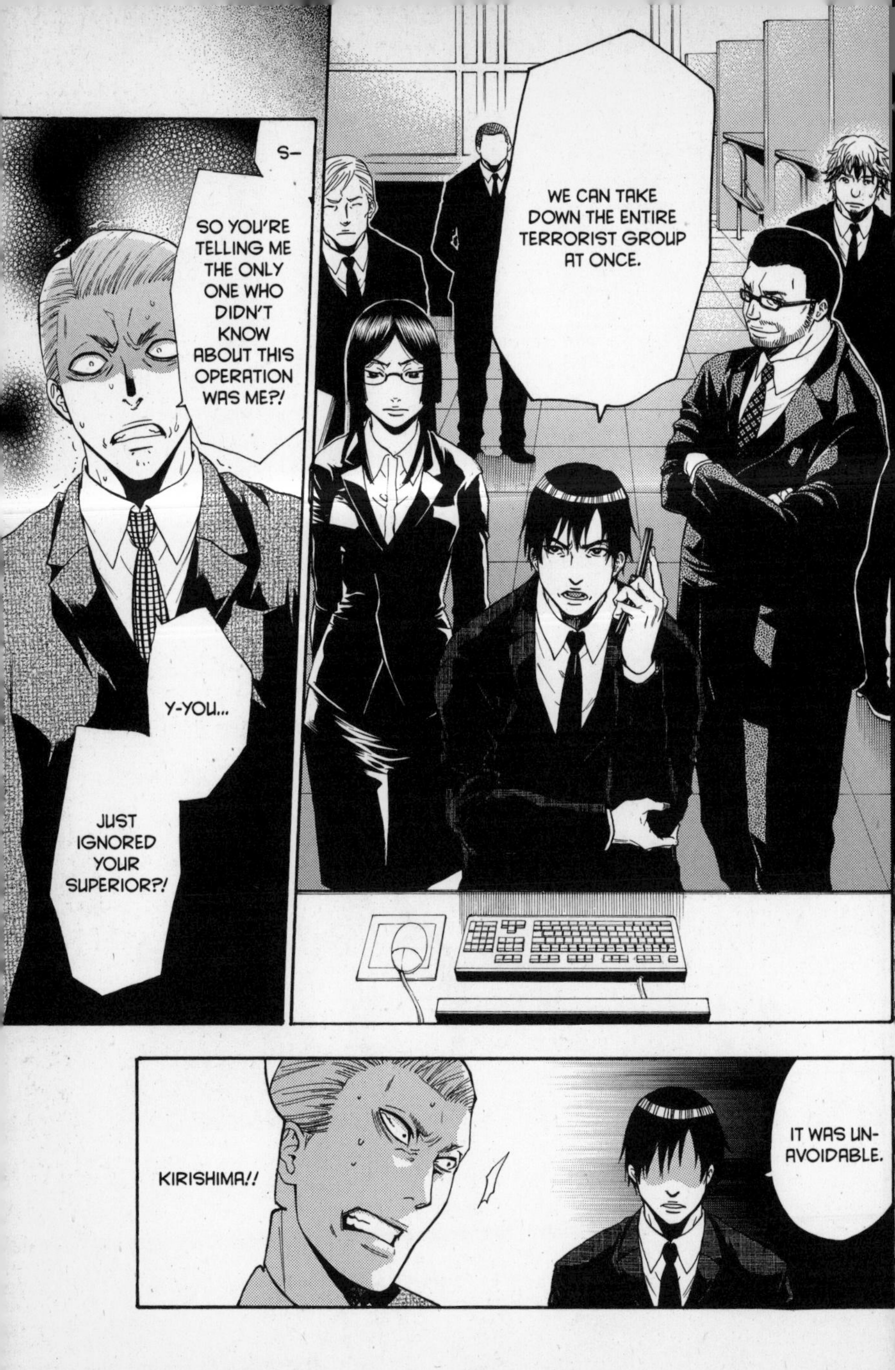
WE CAN TAKE DOWN THE ENTIRE TERRORIST GROUP AT ONCE.
S—
SO YOU'RE TELLING ME THE ONLY ONE WHO DIDN'T KNOW ABOUT THIS OPERATION WAS ME?!
Y-YOU...
JUST IGNORED YOUR SUPERIOR?!
IT WAS UN-AVOIDABLE.
KIRISHIMA!!

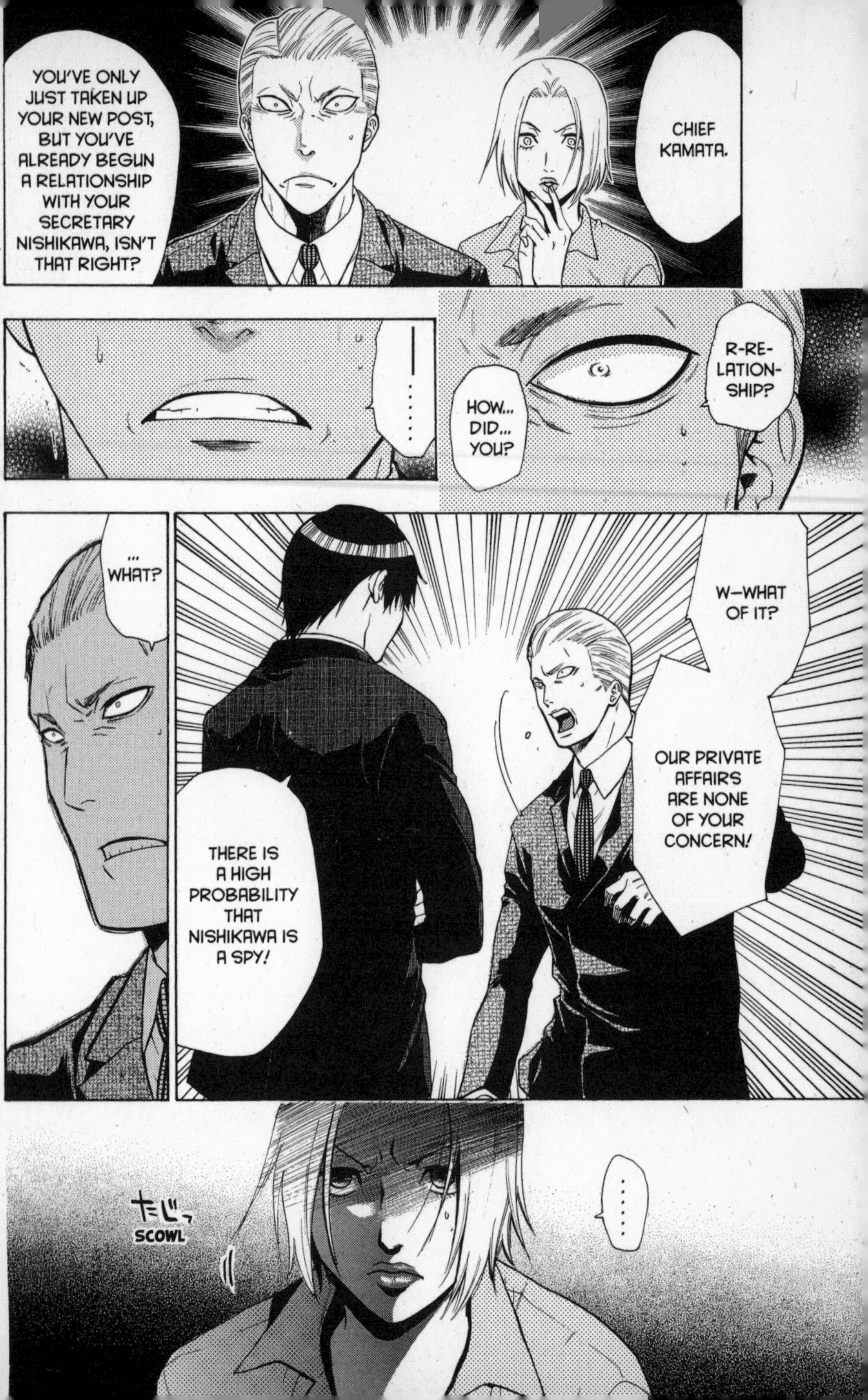
CHIEF KAMATA.
YOU'VE ONLY JUST TAKEN UP YOUR NEW POST, BUT YOU'VE ALREADY BEGUN A RELATIONSHIP WITH YOUR SECRETARY NISHIKAWA, ISN'T THAT RIGHT?
R-RE-LATION-SHIP?
HOW... DID... YOU?
......
W—WHAT OF IT?
OUR PRIVATE AFFAIRS ARE NONE OF YOUR CONCERN!
THERE IS A HIGH PROBABILITY THAT NISHIKAWA IS A SPY!
... WHAT?
SCOWL
......

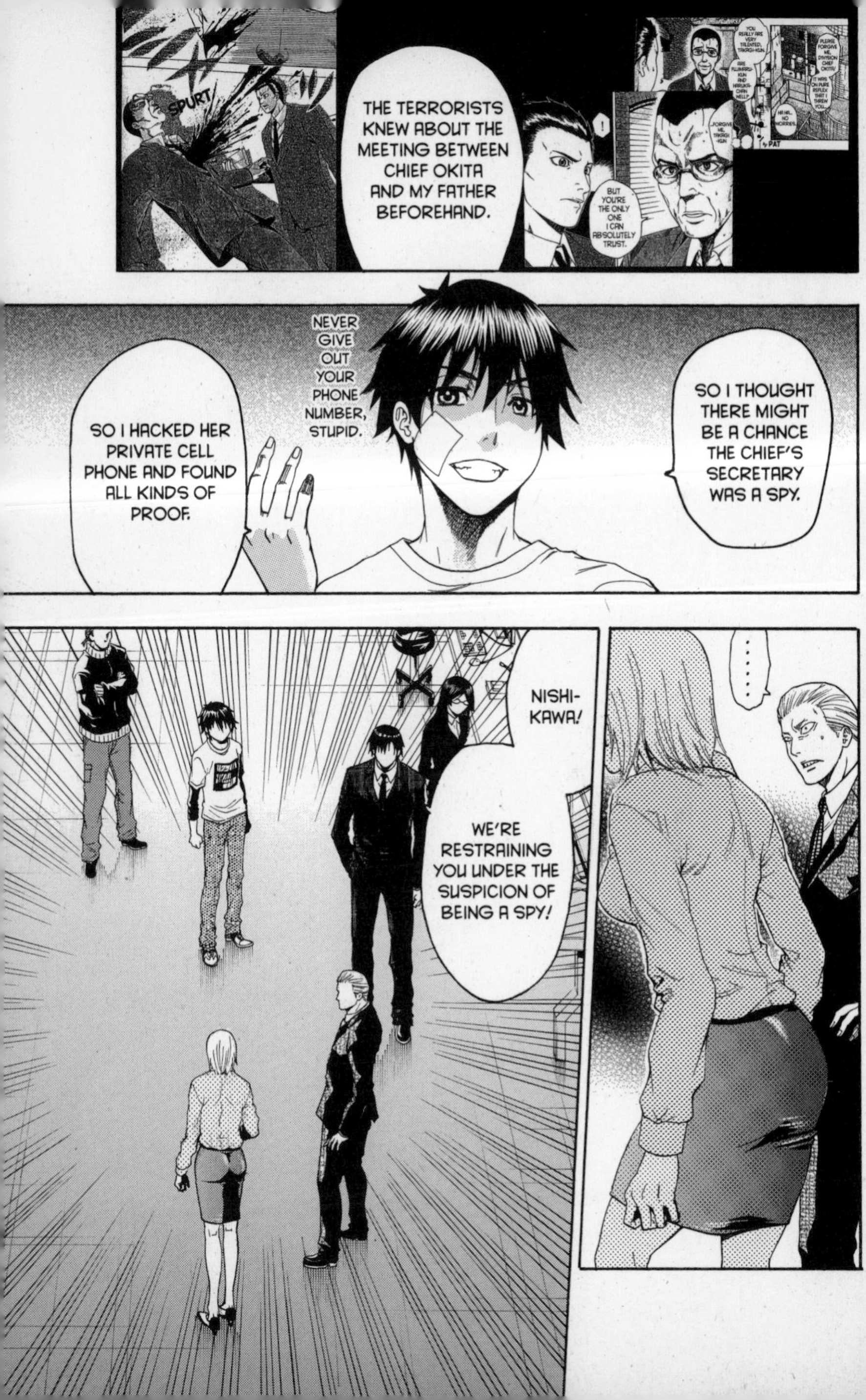
PLEASE FORGIVE ME, DIVISION CHIEF OKITA!
IT WAS ON PURE REFLEX THAT I THREW YOU.
HA HA... NO WORRIES.
PAT
YOU REALLY ARE VERY TALENTED, TAKAGI-KUN.
ARE FUJIMARU-KUN AND HARUKA-CHAN WELL?
...FORGIVE ME, TAKAGI-KUN
!
BUT YOU'RE THE ONLY ONE I CAN ABSOLUTELY TRUST.
THE TERRORISTS KNEW ABOUT THE MEETING BETWEEN CHIEF OKITA AND MY FATHER BEFOREHAND.
SPURT
SO I THOUGHT THERE MIGHT BE A CHANCE THE CHIEF'S SECRETARY WAS A SPY.
NEVER GIVE OUT YOUR PHONE NUMBER, STUPID.
SO I HACKED HER PRIVATE CELL PHONE AND FOUND ALL KINDS OF PROOF.
......
NISHIKAWA!
WE'RE RESTRAINING YOU UNDER THE SUSPICION OF BEING A SPY!

DAMN...

BZZT

URGH—

BRRR

AAGH!!!

ZZZT

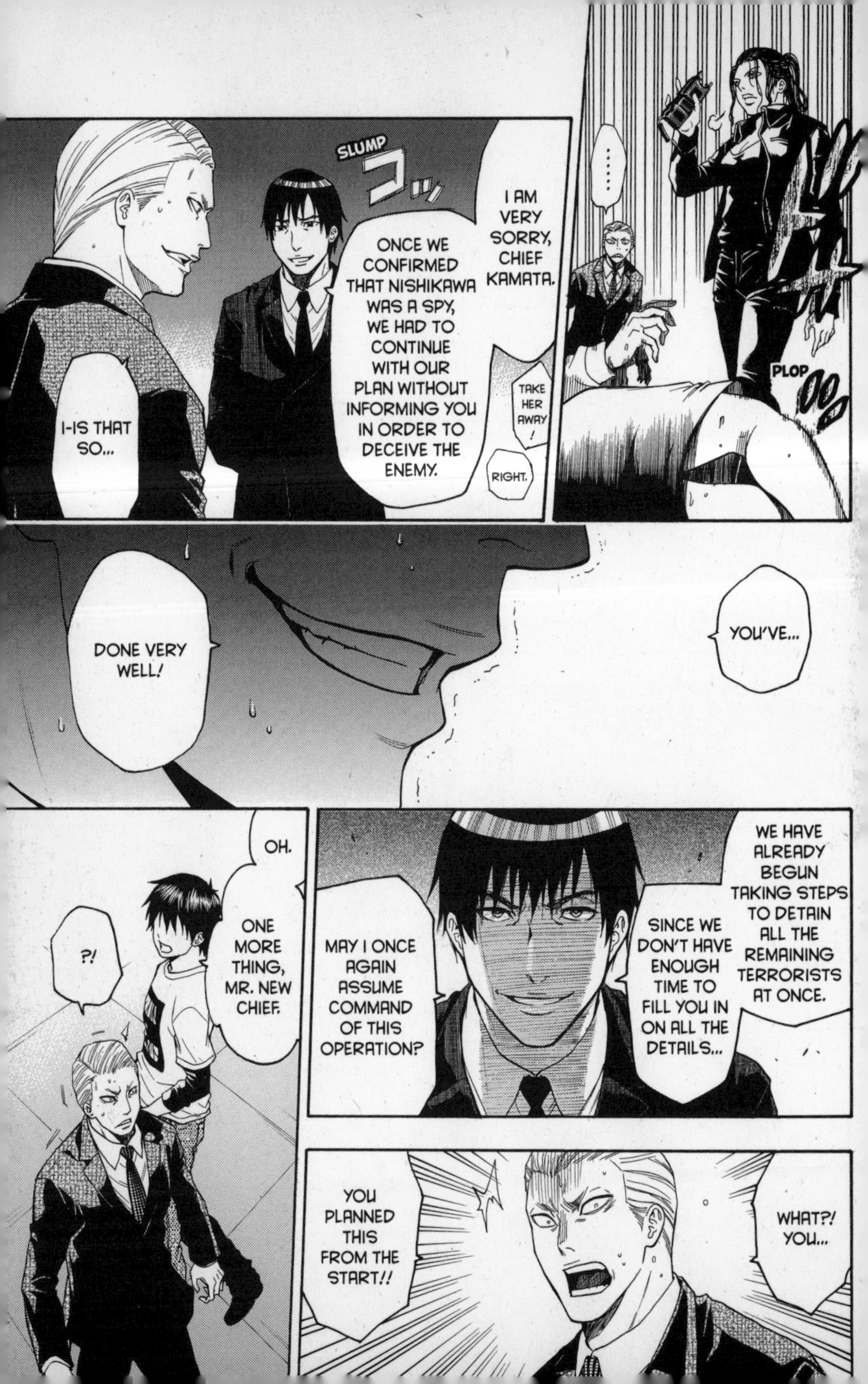
......
TAKE HER AWAY!
RIGHT.
PLOP
SLUMP
I AM VERY SORRY, CHIEF KAMATA.
ONCE WE CONFIRMED THAT NISHIKAWA WAS A SPY, WE HAD TO CONTINUE WITH OUR PLAN WITHOUT INFORMING YOU IN ORDER TO DECEIVE THE ENEMY.
I-IS THAT SO...
YOU'VE...
DONE VERY WELL!
WE HAVE ALREADY BEGUN TAKING STEPS TO DETAIN ALL THE REMAINING TERRORISTS AT ONCE.
SINCE WE DON'T HAVE ENOUGH TIME TO FILL YOU IN ON ALL THE DETAILS...
MAY I ONCE AGAIN ASSUME COMMAND OF THIS OPERATION?
WHAT?! YOU...
YOU PLANNED THIS FROM THE START!!
OH.
ONE MORE THING, MR. NEW CHIEF.
?!

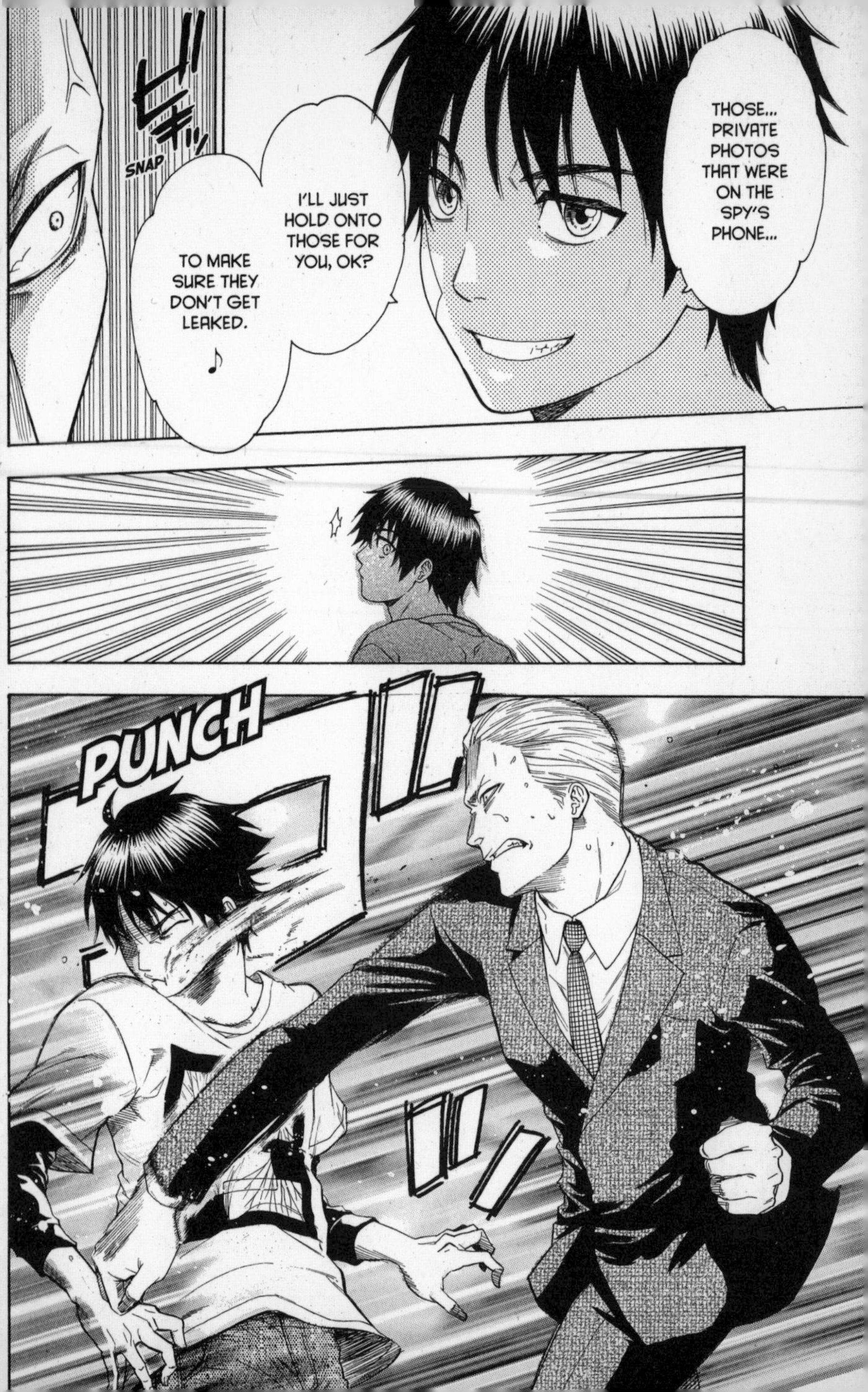
THOSE... PRIVATE PHOTOS THAT WERE ON THE SPY'S PHONE...
I'LL JUST HOLD ONTO THOSE FOR YOU, OK?
TO MAKE SURE THEY DON'T GET LEAKED. ♪
SNAP
PUNCH

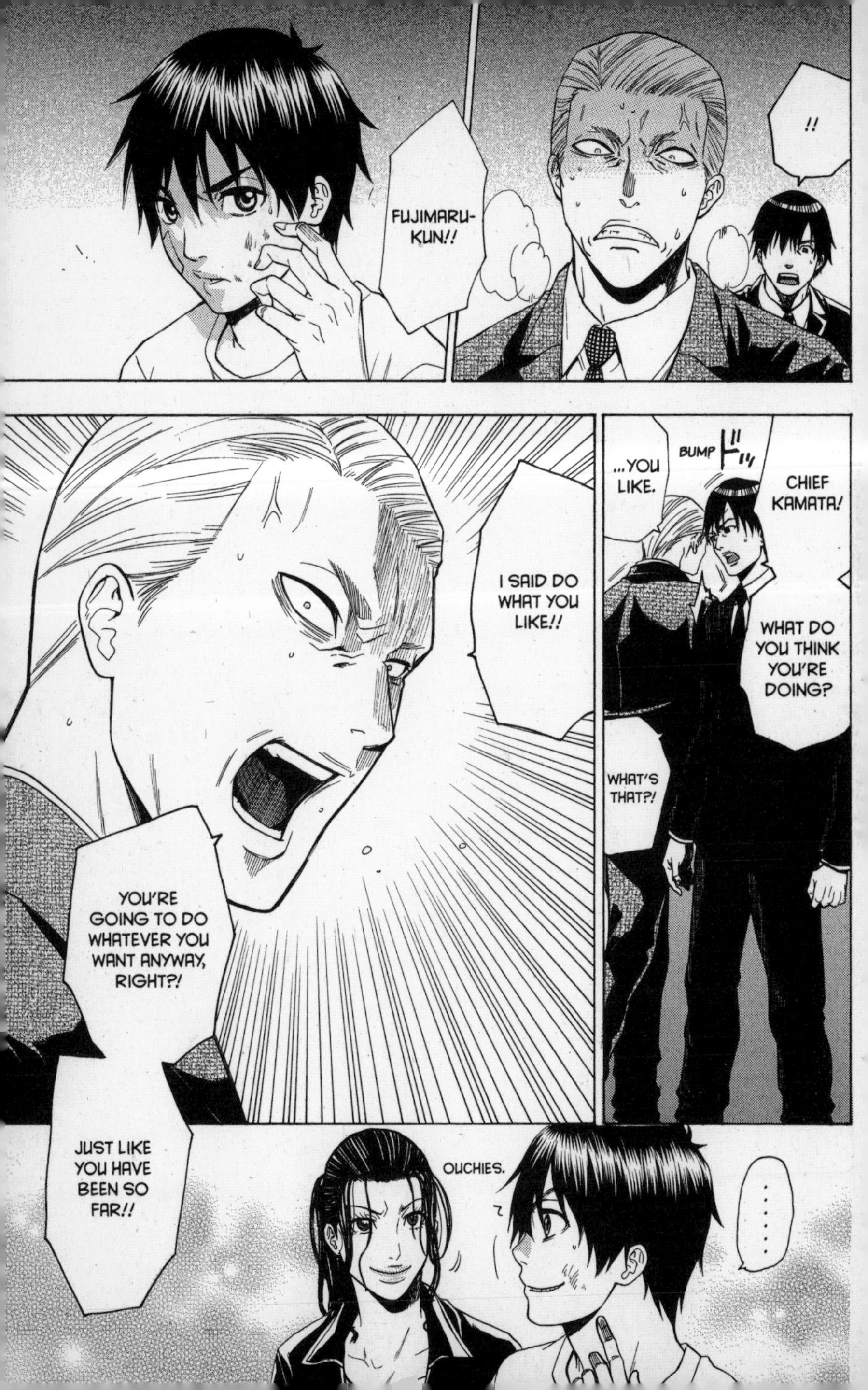
!!
FUJIMARU-KUN!!
...YOU LIKE.
BUMP ドッ
CHIEF KAMATA!
WHAT DO YOU THINK YOU'RE DOING?
WHAT'S THAT?!
I SAID DO WHAT YOU LIKE!!
YOU'RE GOING TO DO WHATEVER YOU WANT ANYWAY, RIGHT?!
JUST LIKE YOU HAVE BEEN SO FAR!!
......
OUCHIES.

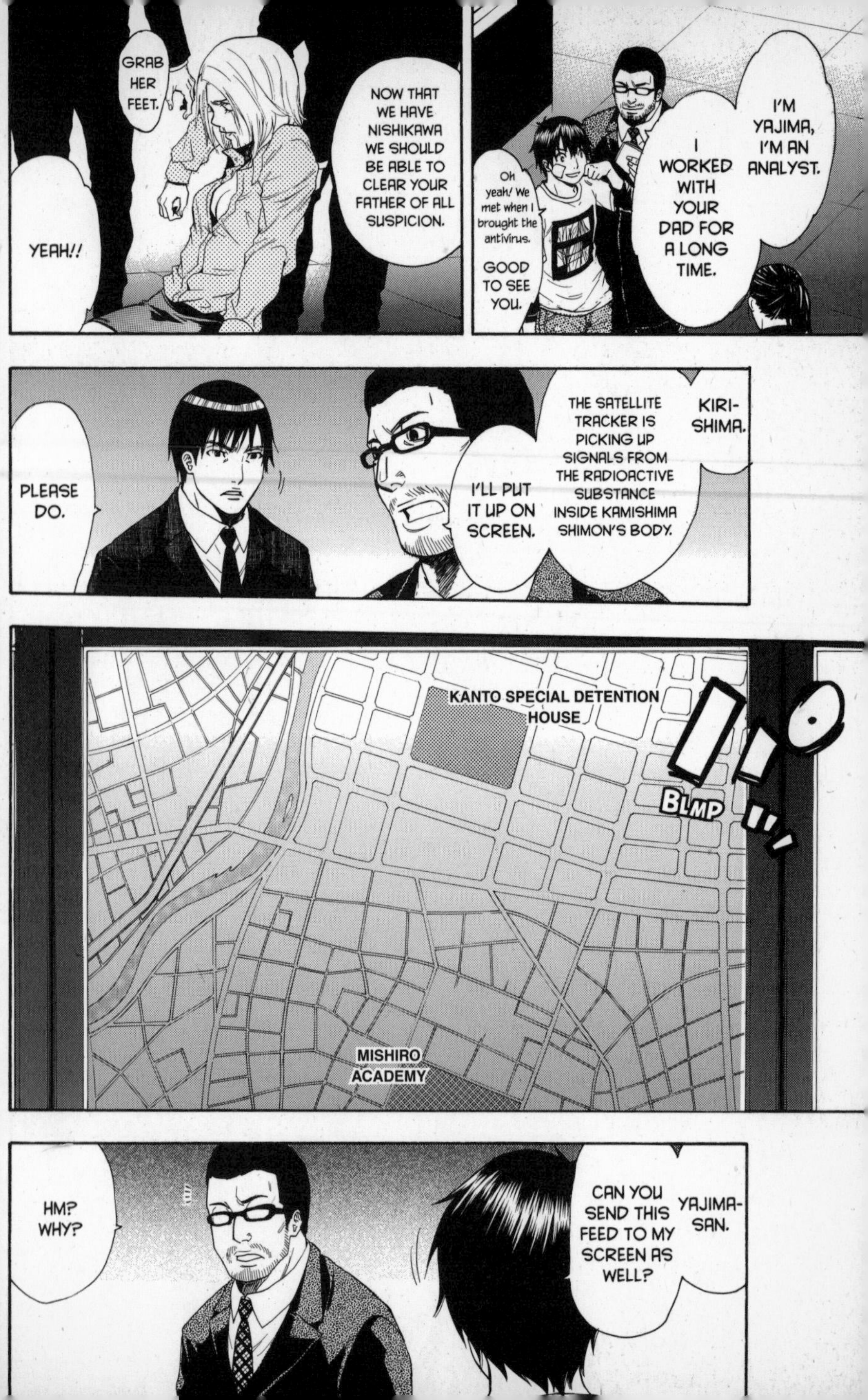
I'M YAJIMA, I'M AN ANALYST.
I WORKED WITH YOUR DAD FOR A LONG TIME.
Oh yeah! We met when I brought the antivirus.
GOOD TO SEE YOU.
NOW THAT WE HAVE NISHIKAWA WE SHOULD BE ABLE TO CLEAR YOUR FATHER OF ALL SUSPICION.
GRAB HER FEET.
YEAH!!
KIRI-SHIMA.
THE SATELLITE TRACKER IS PICKING UP SIGNALS FROM THE RADIOACTIVE SUBSTANCE INSIDE KAMISHIMA SHIMON'S BODY.
I'LL PUT IT UP ON SCREEN.
PLEASE DO.
BLMP
KANTO SPECIAL DETENTION HOUSE
MISHIRO ACADEMY
YAJIMA-SAN.
CAN YOU SEND THIS FEED TO MY SCREEN AS WELL?
HM? WHY?

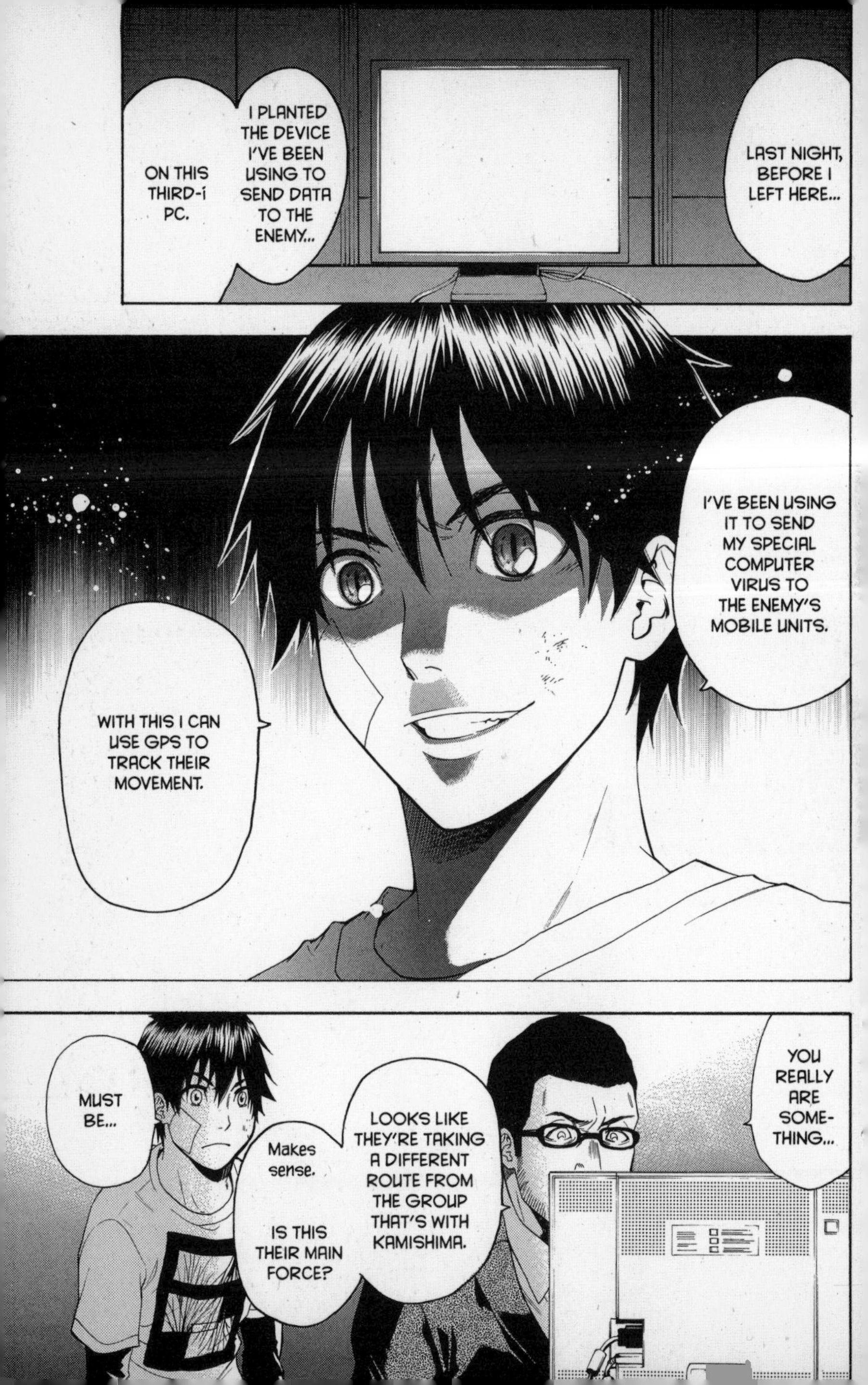
LAST NIGHT, BEFORE I LEFT HERE...
I PLANTED THE DEVICE I'VE BEEN USING TO SEND DATA TO THE ENEMY...
ON THIS THIRD-i PC.
I'VE BEEN USING IT TO SEND MY SPECIAL COMPUTER VIRUS TO THE ENEMY'S MOBILE UNITS.
WITH THIS I CAN USE GPS TO TRACK THEIR MOVEMENT.
YOU REALLY ARE SOME-THING...
LOOKS LIKE THEY'RE TAKING A DIFFERENT ROUTE FROM THE GROUP THAT'S WITH KAMISHIMA.
Makes sense.
IS THIS THEIR MAIN FORCE?
MUST BE...

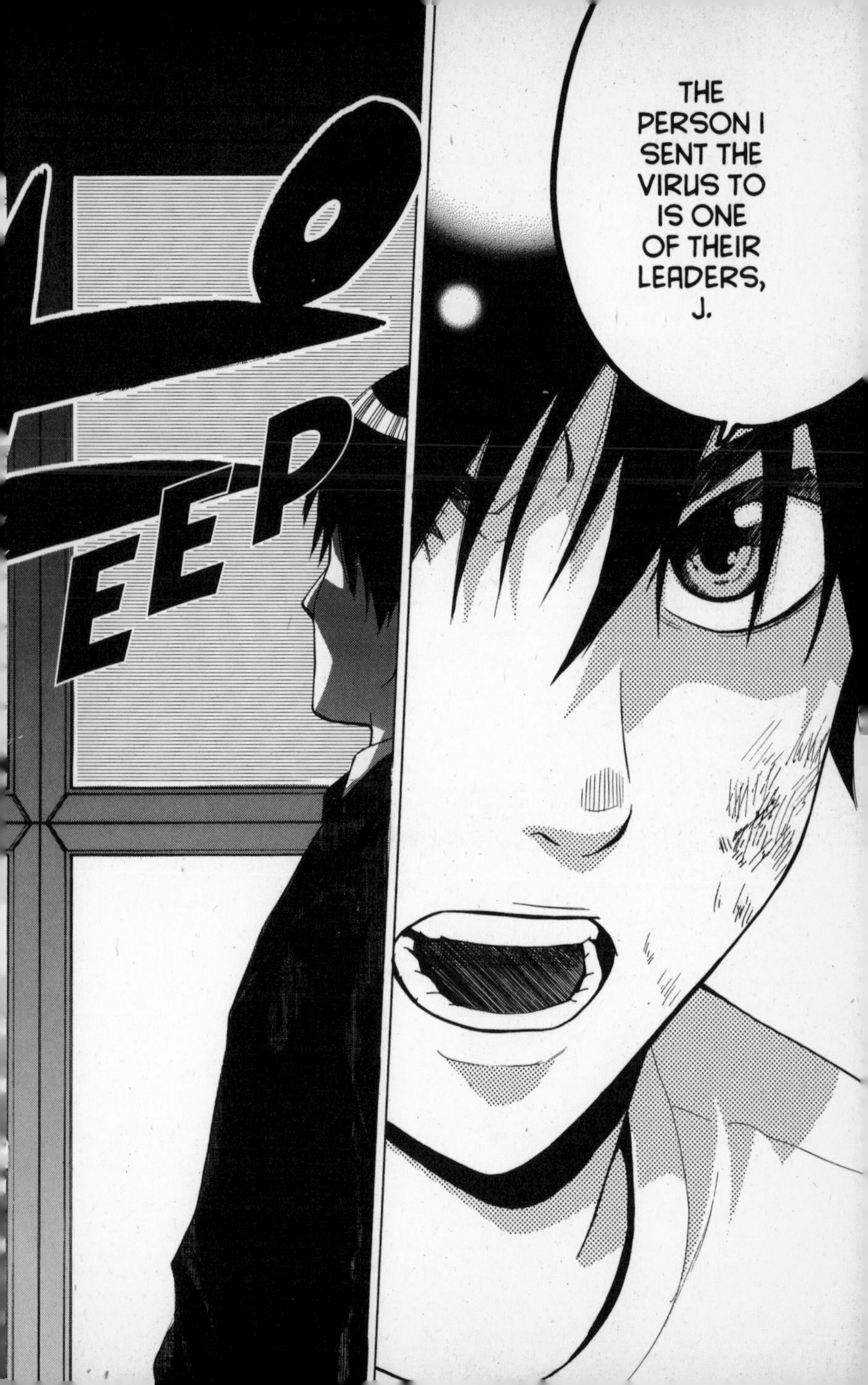
THE PERSON I SENT THE VIRUS TO IS ONE OF THEIR LEADERS, J.
EEP

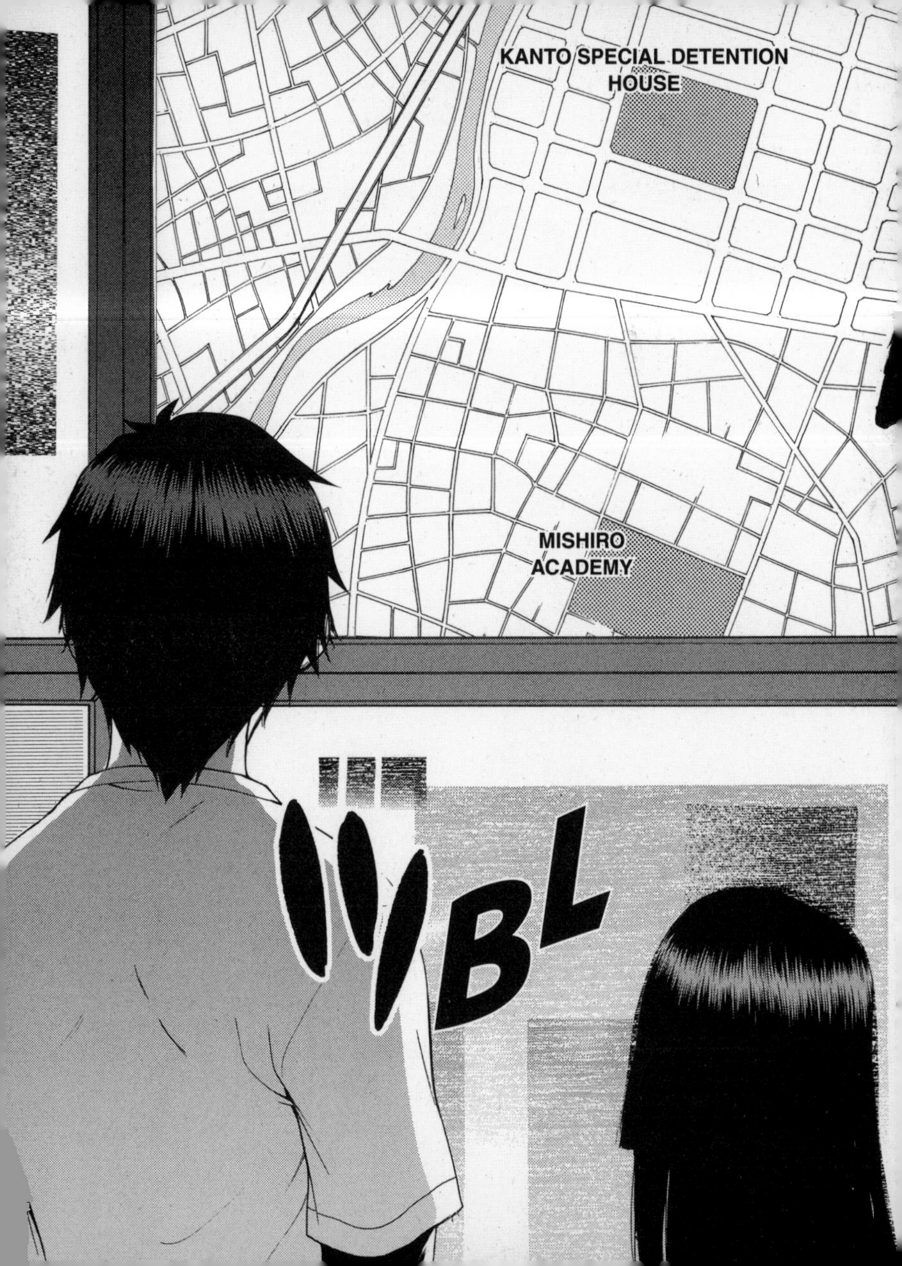
KANTO SPECIAL DETENTION HOUSE
MISHIRO ACADEMY
BL

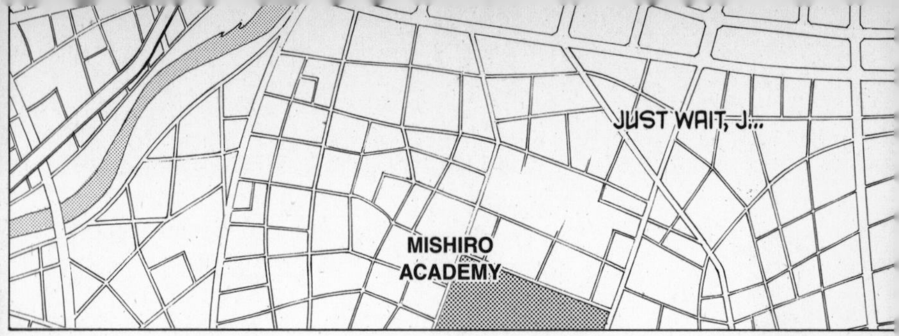
JUST WAIT, J...
MISHIRO ACADEMY

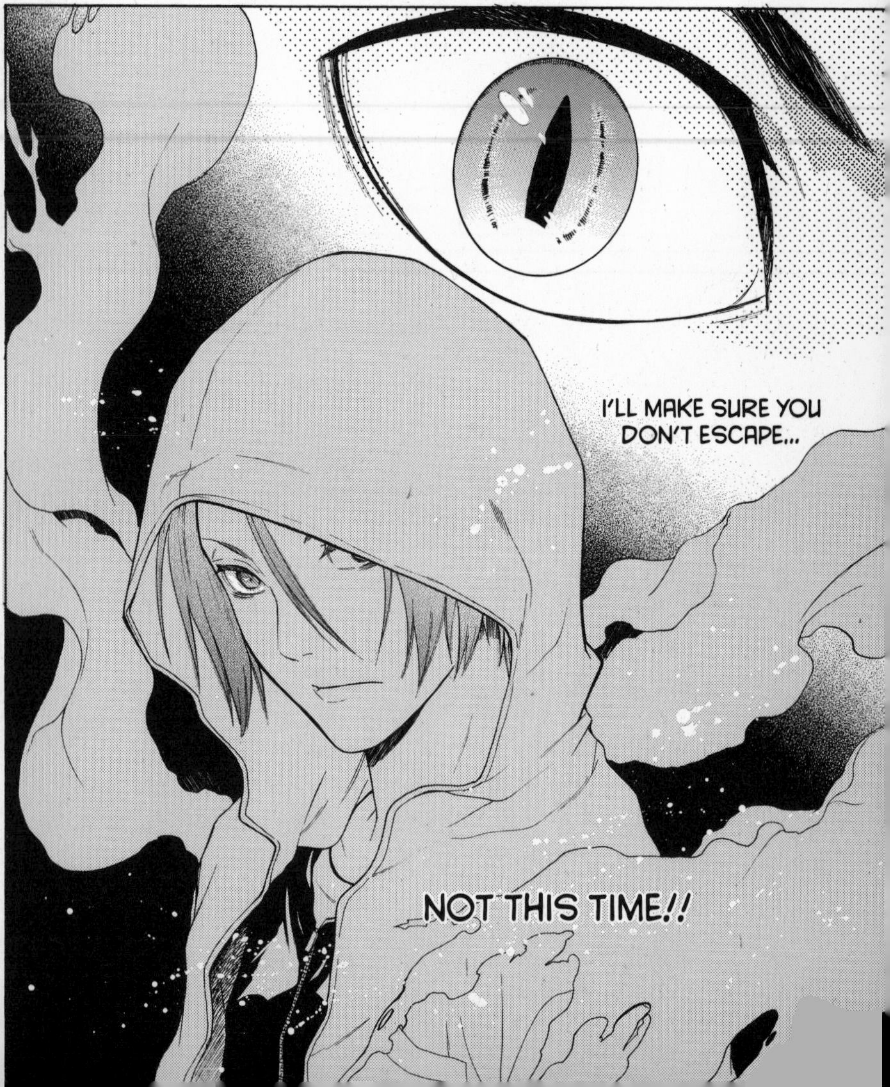
I'LL MAKE SURE YOU DON'T ESCAPE...
NOT THIS TIME!!

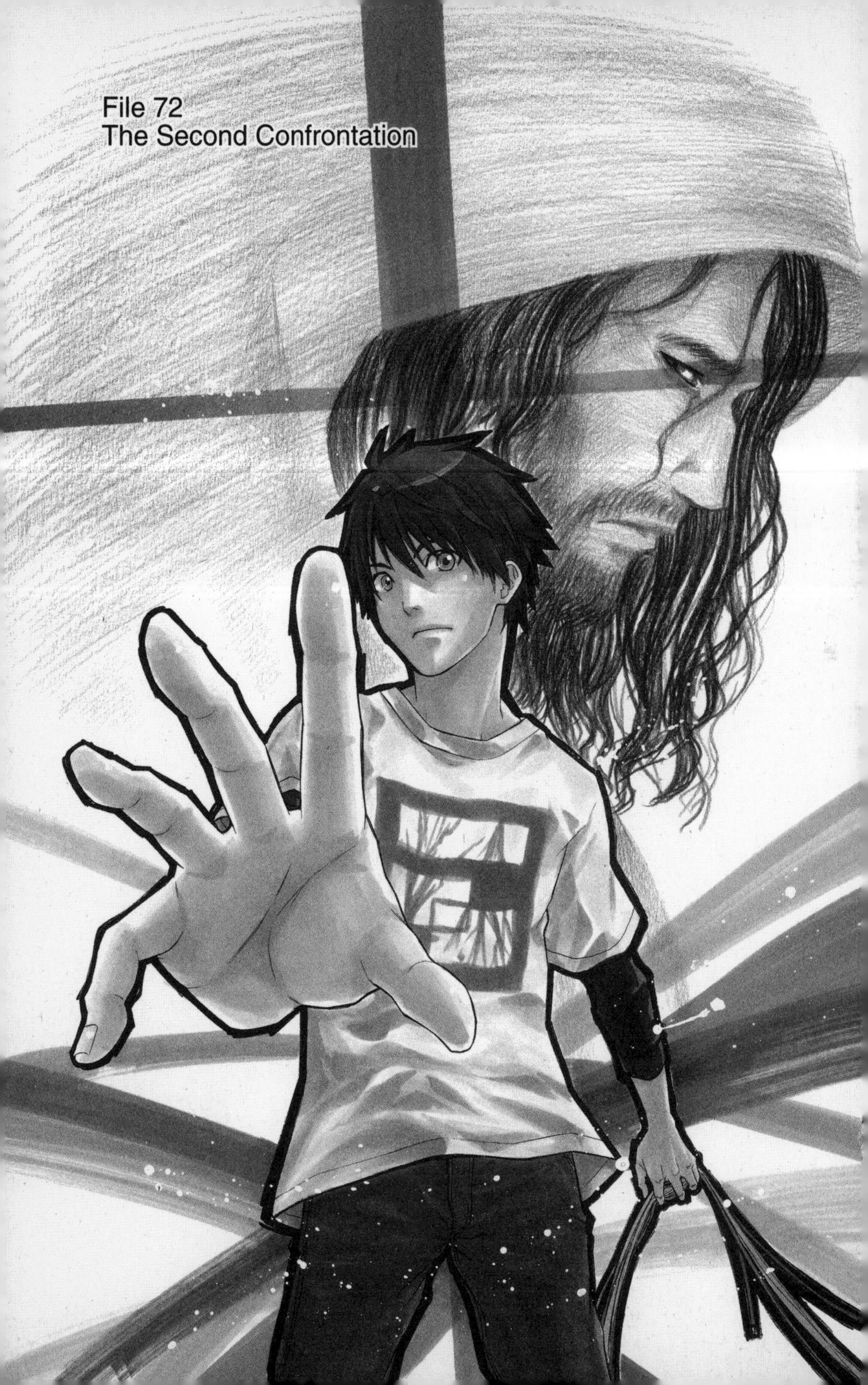
File 72
The Second Confrontation

CAIN AND ABEL: THEIR NAMES DERIVE FROM THE BOOK OF GENESIS IN THE OLD TESTAMENT. IN THE STORY, GOD TOOK JOY IN THE OFFERING THAT ABEL, THE YOUNGER OF THE TWO BROTHERS, MADE TO HIM, AND CAIN, IN A JEALOUS RAGE, KILLED ABEL. THEIR PARENTS WERE BELIEVERS IN THE RELIGIOUS CULT, AND BOTH DIED IN THE FAILED ATTEMPT TO RESCUE THE LEADER TWO YEARS AGO. AS THEY WERE INDOCTRINATED INTO THE CULT BY THEIR PARENTS, THEY BELIEVE IN IT WITH ALL THEIR HEARTS. THEY OBEY K AND J, WHO STAND IN FOR THE LEADER, WITHOUT QUESTION OR HESITATION.

CAIN: SHE SEEMS THE MORE DECENT OF THE TWO BUT SHE IS ACTUALLY THE MOST DANGEROUS. THE TWO SISTERS HAVE AN EXTREMELY WARPED SENSE OF AFFECTION FOR ONE ANOTHER. ABEL IS EVERYTHING TO CAIN AND HER SAFETY IS THE ONLY MEASURE BY WHICH SHE WEIGHS ALL OF HER ACTIONS. IF EVER THE SITUATION AROSE WHERE SOMEONE WAS GOING TO SEPARATE THE TWO, CAIN WOULD KILL THEM WITHOUT A MOMENT'S HESITATION. ABEL'S OPINION ON THE MATTER WOULD BE OF NO IMPORTANCE TO CAIN.

ABEL: HER SISTER CAIN IS EVERYTHING TO HER AS SHE IS UTTERLY DEPENDENT ON HER. IF CAIN LEAVES HER SIDE WITHOUT TELLING HER, SHE QUICKLY GROWS UNEASY AND BECOMES NERVOUS. HER TEMPO IS QUITE DIFFERENT FROM MOST PEOPLE. THOUGH SHE USUALLY LOOKS SPACED OUT, SHE ALSO HAS A SADISTIC STREAK. WHEN SHE GETS WORKED UP, SHE BEGINS VIOLENTLY HAVING FUN, MUCH LIKE A CAT PLAYING WITH HER PREY. HER THOUGHTS ABOUT K AND J DON'T RUN TOO DEEP. TO HER, THEY ARE SIMPLY PEOPLE SHE HAS TO LISTEN TO. SHE TRULY BELIEVES IN THE CAUSE OF THE CULT, BUT IN HER PERSONAL HIERARCHY CAIN WILL ALWAYS COME FIRST.

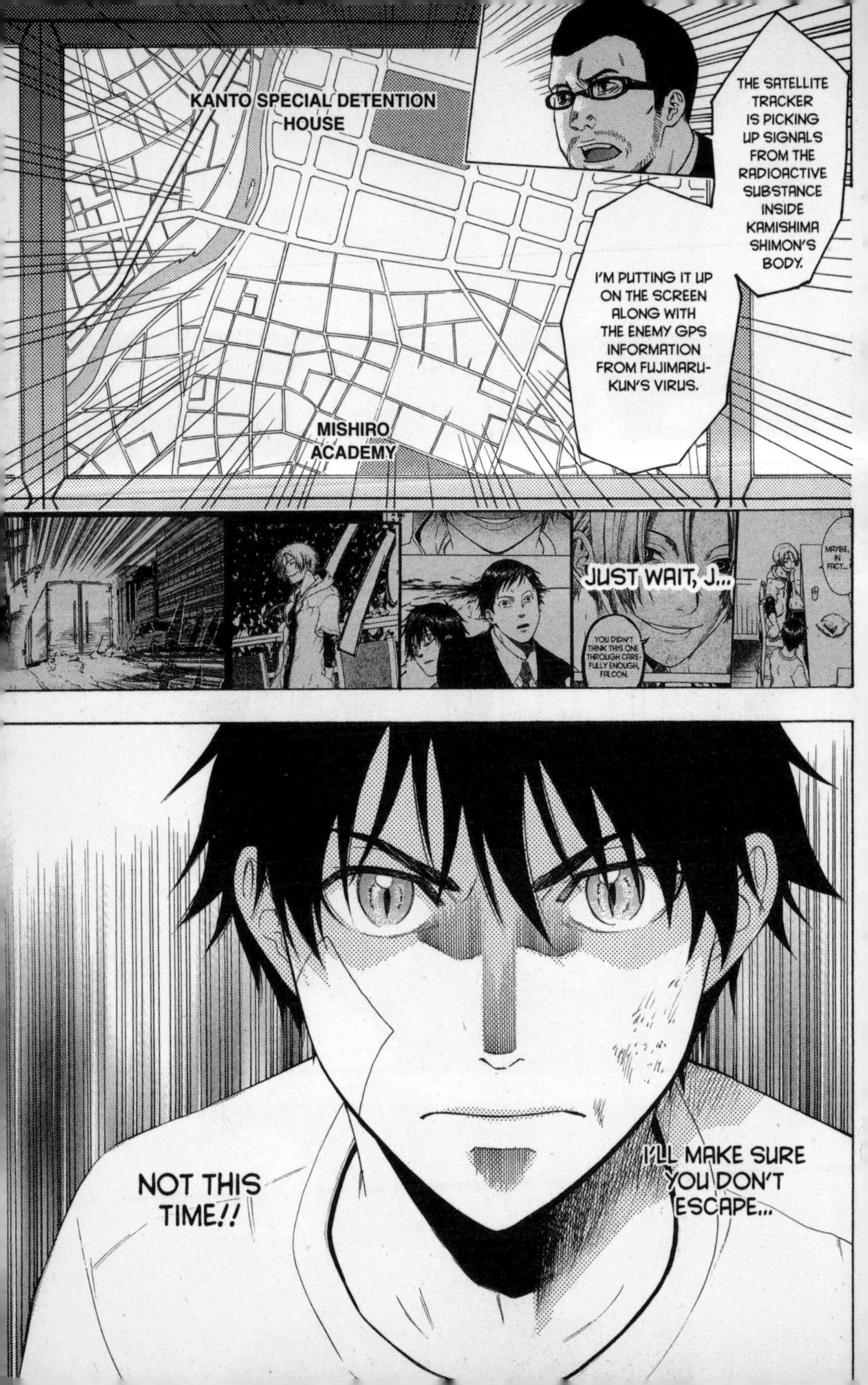
THE SATELLITE TRACKER IS PICKING UP SIGNALS FROM THE RADIOACTIVE SUBSTANCE INSIDE KAMISHIMA SHIMON'S BODY.
I'M PUTTING IT UP ON THE SCREEN ALONG WITH THE ENEMY GPS INFORMATION FROM FUJIMARU-KUN'S VIRUS.
KANTO SPECIAL DETENTION HOUSE
MISHIRO ACADEMY
MAYBE, IN FACT...
JUST WAIT, J...
YOU DIDN'T THINK THIS ONE THROUGH CARE-FULLY ENOUGH, FALCON.
I'LL MAKE SURE YOU DON'T ESCAPE...
NOT THIS TIME!!

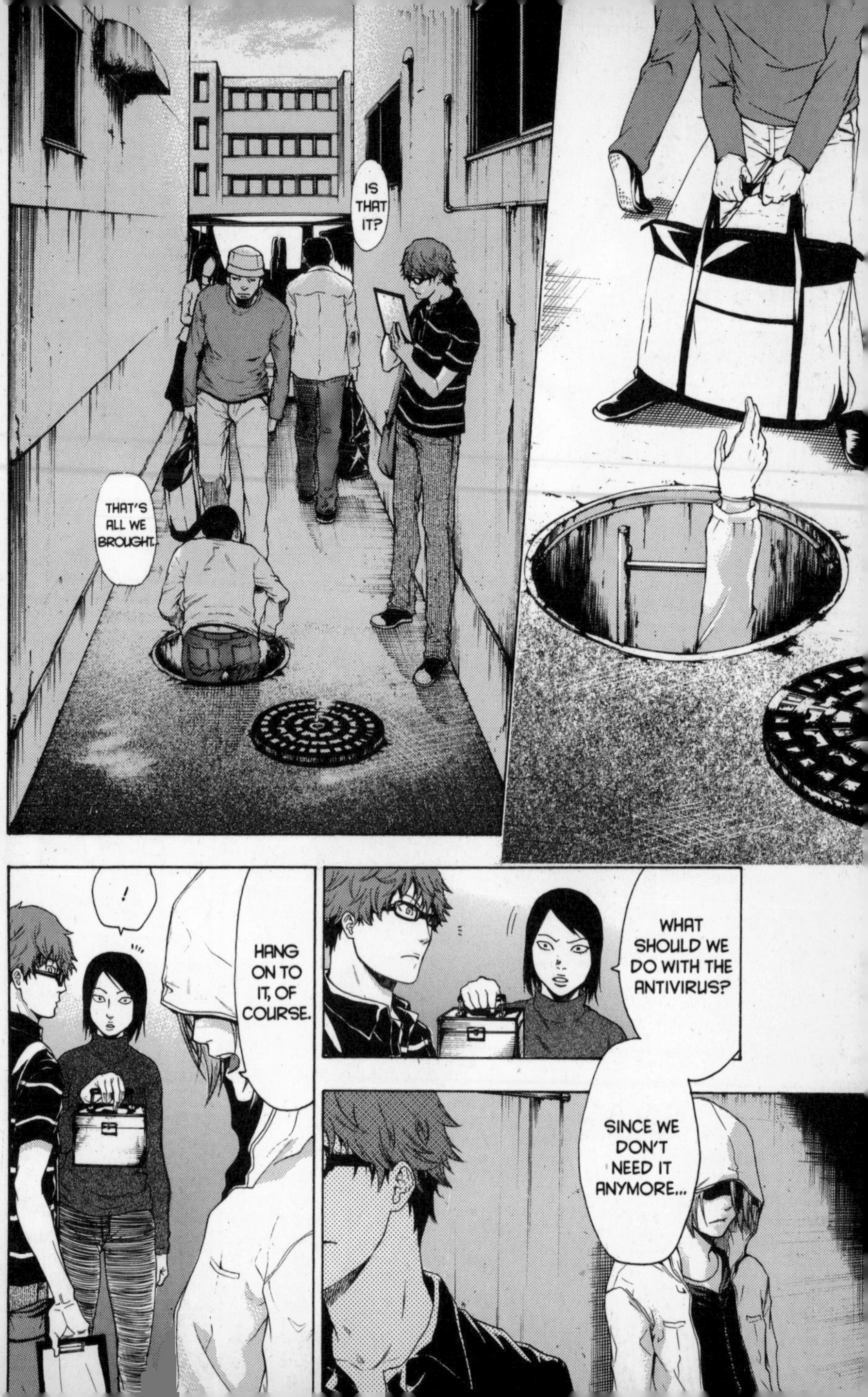
IS THAT IT?
THAT'S ALL WE BROUGHT.
WHAT SHOULD WE DO WITH THE ANTIVIRUS?
SINCE WE DON'T NEED IT ANYMORE...
HANG ON TO IT, OF COURSE.
!

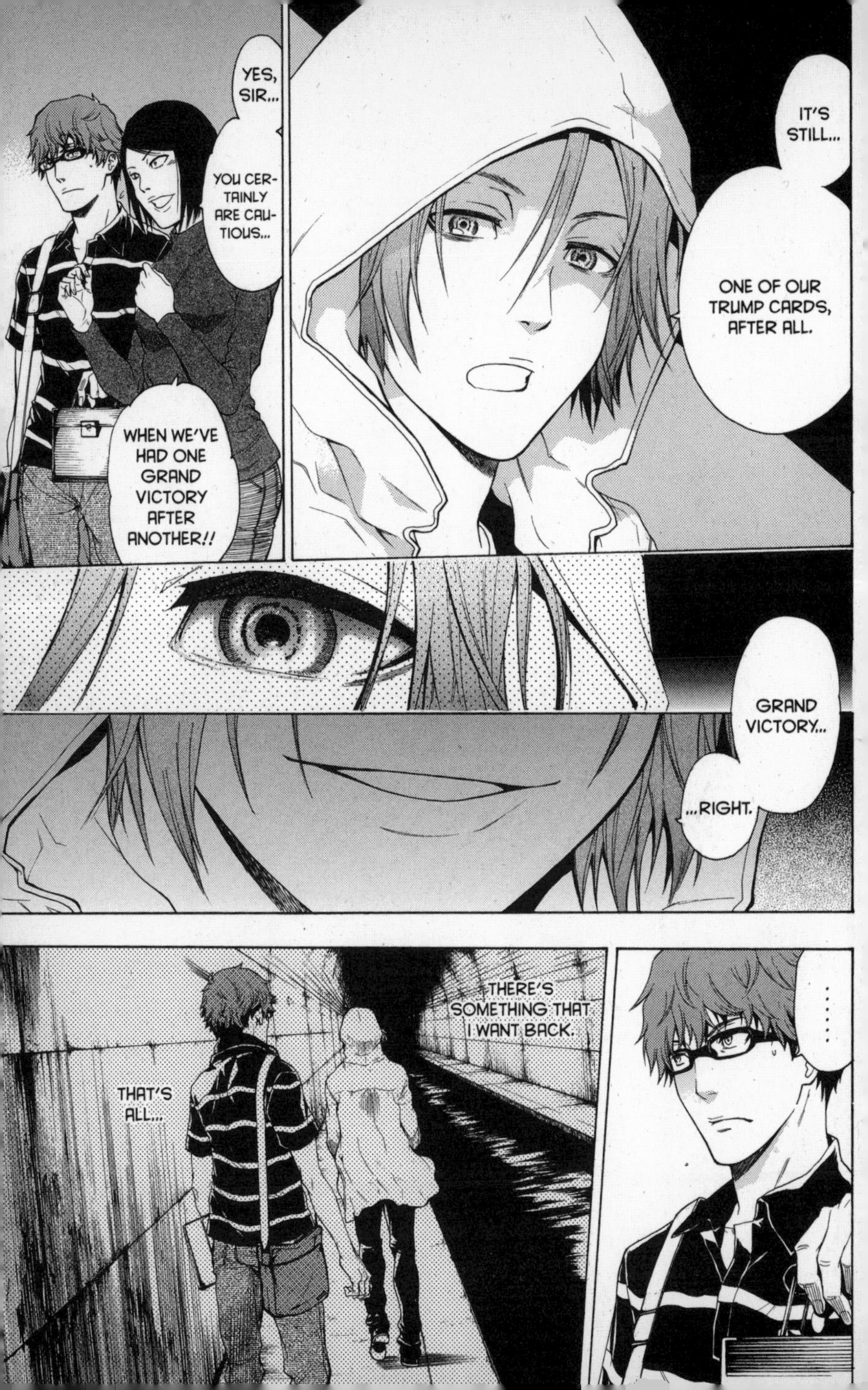
IT'S STILL...
ONE OF OUR TRUMP CARDS, AFTER ALL.
YES, SIR...
YOU CERTAINLY ARE CAUTIOUS...
WHEN WE'VE HAD ONE GRAND VICTORY AFTER ANOTHER!!
GRAND VICTORY...
...RIGHT.
......
THERE'S SOMETHING THAT I WANT BACK.
THAT'S ALL...

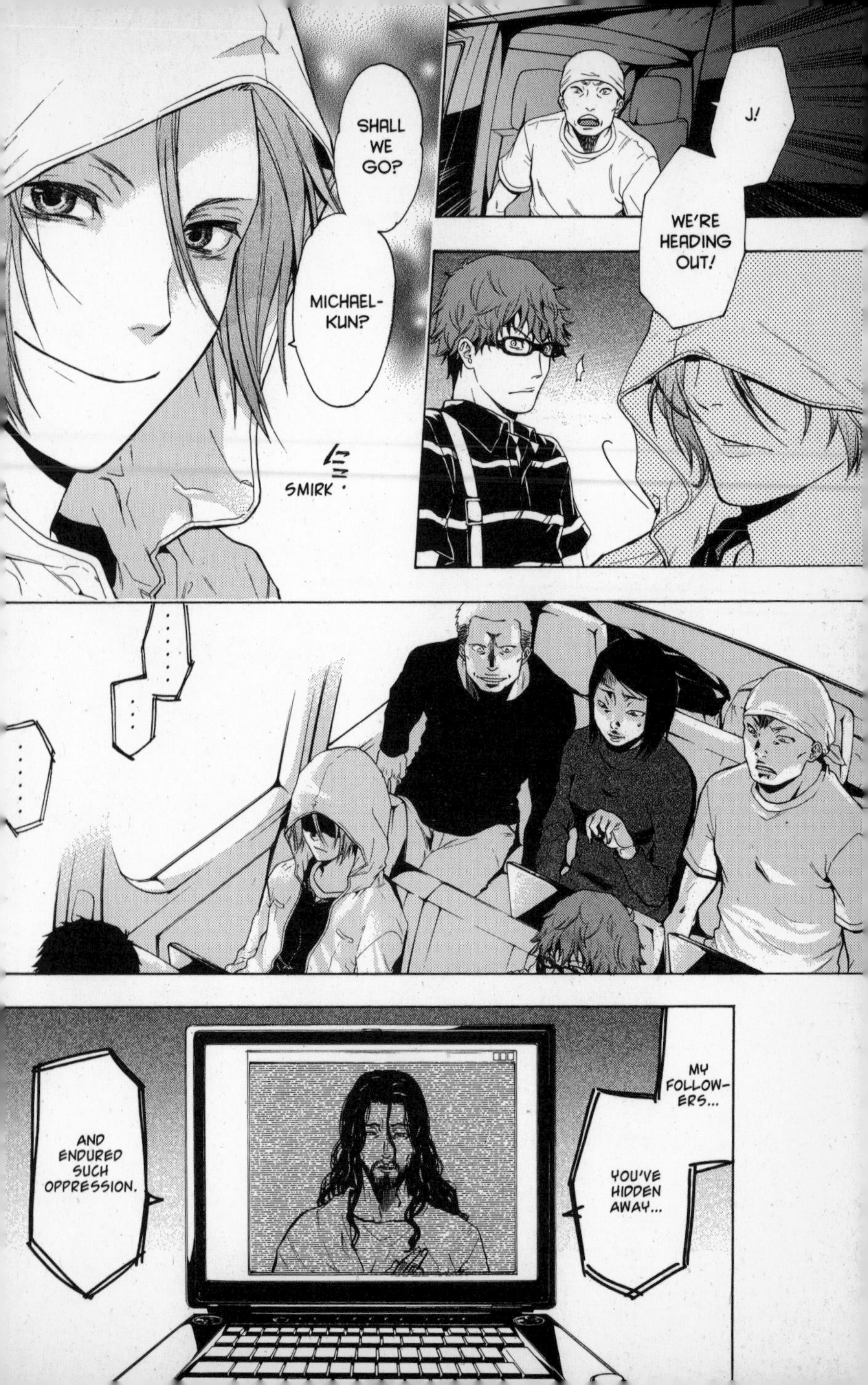
J!
WE'RE HEADING OUT!
SHALL WE GO?
MICHAEL-KUN?
SMIRK
...
...
MY FOLLOWERS...
YOU'VE HIDDEN AWAY...
AND ENDURED SUCH OPPRESSION.

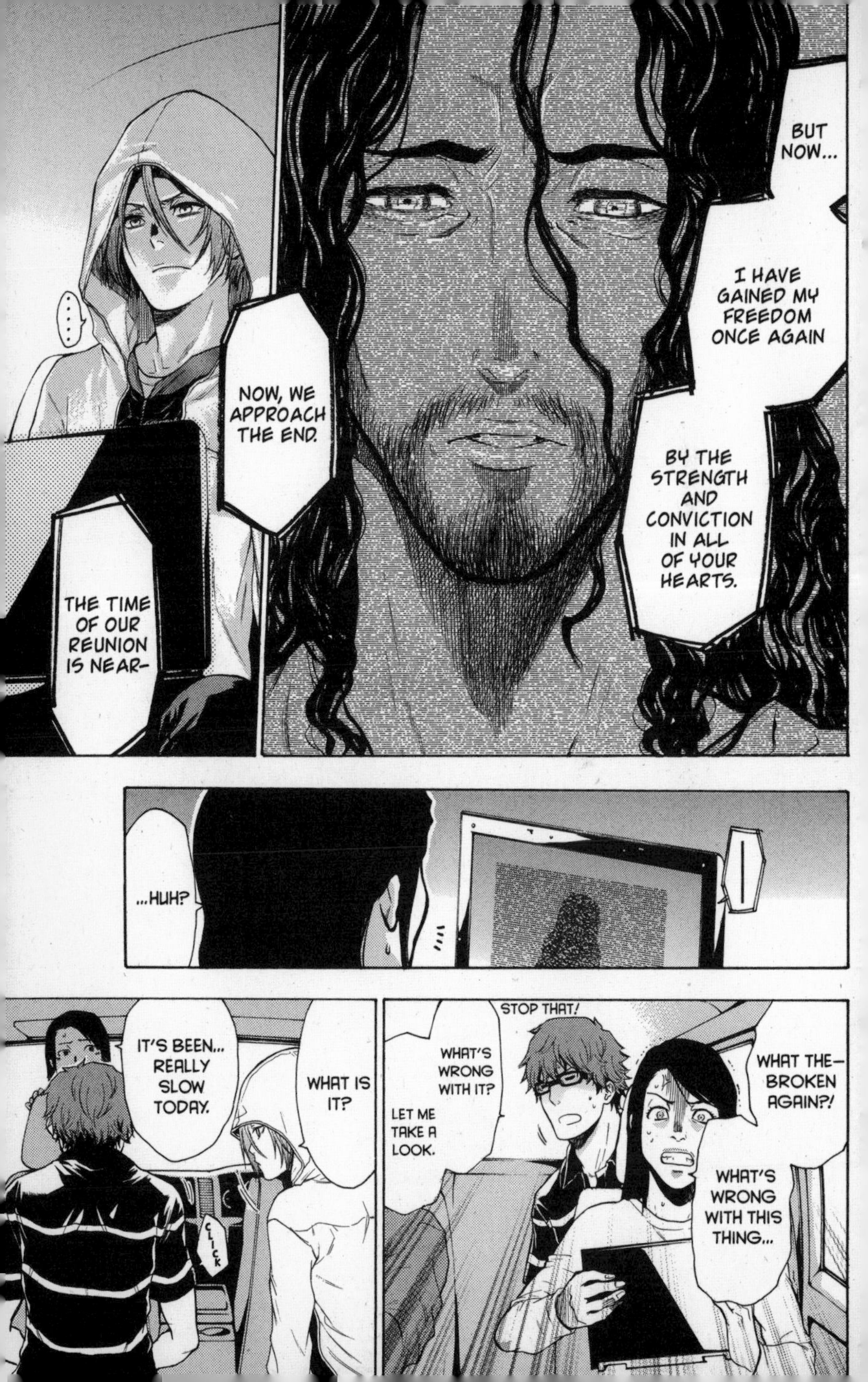
BUT NOW...
I HAVE GAINED MY FREEDOM ONCE AGAIN
BY THE STRENGTH AND CONVICTION IN ALL OF YOUR HEARTS.
NOW, WE APPROACH THE END.
THE TIME OF OUR REUNION IS NEAR-
......
...HUH?
WHAT THE— BROKEN AGAIN?!
STOP THAT!
WHAT'S WRONG WITH IT?
LET ME TAKE A LOOK.
WHAT'S WRONG WITH THIS THING...
WHAT IS IT?
IT'S BEEN... REALLY SLOW TODAY.
CLICK

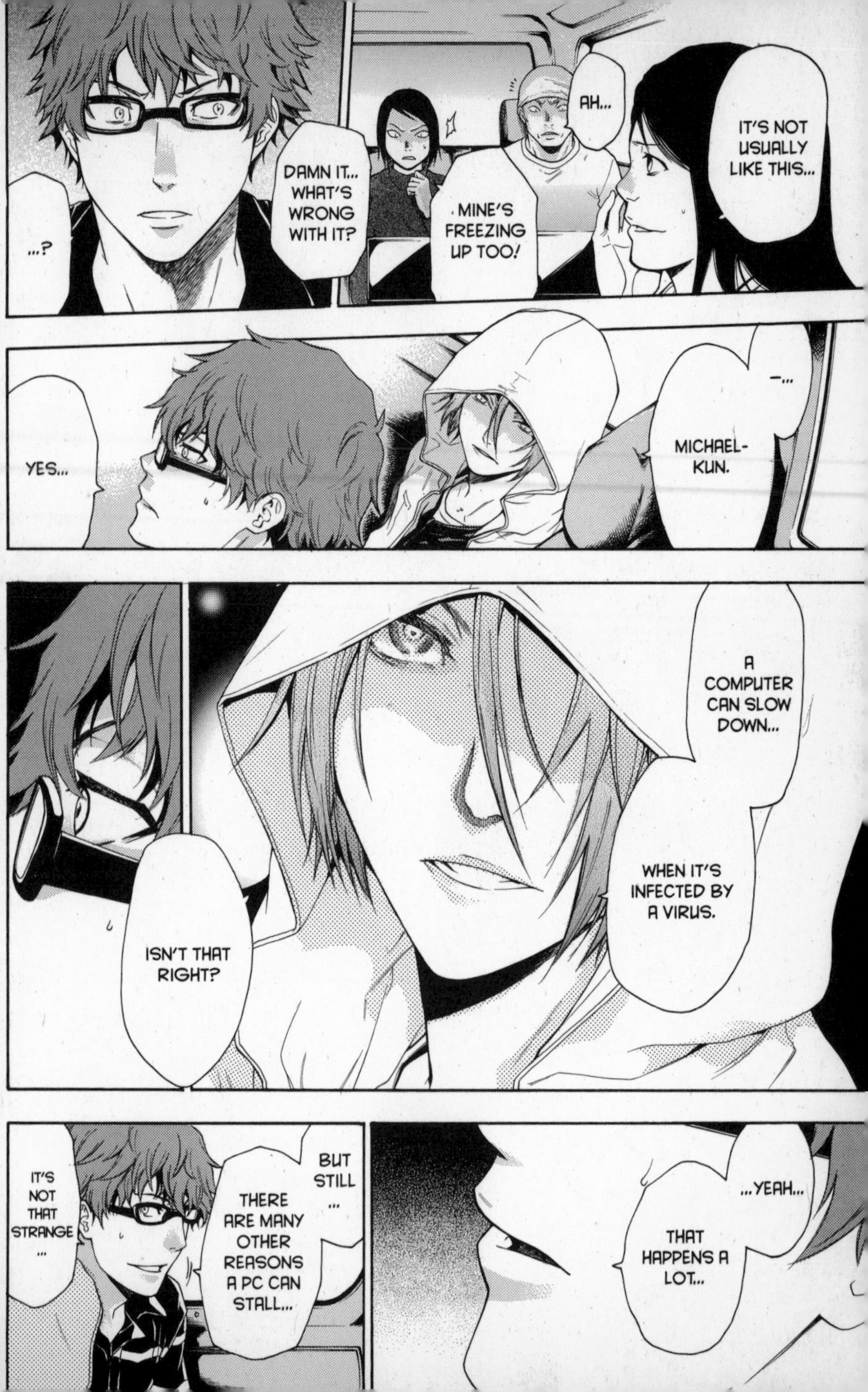
IT'S NOT USUALLY LIKE THIS...
AH...
MINE'S FREEZING UP TOO!
DAMN IT... WHAT'S WRONG WITH IT?
...?
–...
MICHAEL-KUN.
YES...
A COMPUTER CAN SLOW DOWN...
WHEN IT'S INFECTED BY A VIRUS.
ISN'T THAT RIGHT?
...YEAH...
THAT HAPPENS A LOT...
BUT STILL ...
THERE ARE MANY OTHER REASONS A PC CAN STALL...
IT'S NOT THAT STRANGE ...

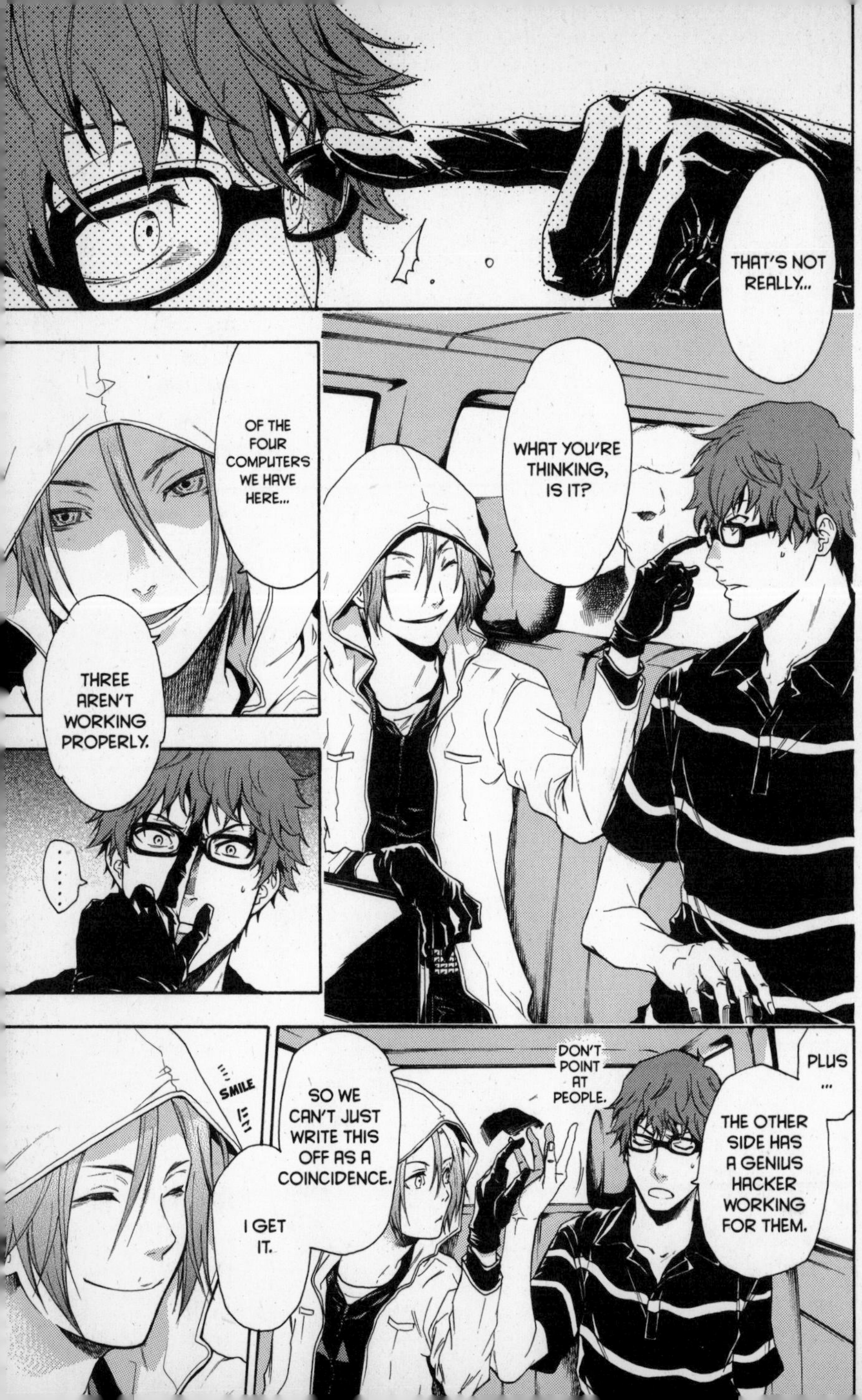
THAT'S NOT REALLY...
WHAT YOU'RE THINKING, IS IT?
OF THE FOUR COMPUTERS WE HAVE HERE...
THREE AREN'T WORKING PROPERLY.
......
PLUS ...
THE OTHER SIDE HAS A GENIUS HACKER WORKING FOR THEM.
DON'T POINT AT PEOPLE.
SO WE CAN'T JUST WRITE THIS OFF AS A COINCIDENCE.
I GET IT.
SMILE

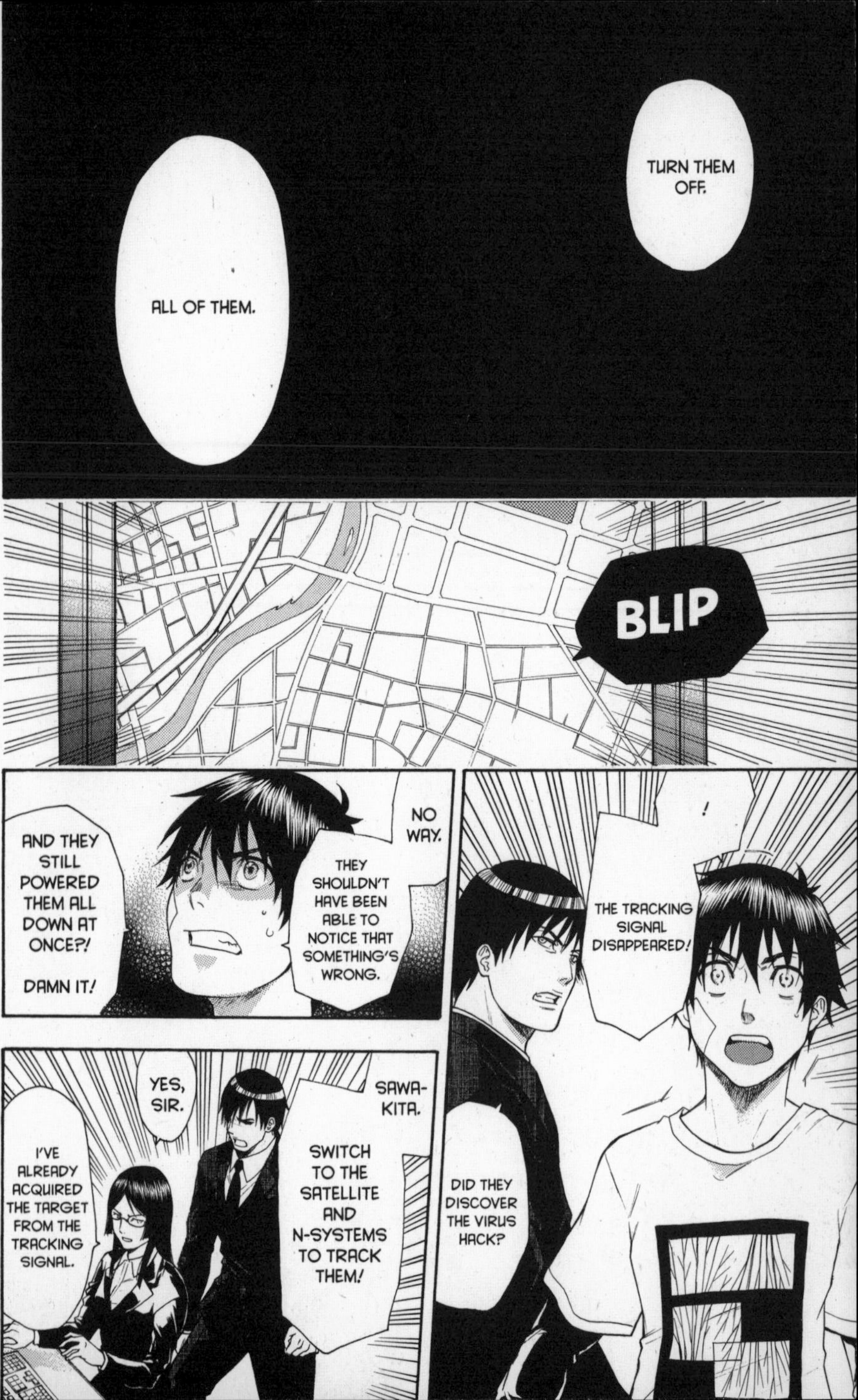
TURN THEM OFF.
ALL OF THEM.
BLIP
!
THE TRACKING SIGNAL DISAPPEARED!
DID THEY DISCOVER THE VIRUS HACK?
NO WAY.
THEY SHOULDN'T HAVE BEEN ABLE TO NOTICE THAT SOMETHING'S WRONG.
AND THEY STILL POWERED THEM ALL DOWN AT ONCE?!
DAMN IT!
SAWA-KITA.
SWITCH TO THE SATELLITE AND N-SYSTEMS TO TRACK THEM!
YES, SIR.
I'VE ALREADY ACQUIRED THE TARGET FROM THE TRACKING SIGNAL.

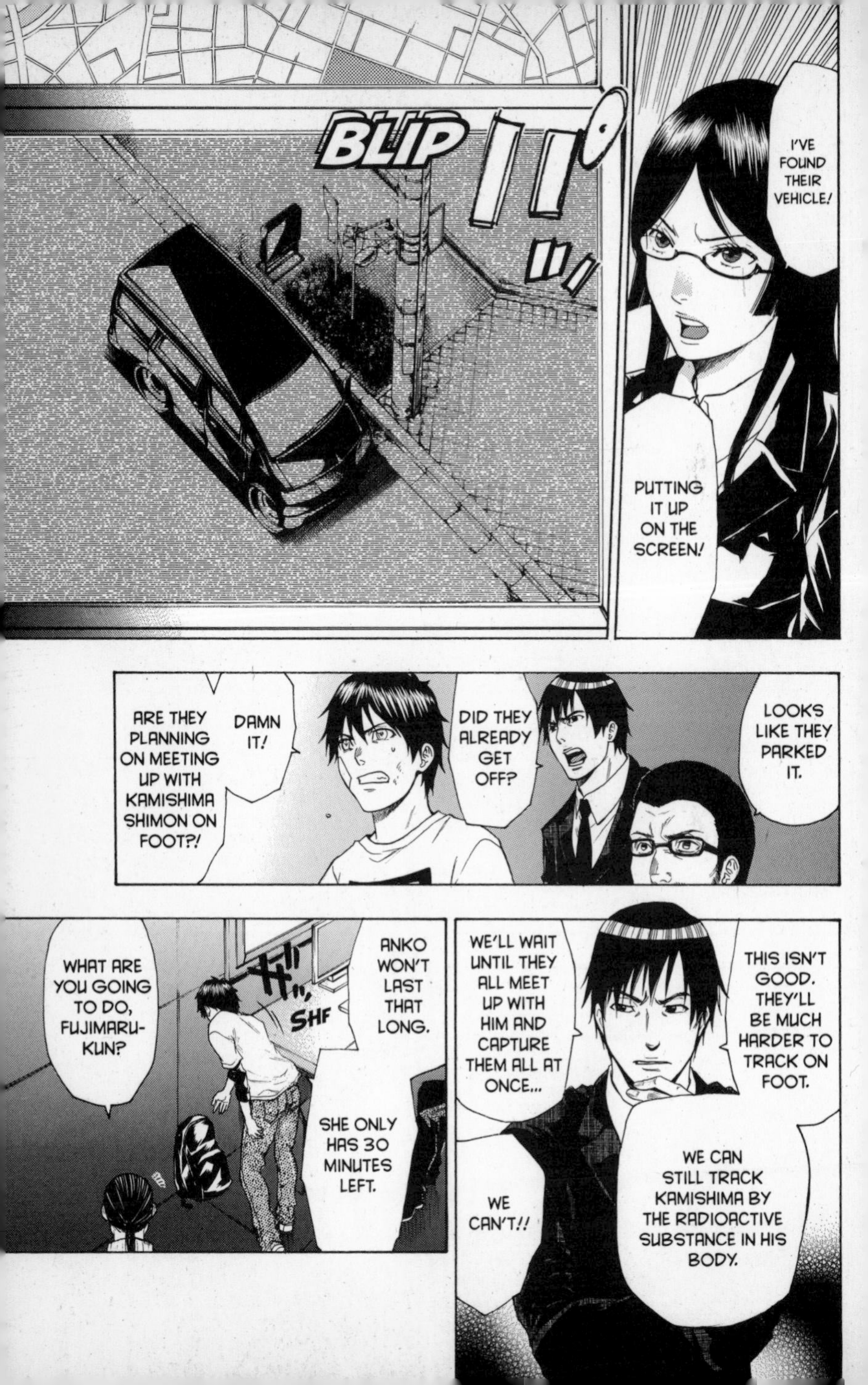
I'VE FOUND THEIR VEHICLE!
PUTTING IT UP ON THE SCREEN!
BLIP
LOOKS LIKE THEY PARKED IT.
DID THEY ALREADY GET OFF?
DAMN IT!
ARE THEY PLANNING ON MEETING UP WITH KAMISHIMA SHIMON ON FOOT?!
THIS ISN'T GOOD. THEY'LL BE MUCH HARDER TO TRACK ON FOOT.
WE'LL WAIT UNTIL THEY ALL MEET UP WITH HIM AND CAPTURE THEM ALL AT ONCE...
WE CAN STILL TRACK KAMISHIMA BY THE RADIOACTIVE SUBSTANCE IN HIS BODY.
WE CAN'T!!
ANKO WON'T LAST THAT LONG.
SHE ONLY HAS 30 MINUTES LEFT.
SHF
WHAT ARE YOU GOING TO DO, FUJIMARU-KUN?

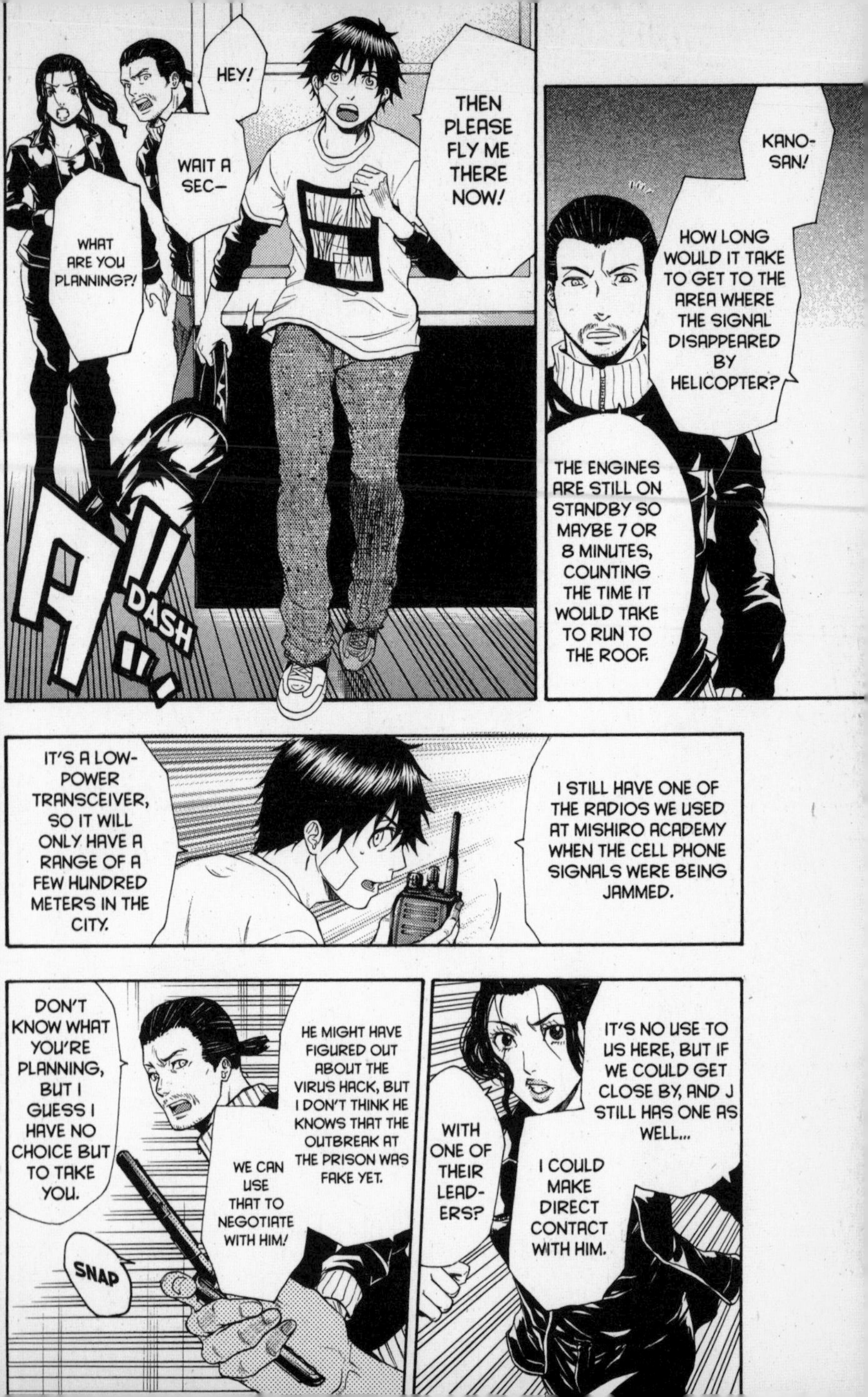
KANO-SAN!
HOW LONG WOULD IT TAKE TO GET TO THE AREA WHERE THE SIGNAL DISAPPEARED BY HELICOPTER?
THE ENGINES ARE STILL ON STANDBY SO MAYBE 7 OR 8 MINUTES, COUNTING THE TIME IT WOULD TAKE TO RUN TO THE ROOF.
THEN PLEASE FLY ME THERE NOW!
HEY!
WAIT A SEC—
WHAT ARE YOU PLANNING?!
DASH
I STILL HAVE ONE OF THE RADIOS WE USED AT MISHIRO ACADEMY WHEN THE CELL PHONE SIGNALS WERE BEING JAMMED.
IT'S A LOW-POWER TRANSCEIVER, SO IT WILL ONLY HAVE A RANGE OF A FEW HUNDRED METERS IN THE CITY.
IT'S NO USE TO US HERE, BUT IF WE COULD GET CLOSE BY, AND J STILL HAS ONE AS WELL...
I COULD MAKE DIRECT CONTACT WITH HIM.
WITH ONE OF THEIR LEAD-ERS?
HE MIGHT HAVE FIGURED OUT ABOUT THE VIRUS HACK, BUT I DON'T THINK HE KNOWS THAT THE OUTBREAK AT THE PRISON WAS FAKE YET.
WE CAN USE THAT TO NEGOTIATE WITH HIM!
DON'T KNOW WHAT YOU'RE PLANNING, BUT I GUESS I HAVE NO CHOICE BUT TO TAKE YOU.
SNAP

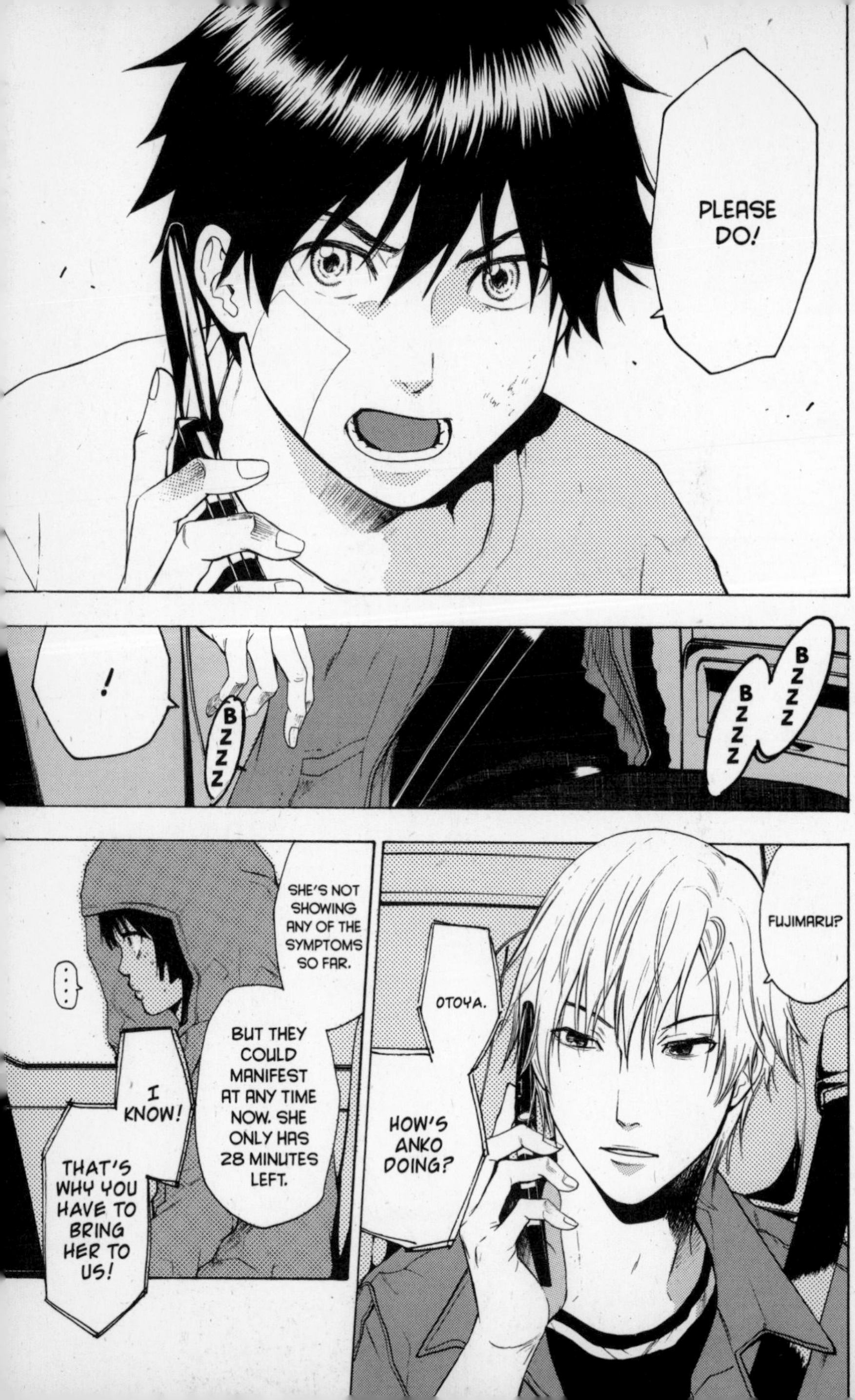
PLEASE DO!
BZZZ
BZZZ
BZZZ
!
FUJIMARU?
OTOYA.
HOW'S ANKO DOING?
SHE'S NOT SHOWING ANY OF THE SYMPTOMS SO FAR.
...
BUT THEY COULD MANIFEST AT ANY TIME NOW. SHE ONLY HAS 28 MINUTES LEFT.
I KNOW!
THAT'S WHY YOU HAVE TO BRING HER TO US!

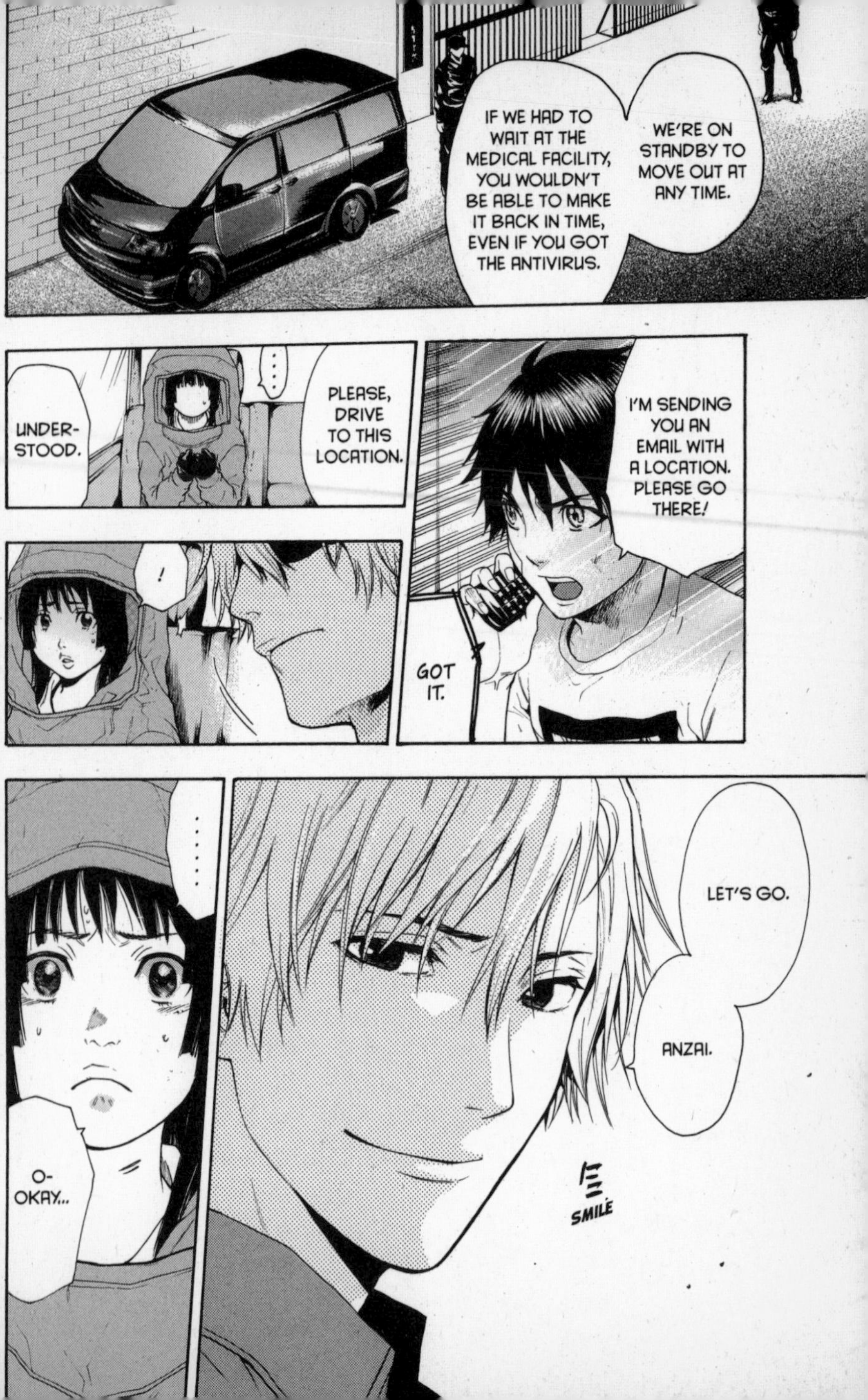

WE'RE ON STANDBY TO MOVE OUT AT ANY TIME.
IF WE HAD TO WAIT AT THE MEDICAL FACILITY, YOU WOULDN'T BE ABLE TO MAKE IT BACK IN TIME, EVEN IF YOU GOT THE ANTIVIRUS.
I'M SENDING YOU AN EMAIL WITH A LOCATION. PLEASE GO THERE!
GOT IT.
PLEASE, DRIVE TO THIS LOCATION.
...
UNDER-STOOD.
!
LET'S GO.
ANZAI.
SMILE
....
O-OKAY...

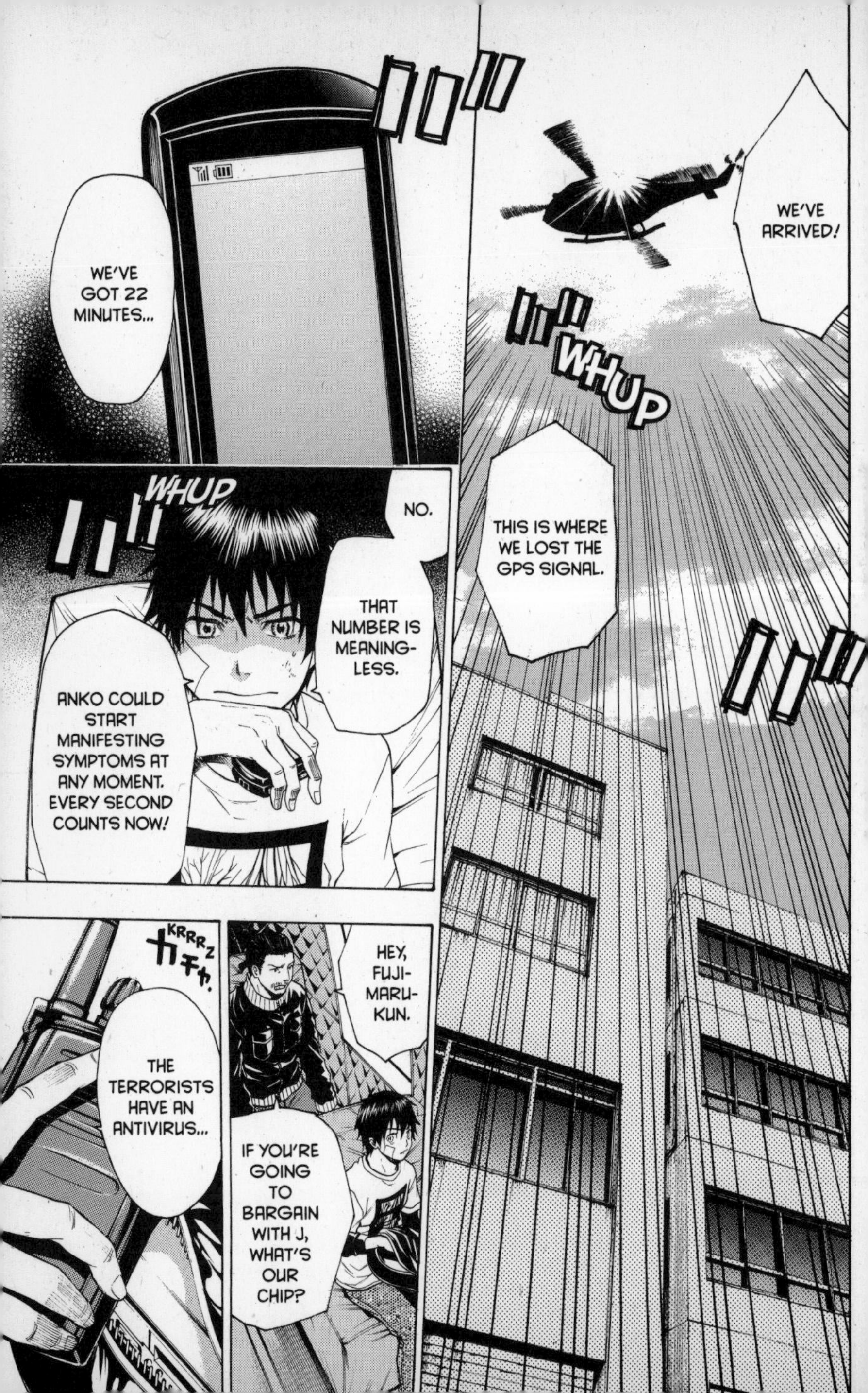
WE'VE ARRIVED!
WHUP
THIS IS WHERE WE LOST THE GPS SIGNAL.
WE'VE GOT 22 MINUTES...
WHUP
NO.
THAT NUMBER IS MEANING-LESS.
ANKO COULD START MANIFESTING SYMPTOMS AT ANY MOMENT. EVERY SECOND COUNTS NOW!
HEY, FUJI-MARU-KUN.
IF YOU'RE GOING TO BARGAIN WITH J, WHAT'S OUR CHIP?
KRRRZ
カチャ
THE TERRORISTS HAVE AN ANTIVIRUS...

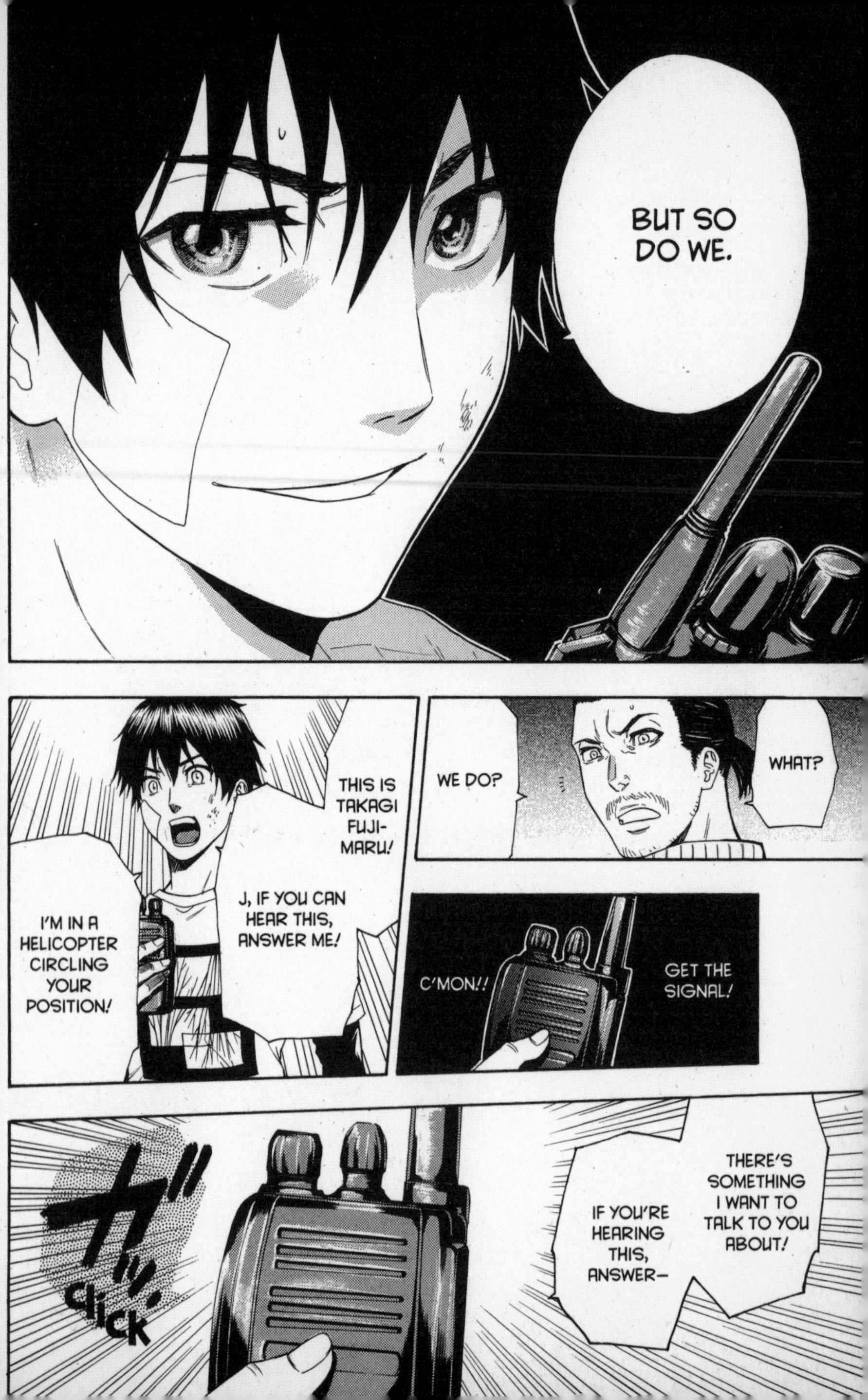
BUT SO DO WE.
WHAT?
WE DO?
GET THE SIGNAL!
C'MON!!
THIS IS TAKAGI FUJI-MARU!
J, IF YOU CAN HEAR THIS, ANSWER ME!
I'M IN A HELICOPTER CIRCLING YOUR POSITION!
THERE'S SOMETHING I WANT TO TALK TO YOU ABOUT!
IF YOU'RE HEARING THIS, ANSWER—
ガッ
CLICK

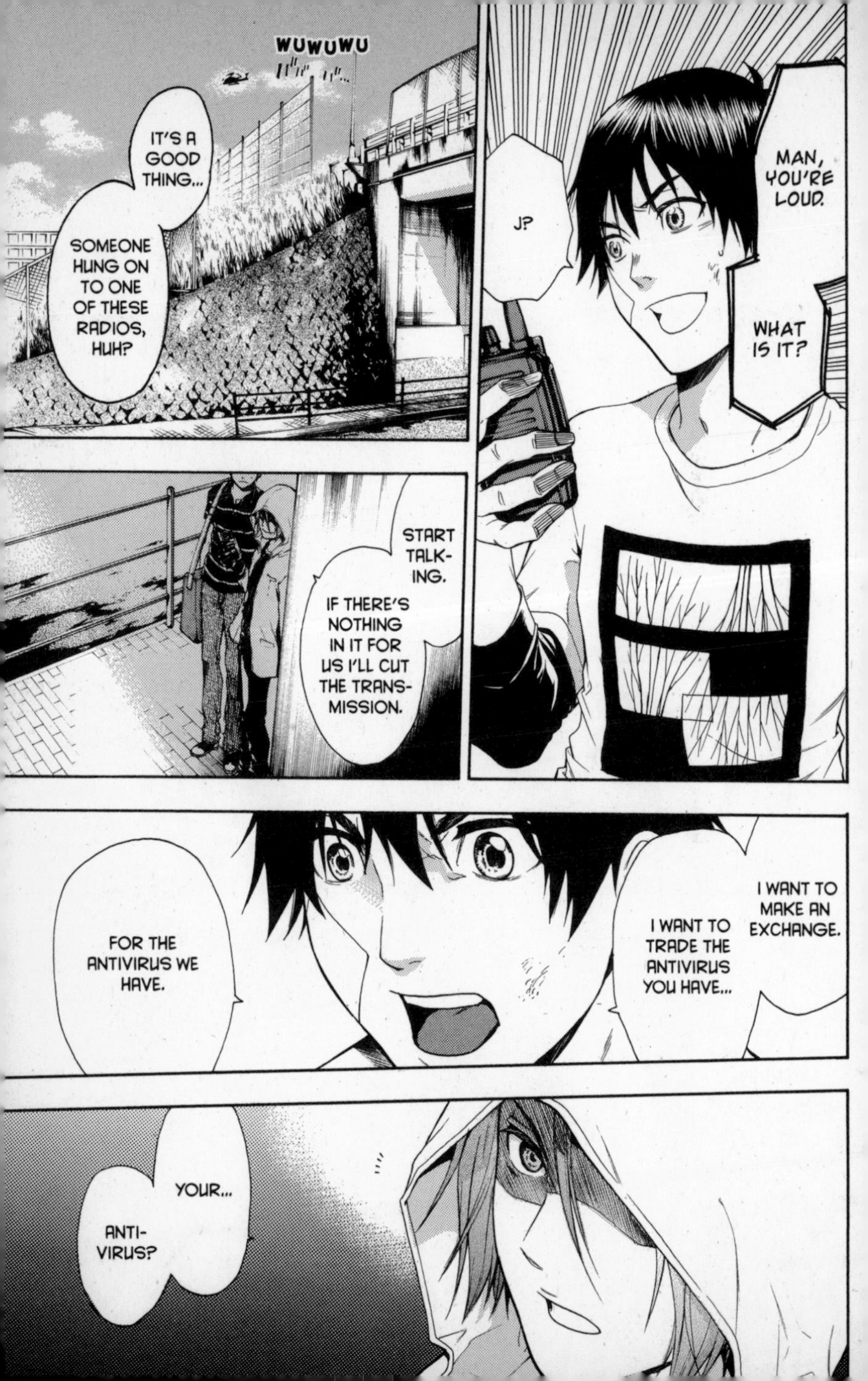
MAN, YOU'RE LOUD.
J?
WHAT IS IT?
WUWUWU
IT'S A GOOD THING...
SOMEONE HUNG ON TO ONE OF THESE RADIOS, HUH?
START TALK-ING.
IF THERE'S NOTHING IN IT FOR US I'LL CUT THE TRANS-MISSION.
I WANT TO MAKE AN EXCHANGE.
I WANT TO TRADE THE ANTIVIRUS YOU HAVE...
FOR THE ANTIVIRUS WE HAVE.
YOUR...
ANTI-VIRUS?

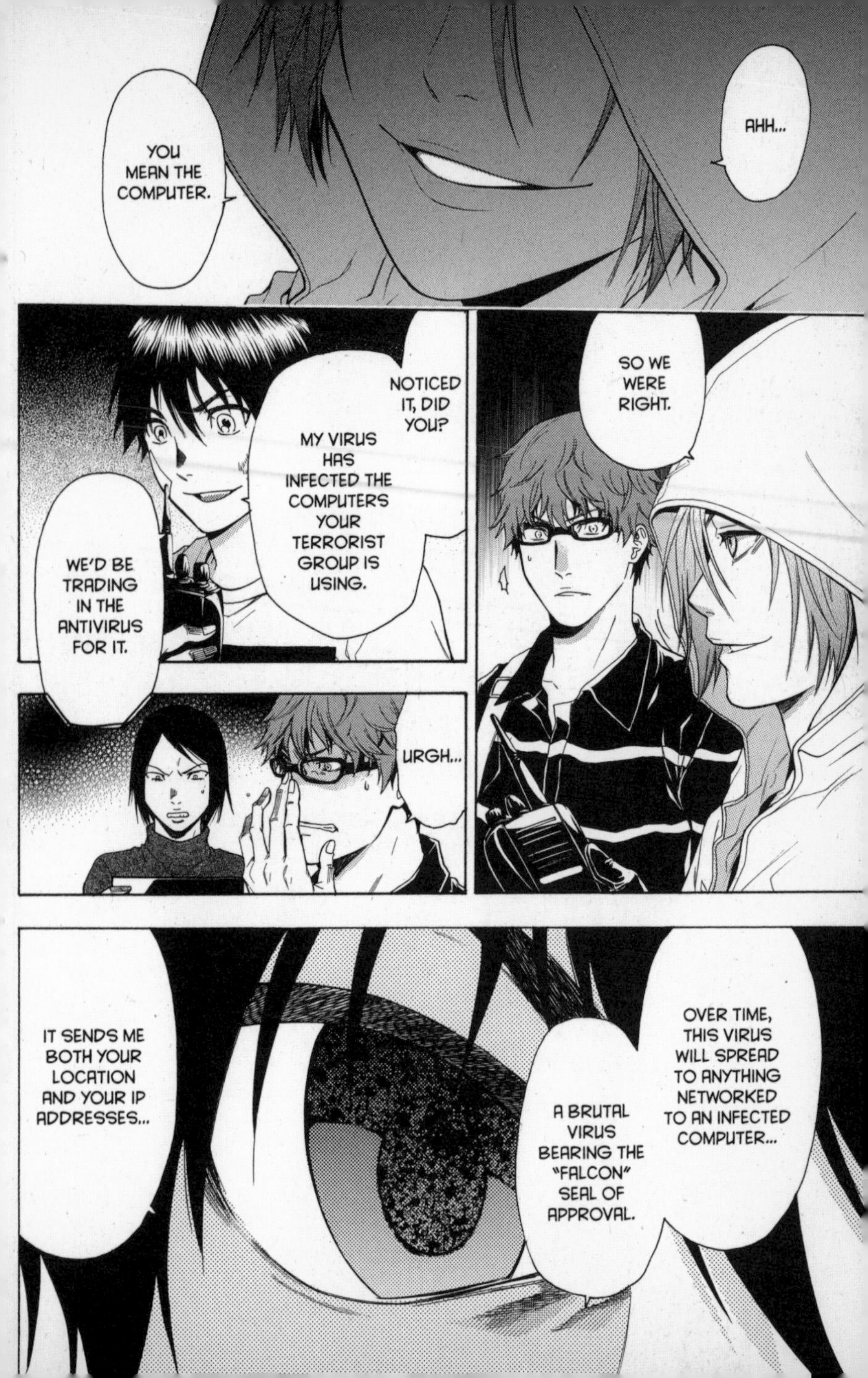
AHH...
YOU MEAN THE COMPUTER.
SO WE WERE RIGHT.
NOTICED IT, DID YOU?
MY VIRUS HAS INFECTED THE COMPUTERS YOUR TERRORIST GROUP IS USING.
WE'D BE TRADING IN THE ANTIVIRUS FOR IT.
URGH...
OVER TIME, THIS VIRUS WILL SPREAD TO ANYTHING NETWORKED TO AN INFECTED COMPUTER...
A BRUTAL VIRUS BEARING THE "FALCON" SEAL OF APPROVAL.
IT SENDS ME BOTH YOUR LOCATION AND YOUR IP ADDRESSES...

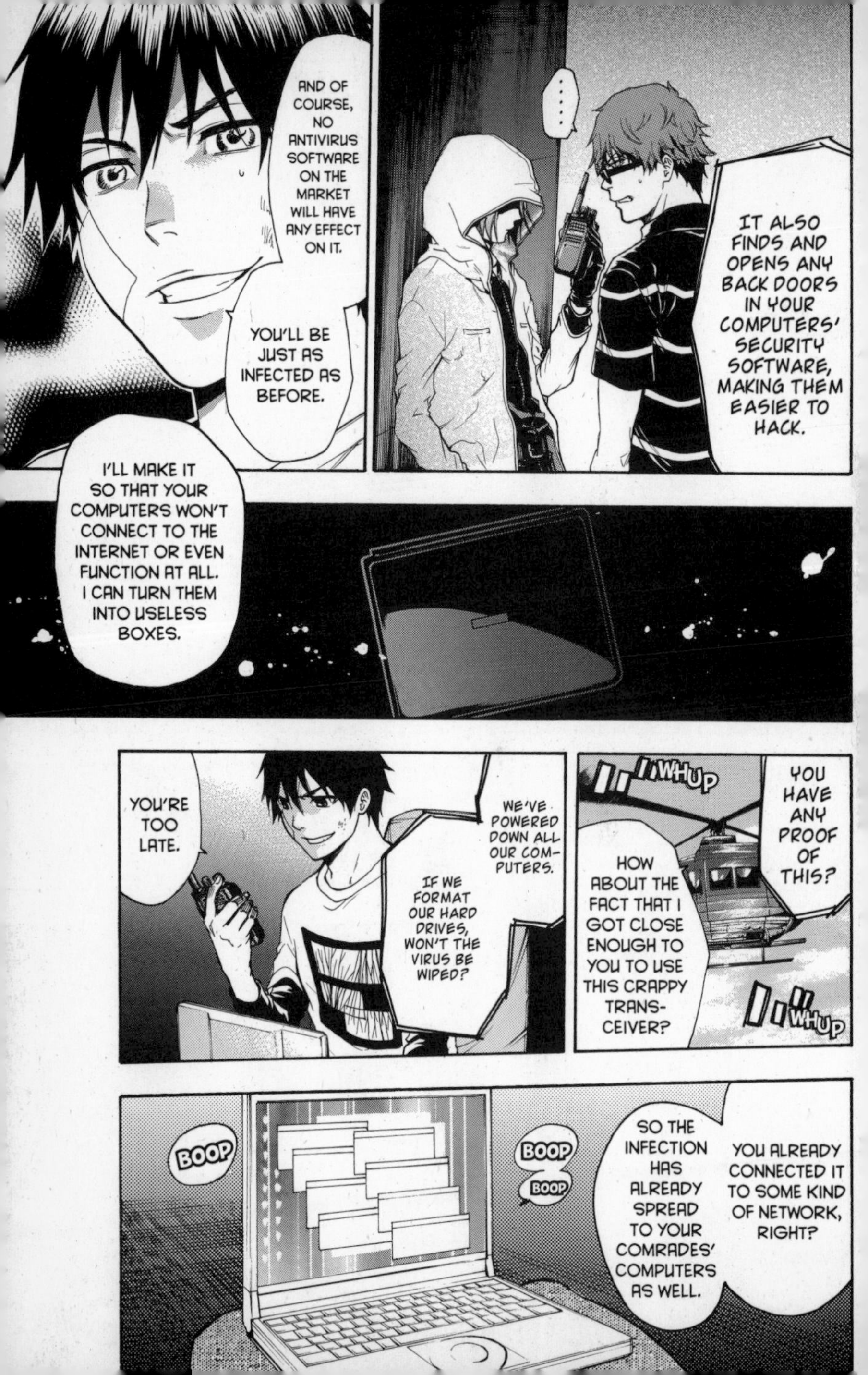
IT ALSO FINDS AND OPENS ANY BACK DOORS IN YOUR COMPUTERS' SECURITY SOFTWARE, MAKING THEM EASIER TO HACK.
.....
AND OF COURSE, NO ANTIVIRUS SOFTWARE ON THE MARKET WILL HAVE ANY EFFECT ON IT.
YOU'LL BE JUST AS INFECTED AS BEFORE.
I'LL MAKE IT SO THAT YOUR COMPUTERS WON'T CONNECT TO THE INTERNET OR EVEN FUNCTION AT ALL. I CAN TURN THEM INTO USELESS BOXES.
YOU HAVE ANY PROOF OF THIS?
WHUP
HOW ABOUT THE FACT THAT I GOT CLOSE ENOUGH TO YOU TO USE THIS CRAPPY TRANS-CEIVER?
WHUP
WE'VE POWERED DOWN ALL OUR COM-PUTERS.
IF WE FORMAT OUR HARD DRIVES, WON'T THE VIRUS BE WIPED?
YOU'RE TOO LATE.
YOU ALREADY CONNECTED IT TO SOME KIND OF NETWORK, RIGHT?
SO THE INFECTION HAS ALREADY SPREAD TO YOUR COMRADES' COMPUTERS AS WELL.
BOOP
BOOP
BOOP

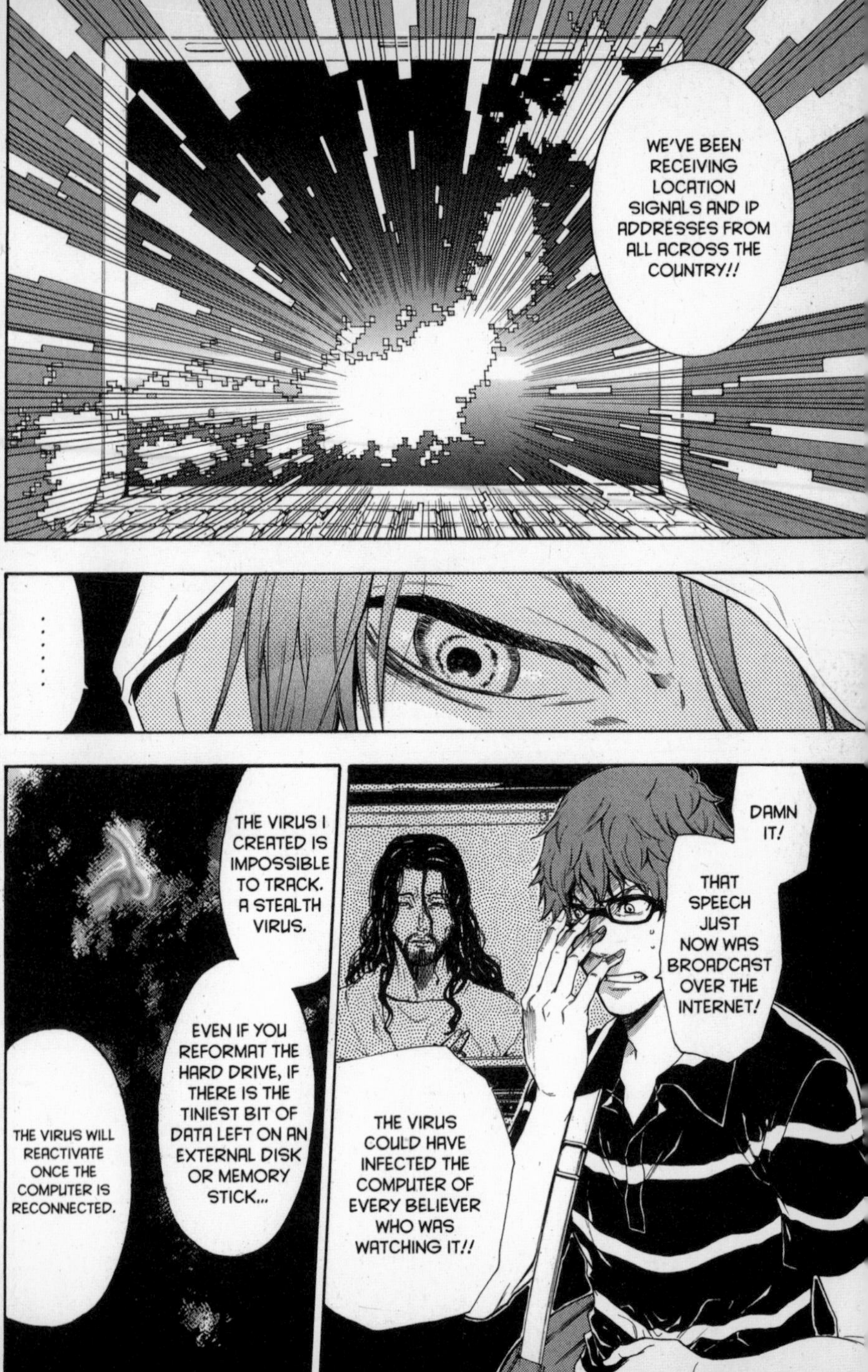

WE'VE BEEN RECEIVING LOCATION SIGNALS AND IP ADDRESSES FROM ALL ACROSS THE COUNTRY!!
......
DAMN IT!
THAT SPEECH JUST NOW WAS BROADCAST OVER THE INTERNET!
THE VIRUS COULD HAVE INFECTED THE COMPUTER OF EVERY BELIEVER WHO WAS WATCHING IT!!
THE VIRUS I CREATED IS IMPOSSIBLE TO TRACK. A STEALTH VIRUS.
EVEN IF YOU REFORMAT THE HARD DRIVE, IF THERE IS THE TINIEST BIT OF DATA LEFT ON AN EXTERNAL DISK OR MEMORY STICK...
THE VIRUS WILL REACTIVATE ONCE THE COMPUTER IS RECONNECTED.

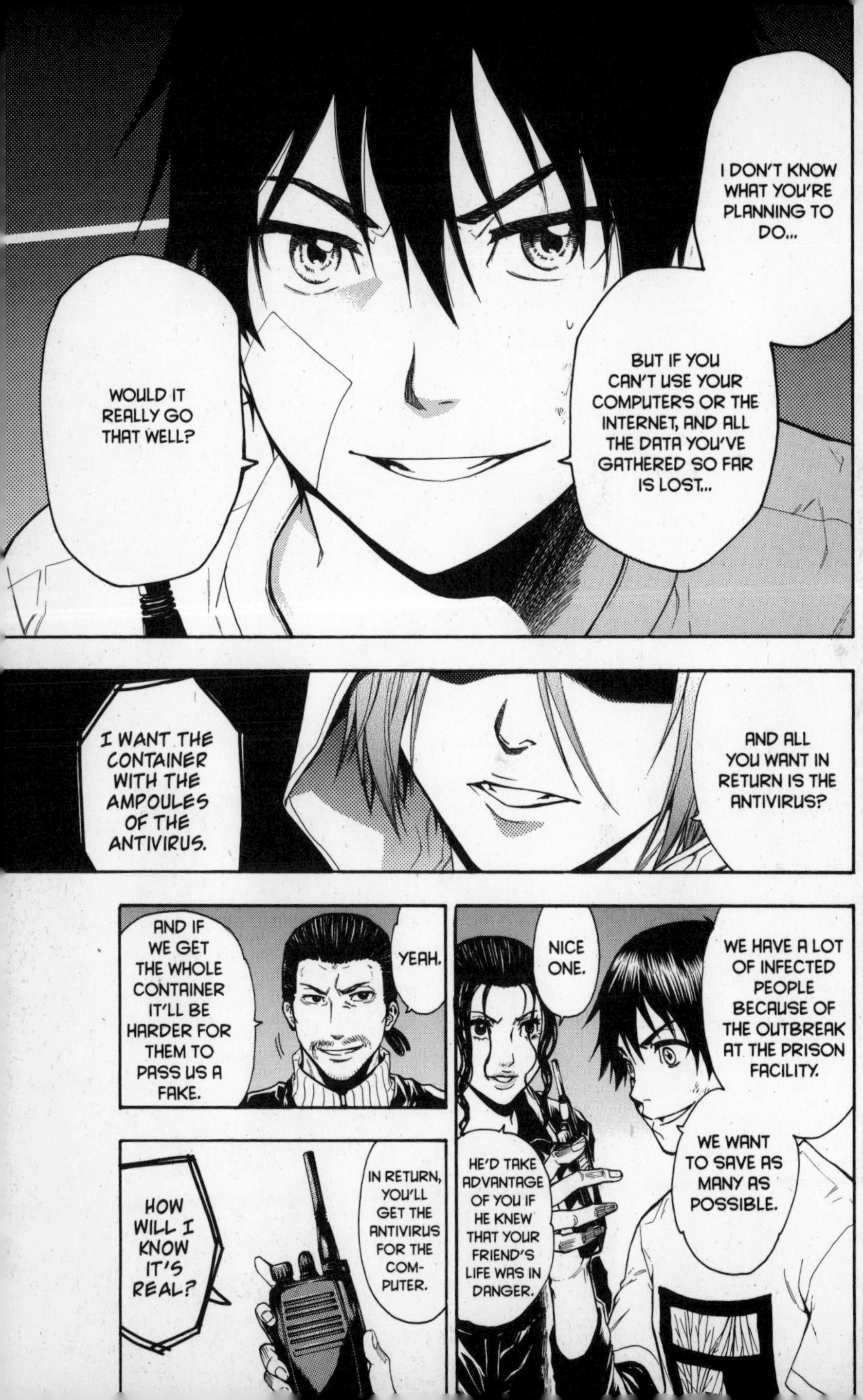
I DON'T KNOW WHAT YOU'RE PLANNING TO DO...
BUT IF YOU CAN'T USE YOUR COMPUTERS OR THE INTERNET, AND ALL THE DATA YOU'VE GATHERED SO FAR IS LOST...
WOULD IT REALLY GO THAT WELL?
AND ALL YOU WANT IN RETURN IS THE ANTIVIRUS?
I WANT THE CONTAINER WITH THE AMPOULES OF THE ANTIVIRUS.
WE HAVE A LOT OF INFECTED PEOPLE BECAUSE OF THE OUTBREAK AT THE PRISON FACILITY.
NICE ONE.
WE WANT TO SAVE AS MANY AS POSSIBLE.
HE'D TAKE ADVANTAGE OF YOU IF HE KNEW THAT YOUR FRIEND'S LIFE WAS IN DANGER.
YEAH.
AND IF WE GET THE WHOLE CONTAINER IT'LL BE HARDER FOR THEM TO PASS US A FAKE.
IN RETURN, YOU'LL GET THE ANTIVIRUS FOR THE COM-PUTER.
HOW WILL I KNOW IT'S REAL?

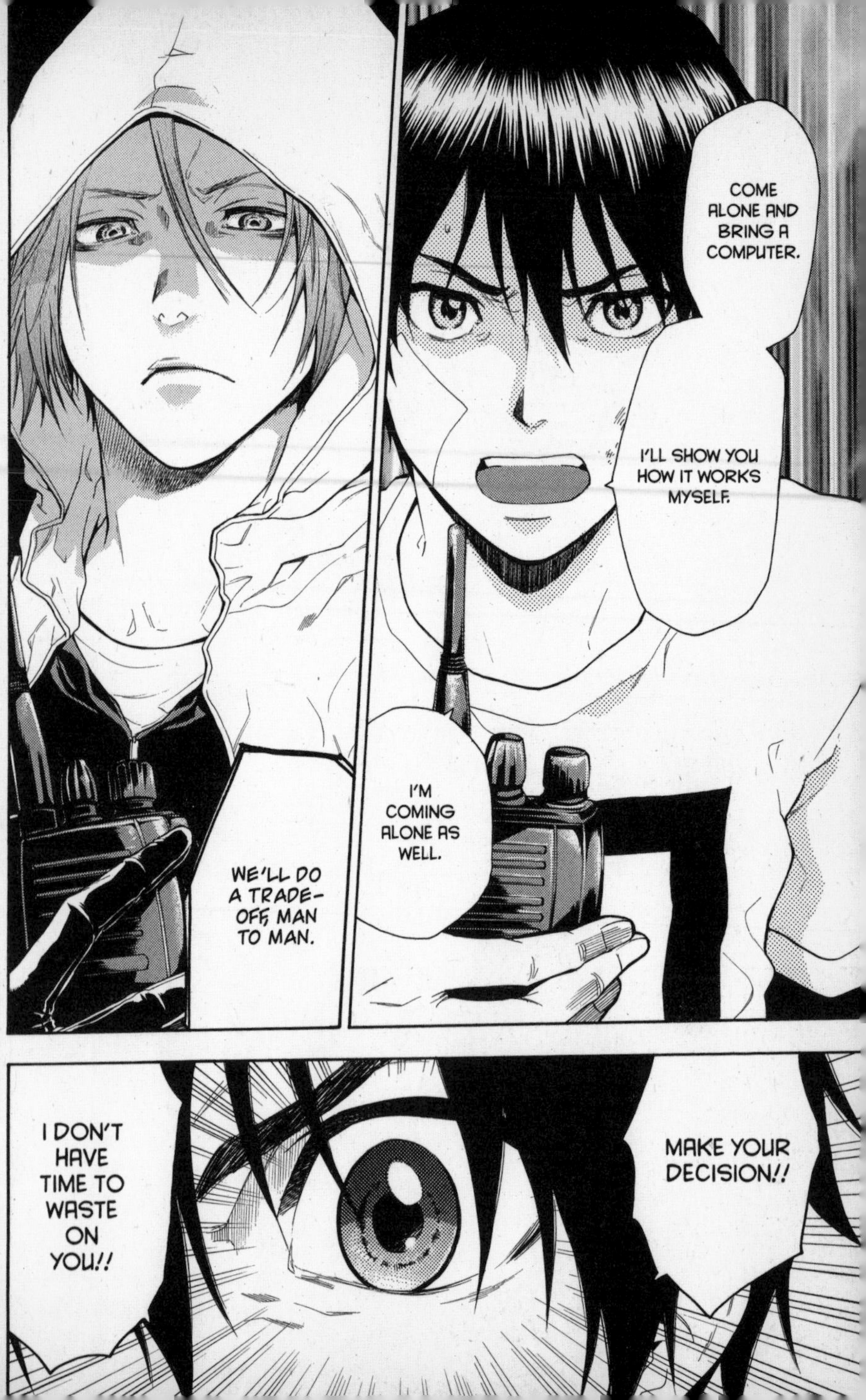
COME ALONE AND BRING A COMPUTER.
I'LL SHOW YOU HOW IT WORKS MYSELF.
I'M COMING ALONE AS WELL.
WE'LL DO A TRADE-OFF, MAN TO MAN.
MAKE YOUR DECISION!!
I DON'T HAVE TIME TO WASTE ON YOU!!

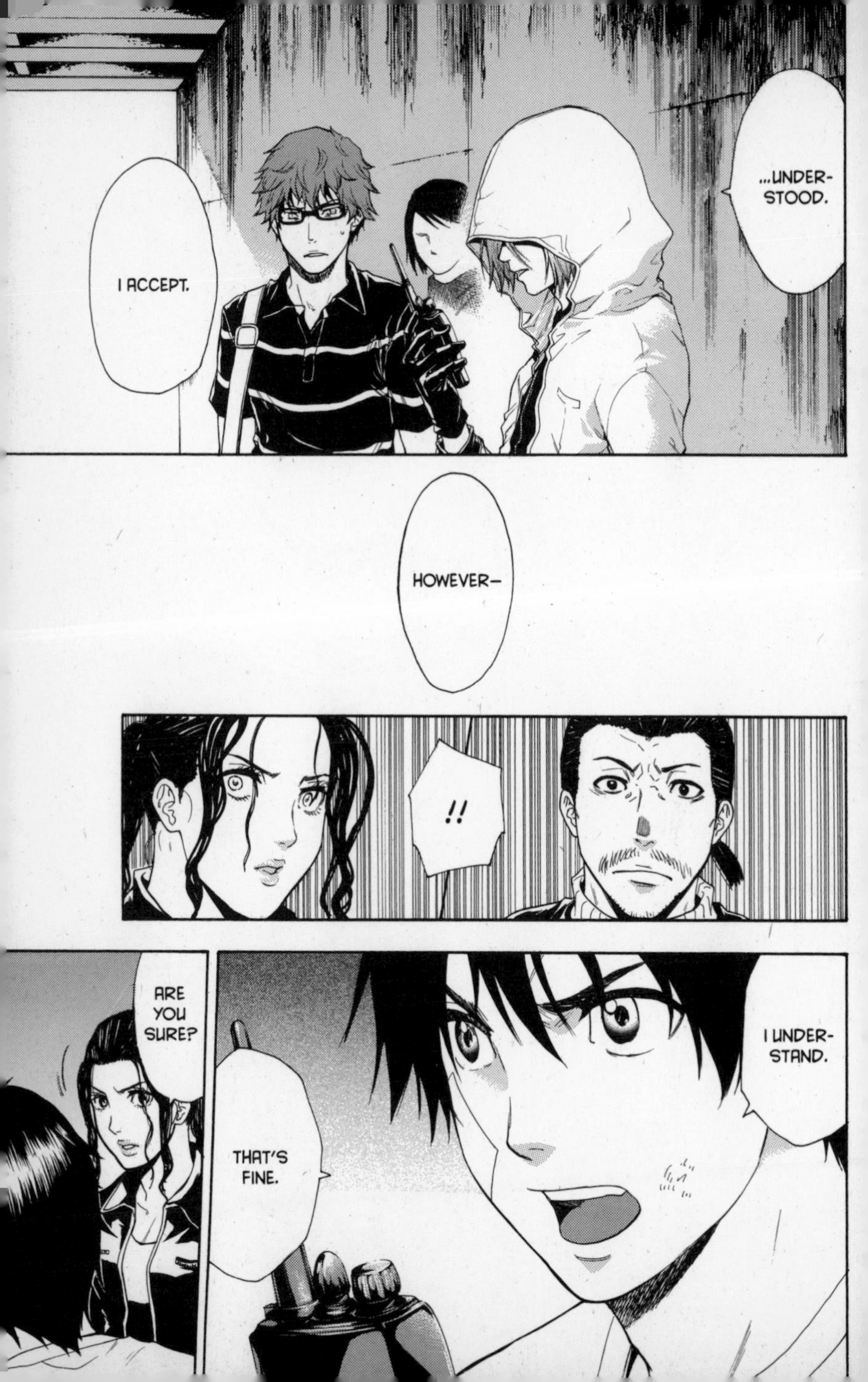
...UNDER-STOOD.
I ACCEPT.
HOWEVER–
!!
I UNDER-STAND.
THAT'S FINE.
ARE YOU SURE?

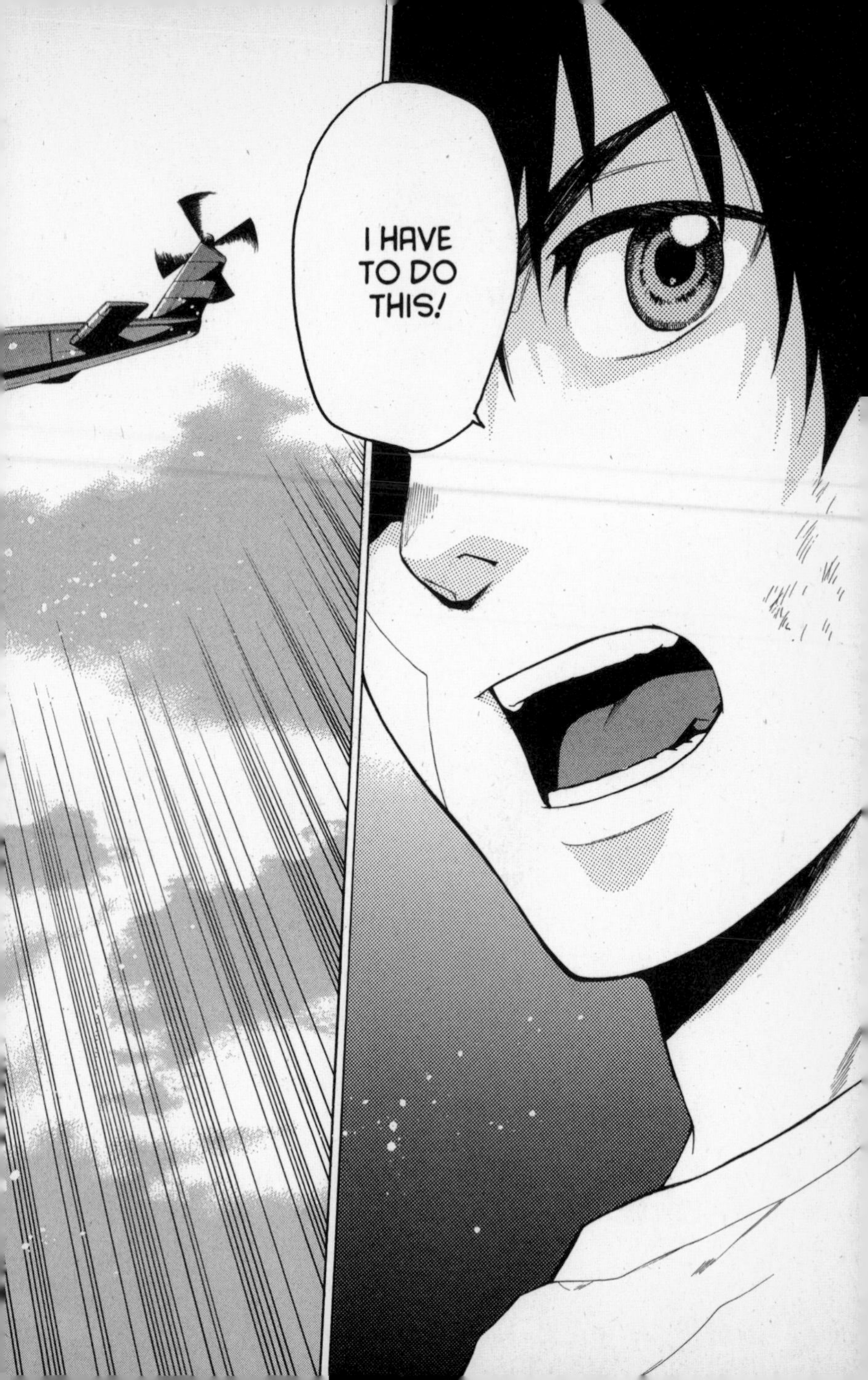
I HAVE TO DO THIS!

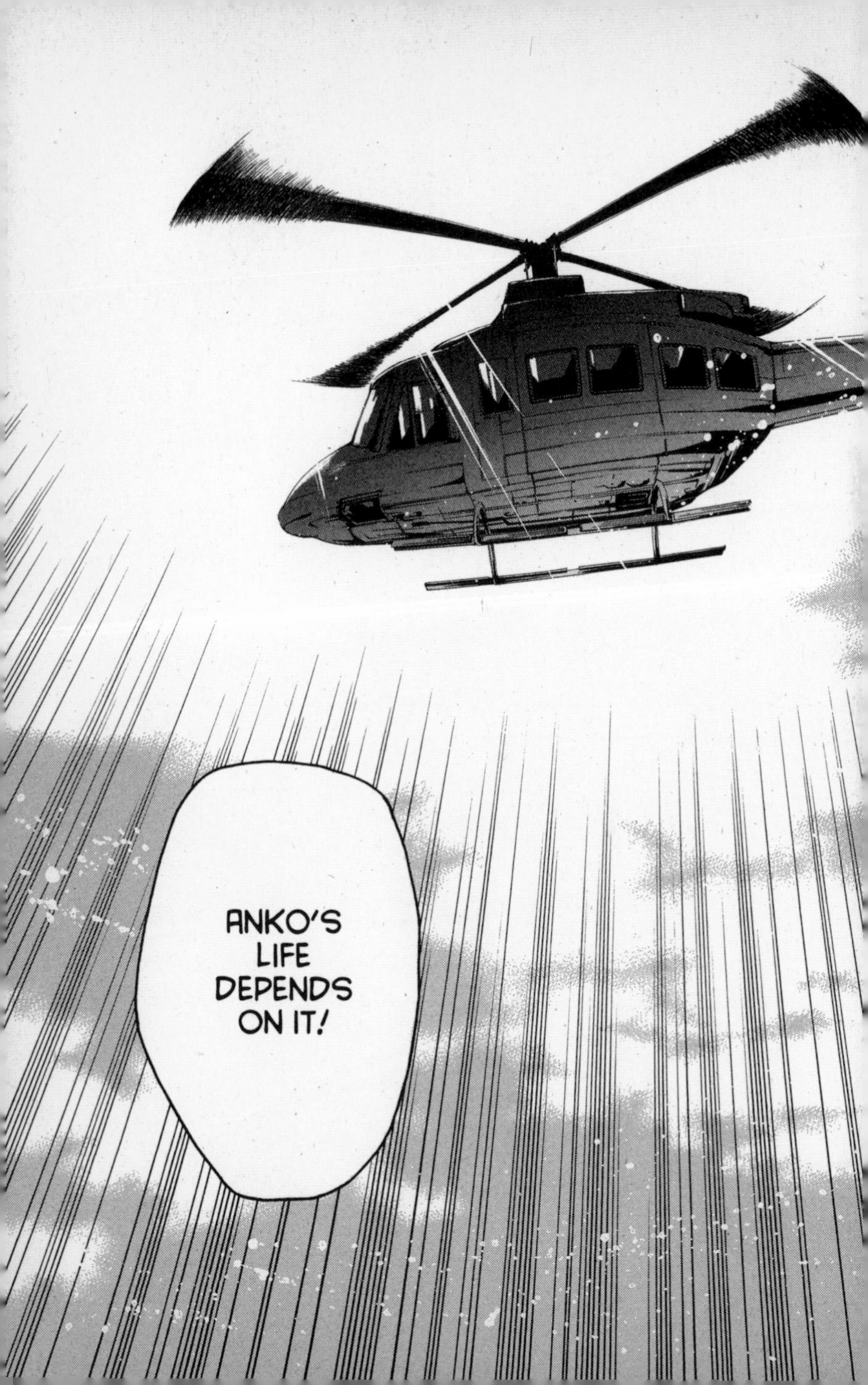
ANKO'S LIFE DEPENDS ON IT!

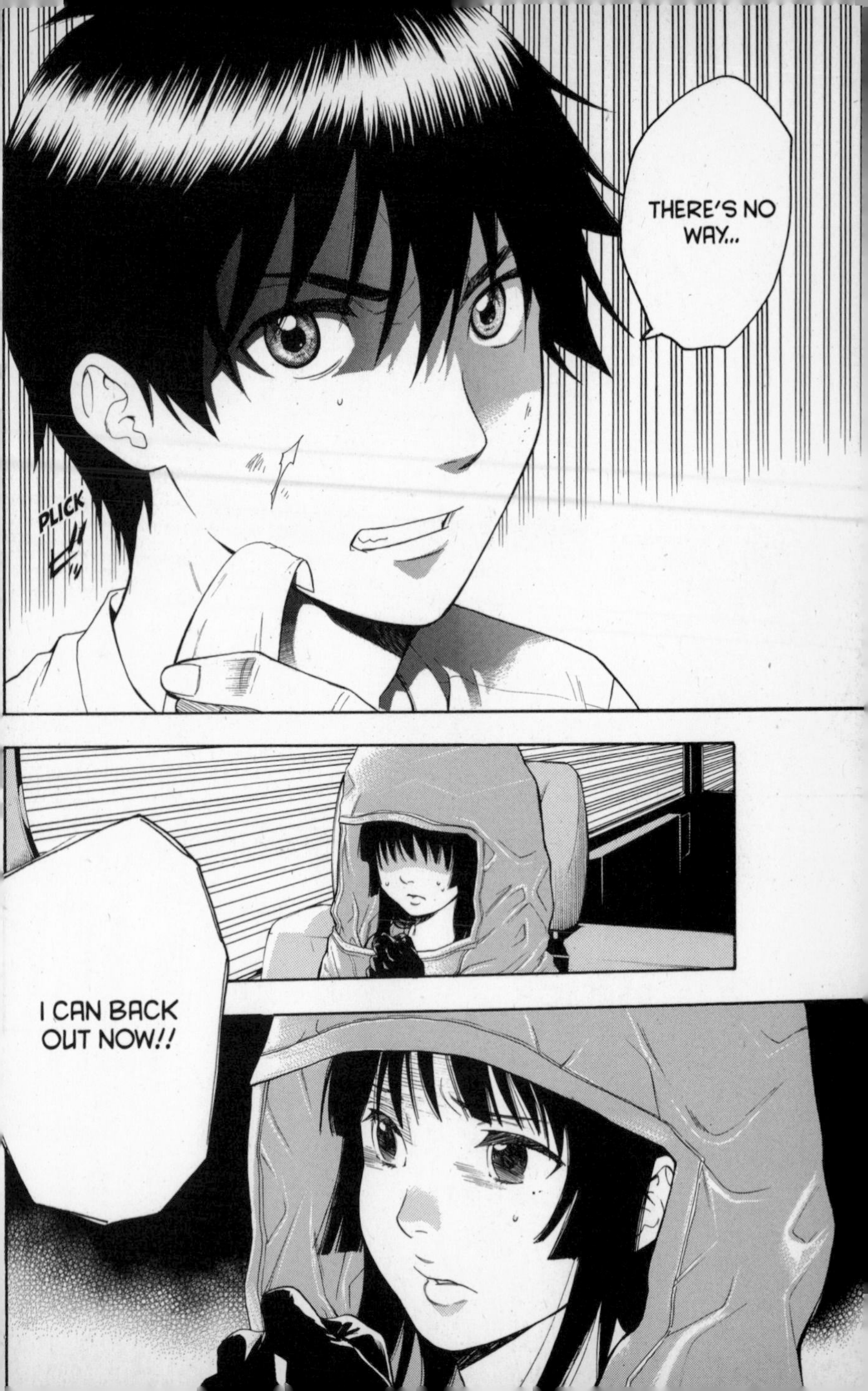
THERE'S NO WAY...
PLICK
I CAN BACK OUT NOW!!

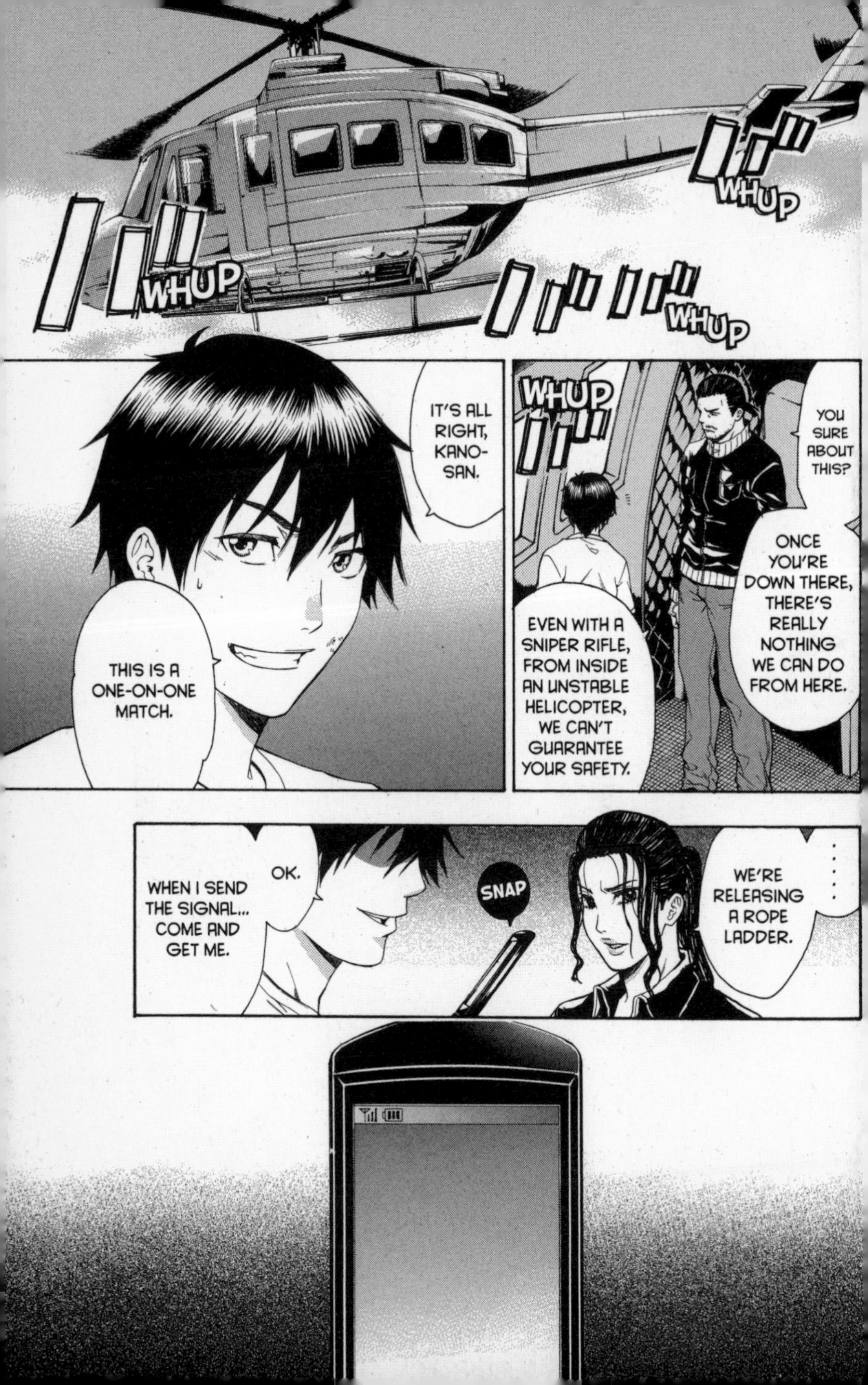
WHUP
WHUP
WHUP
WHUP
YOU SURE ABOUT THIS?
ONCE YOU'RE DOWN THERE, THERE'S REALLY NOTHING WE CAN DO FROM HERE.
EVEN WITH A SNIPER RIFLE, FROM INSIDE AN UNSTABLE HELICOPTER, WE CAN'T GUARANTEE YOUR SAFETY.
IT'S ALL RIGHT, KANO-SAN.
THIS IS A ONE-ON-ONE MATCH.
......
WE'RE RELEASING A ROPE LADDER.
SNAP
OK.
WHEN I SEND THE SIGNAL... COME AND GET ME.

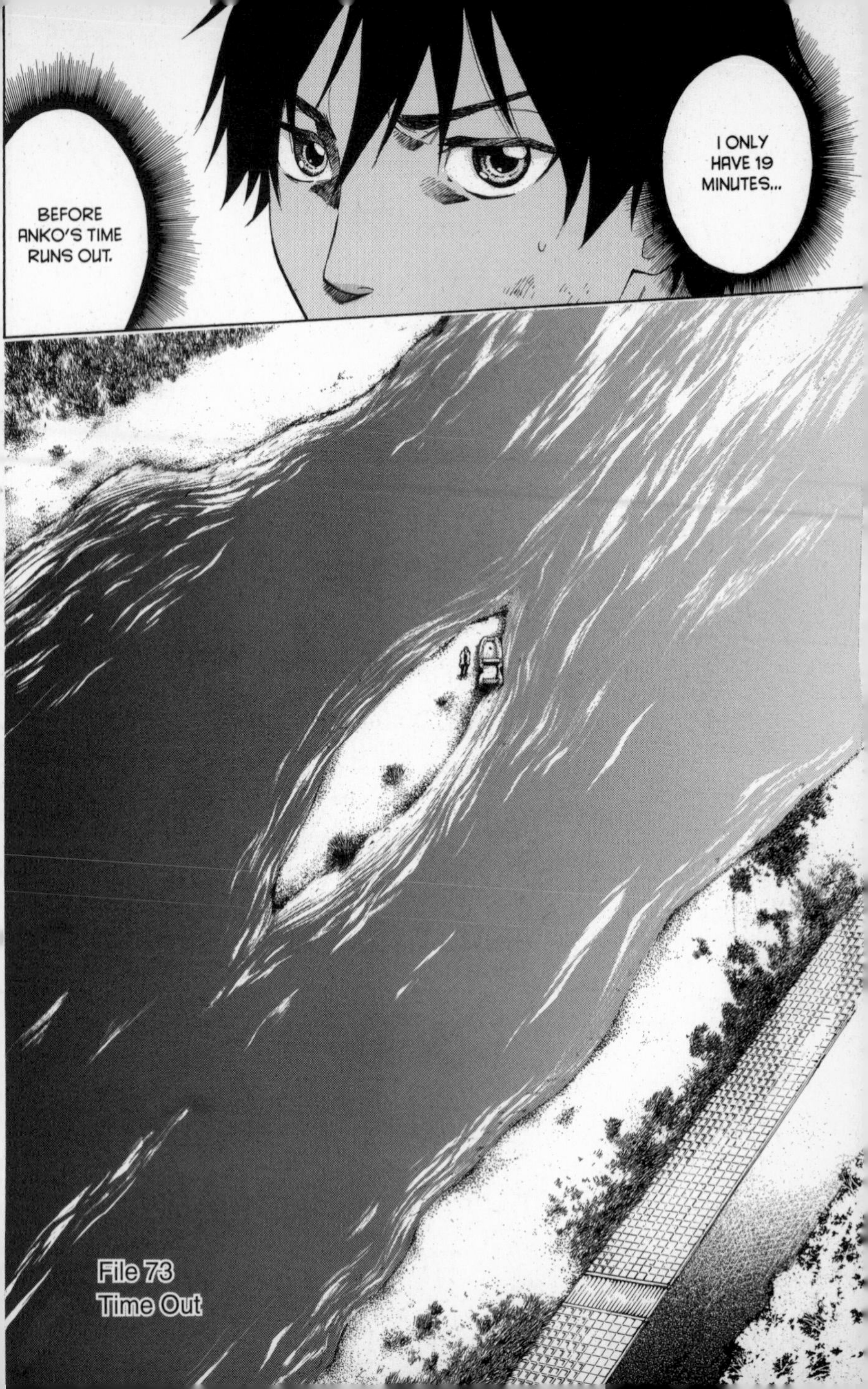
I ONLY HAVE 19 MINUTES...
BEFORE ANKO'S TIME RUNS OUT.
File 73
Time Out

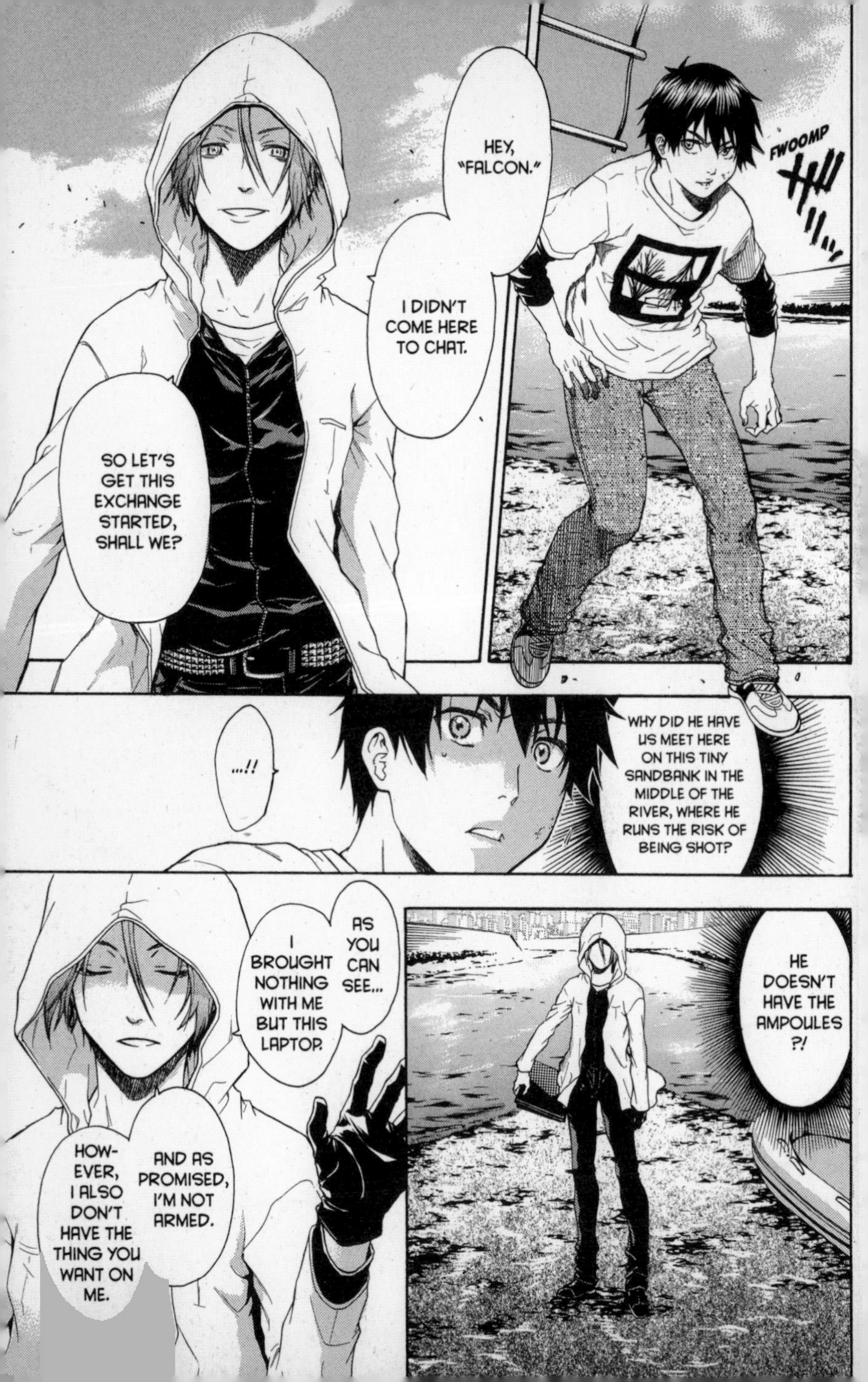
FWOOMP
HEY, "FALCON."
I DIDN'T COME HERE TO CHAT.
SO LET'S GET THIS EXCHANGE STARTED, SHALL WE?
WHY DID HE HAVE US MEET HERE ON THIS TINY SANDBANK IN THE MIDDLE OF THE RIVER, WHERE HE RUNS THE RISK OF BEING SHOT?
...!!
HE DOESN'T HAVE THE AMPOULES?!
AS YOU CAN SEE...
I BROUGHT NOTHING WITH ME BUT THIS LAPTOP.
AND AS PROMISED, I'M NOT ARMED.
HOW-EVER, I ALSO DON'T HAVE THE THING YOU WANT ON ME.

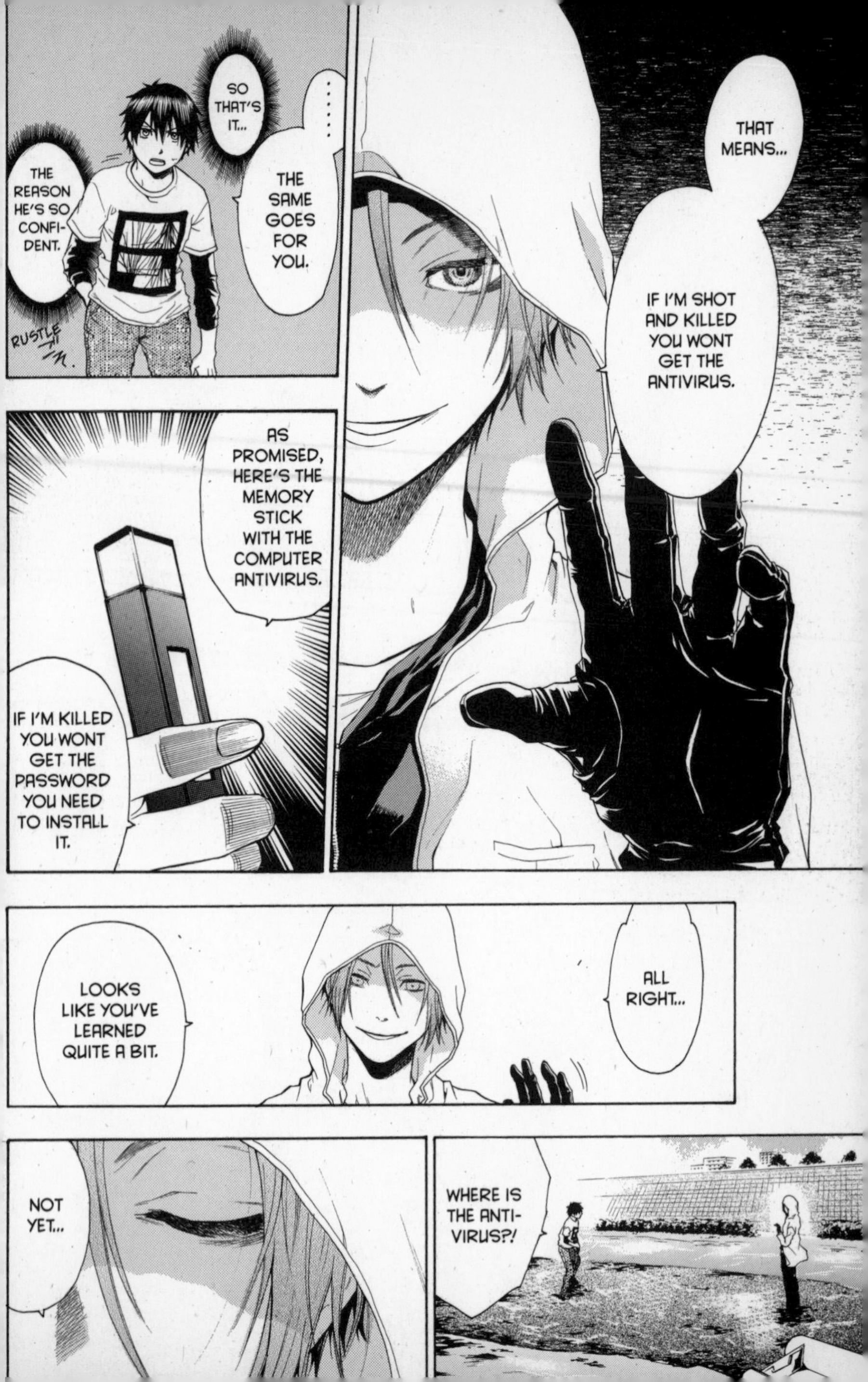
THAT MEANS...
IF I'M SHOT AND KILLED YOU WONT GET THE ANTIVIRUS.
......
THE SAME GOES FOR YOU.
SO THAT'S IT...
THE REASON HE'S SO CONFI-DENT.
RUSTLE
AS PROMISED, HERE'S THE MEMORY STICK WITH THE COMPUTER ANTIVIRUS.
IF I'M KILLED YOU WONT GET THE PASSWORD YOU NEED TO INSTALL IT.
ALL RIGHT...
LOOKS LIKE YOU'VE LEARNED QUITE A BIT.
WHERE IS THE ANTI-VIRUS?!
NOT YET...

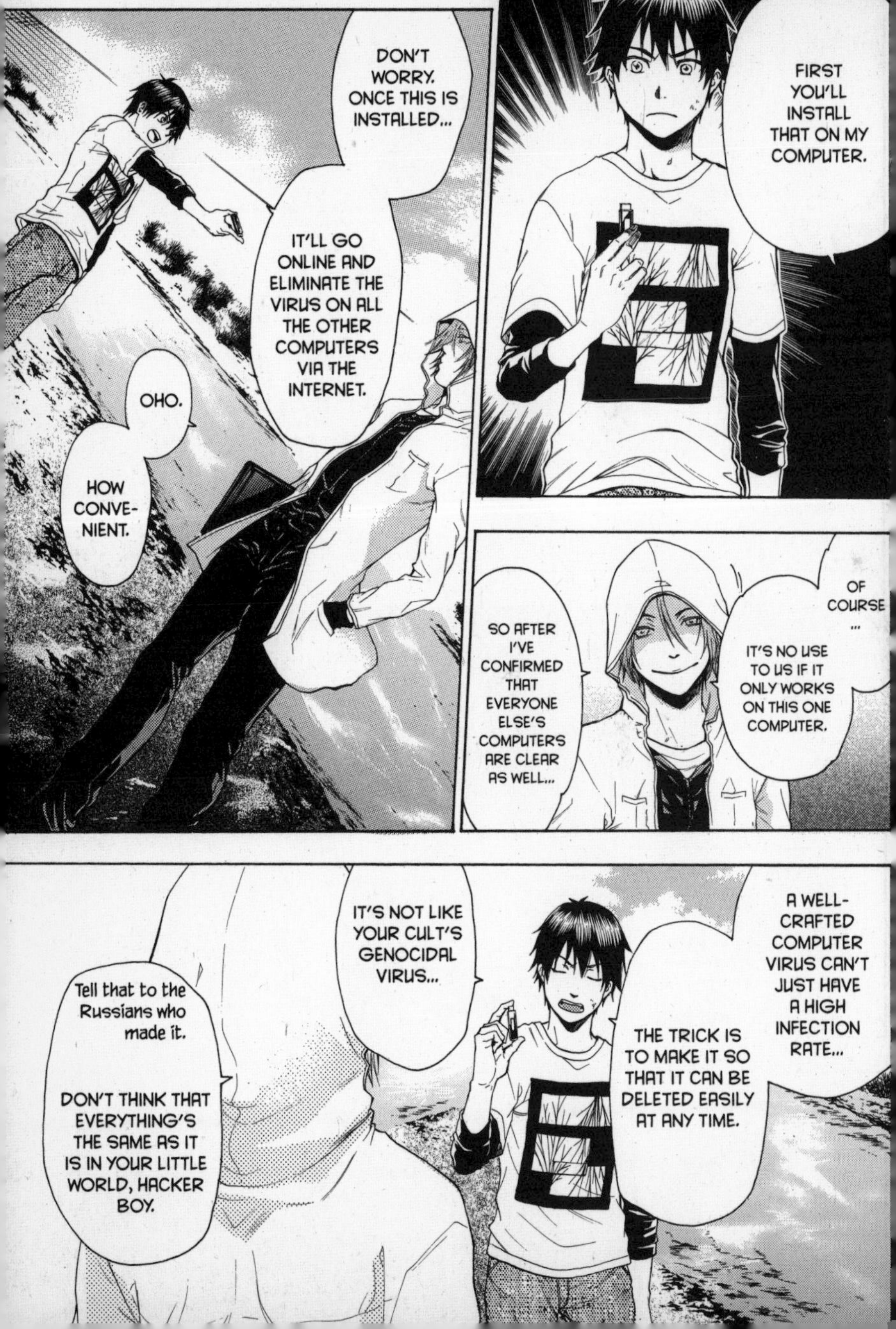
FIRST YOU'LL INSTALL THAT ON MY COMPUTER.
OF COURSE...
IT'S NO USE TO US IF IT ONLY WORKS ON THIS ONE COMPUTER.
SO AFTER I'VE CONFIRMED THAT EVERYONE ELSE'S COMPUTERS ARE CLEAR AS WELL...
DON'T WORRY. ONCE THIS IS INSTALLED...
IT'LL GO ONLINE AND ELIMINATE THE VIRUS ON ALL THE OTHER COMPUTERS VIA THE INTERNET.
OHO.
HOW CONVE-NIENT.
A WELL-CRAFTED COMPUTER VIRUS CAN'T JUST HAVE A HIGH INFECTION RATE...
THE TRICK IS TO MAKE IT SO THAT IT CAN BE DELETED EASILY AT ANY TIME.
IT'S NOT LIKE YOUR CULT'S GENOCIDAL VIRUS...
Tell that to the Russians who made it.
DON'T THINK THAT EVERYTHING'S THE SAME AS IT IS IN YOUR LITTLE WORLD, HACKER BOY.

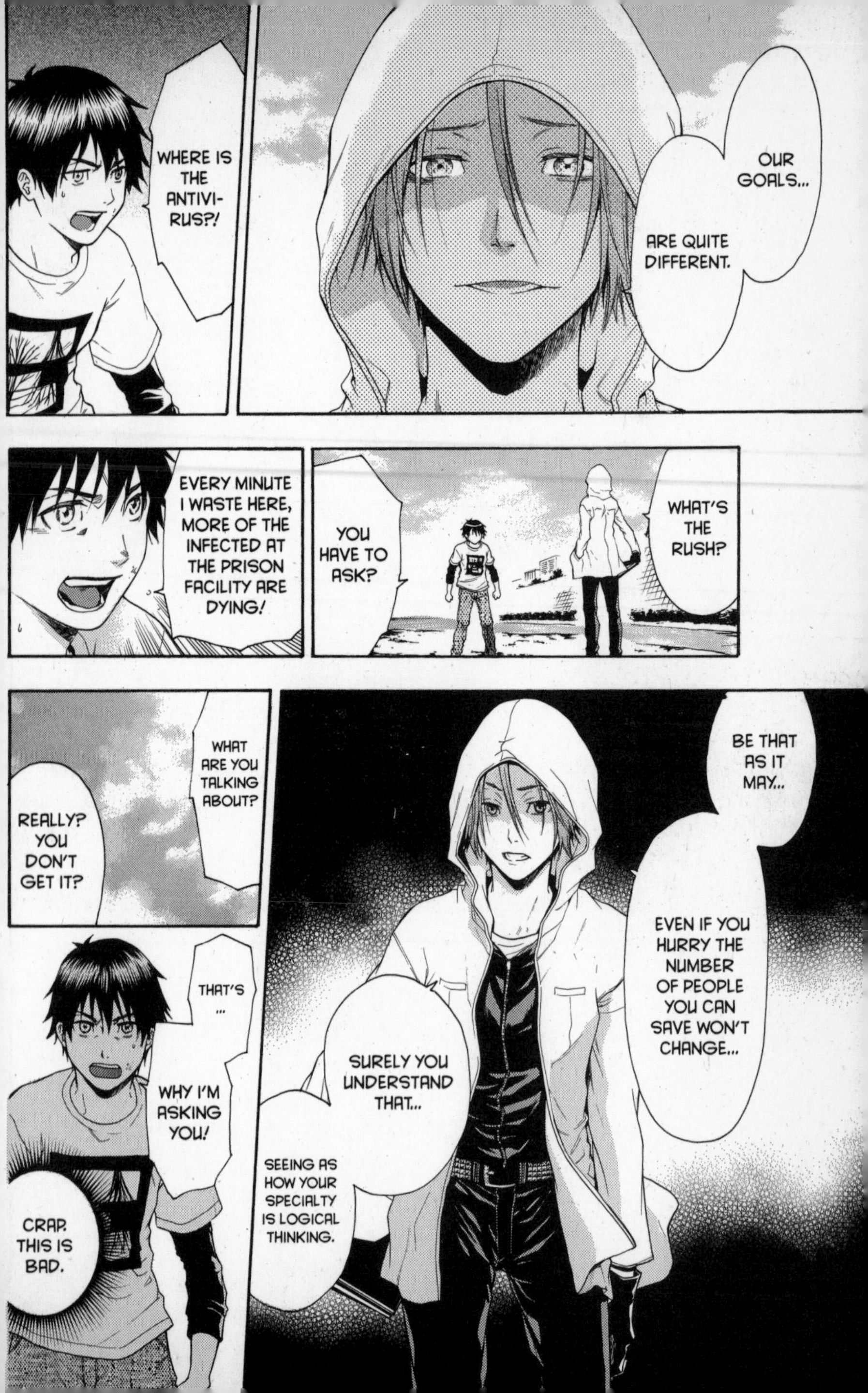
OUR GOALS...
ARE QUITE DIFFERENT.
WHERE IS THE ANTIVI-RUS?!
WHAT'S THE RUSH?
YOU HAVE TO ASK?
EVERY MINUTE I WASTE HERE, MORE OF THE INFECTED AT THE PRISON FACILITY ARE DYING!
BE THAT AS IT MAY...
EVEN IF YOU HURRY THE NUMBER OF PEOPLE YOU CAN SAVE WON'T CHANGE...
SURELY YOU UNDERSTAND THAT...
SEEING AS HOW YOUR SPECIALTY IS LOGICAL THINKING.
WHAT ARE YOU TALKING ABOUT?
REALLY? YOU DON'T GET IT?
THAT'S ...
WHY I'M ASKING YOU!
CRAP. THIS IS BAD.

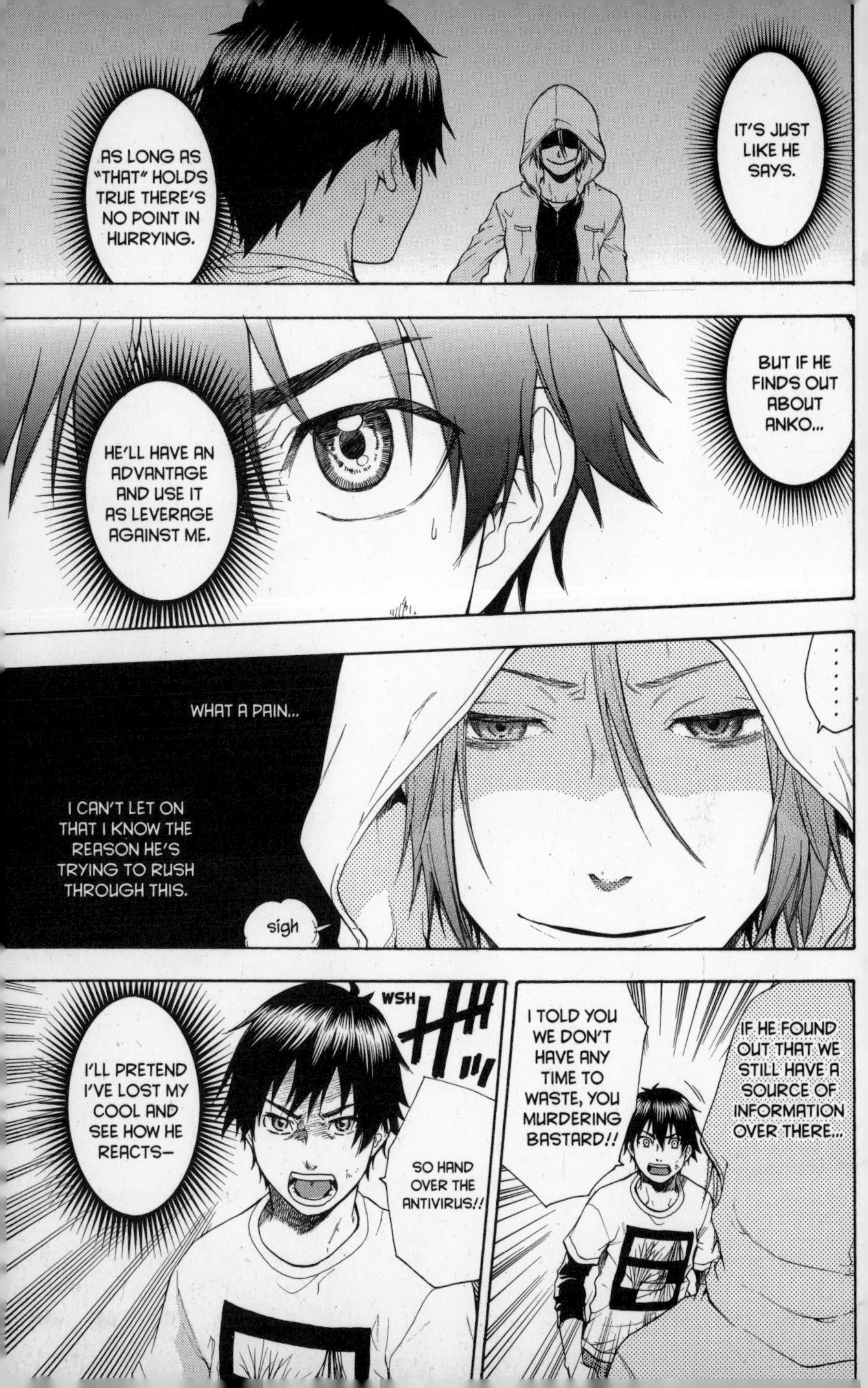
IT'S JUST LIKE HE SAYS.
AS LONG AS "THAT" HOLDS TRUE THERE'S NO POINT IN HURRYING.
BUT IF HE FINDS OUT ABOUT ANKO...
HE'LL HAVE AN ADVANTAGE AND USE IT AS LEVERAGE AGAINST ME.
......
WHAT A PAIN...
I CAN'T LET ON THAT I KNOW THE REASON HE'S TRYING TO RUSH THROUGH THIS.
sigh
IF HE FOUND OUT THAT WE STILL HAVE A SOURCE OF INFORMATION OVER THERE...
I TOLD YOU WE DON'T HAVE ANY TIME TO WASTE, YOU MURDERING BASTARD!!
WSH
SO HAND OVER THE ANTIVIRUS!!
I'LL PRETEND I'VE LOST MY COOL AND SEE HOW HE REACTS—

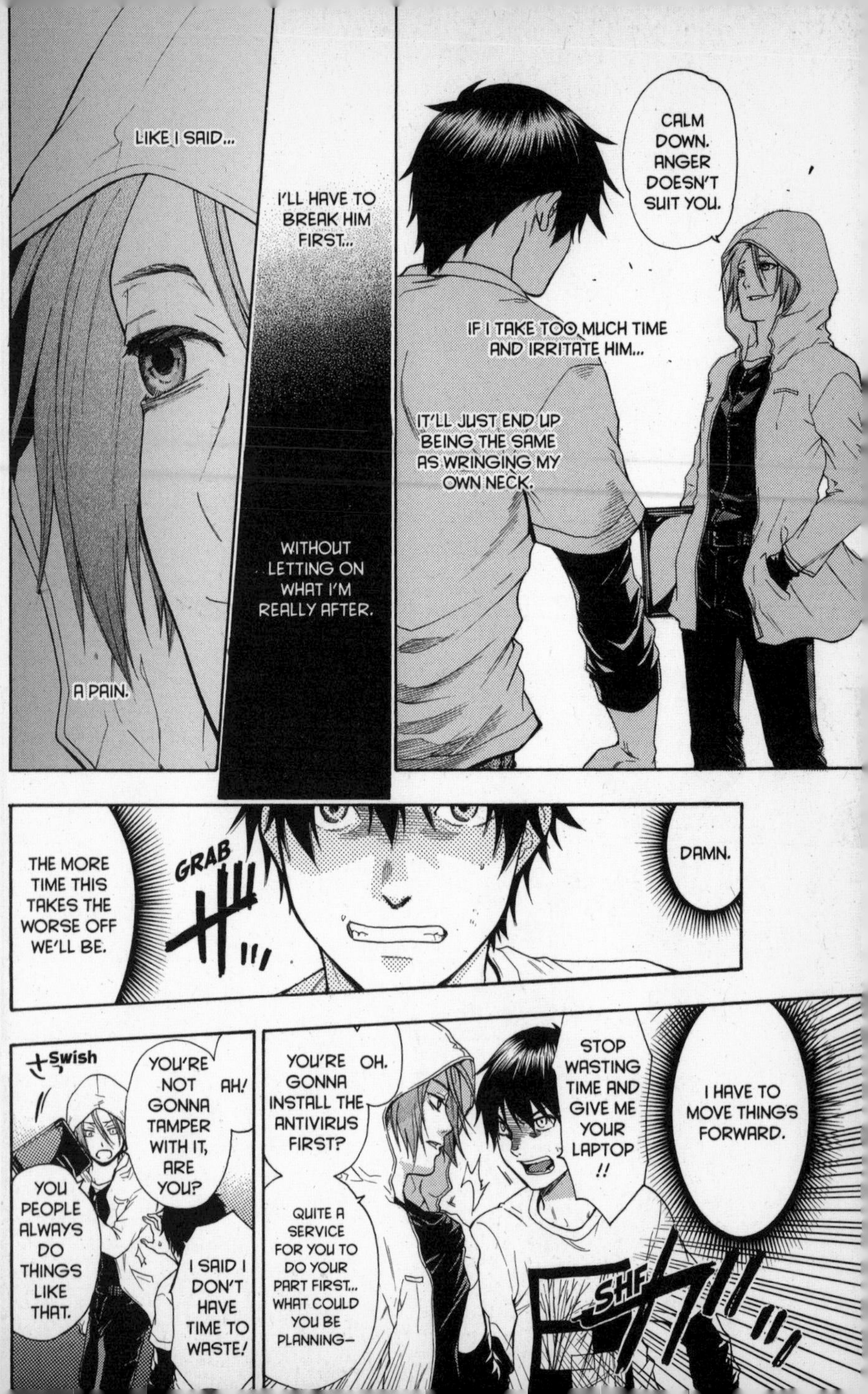
CALM DOWN. ANGER DOESN'T SUIT YOU.
IF I TAKE TOO MUCH TIME AND IRRITATE HIM...
IT'LL JUST END UP BEING THE SAME AS WRINGING MY OWN NECK.
I'LL HAVE TO BREAK HIM FIRST...
WITHOUT LETTING ON WHAT I'M REALLY AFTER.
LIKE I SAID...
A PAIN.
DAMN.
GRAB
THE MORE TIME THIS TAKES THE WORSE OFF WE'LL BE.
I HAVE TO MOVE THINGS FORWARD.
STOP WASTING TIME AND GIVE ME YOUR LAPTOP!!
SHF
OH.
YOU'RE GONNA INSTALL THE ANTIVIRUS FIRST?
QUITE A SERVICE FOR YOU TO DO YOUR PART FIRST... WHAT COULD YOU BE PLANNING—
AH!
YOU'RE NOT GONNA TAMPER WITH IT, ARE YOU?
Swish
YOU PEOPLE ALWAYS DO THINGS LIKE THAT.
I SAID I DON'T HAVE TIME TO WASTE!

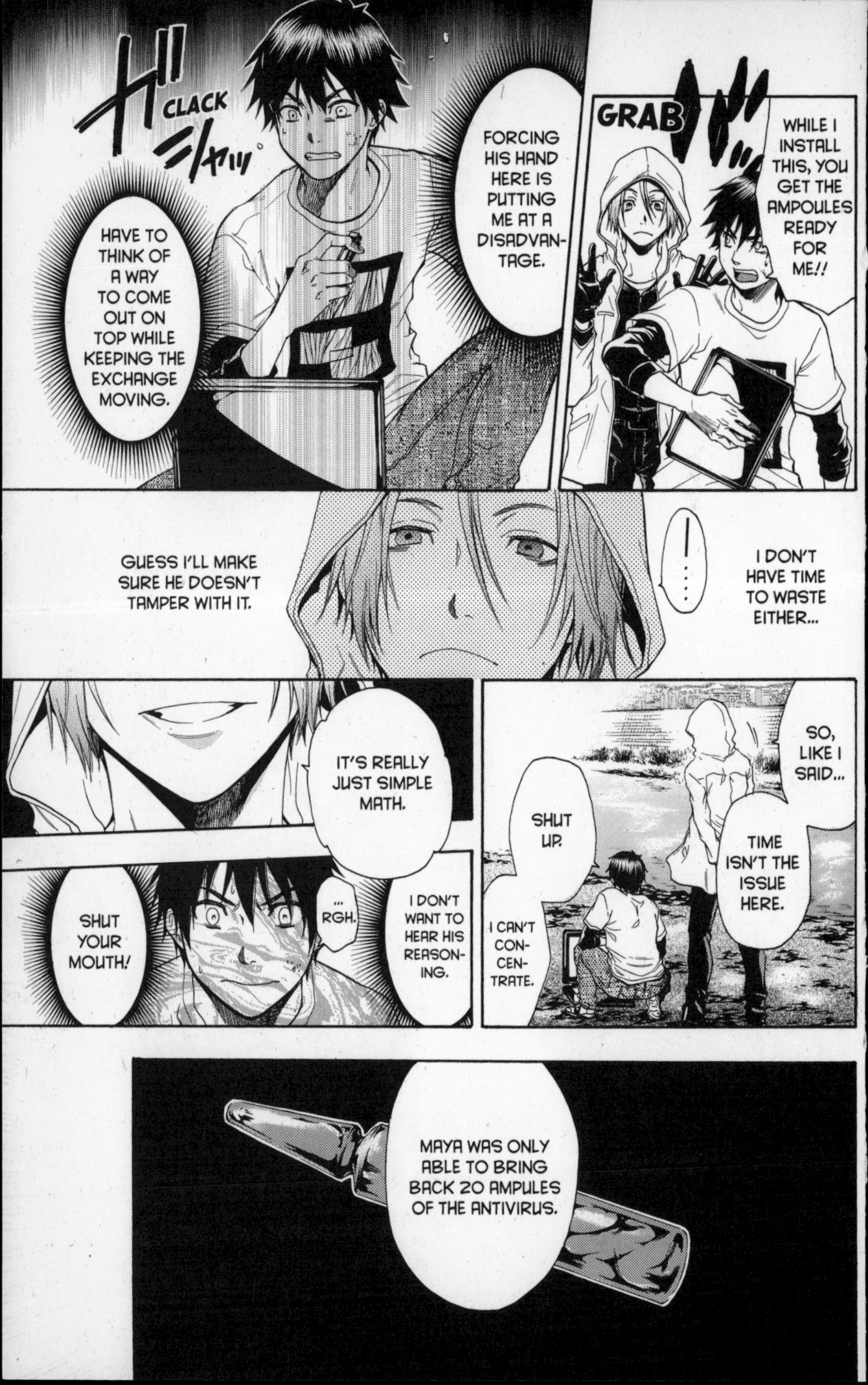
GRAB
WHILE I INSTALL THIS, YOU GET THE AMPOULES READY FOR ME!!
FORCING HIS HAND HERE IS PUTTING ME AT A DISADVANTAGE.
ガシャッ
CLACK
HAVE TO THINK OF A WAY TO COME OUT ON TOP WHILE KEEPING THE EXCHANGE MOVING.
I DON'T HAVE TIME TO WASTE EITHER...
!....
GUESS I'LL MAKE SURE HE DOESN'T TAMPER WITH IT.
SO, LIKE I SAID...
TIME ISN'T THE ISSUE HERE.
SHUT UP.
I CAN'T CONCENTRATE.
IT'S REALLY JUST SIMPLE MATH.
I DON'T WANT TO HEAR HIS REASONING.
...RGH.
SHUT YOUR MOUTH!
MAYA WAS ONLY ABLE TO BRING BACK 20 AMPULES OF THE ANTIVIRUS.

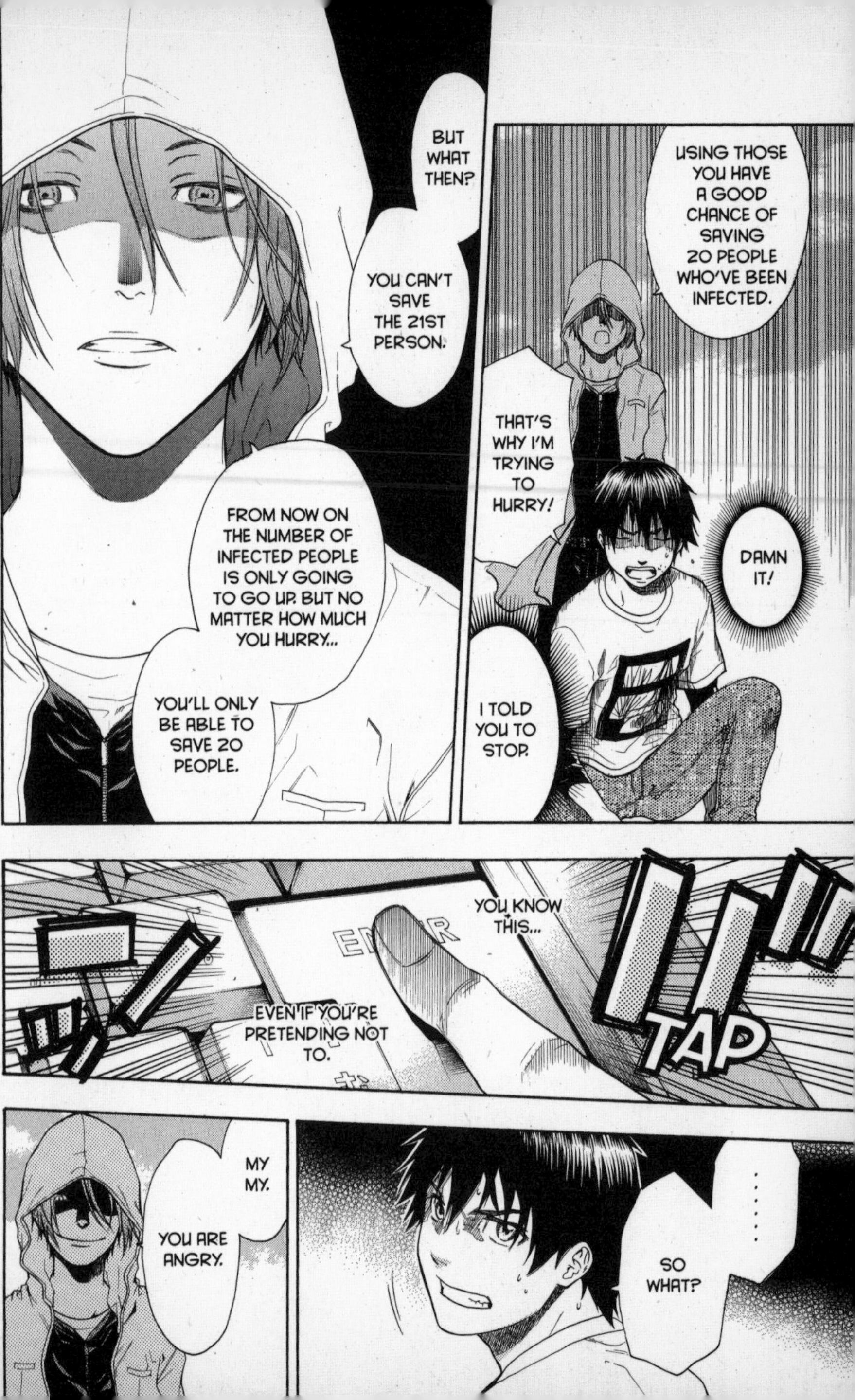
USING THOSE YOU HAVE A GOOD CHANCE OF SAVING 20 PEOPLE WHO'VE BEEN INFECTED.
THAT'S WHY I'M TRYING TO HURRY!
DAMN IT!
I TOLD YOU TO STOP.
BUT WHAT THEN?
YOU CAN'T SAVE THE 21ST PERSON.
FROM NOW ON THE NUMBER OF INFECTED PEOPLE IS ONLY GOING TO GO UP. BUT NO MATTER HOW MUCH YOU HURRY...
YOU'LL ONLY BE ABLE TO SAVE 20 PEOPLE.
TAP
YOU KNOW THIS...
EVEN IF YOU'RE PRETENDING NOT TO.
......
SO WHAT?
MY MY.
YOU ARE ANGRY.

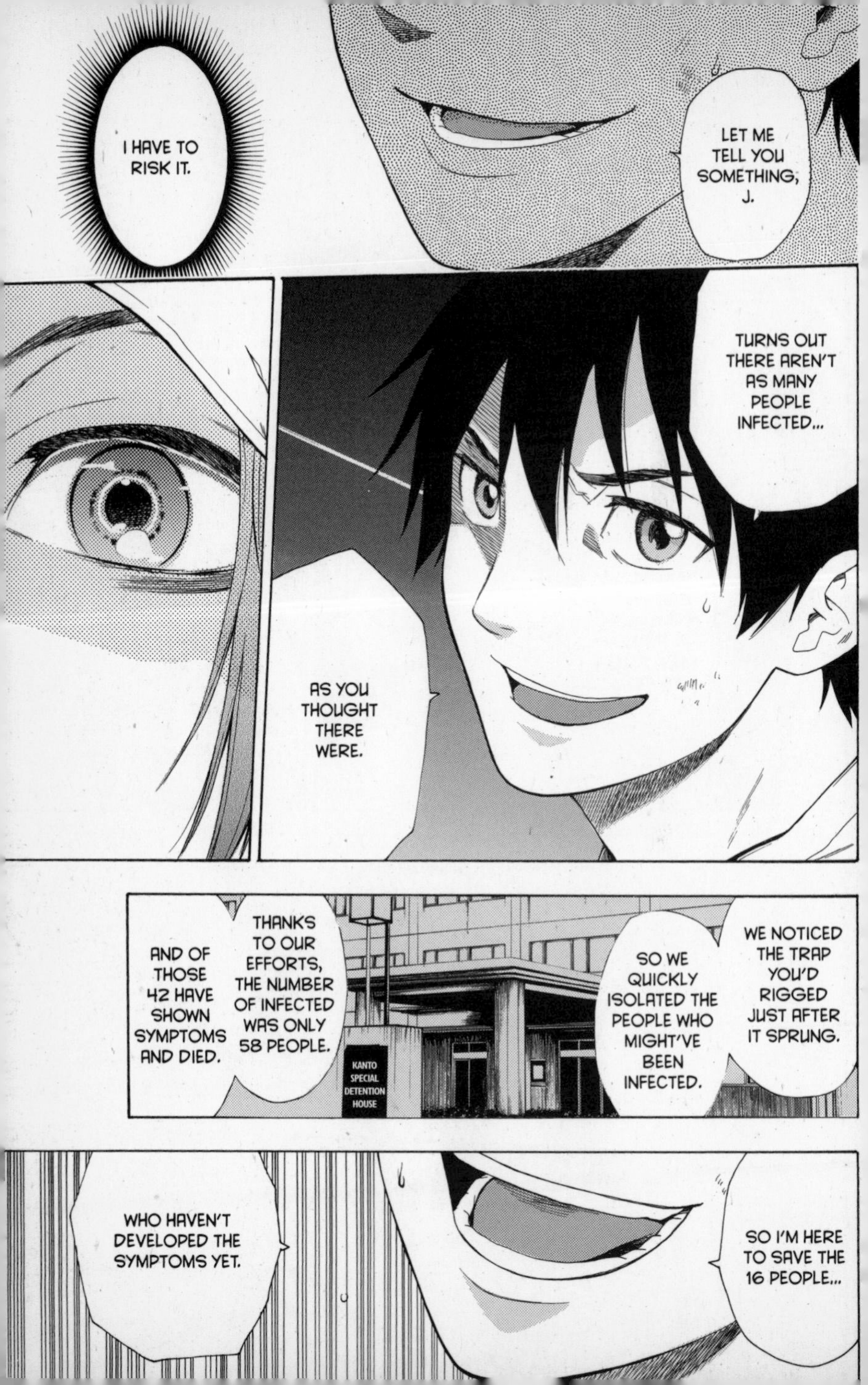
LET ME TELL YOU SOMETHING, J.
I HAVE TO RISK IT.
TURNS OUT THERE AREN'T AS MANY PEOPLE INFECTED...
AS YOU THOUGHT THERE WERE.
WE NOTICED THE TRAP YOU'D RIGGED JUST AFTER IT SPRUNG.
SO WE QUICKLY ISOLATED THE PEOPLE WHO MIGHT'VE BEEN INFECTED.
KANTO SPECIAL DETENTION HOUSE
THANKS TO OUR EFFORTS, THE NUMBER OF INFECTED WAS ONLY 58 PEOPLE.
AND OF THOSE 42 HAVE SHOWN SYMPTOMS AND DIED.
SO I'M HERE TO SAVE THE 16 PEOPLE...
WHO HAVEN'T DEVELOPED THE SYMPTOMS YET.

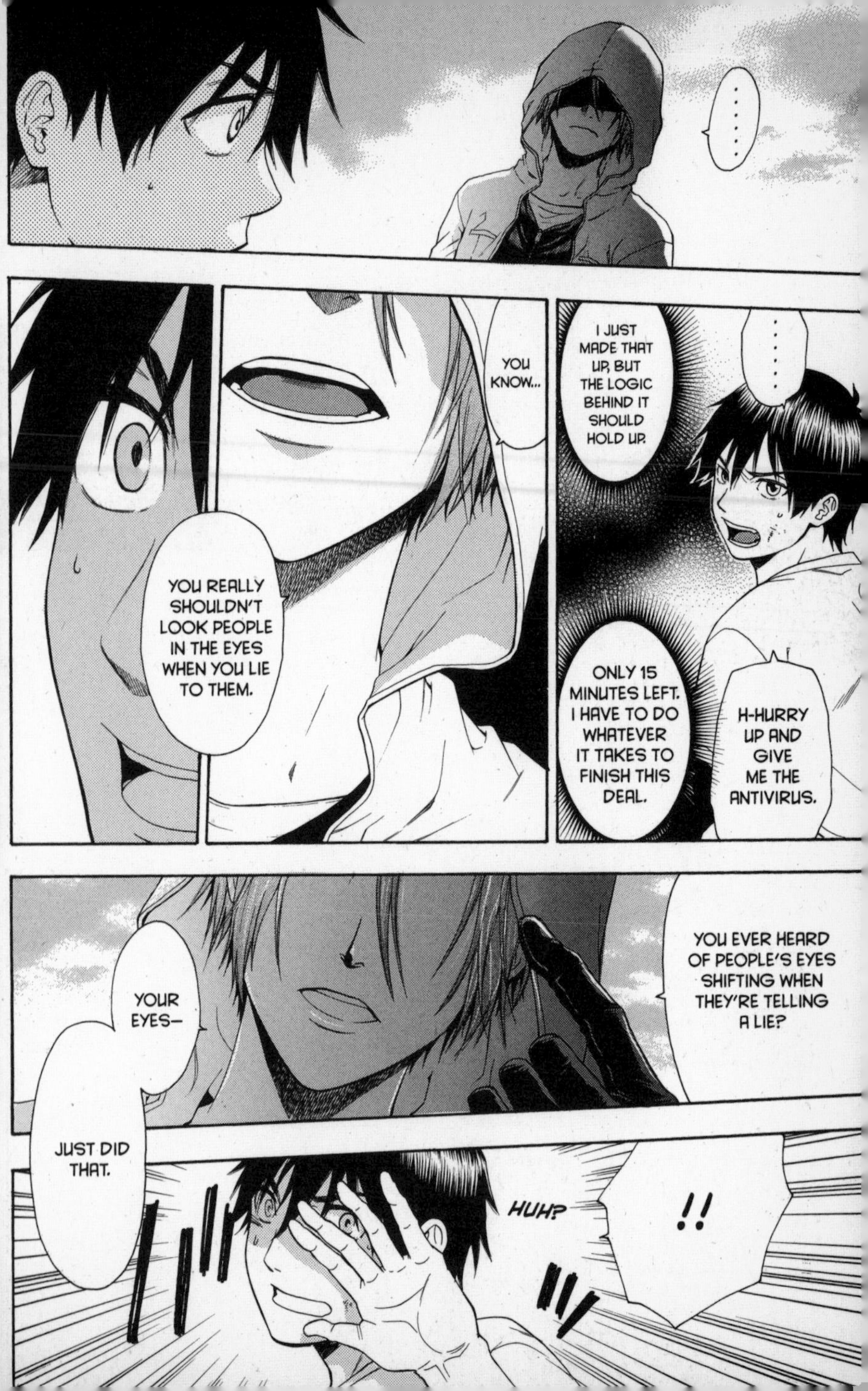
......
......
I JUST MADE THAT UP, BUT THE LOGIC BEHIND IT SHOULD HOLD UP.
H-HURRY UP AND GIVE ME THE ANTIVIRUS.
ONLY 15 MINUTES LEFT. I HAVE TO DO WHATEVER IT TAKES TO FINISH THIS DEAL.
YOU KNOW...
YOU REALLY SHOULDN'T LOOK PEOPLE IN THE EYES WHEN YOU LIE TO THEM.
YOU EVER HEARD OF PEOPLE'S EYES SHIFTING WHEN THEY'RE TELLING A LIE?
YOUR EYES—
JUST DID THAT.
!!
HUH?

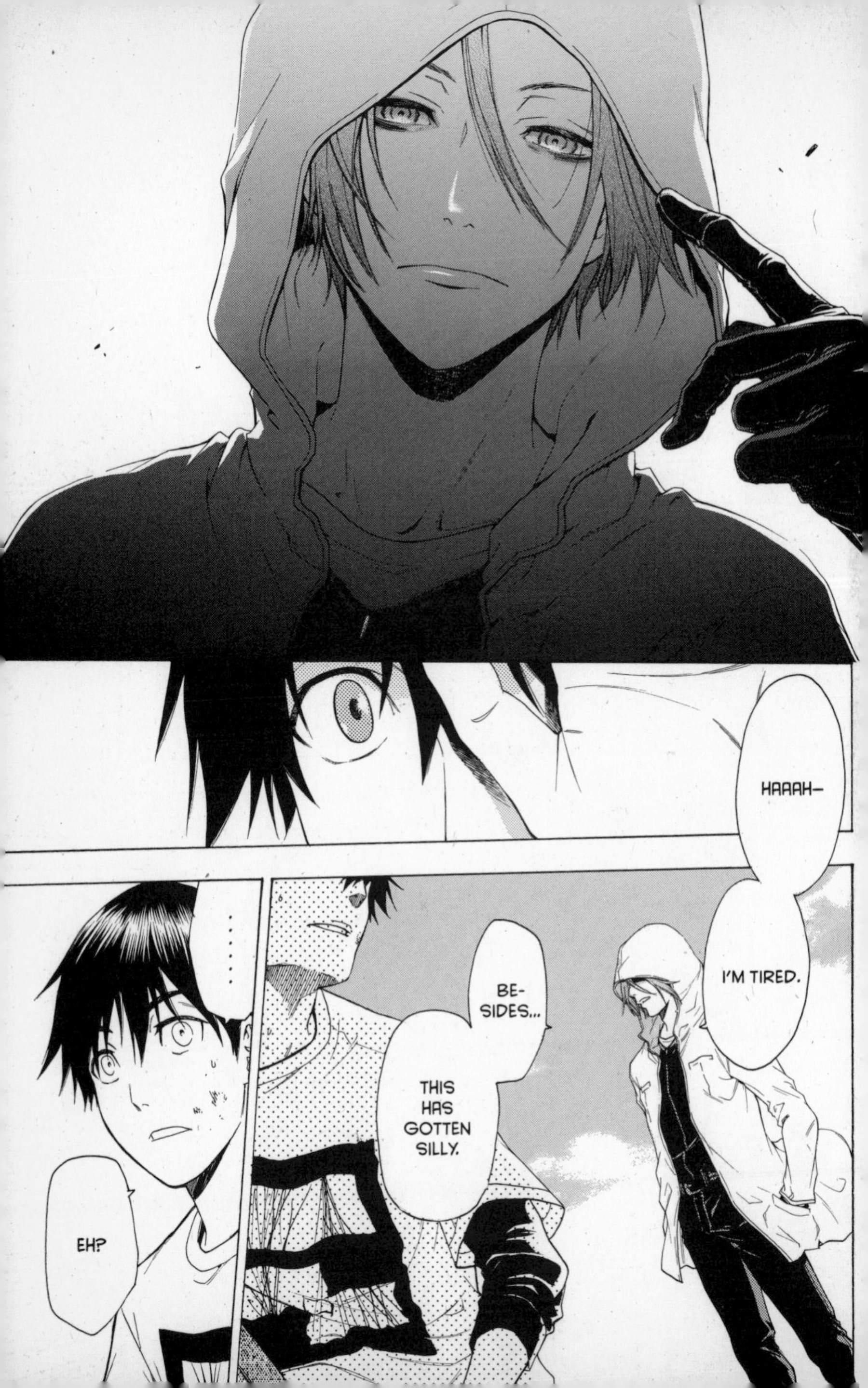
HAAAH—
I'M TIRED.
BE-SIDES...
THIS HAS GOTTEN SILLY.
......
EH?

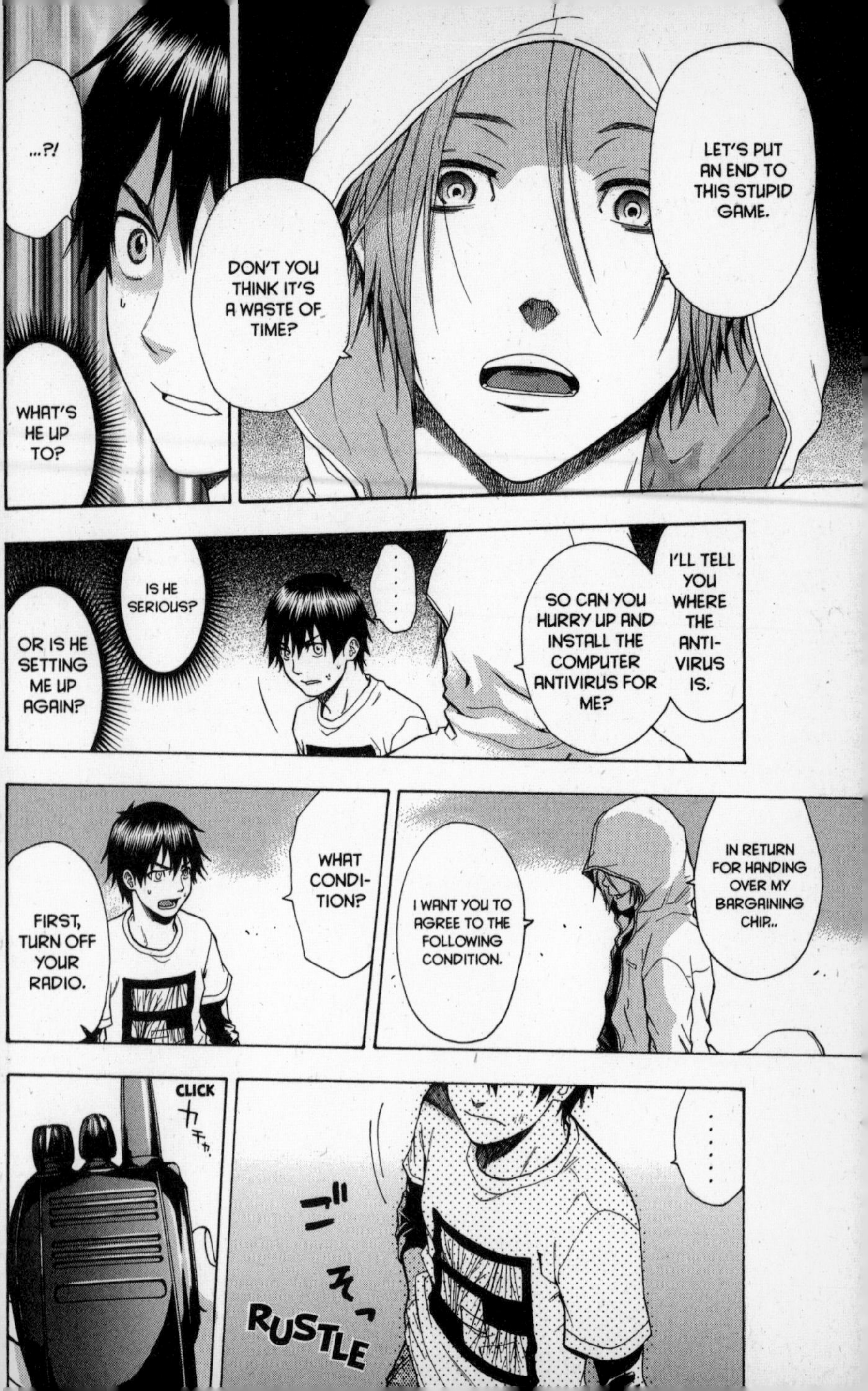
LET'S PUT AN END TO THIS STUPID GAME.
DON'T YOU THINK IT'S A WASTE OF TIME?
...?!
WHAT'S HE UP TO?
I'LL TELL YOU WHERE THE ANTI-VIRUS IS.
SO CAN YOU HURRY UP AND INSTALL THE COMPUTER ANTIVIRUS FOR ME?
......
IS HE SERIOUS?
OR IS HE SETTING ME UP AGAIN?
IN RETURN FOR HANDING OVER MY BARGAINING CHIP...
I WANT YOU TO AGREE TO THE FOLLOWING CONDITION.
WHAT CONDI-TION?
FIRST, TURN OFF YOUR RADIO.
......
RUSTLE
CLICK

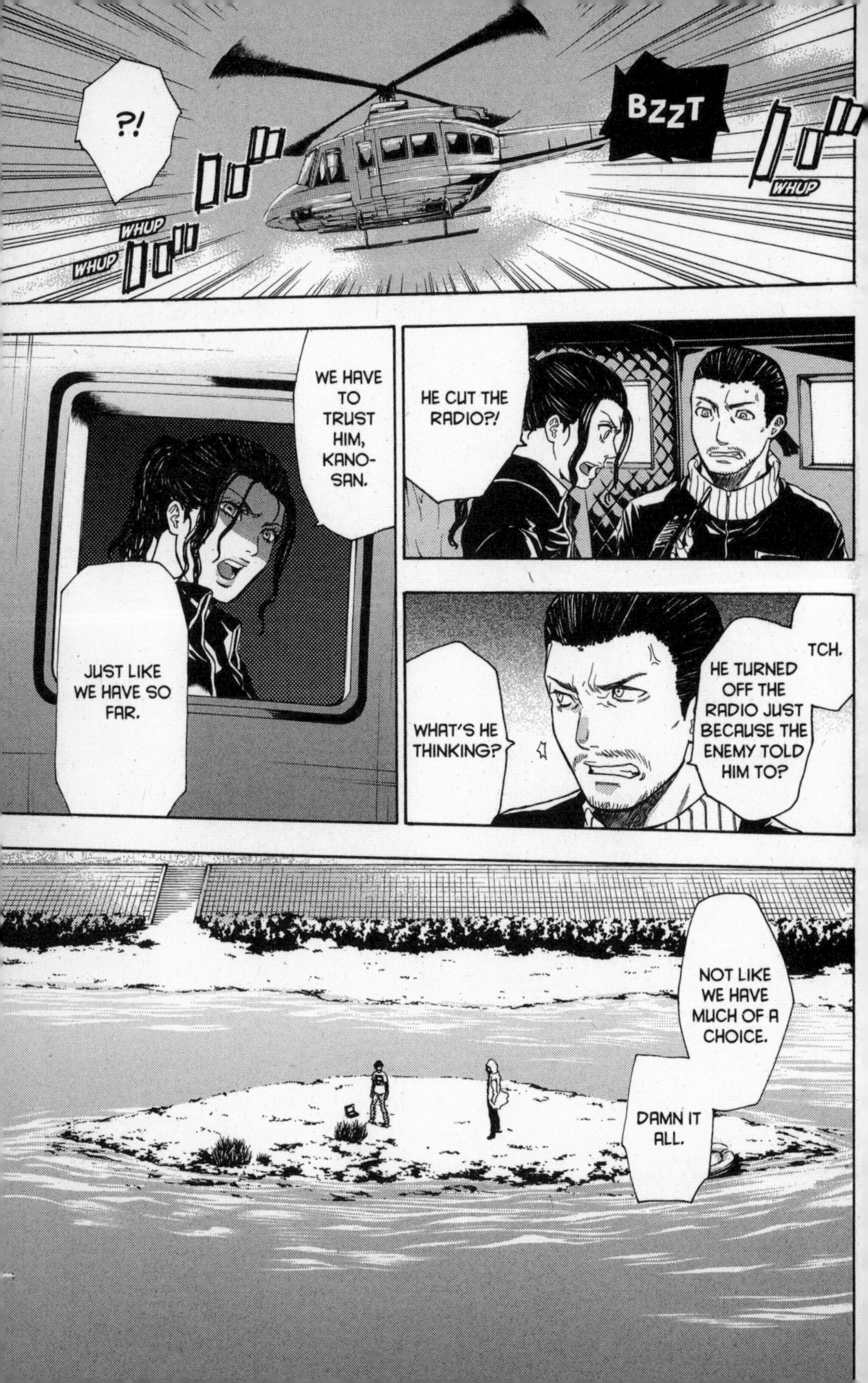
BZZT
WHUP
?!
WHUP
WHUP
HE CUT THE RADIO?!
TCH.
HE TURNED OFF THE RADIO JUST BECAUSE THE ENEMY TOLD HIM TO?
WHAT'S HE THINKING?
WE HAVE TO TRUST HIM, KANO-SAN.
JUST LIKE WE HAVE SO FAR.
NOT LIKE WE HAVE MUCH OF A CHOICE.
DAMN IT ALL.

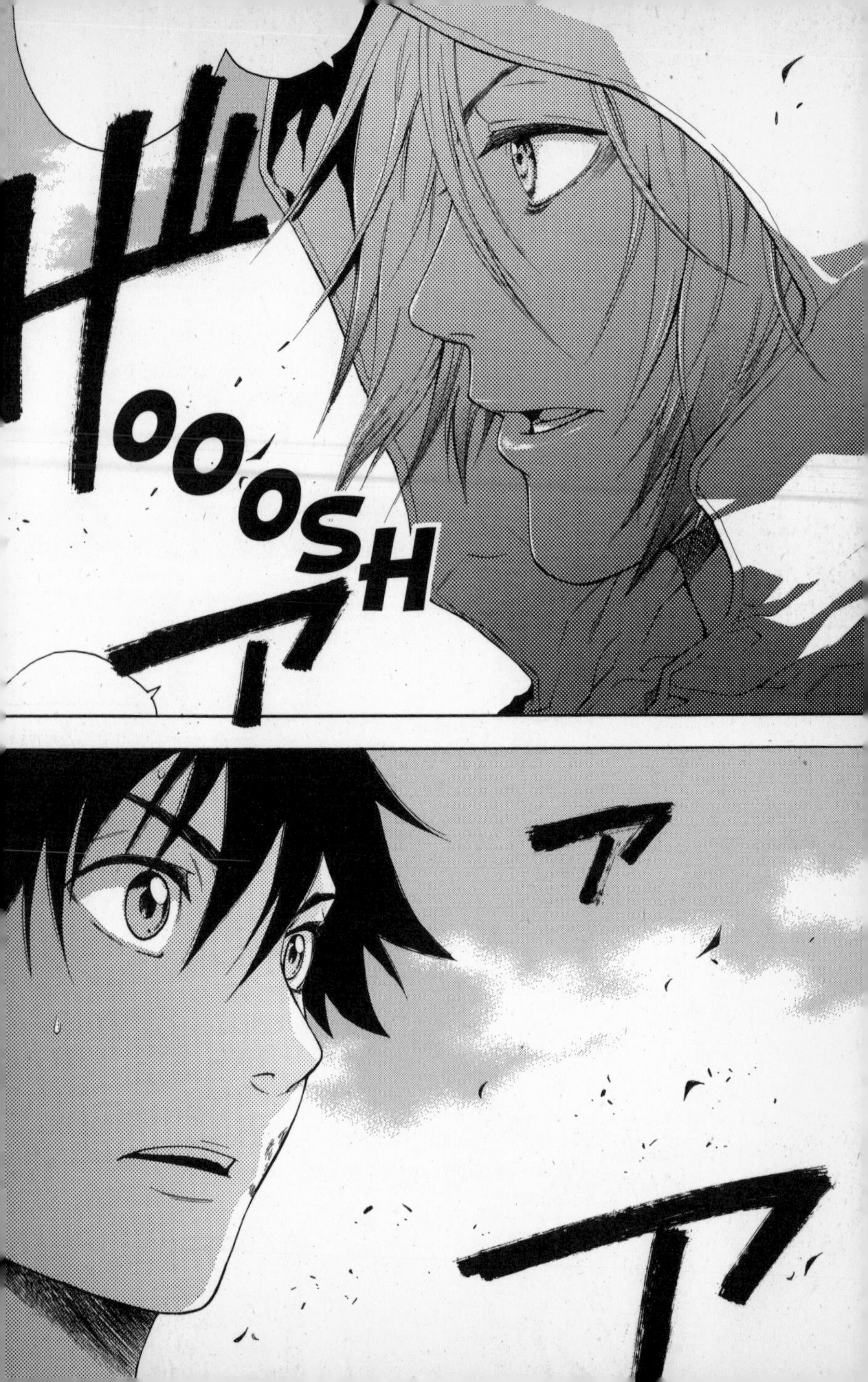
WHOOOSH

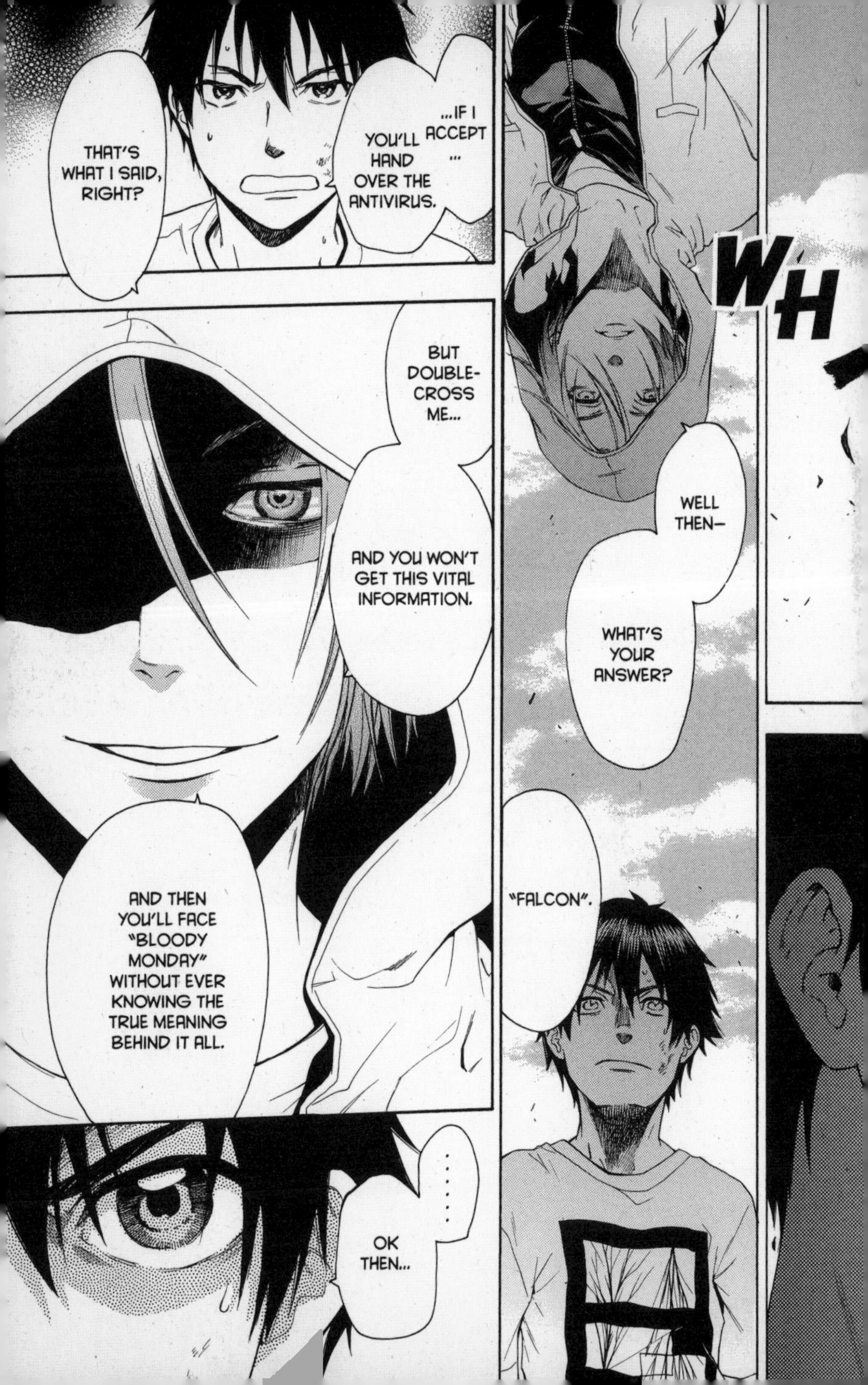
WH
WELL THEN—
WHAT'S YOUR ANSWER?
"FALCON".
...IF I ACCEPT ...
YOU'LL HAND OVER THE ANTIVIRUS.
THAT'S WHAT I SAID, RIGHT?
BUT DOUBLE-CROSS ME...
AND YOU WON'T GET THIS VITAL INFORMATION.
AND THEN YOU'LL FACE "BLOODY MONDAY" WITHOUT EVER KNOWING THE TRUE MEANING BEHIND IT ALL.
......
OK THEN...

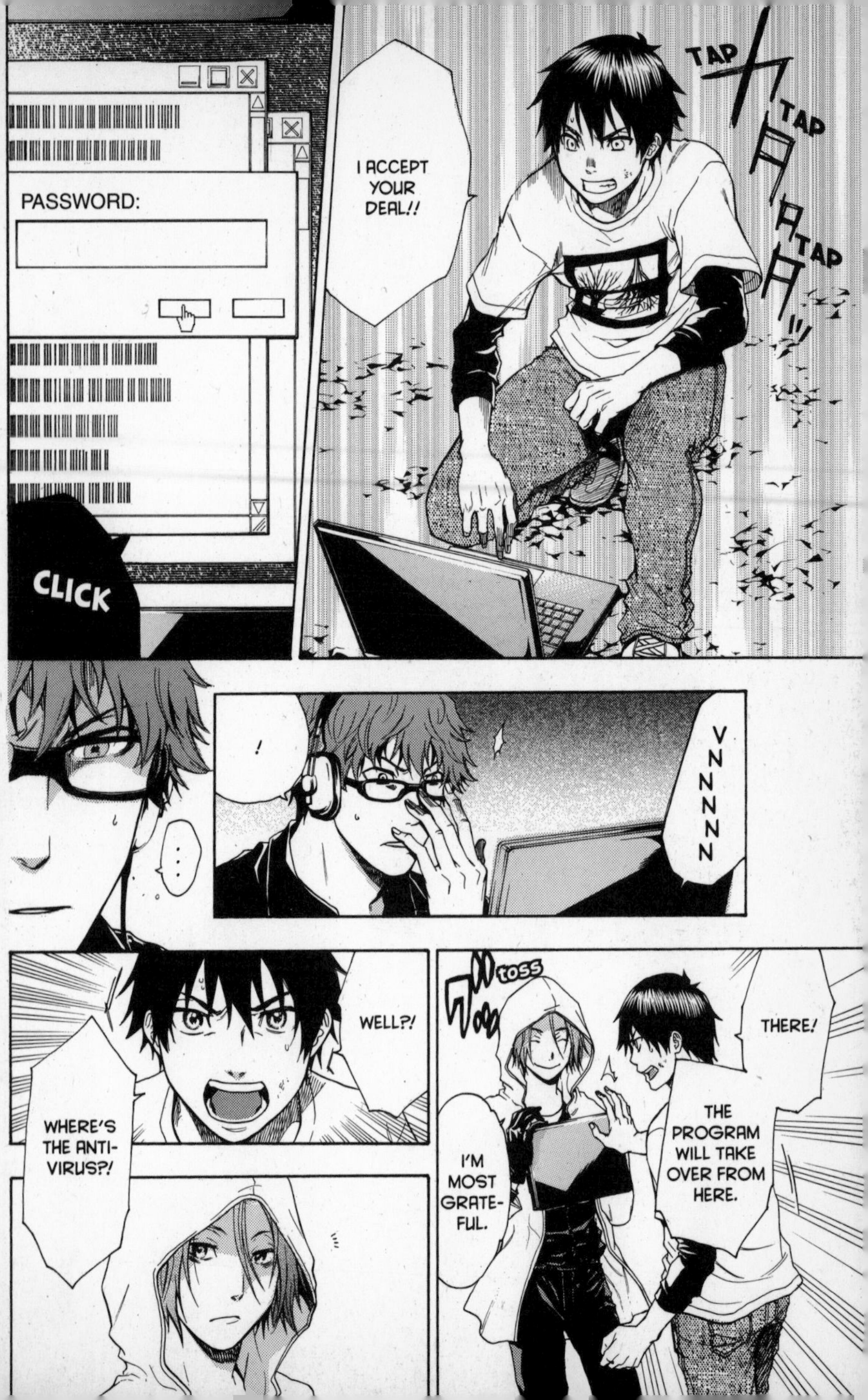
TAP TAP TAP TAP
I ACCEPT YOUR DEAL!!
PASSWORD:
CLICK
VNNNNN
!
...
toss
THERE!
THE PROGRAM WILL TAKE OVER FROM HERE.
I'M MOST GRATEFUL.
WELL?!
WHERE'S THE ANTI-VIRUS?!

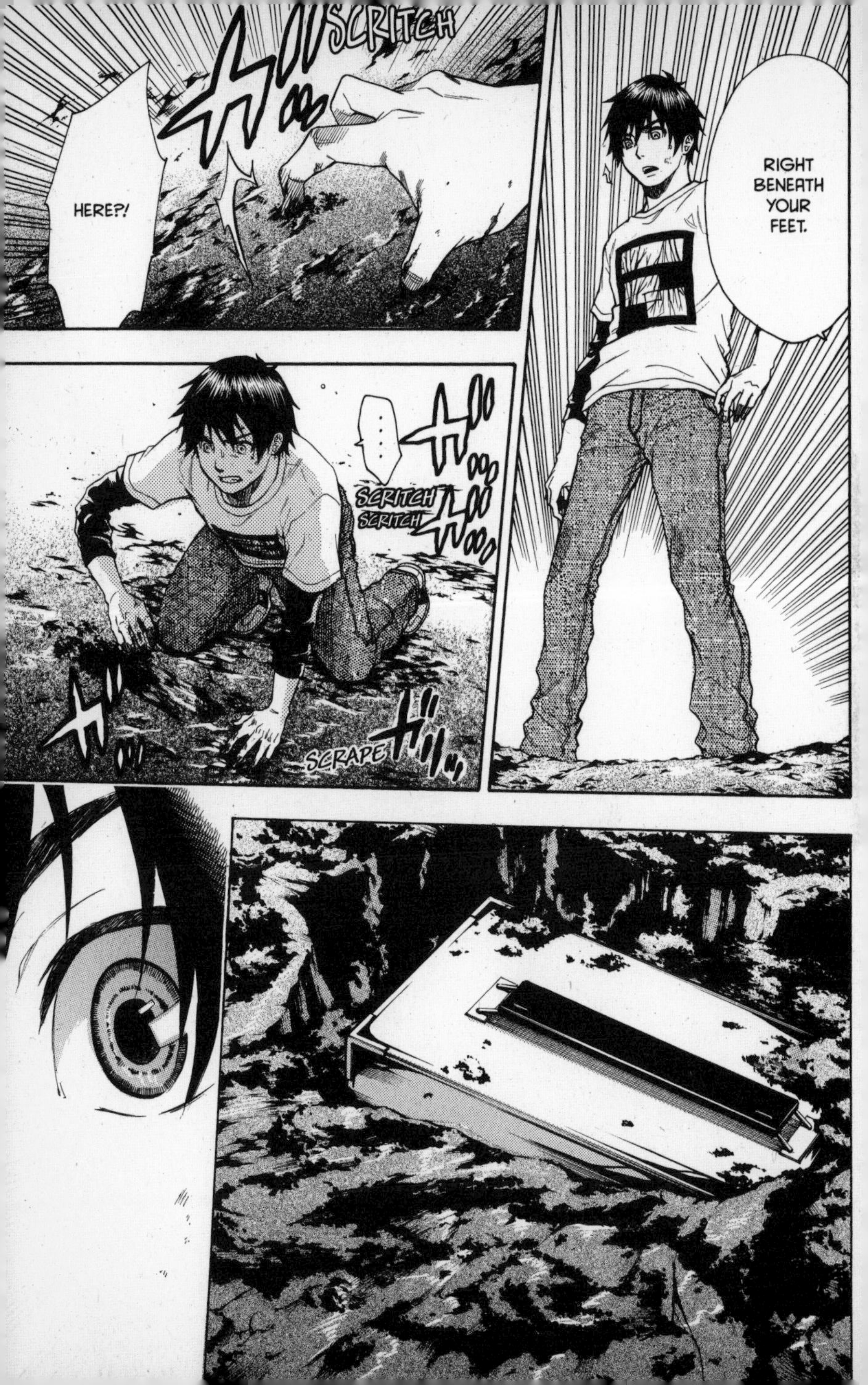
RIGHT BENEATH YOUR FEET.
SCRITCH
HERE?!
......
SCRITCH SCRITCH
SCRAPE

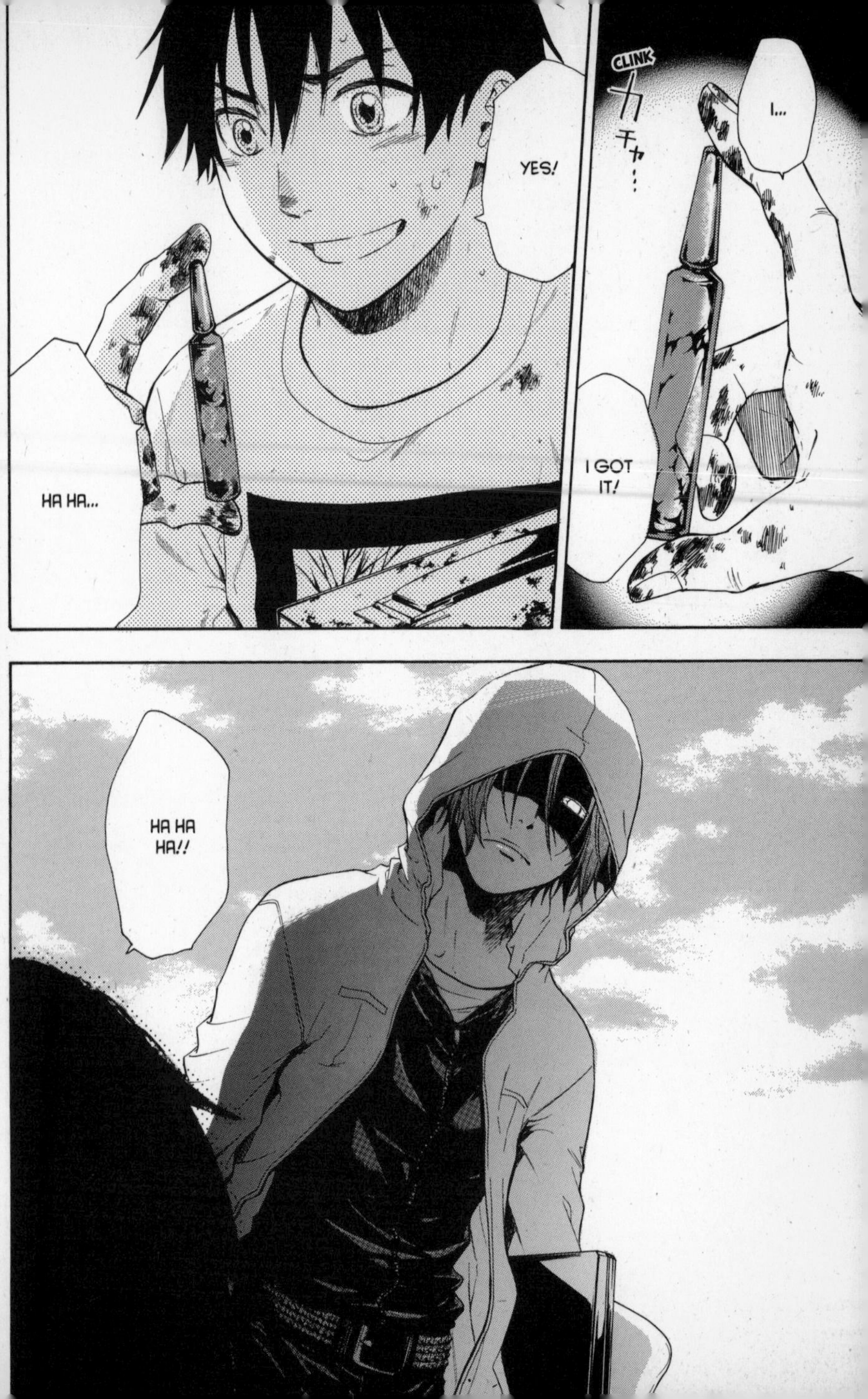
I...
CLINK
カチャ…
I GOT IT!
YES!
HA HA...
HA HA HA!!

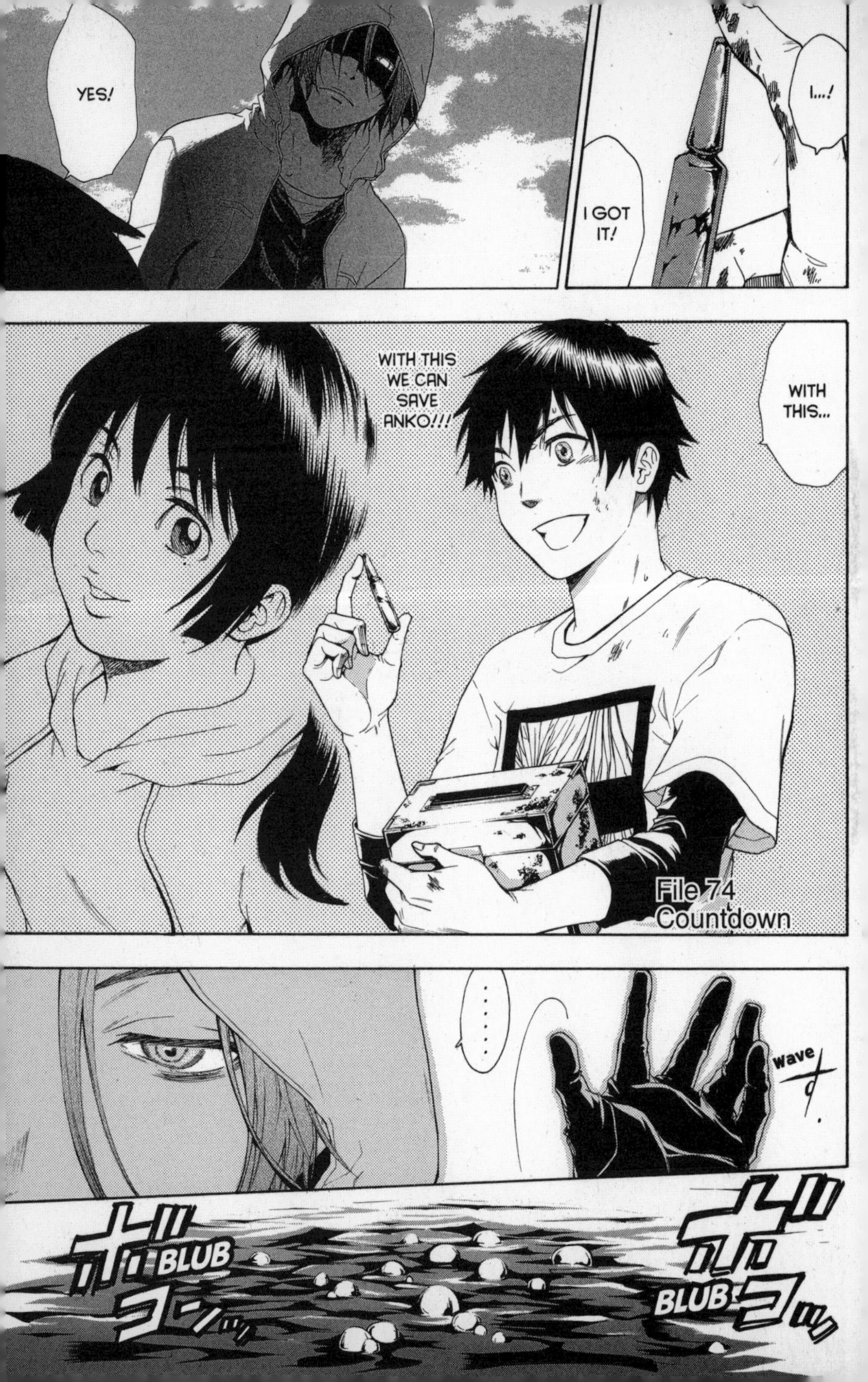
I...!
I GOT IT!
YES!
WITH THIS...
WITH THIS WE CAN SAVE ANKO!!!
File 74
Countdown
......
Wave
BLUB
BLUB

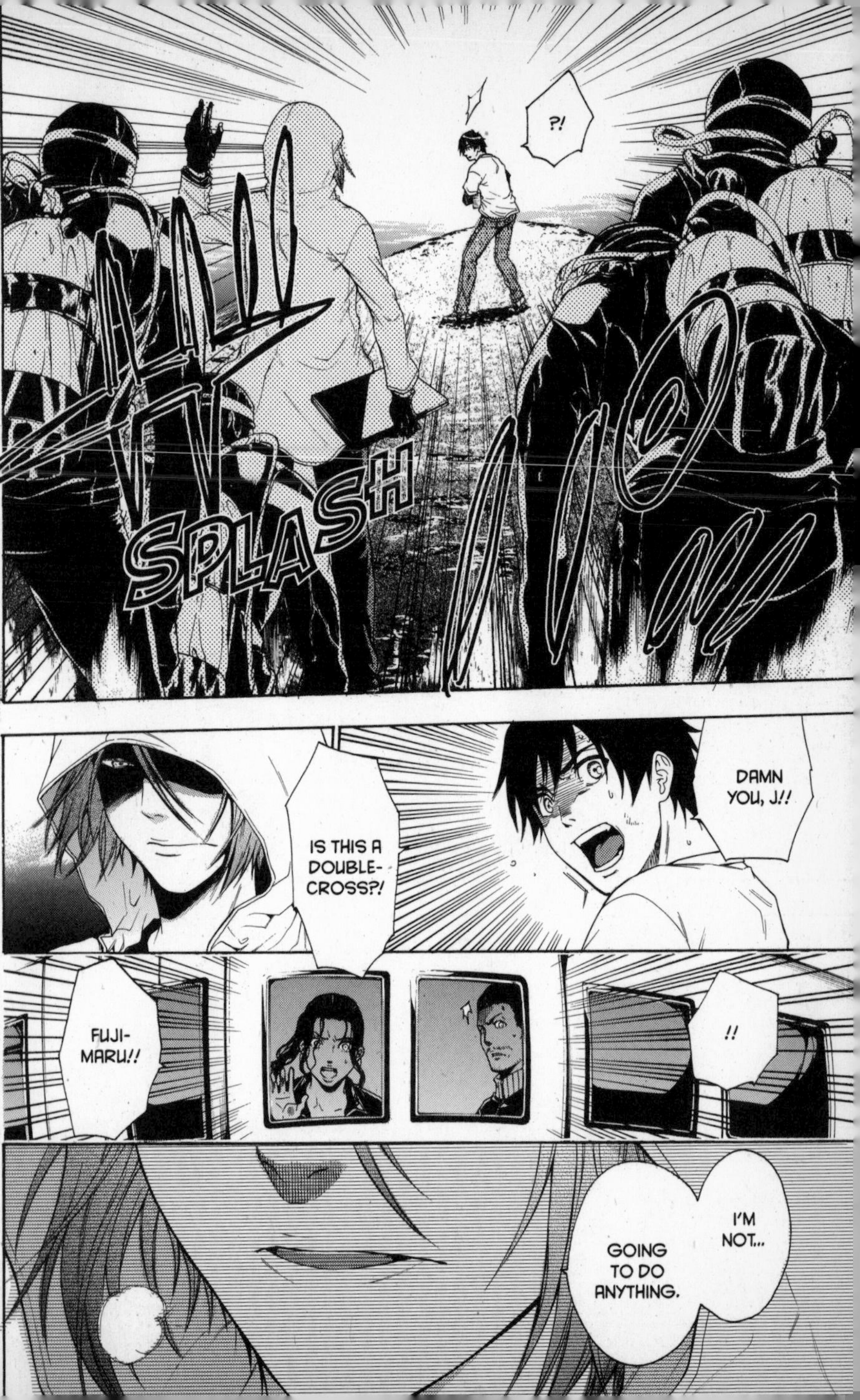
?!
SPLASH
DAMN YOU, J!!
IS THIS A DOUBLE-CROSS?!
!!
FUJI-MARU!!
I'M NOT...
GOING TO DO ANYTHING.

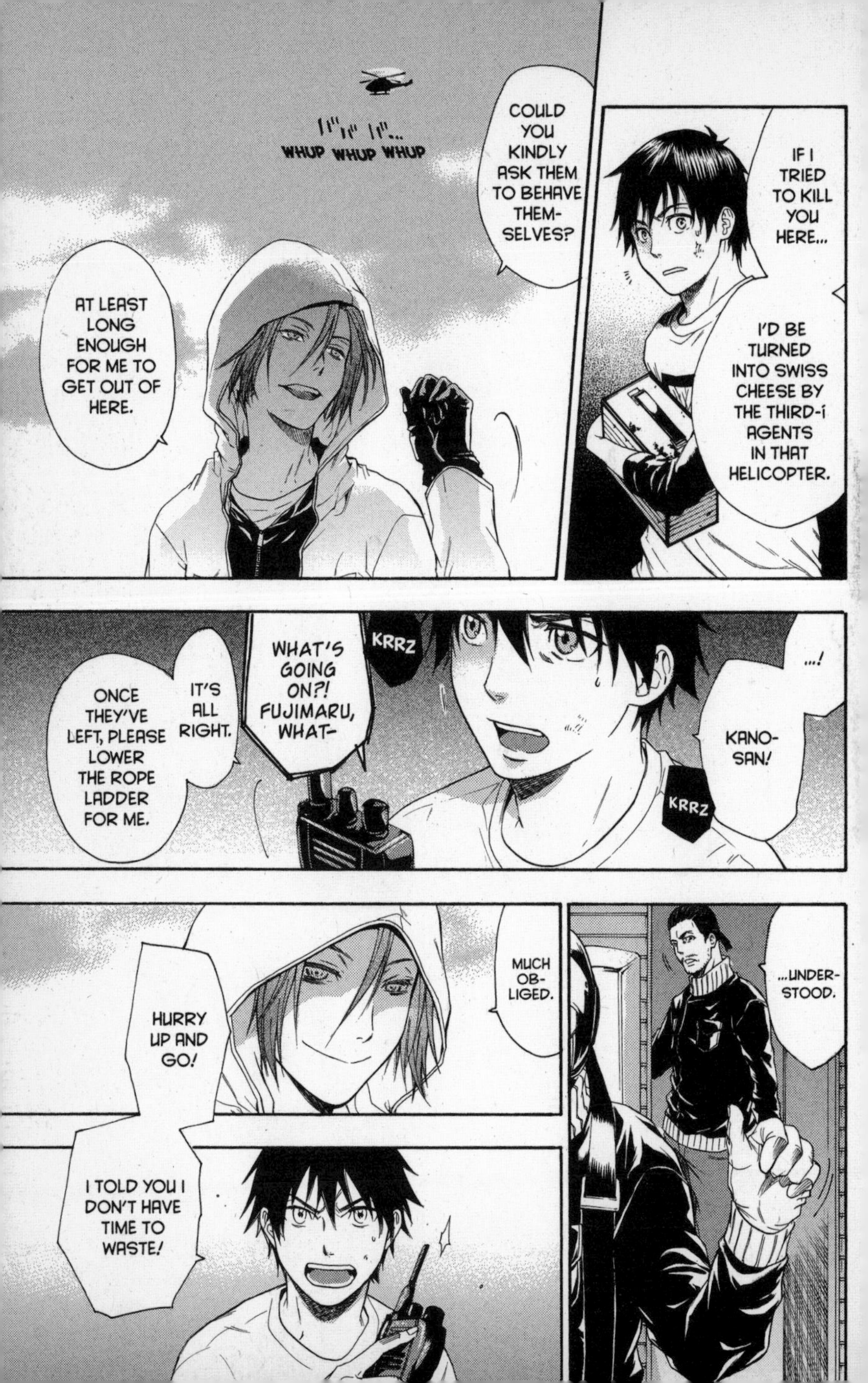
IF I TRIED TO KILL YOU HERE...
I'D BE TURNED INTO SWISS CHEESE BY THE THIRD-i AGENTS IN THAT HELICOPTER.
COULD YOU KINDLY ASK THEM TO BEHAVE THEM-SELVES?
WHUP WHUP WHUP
AT LEAST LONG ENOUGH FOR ME TO GET OUT OF HERE.
...!
KANO-SAN!
KRRZ
KRRZ
WHAT'S GOING ON?! FUJIMARU, WHAT-
IT'S ALL RIGHT.
ONCE THEY'VE LEFT, PLEASE LOWER THE ROPE LADDER FOR ME.
...UNDER-STOOD.
MUCH OB-LIGED.
HURRY UP AND GO!
I TOLD YOU I DON'T HAVE TIME TO WASTE!

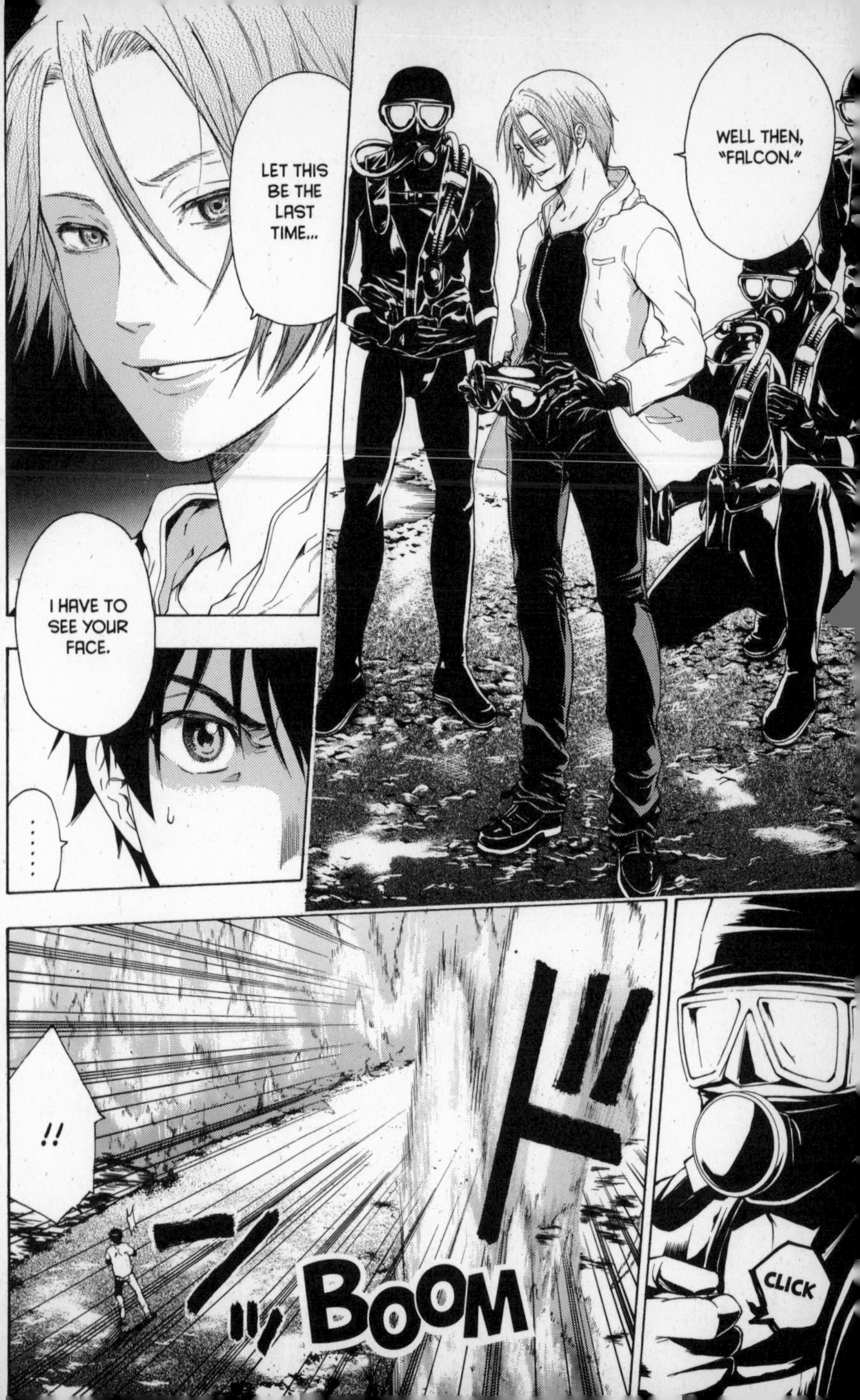
WELL THEN, "FALCON."
LET THIS BE THE LAST TIME...
I HAVE TO SEE YOUR FACE.
......
CLICK
BOOM
!!

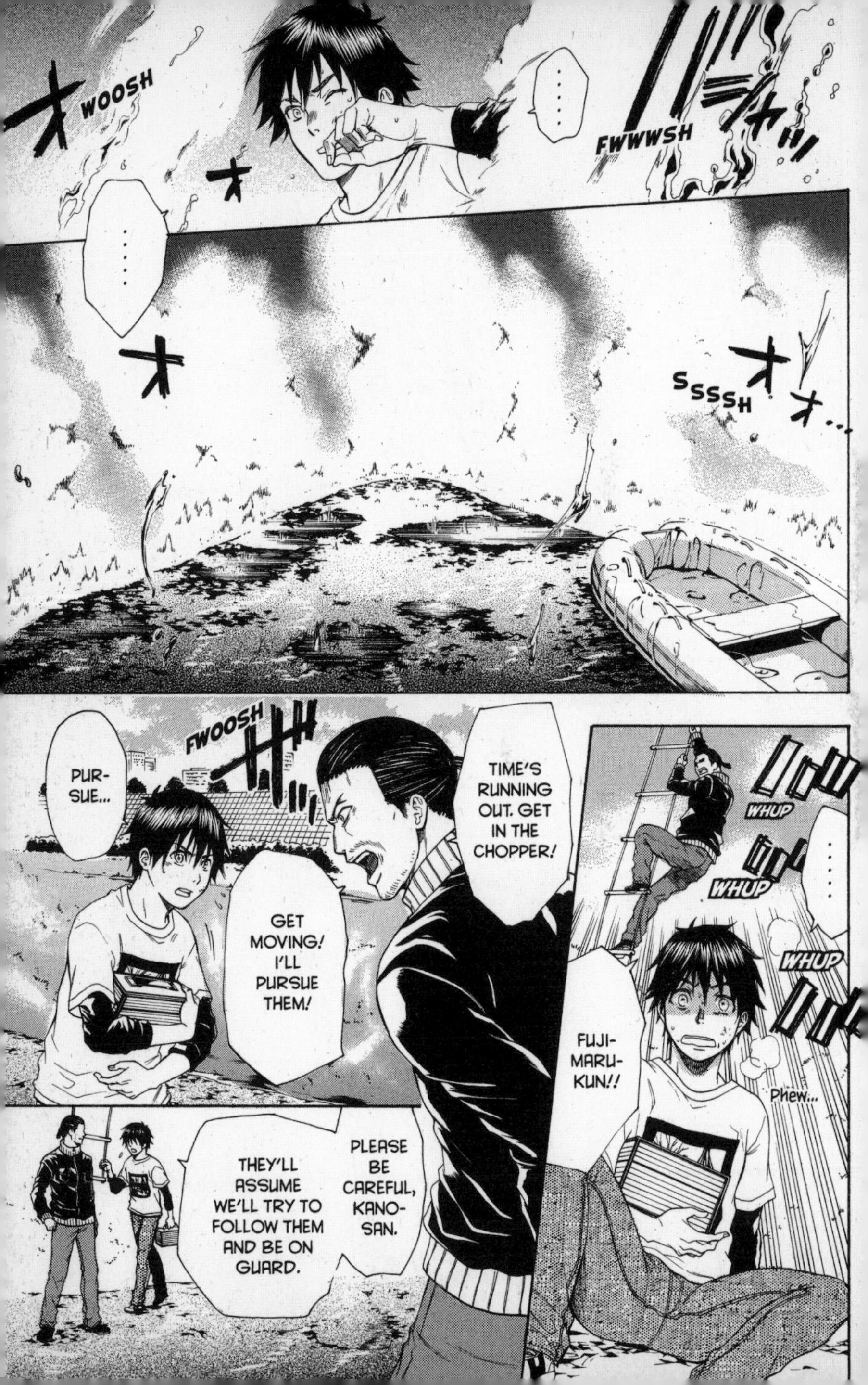
FWWWSH
......
WOOSH
......
SSSSH
WHUP
......
WHUP
WHUP
FUJI-MARU-KUN!!
Phew...
TIME'S RUNNING OUT. GET IN THE CHOPPER!
FWOOSH
GET MOVING! I'LL PURSUE THEM!
PUR-SUE...
PLEASE BE CAREFUL, KANO-SAN.
THEY'LL ASSUME WE'LL TRY TO FOLLOW THEM AND BE ON GUARD.

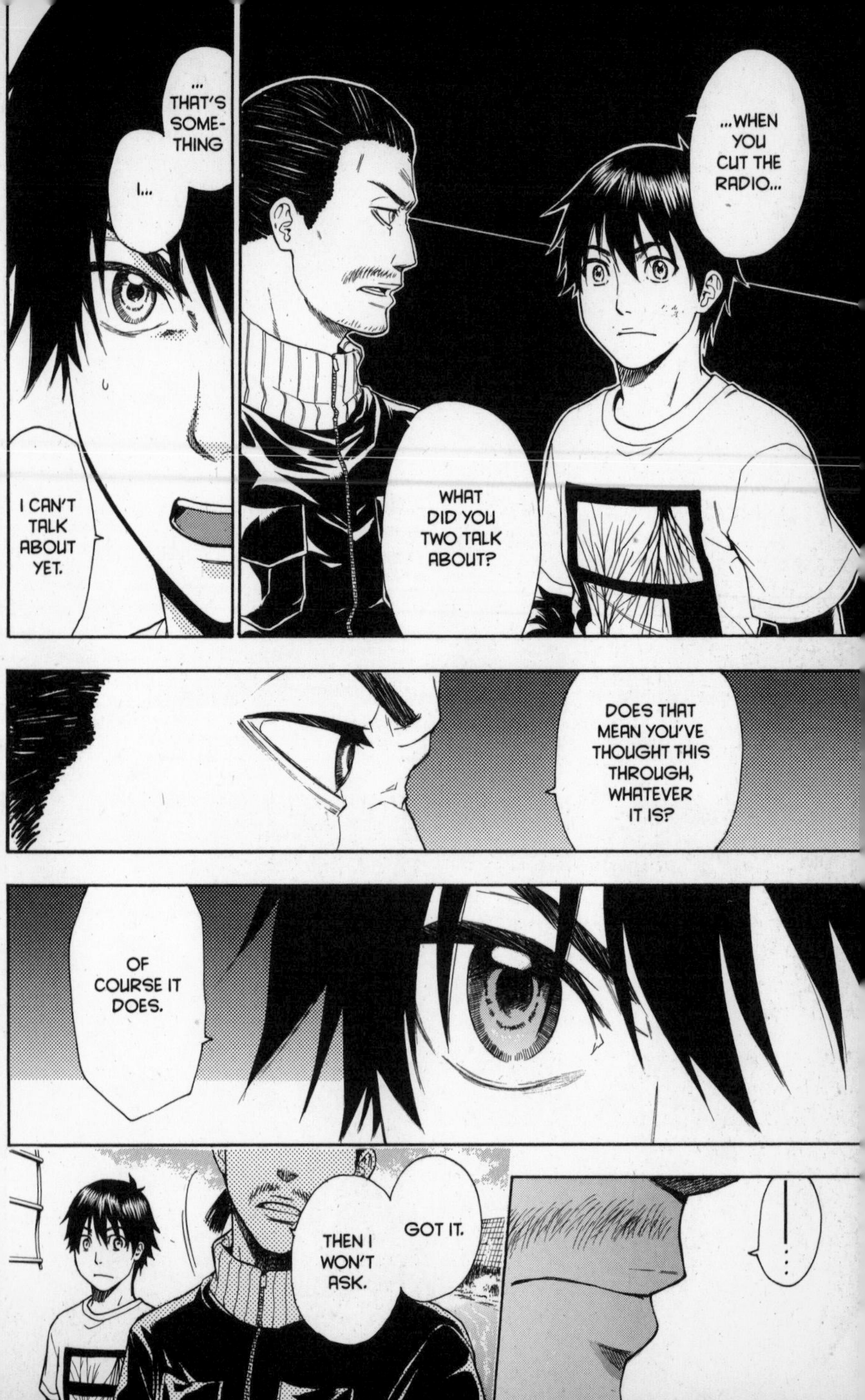
...WHEN YOU CUT THE RADIO...
WHAT DID YOU TWO TALK ABOUT?
...THAT'S SOME-THING
I...
I CAN'T TALK ABOUT YET.
DOES THAT MEAN YOU'VE THOUGHT THIS THROUGH, WHATEVER IT IS?
OF COURSE IT DOES.
!...
GOT IT.
THEN I WON'T ASK.

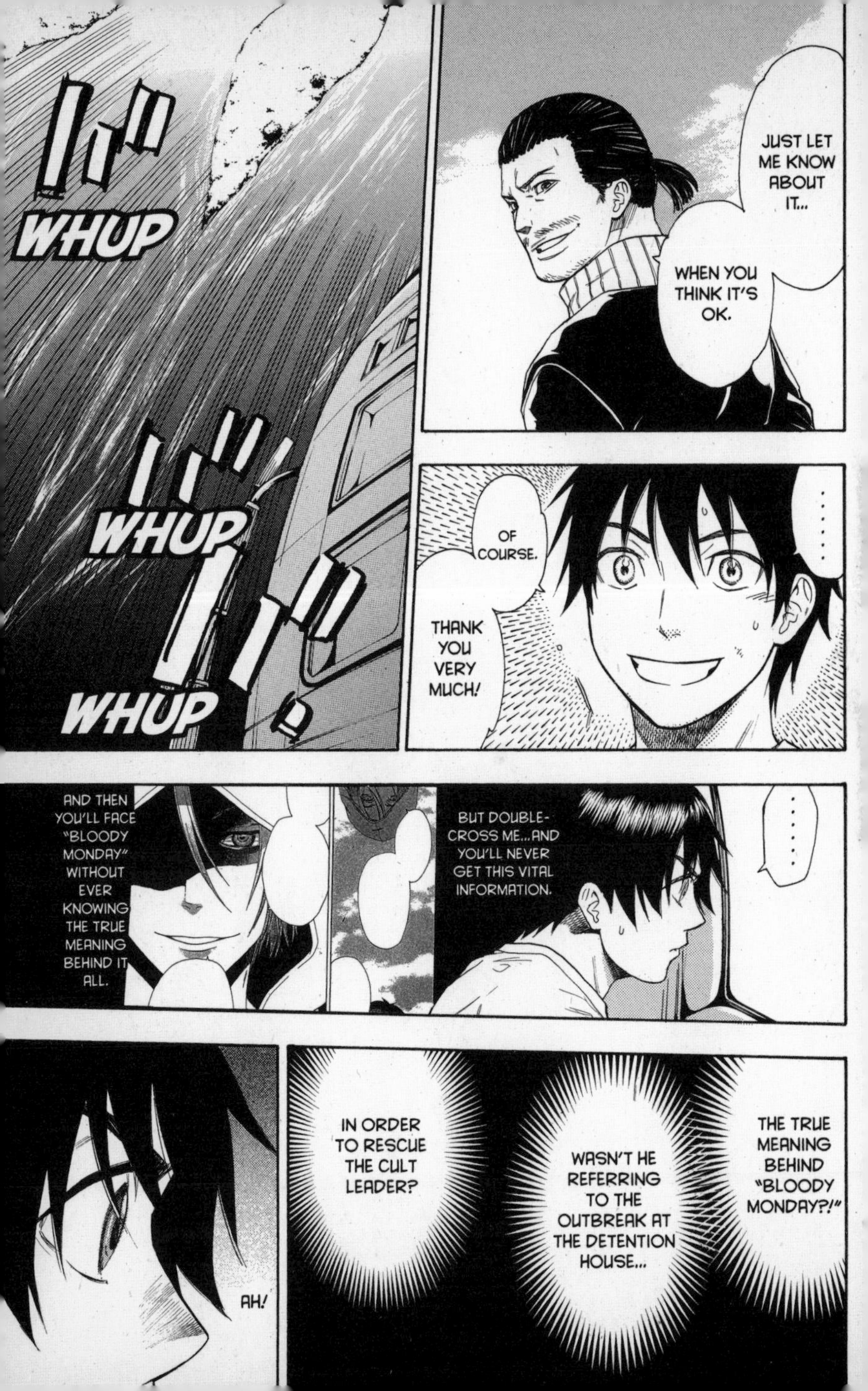

JUST LET ME KNOW ABOUT IT...
WHEN YOU THINK IT'S OK.
......
OF COURSE.
THANK YOU VERY MUCH!
WHUP
WHUP
WHUP
......
BUT DOUBLE-CROSS ME...AND YOU'LL NEVER GET THIS VITAL INFORMATION.
AND THEN YOU'LL FACE "BLOODY MONDAY" WITHOUT EVER KNOWING THE TRUE MEANING BEHIND IT ALL.
THE TRUE MEANING BEHIND "BLOODY MONDAY?!"
WASN'T HE REFERRING TO THE OUTBREAK AT THE DETENTION HOUSE...
IN ORDER TO RESCUE THE CULT LEADER?
AH!

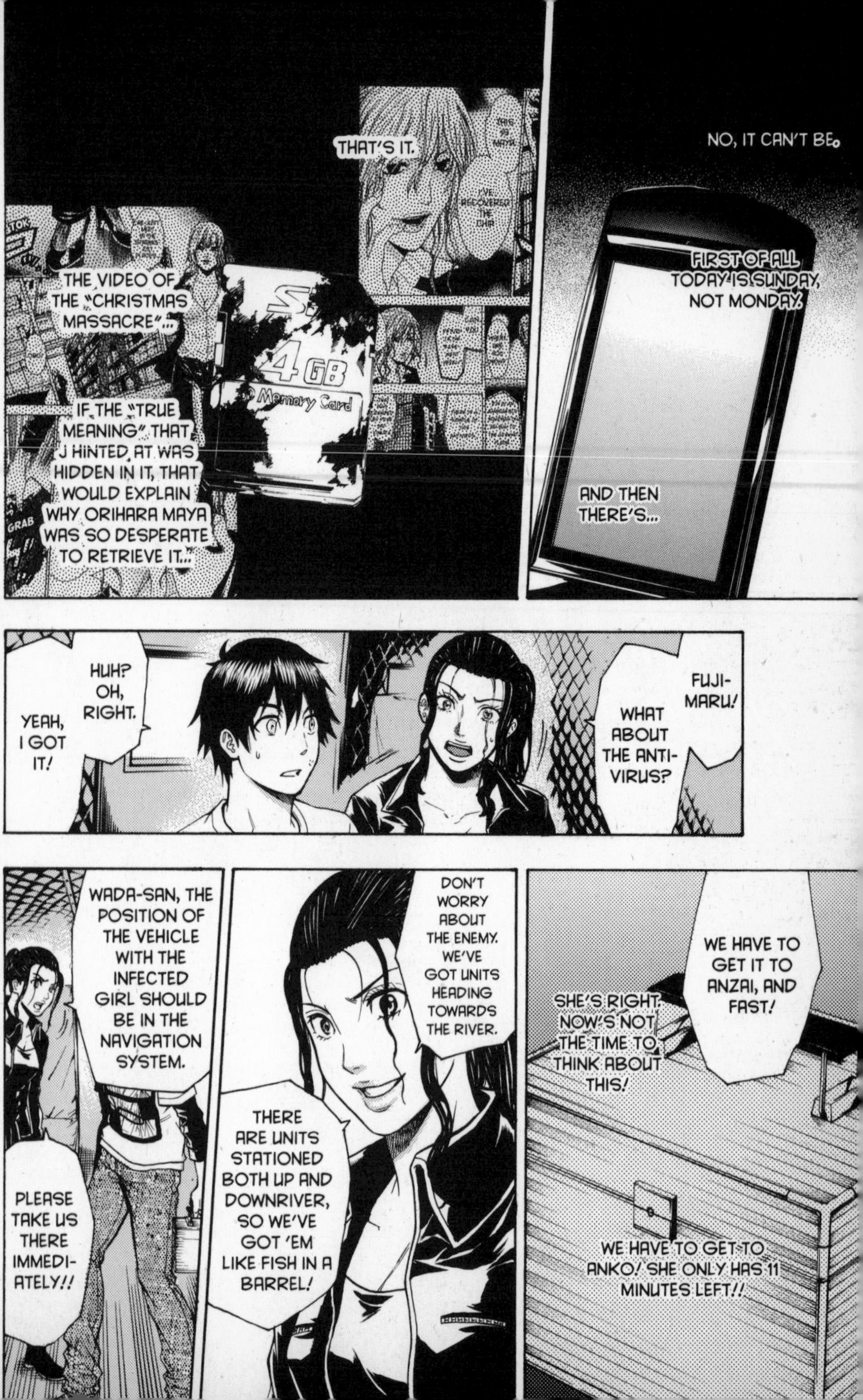
NO, IT CAN'T BE.
FIRST OF ALL TODAY IS SUNDAY, NOT MONDAY.
AND THEN THERE'S...
THAT'S IT.
THE VIDEO OF THE "CHRISTMAS MASSACRE"...
4 GB
Memory Card
IF THE "TRUE MEANING" THAT J HINTED AT WAS HIDDEN IN IT, THAT WOULD EXPLAIN WHY ORIHARA MAYA WAS SO DESPERATE TO RETRIEVE IT...
FUJI-MARU!
WHAT ABOUT THE ANTI-VIRUS?
HUH? OH, RIGHT.
YEAH, I GOT IT!
WE HAVE TO GET IT TO ANZAI, AND FAST!
SHE'S RIGHT. NOW'S NOT THE TIME TO THINK ABOUT THIS!
WE HAVE TO GET TO ANKO! SHE ONLY HAS 11 MINUTES LEFT!!
DON'T WORRY ABOUT THE ENEMY. WE'VE GOT UNITS HEADING TOWARDS THE RIVER.
THERE ARE UNITS STATIONED BOTH UP AND DOWNRIVER, SO WE'VE GOT 'EM LIKE FISH IN A BARREL!
WADA-SAN, THE POSITION OF THE VEHICLE WITH THE INFECTED GIRL SHOULD BE IN THE NAVIGATION SYSTEM.
PLEASE TAKE US THERE IMMEDIATELY!!

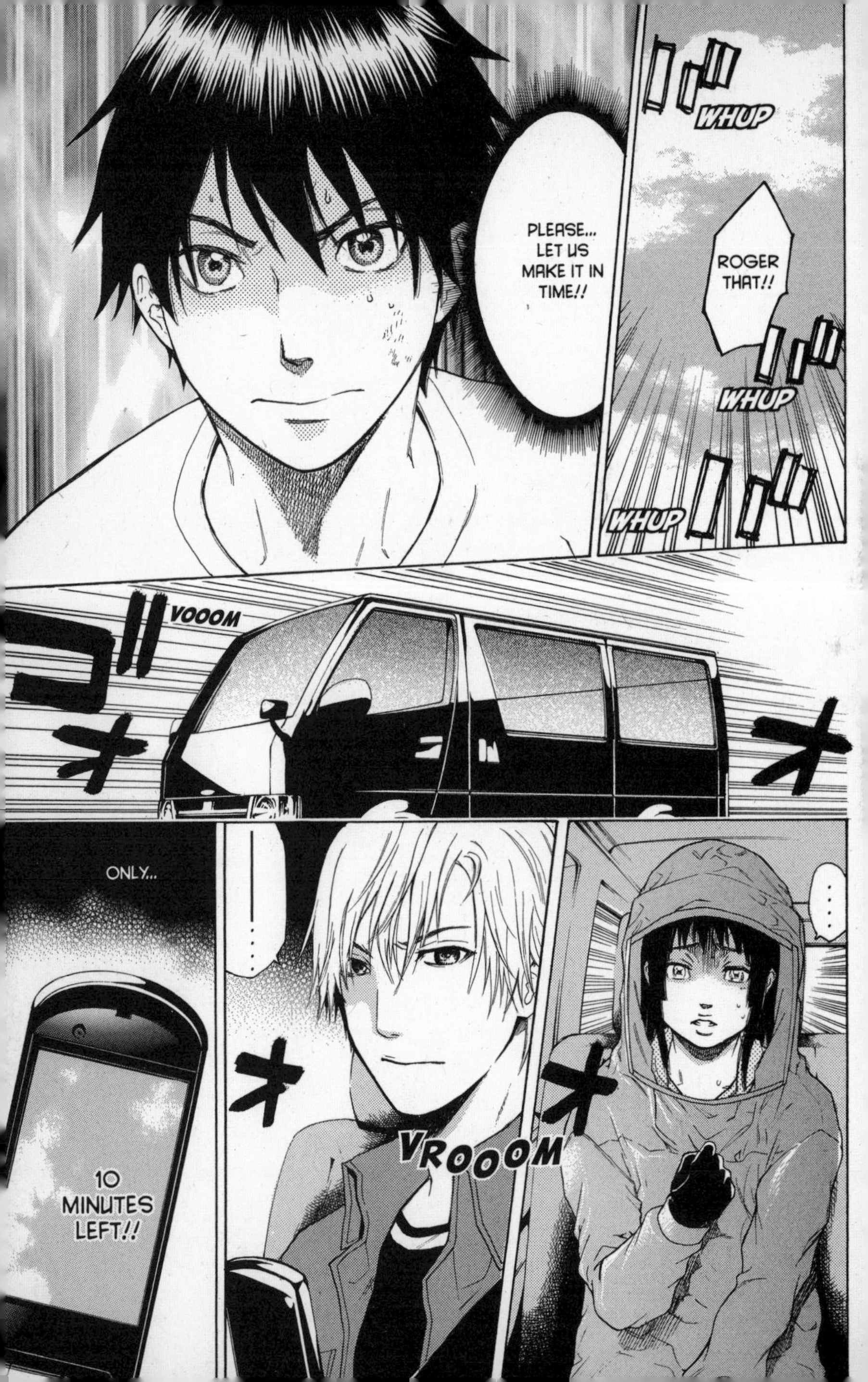
WHUP
ROGER THAT!!
WHUP
WHUP
PLEASE... LET US MAKE IT IN TIME!!
VOOOM
....
!...
VROOOM
ONLY...
10 MINUTES LEFT!!

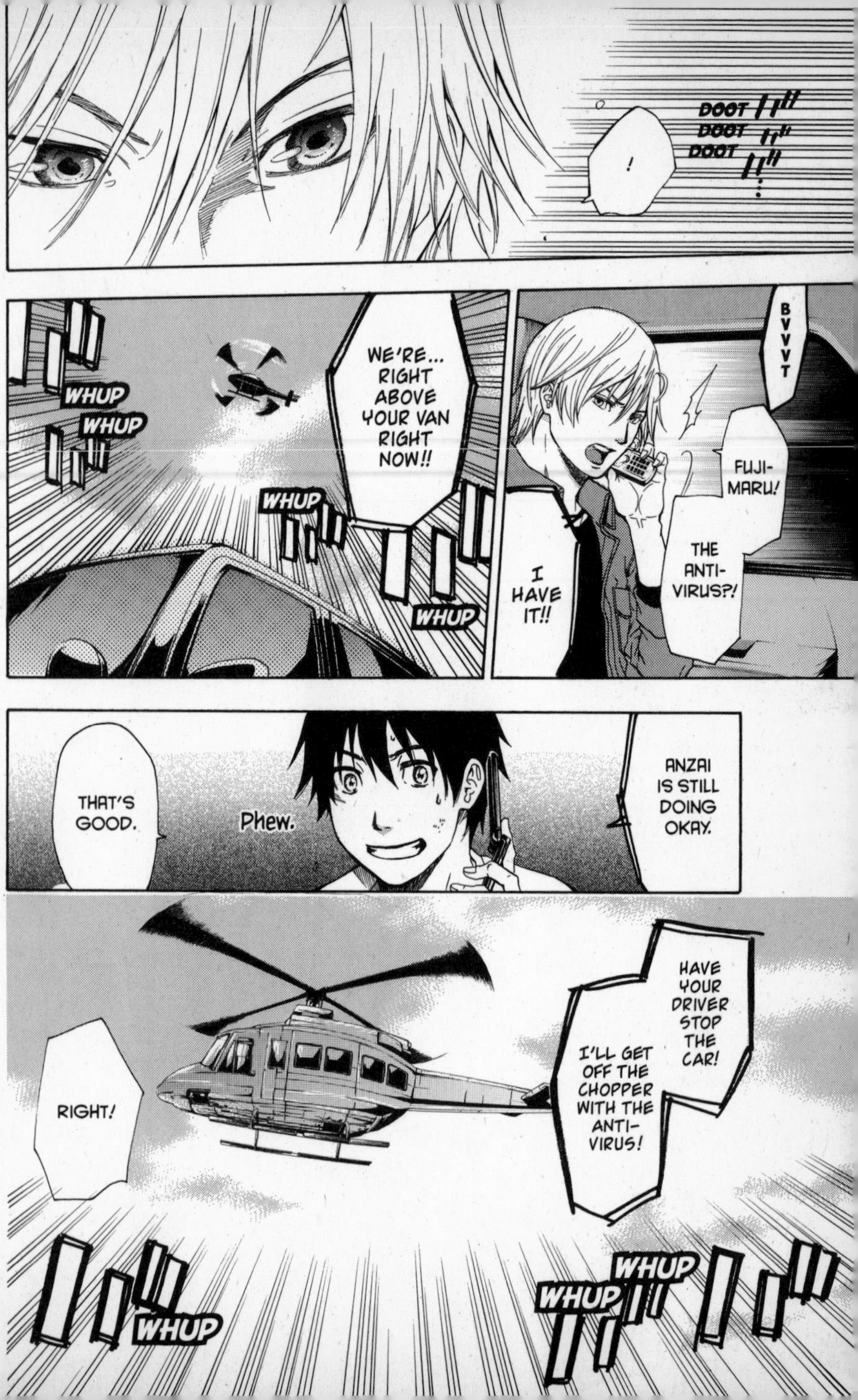
DOOT DOOT DOOT
!
BVVVT
FUJI-MARU!
THE ANTI-VIRUS?!
I HAVE IT!!
WE'RE... RIGHT ABOVE YOUR VAN RIGHT NOW!!
WHUP
WHUP
WHUP
WHUP
ANZAI IS STILL DOING OKAY.
Phew.
THAT'S GOOD.
HAVE YOUR DRIVER STOP THE CAR!
I'LL GET OFF THE CHOPPER WITH THE ANTI-VIRUS!
RIGHT!
WHUP
WHUP
WHUP

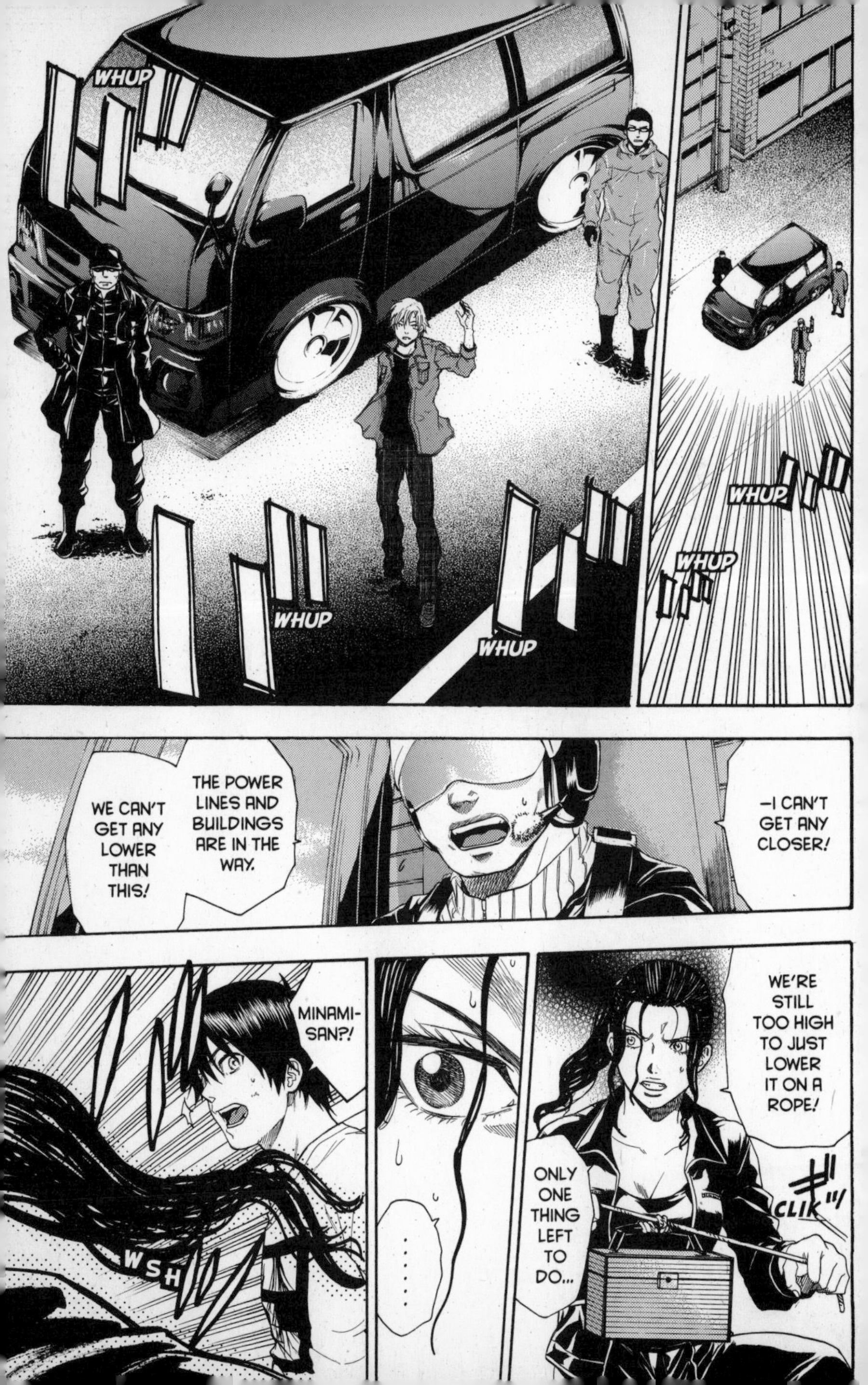
WHUP
WHUP
WHUP
WHUP
WHUP
—I CAN'T GET ANY CLOSER!
THE POWER LINES AND BUILDINGS ARE IN THE WAY.
WE CAN'T GET ANY LOWER THAN THIS!
WE'RE STILL TOO HIGH TO JUST LOWER IT ON A ROPE!
CLIK
ONLY ONE THING LEFT TO DO...
......
MINAMI-SAN?!
WSH

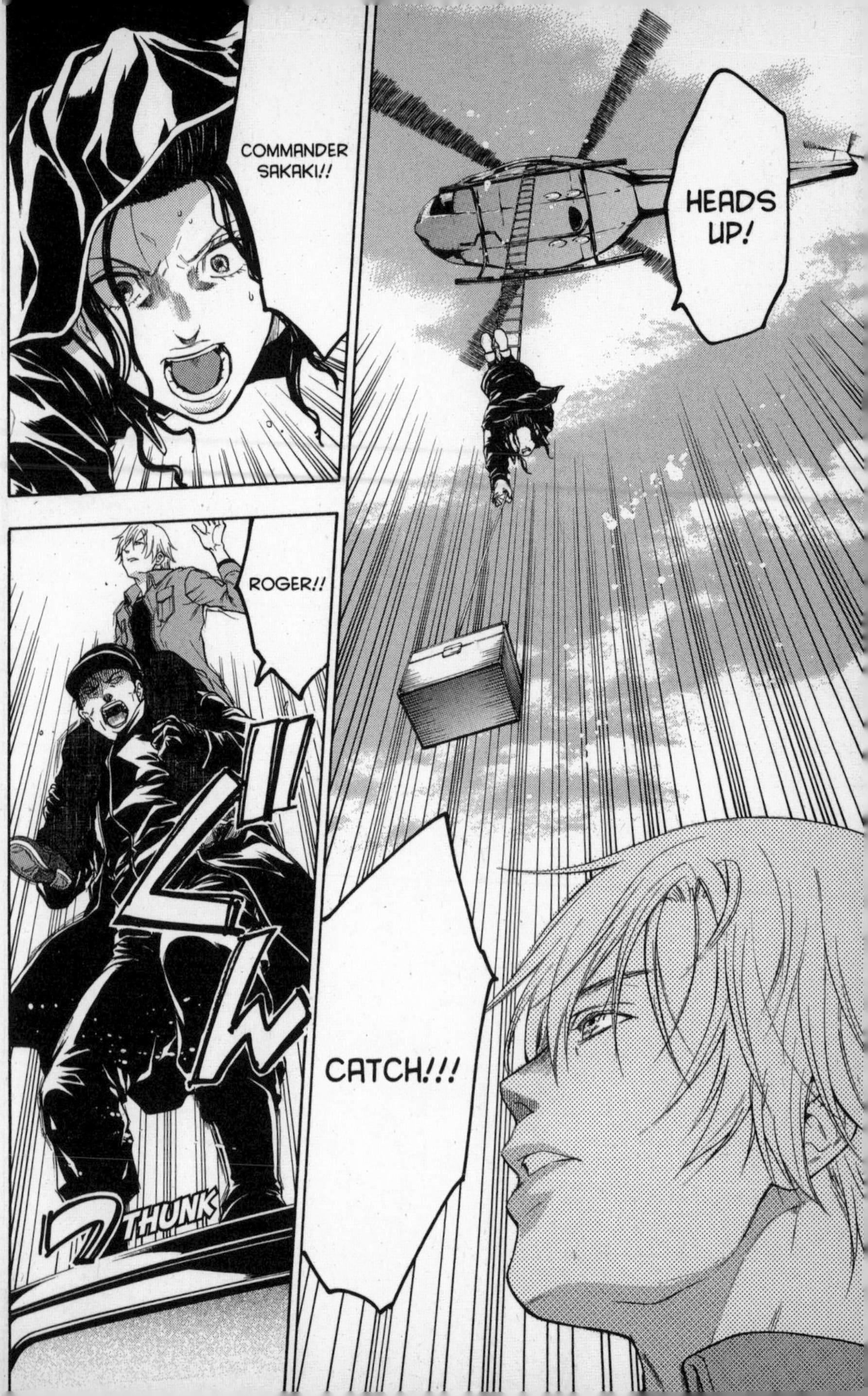
HEADS UP!
CATCH!!!
COMMANDER SAKAKI!!
ROGER!!
THUNK

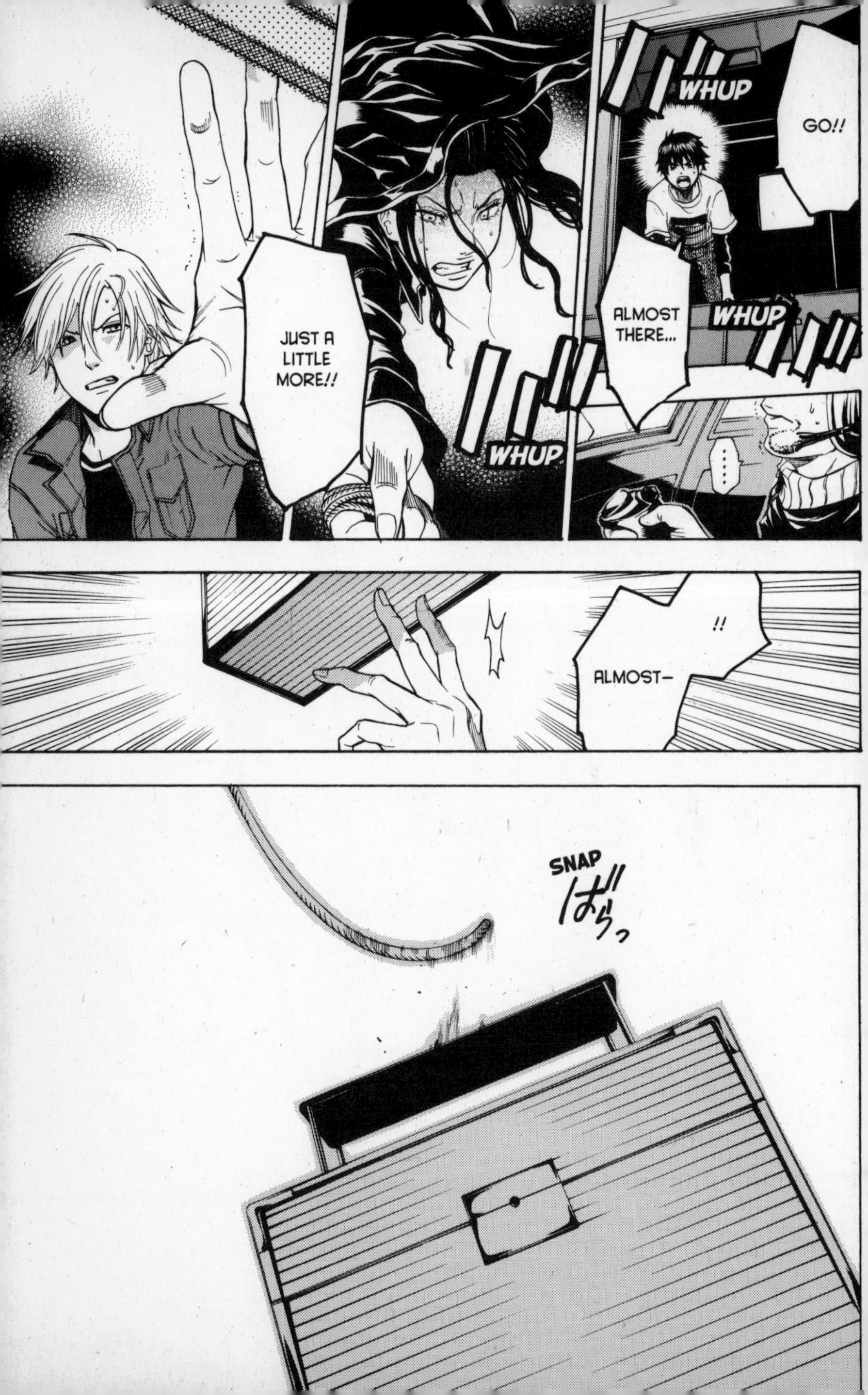
GO!!
WHUP
ALMOST THERE...
WHUP
...
WHUP
JUST A LITTLE MORE!!
!!
ALMOST–
SNAP
ぱらっ

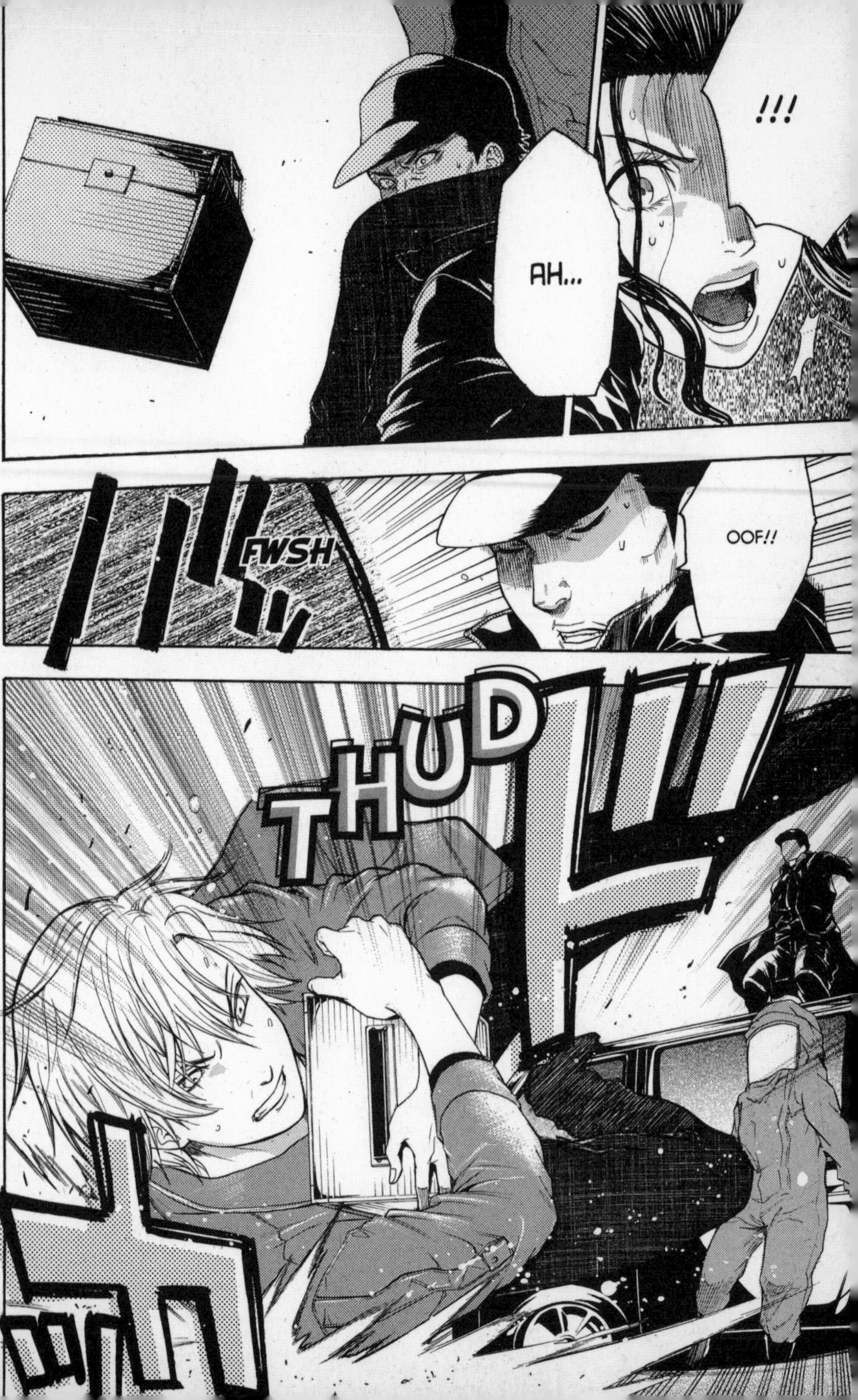
!!!
AH...
OOF!!
FWSH
THUD

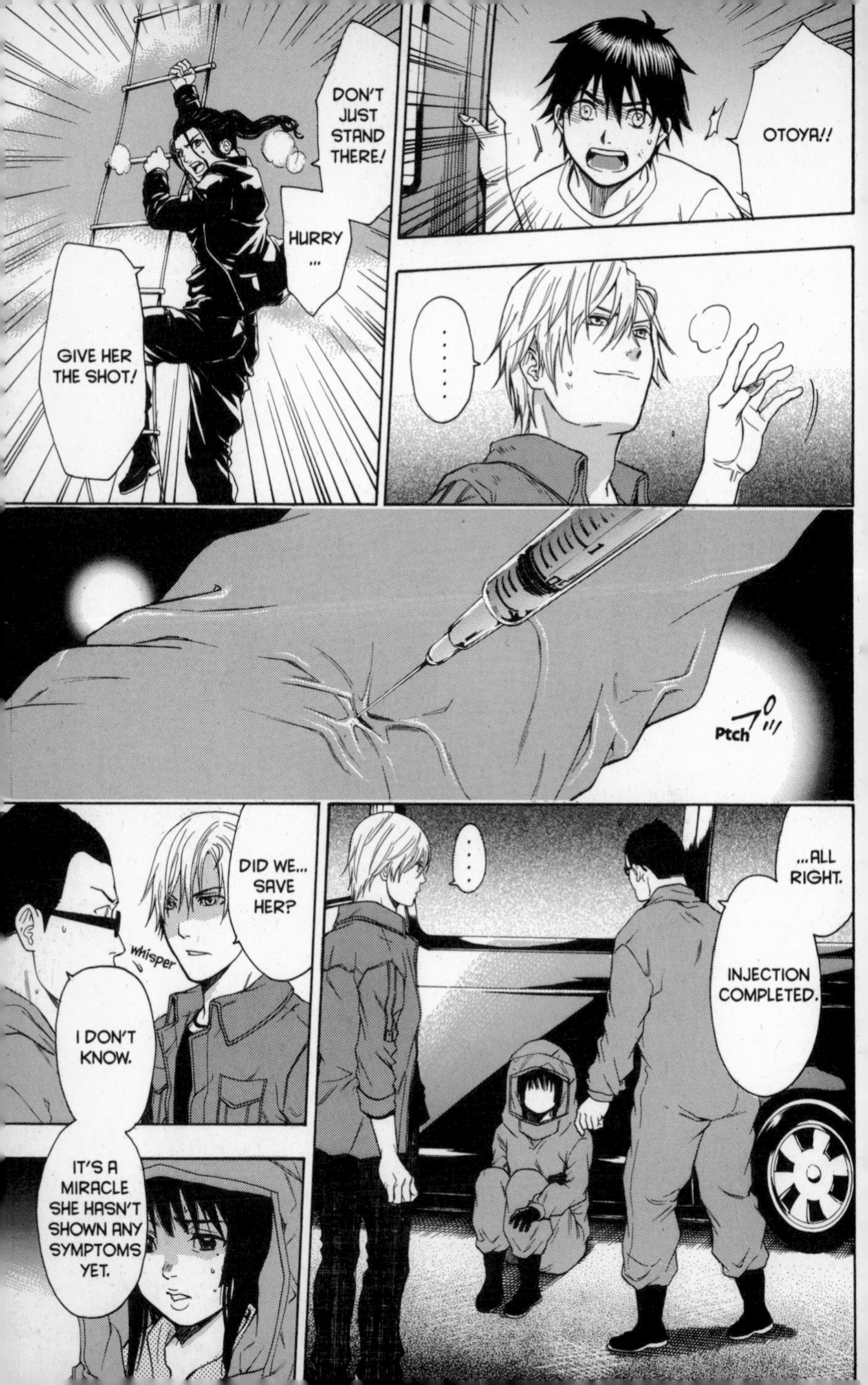
OTOYA!!
......
DON'T JUST STAND THERE!
HURRY ...
GIVE HER THE SHOT!
Ptch
...ALL RIGHT.
INJECTION COMPLETED.
....
DID WE... SAVE HER?
whisper
I DON'T KNOW.
IT'S A MIRACLE SHE HASN'T SHOWN ANY SYMPTOMS YET.

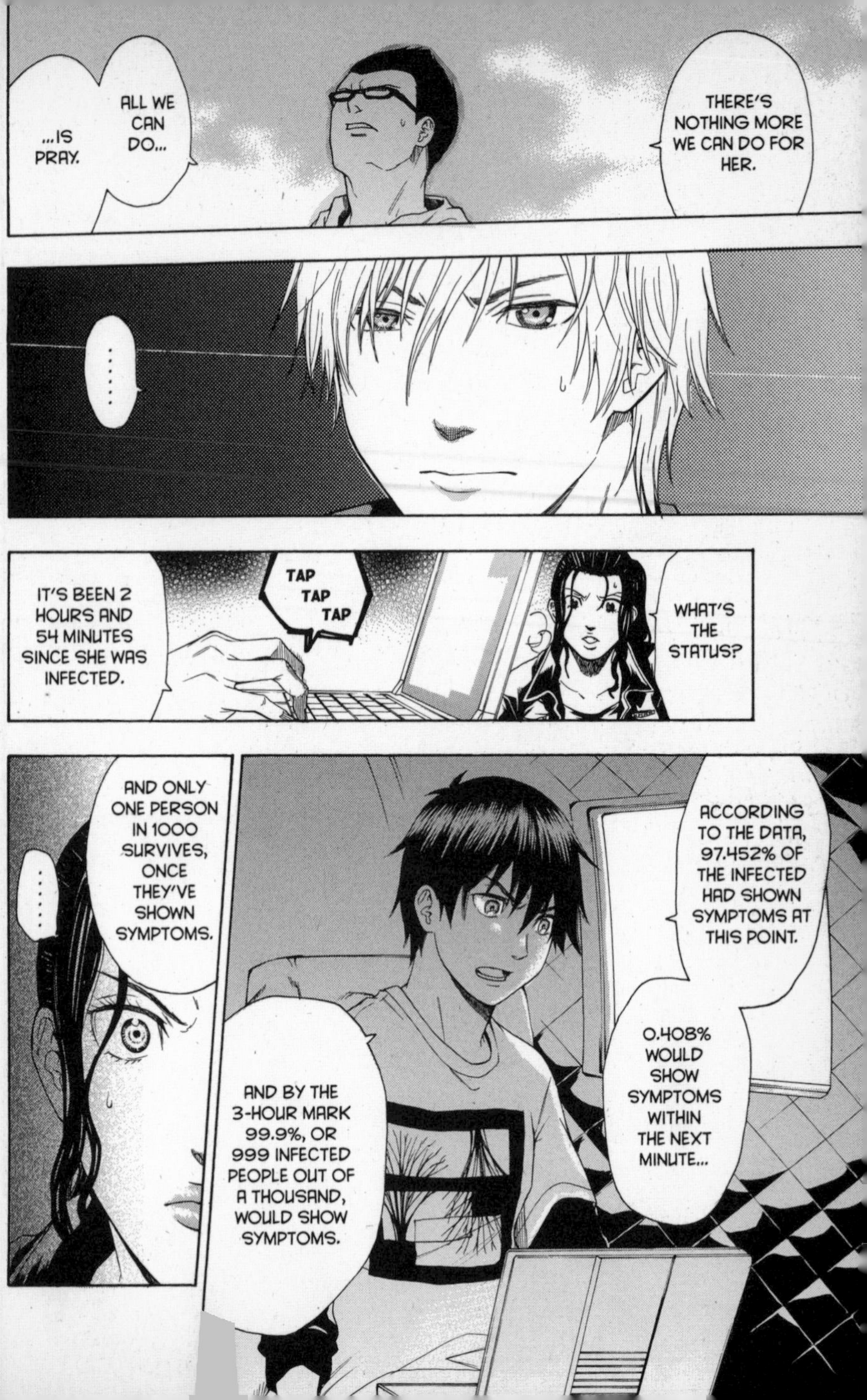
THERE'S NOTHING MORE WE CAN DO FOR HER.
ALL WE CAN DO...
...IS PRAY.
......
WHAT'S THE STATUS?
TAP TAP TAP
IT'S BEEN 2 HOURS AND 54 MINUTES SINCE SHE WAS INFECTED.
ACCORDING TO THE DATA, 97.452% OF THE INFECTED HAD SHOWN SYMPTOMS AT THIS POINT.
0.408% WOULD SHOW SYMPTOMS WITHIN THE NEXT MINUTE...
AND BY THE 3-HOUR MARK 99.9%, OR 999 INFECTED PEOPLE OUT OF A THOUSAND, WOULD SHOW SYMPTOMS.
AND ONLY ONE PERSON IN 1000 SURVIVES, ONCE THEY'VE SHOWN SYMPTOMS.
......

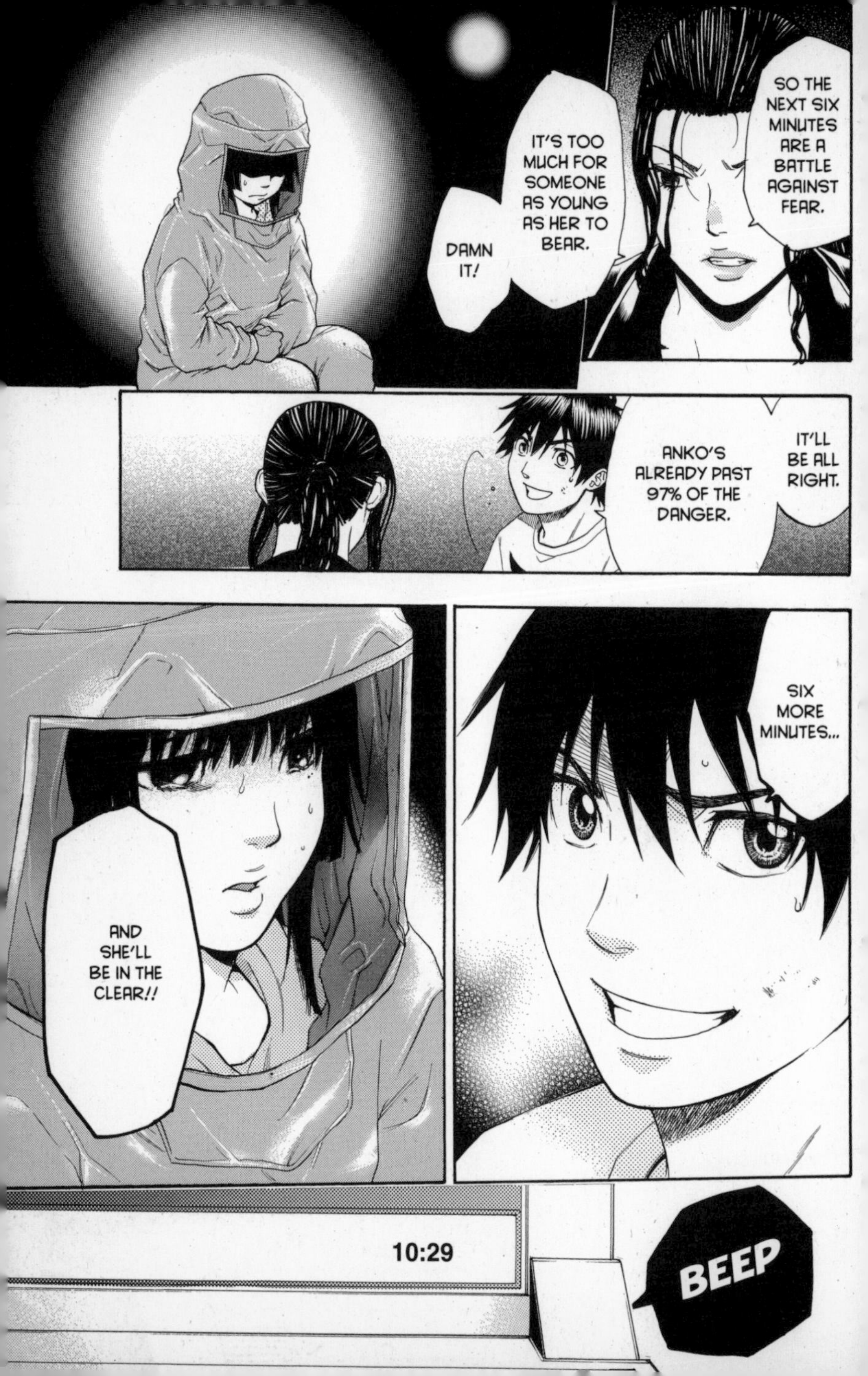
SO THE NEXT SIX MINUTES ARE A BATTLE AGAINST FEAR.
IT'S TOO MUCH FOR SOMEONE AS YOUNG AS HER TO BEAR.
DAMN IT!
IT'LL BE ALL RIGHT.
ANKO'S ALREADY PAST 97% OF THE DANGER.
SIX MORE MINUTES...
AND SHE'LL BE IN THE CLEAR!!
BEEP
10:29

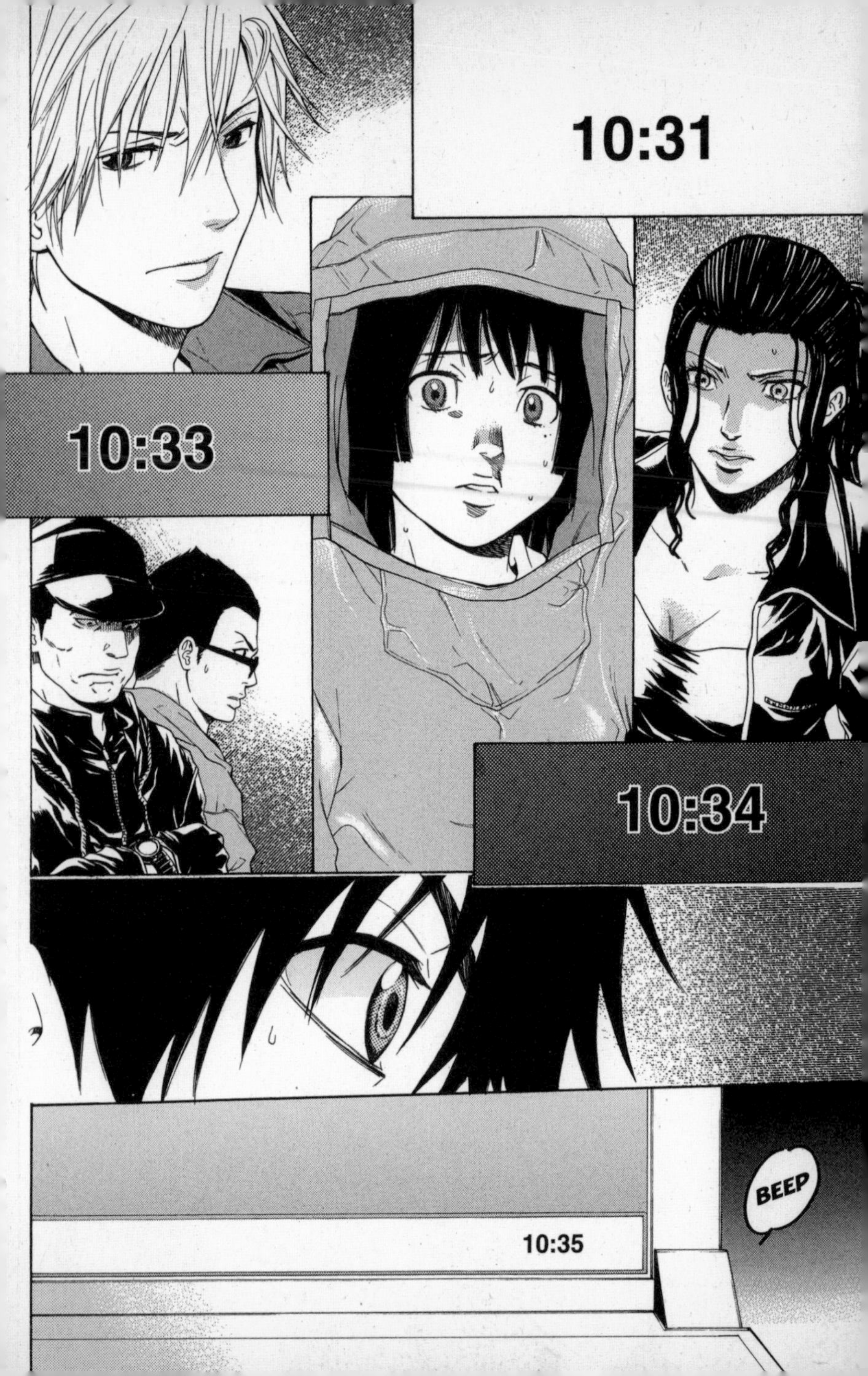
10:31
10:33
10:34
BEEP
10:35

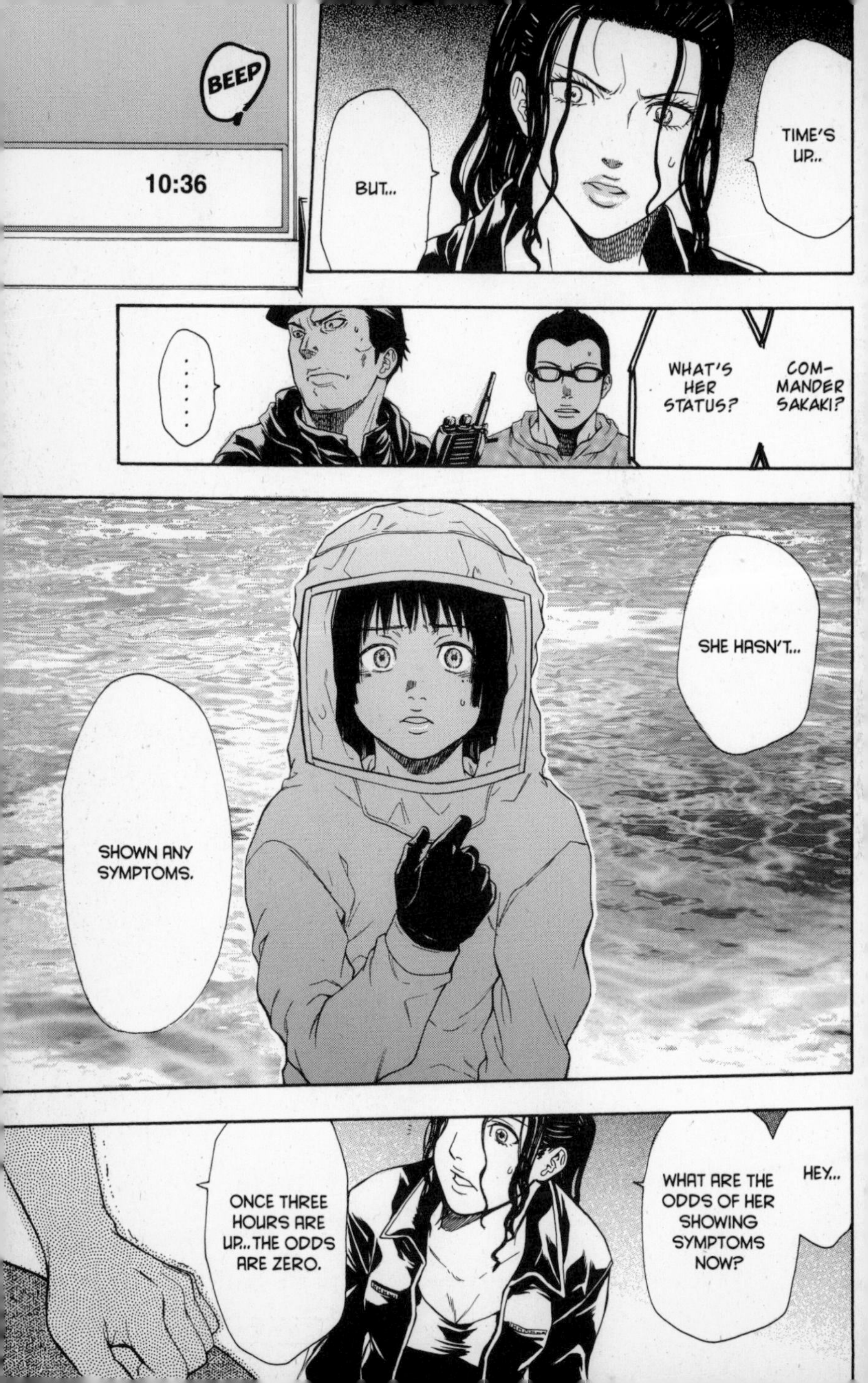
TIME'S UP...
BUT...
BEEP
10:36
COMMANDER SAKAKI?
WHAT'S HER STATUS?
......
SHE HASN'T...
SHOWN ANY SYMPTOMS.
HEY...
WHAT ARE THE ODDS OF HER SHOWING SYMPTOMS NOW?
ONCE THREE HOURS ARE UP... THE ODDS ARE ZERO.

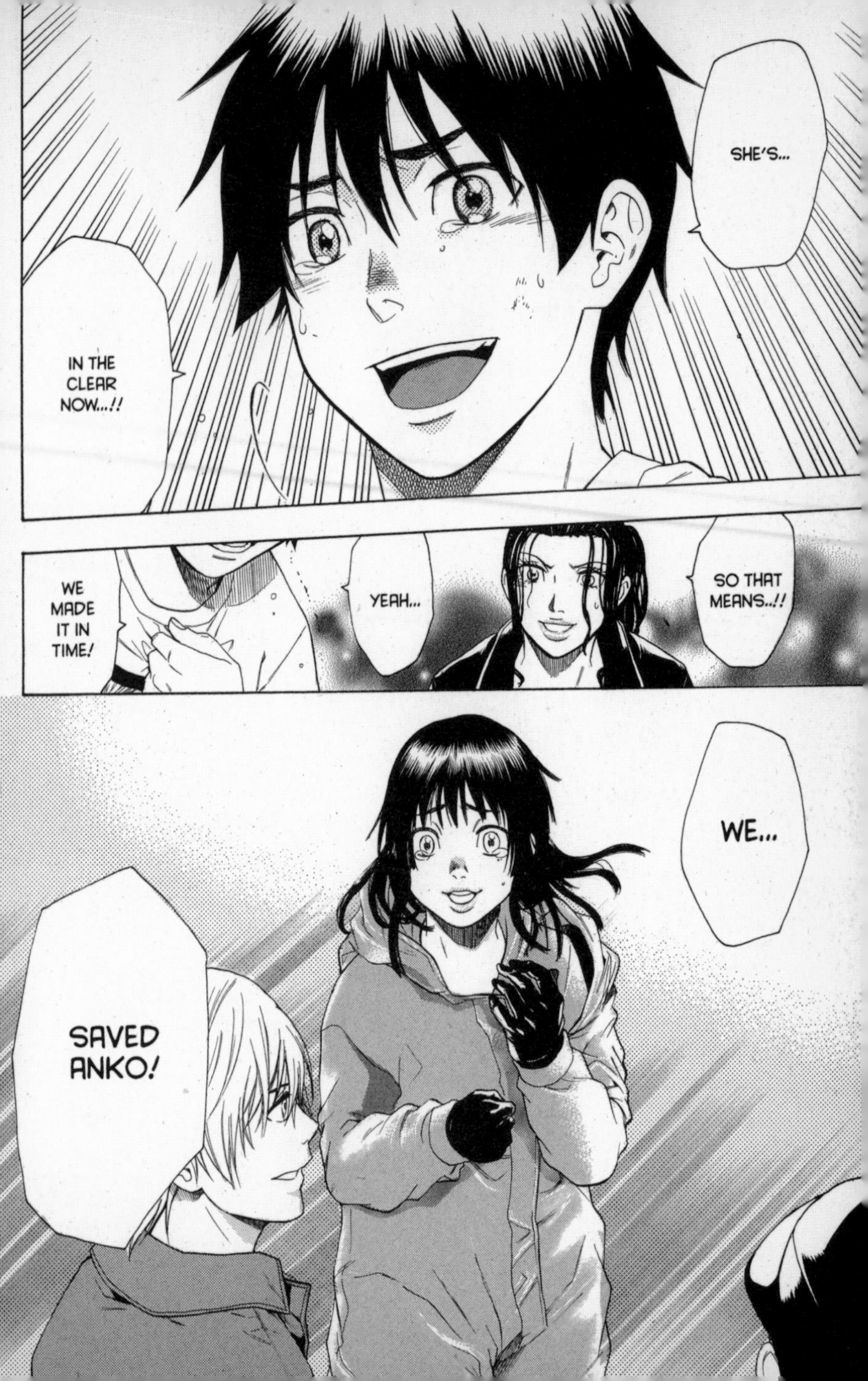
SHE'S...
IN THE CLEAR NOW...!!
SO THAT MEANS..!!
YEAH...
WE MADE IT IN TIME!
WE...
SAVED ANKO!

Chapter 75
The Final Showdown Begins

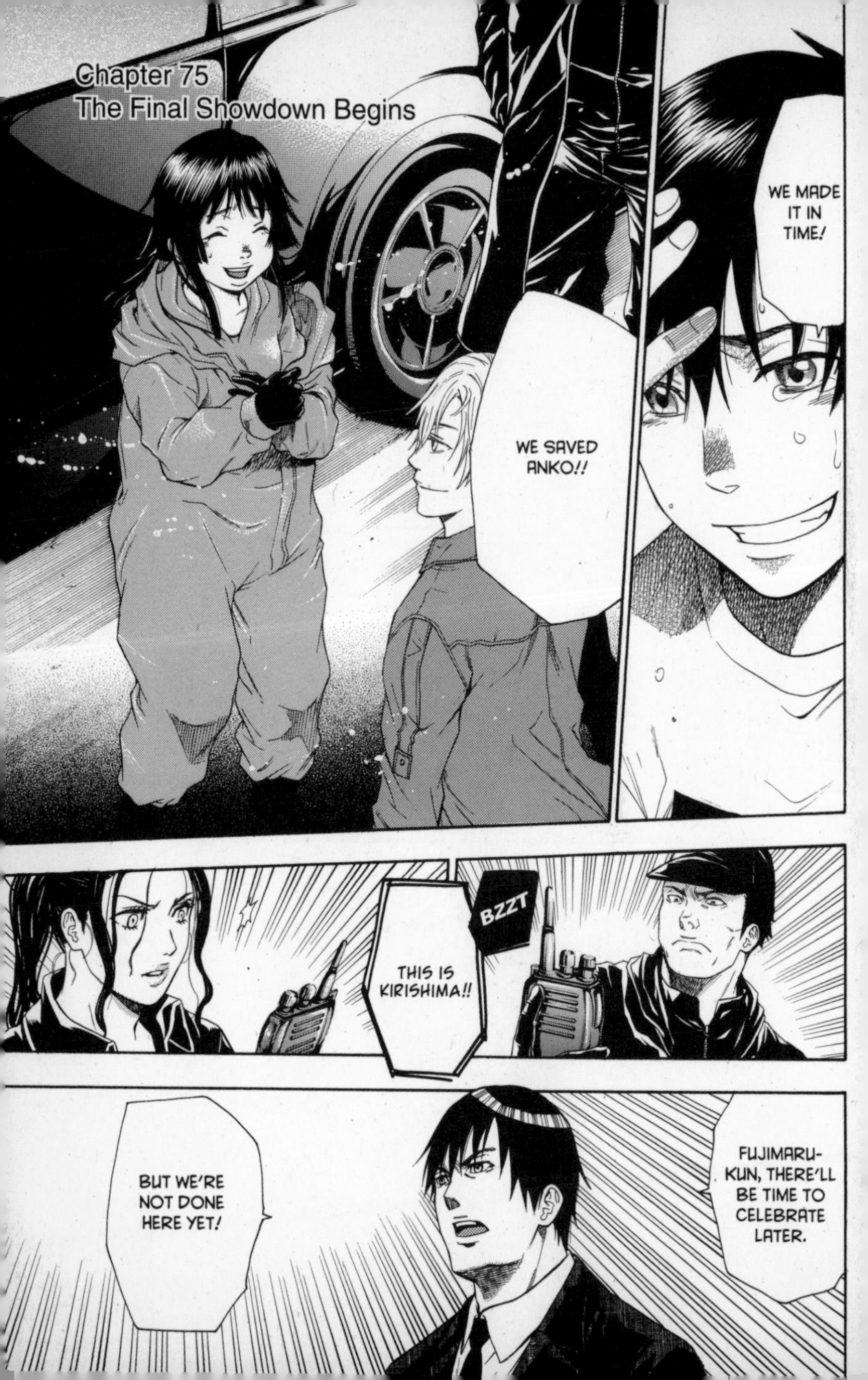

WE MADE IT IN TIME!
WE SAVED ANKO!!
BZZT
THIS IS KIRISHIMA!!
FUJIMARU-KUN, THERE'LL BE TIME TO CELEBRATE LATER.
BUT WE'RE NOT DONE HERE YET!

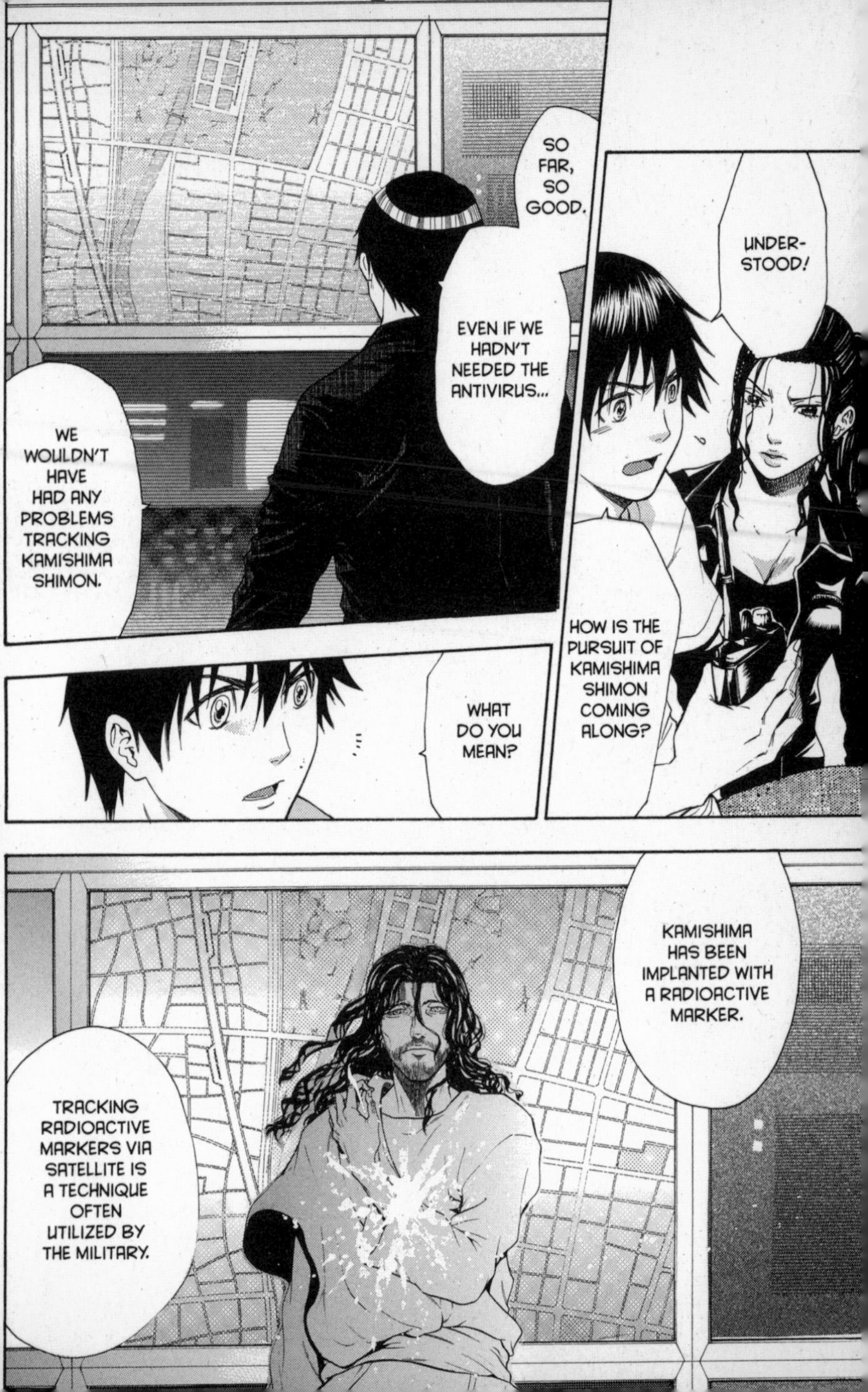
UNDER-STOOD!
HOW IS THE PURSUIT OF KAMISHIMA SHIMON COMING ALONG?
SO FAR, SO GOOD.
EVEN IF WE HADN'T NEEDED THE ANTIVIRUS...
WE WOULDN'T HAVE HAD ANY PROBLEMS TRACKING KAMISHIMA SHIMON.
...!
WHAT DO YOU MEAN?
KAMISHIMA HAS BEEN IMPLANTED WITH A RADIOACTIVE MARKER.
TRACKING RADIOACTIVE MARKERS VIA SATELLITE IS A TECHNIQUE OFTEN UTILIZED BY THE MILITARY.

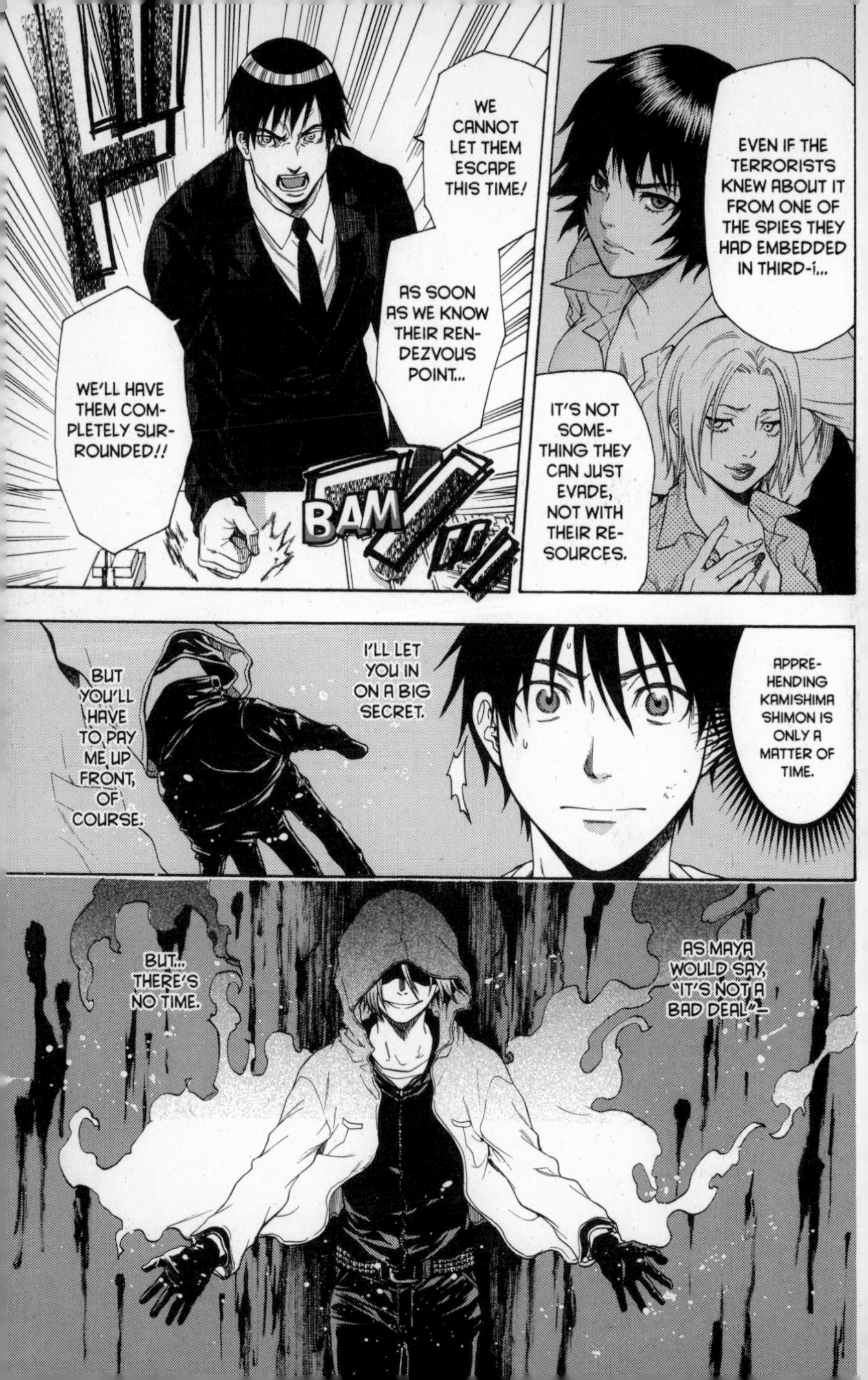
EVEN IF THE TERRORISTS KNEW ABOUT IT FROM ONE OF THE SPIES THEY HAD EMBEDDED IN THIRD-i...
IT'S NOT SOMETHING THEY CAN JUST EVADE, NOT WITH THEIR RESOURCES.
WE CANNOT LET THEM ESCAPE THIS TIME!
AS SOON AS WE KNOW THEIR RENDEZVOUS POINT...
WE'LL HAVE THEM COMPLETELY SURROUNDED!!
BAM
APPREHENDING KAMISHIMA SHIMON IS ONLY A MATTER OF TIME.
I'LL LET YOU IN ON A BIG SECRET.
BUT YOU'LL HAVE TO PAY ME UP FRONT, OF COURSE.
AS MAYA WOULD SAY, "IT'S NOT A BAD DEAL"—
BUT... THERE'S NO TIME.

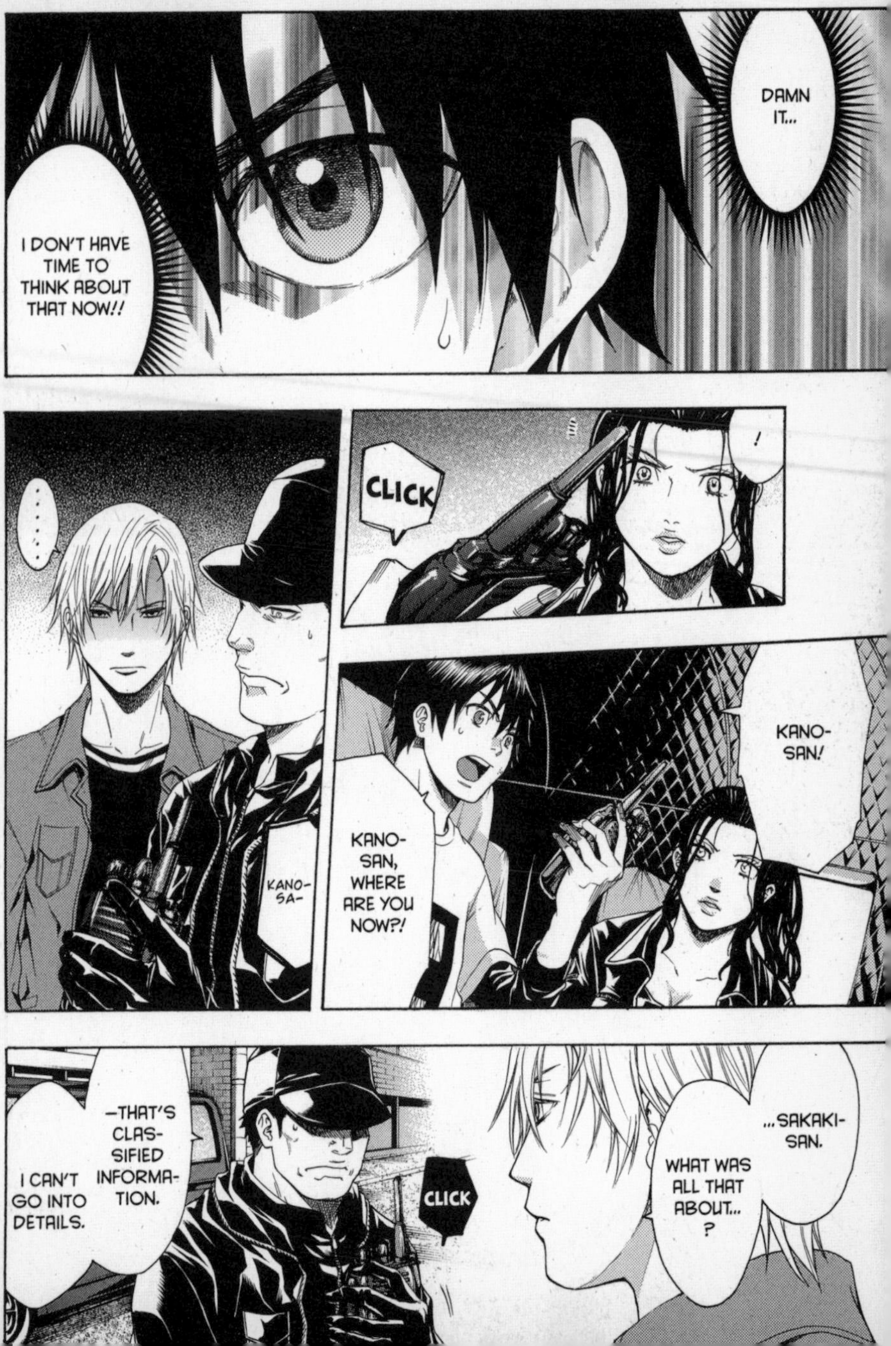
DAMN IT...
I DON'T HAVE TIME TO THINK ABOUT THAT NOW!!
!
CLICK
KANO-SAN!
KANO-SAN, WHERE ARE YOU NOW?!
KANO-SA-
......
...SAKAKI-SAN.
WHAT WAS ALL THAT ABOUT...?
CLICK
—THAT'S CLAS-SIFIED INFORMA-TION.
I CAN'T GO INTO DETAILS.

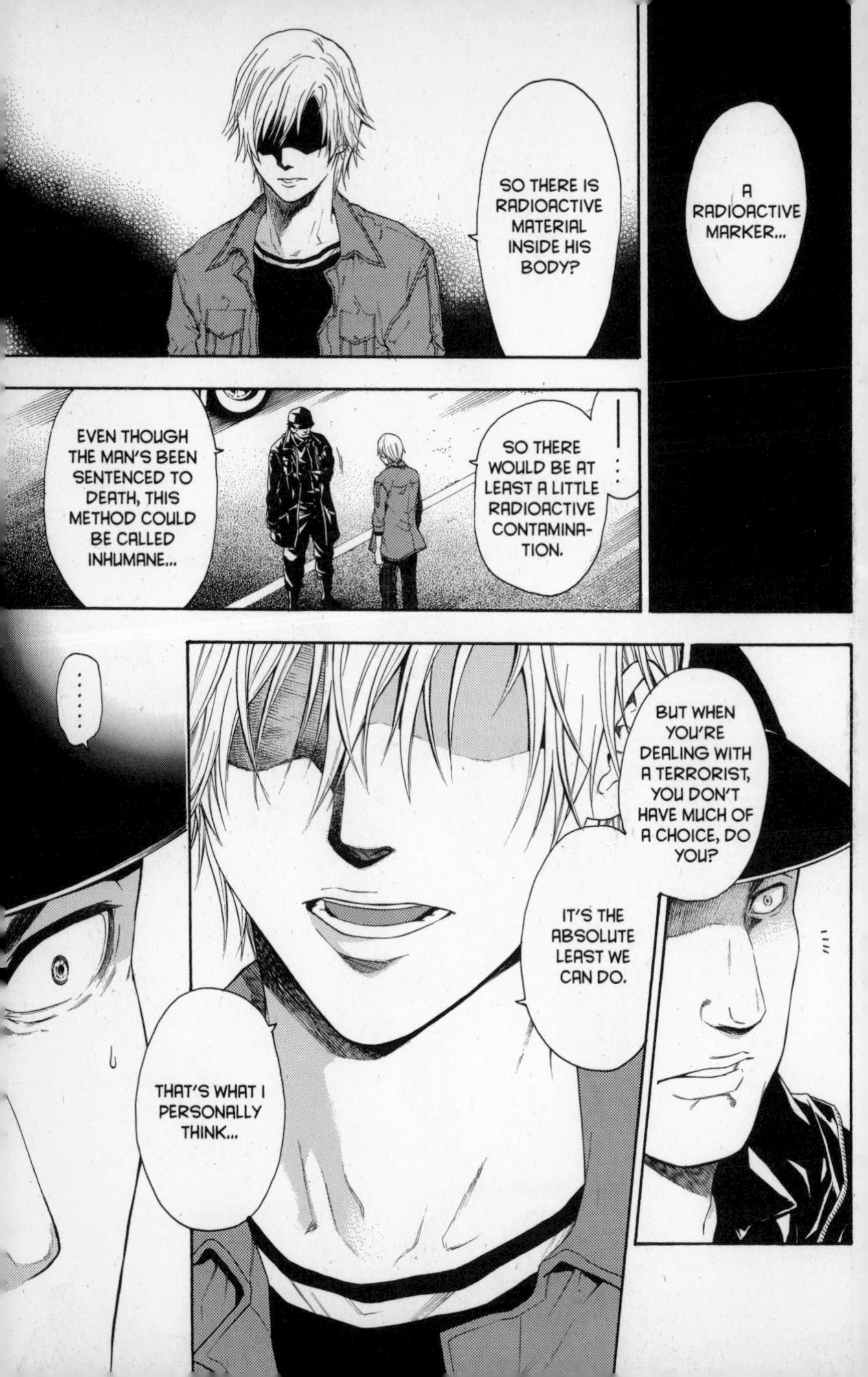
A RADIOACTIVE MARKER...
SO THERE IS RADIOACTIVE MATERIAL INSIDE HIS BODY?
SO THERE WOULD BE AT LEAST A LITTLE RADIOACTIVE CONTAMINATION.
EVEN THOUGH THE MAN'S BEEN SENTENCED TO DEATH, THIS METHOD COULD BE CALLED INHUMANE...
BUT WHEN YOU'RE DEALING WITH A TERRORIST, YOU DON'T HAVE MUCH OF A CHOICE, DO YOU?
IT'S THE ABSOLUTE LEAST WE CAN DO.
......
THAT'S WHAT I PERSONALLY THINK...

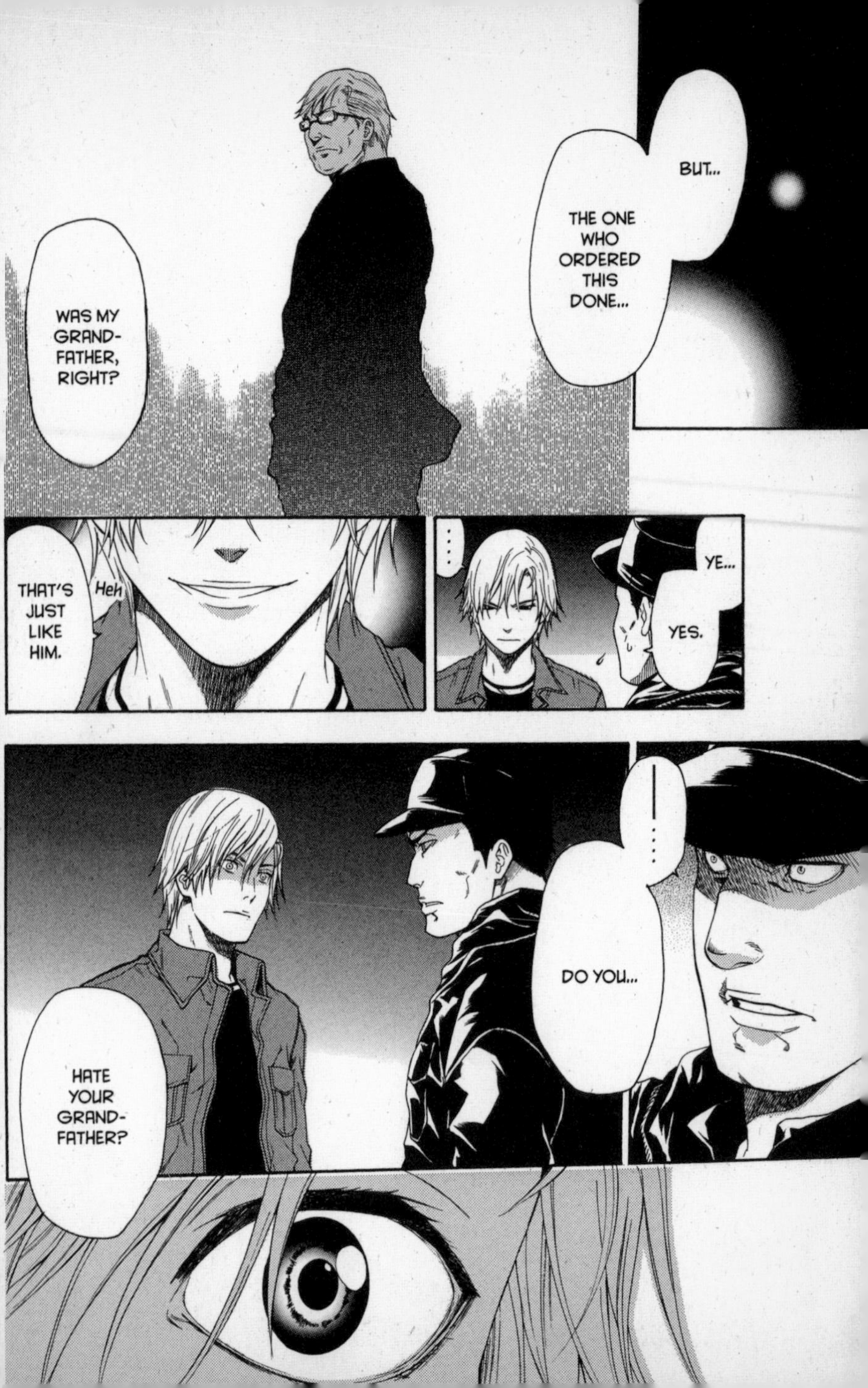
BUT...
THE ONE WHO ORDERED THIS DONE...
WAS MY GRAND-FATHER, RIGHT?
....
YE...
YES.
Heh
THAT'S JUST LIKE HIM.
!....
DO YOU...
HATE YOUR GRAND-FATHER?

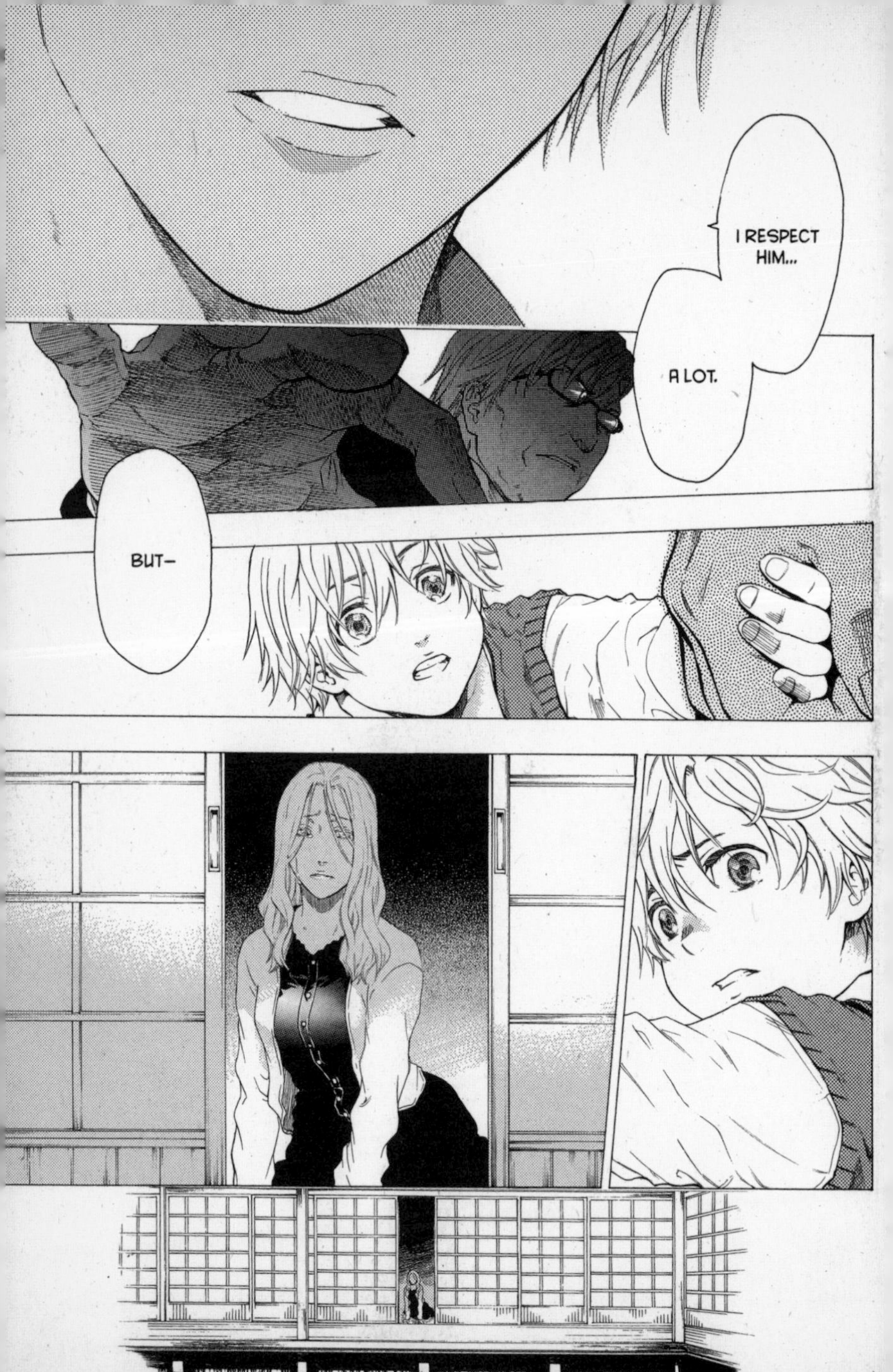
I RESPECT HIM...
A LOT.
BUT-

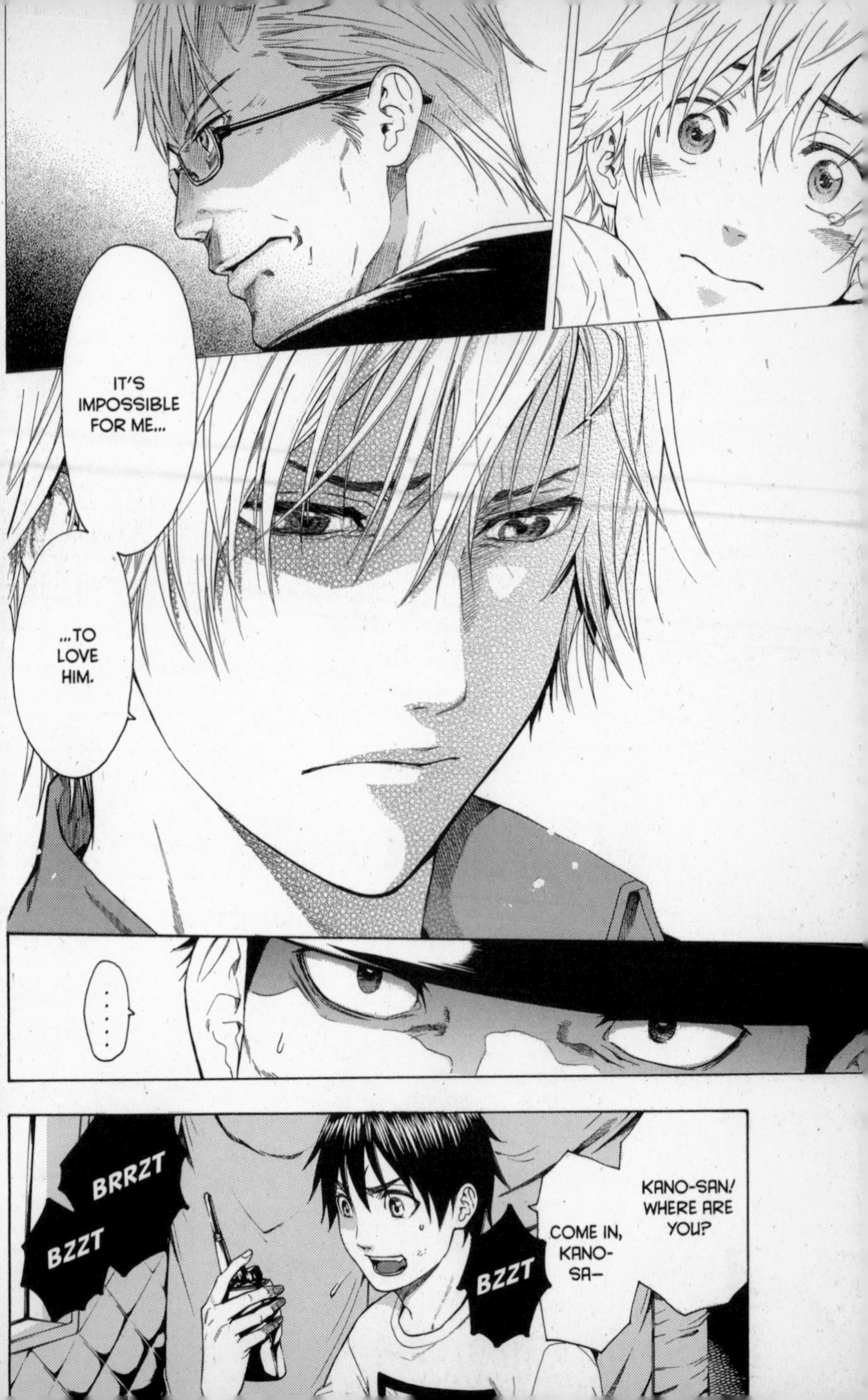
IT'S IMPOSSIBLE FOR ME...
...TO LOVE HIM.
......
KANO-SAN! WHERE ARE YOU?
COME IN, KANO-SA—
BZZT
BRRZT
BZZT

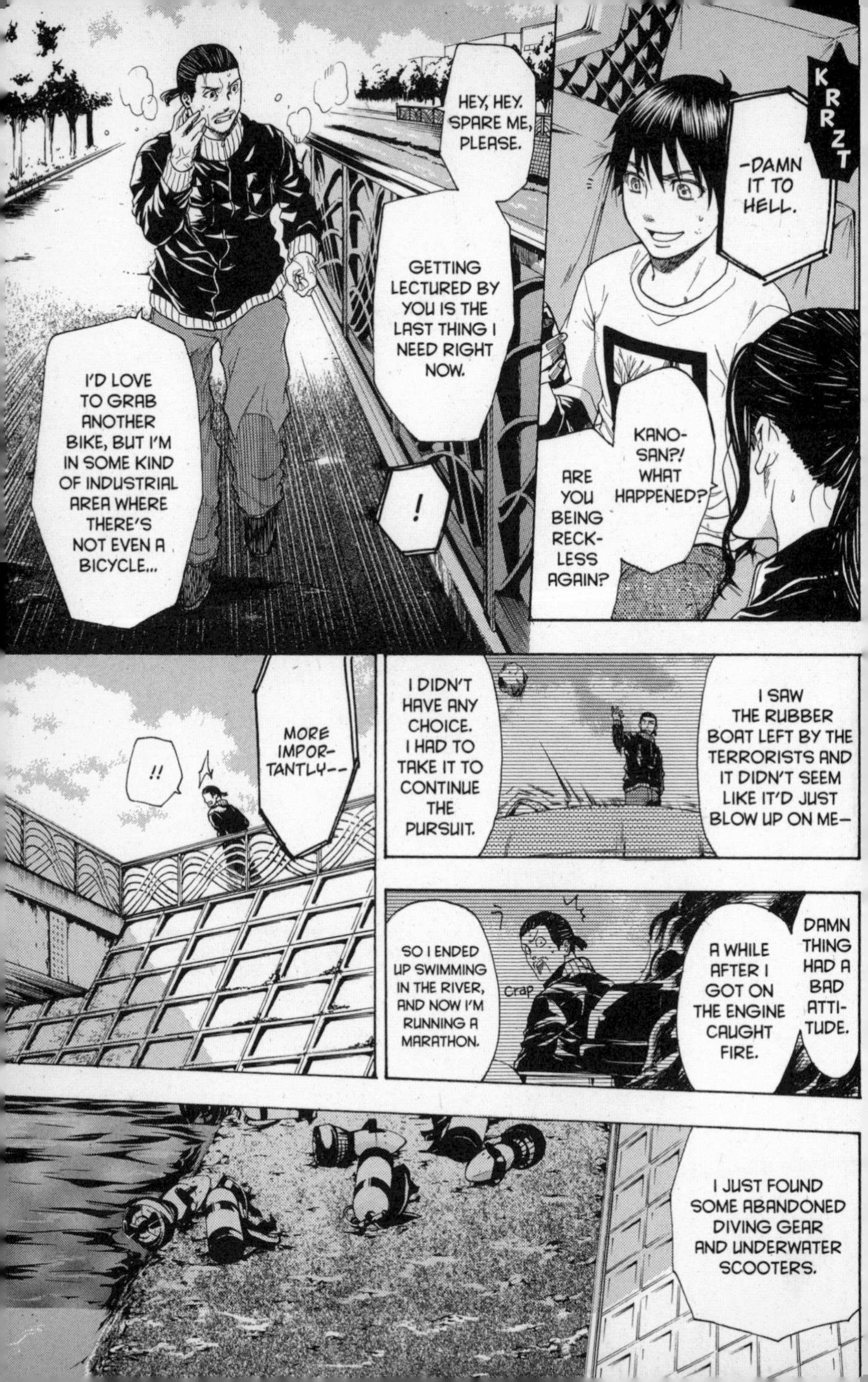
KRRZT
-DAMN IT TO HELL.
KANO-SAN?! WHAT HAPPENED?
ARE YOU BEING RECK-LESS AGAIN?
HEY, HEY. SPARE ME, PLEASE.
GETTING LECTURED BY YOU IS THE LAST THING I NEED RIGHT NOW.
I'D LOVE TO GRAB ANOTHER BIKE, BUT I'M IN SOME KIND OF INDUSTRIAL AREA WHERE THERE'S NOT EVEN A BICYCLE...
!
I SAW THE RUBBER BOAT LEFT BY THE TERRORISTS AND IT DIDN'T SEEM LIKE IT'D JUST BLOW UP ON ME—
I DIDN'T HAVE ANY CHOICE. I HAD TO TAKE IT TO CONTINUE THE PURSUIT.
DAMN THING HAD A BAD ATTI-TUDE.
A WHILE AFTER I GOT ON THE ENGINE CAUGHT FIRE.
Crap
SO I ENDED UP SWIMMING IN THE RIVER, AND NOW I'M RUNNING A MARATHON.
MORE IMPOR-TANTLY--
!!
I JUST FOUND SOME ABANDONED DIVING GEAR AND UNDERWATER SCOOTERS.

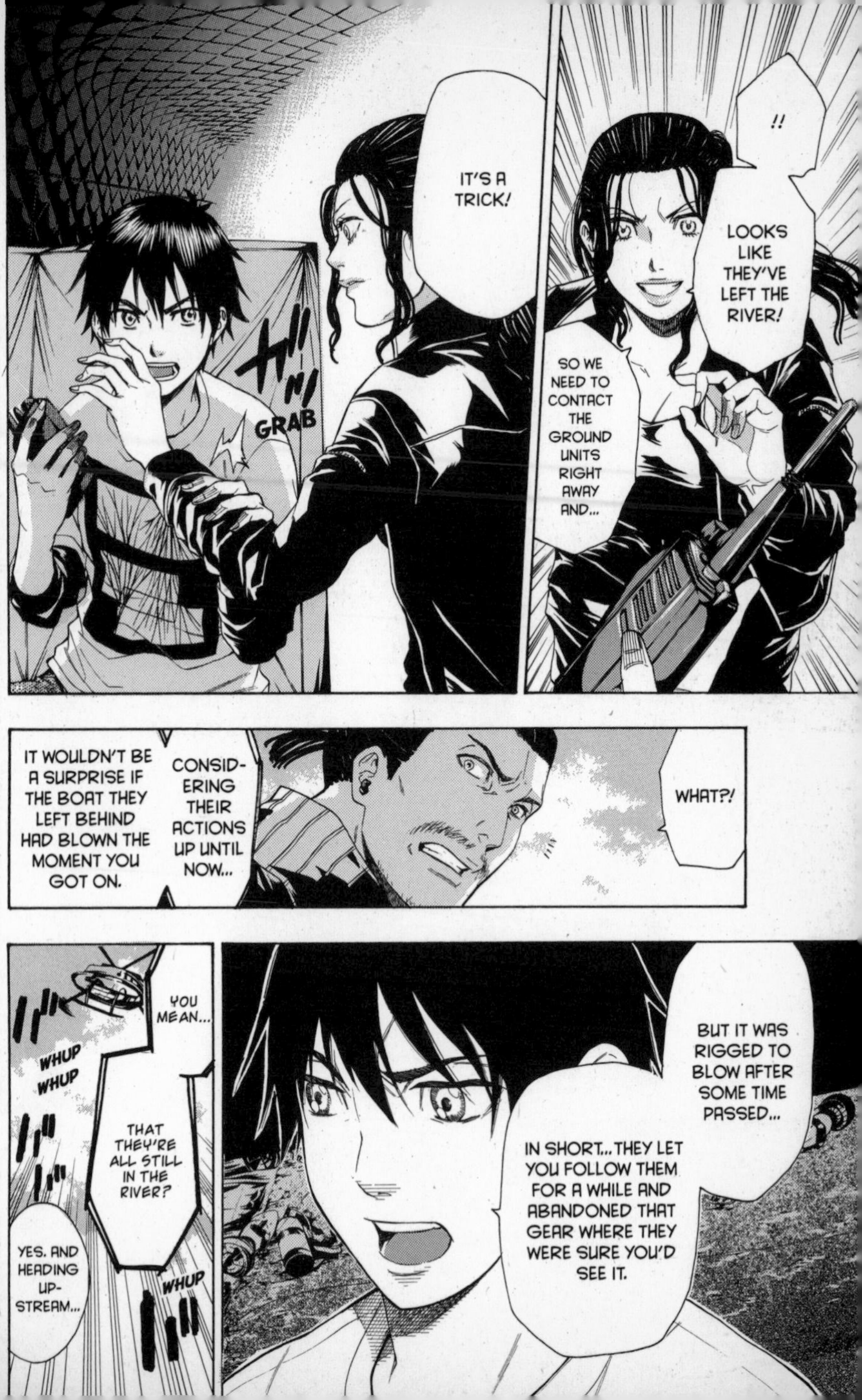
!!
LOOKS LIKE THEY'VE LEFT THE RIVER!
SO WE NEED TO CONTACT THE GROUND UNITS RIGHT AWAY AND...
IT'S A TRICK!
GRAB
WHAT?!
CONSID-ERING THEIR ACTIONS UP UNTIL NOW...
IT WOULDN'T BE A SURPRISE IF THE BOAT THEY LEFT BEHIND HAD BLOWN THE MOMENT YOU GOT ON.
BUT IT WAS RIGGED TO BLOW AFTER SOME TIME PASSED...
IN SHORT... THEY LET YOU FOLLOW THEM FOR A WHILE AND ABANDONED THAT GEAR WHERE THEY WERE SURE YOU'D SEE IT.
YOU MEAN...
WHUP
WHUP
THAT THEY'RE ALL STILL IN THE RIVER?
YES. AND HEADING UP-STREAM...
WHUP

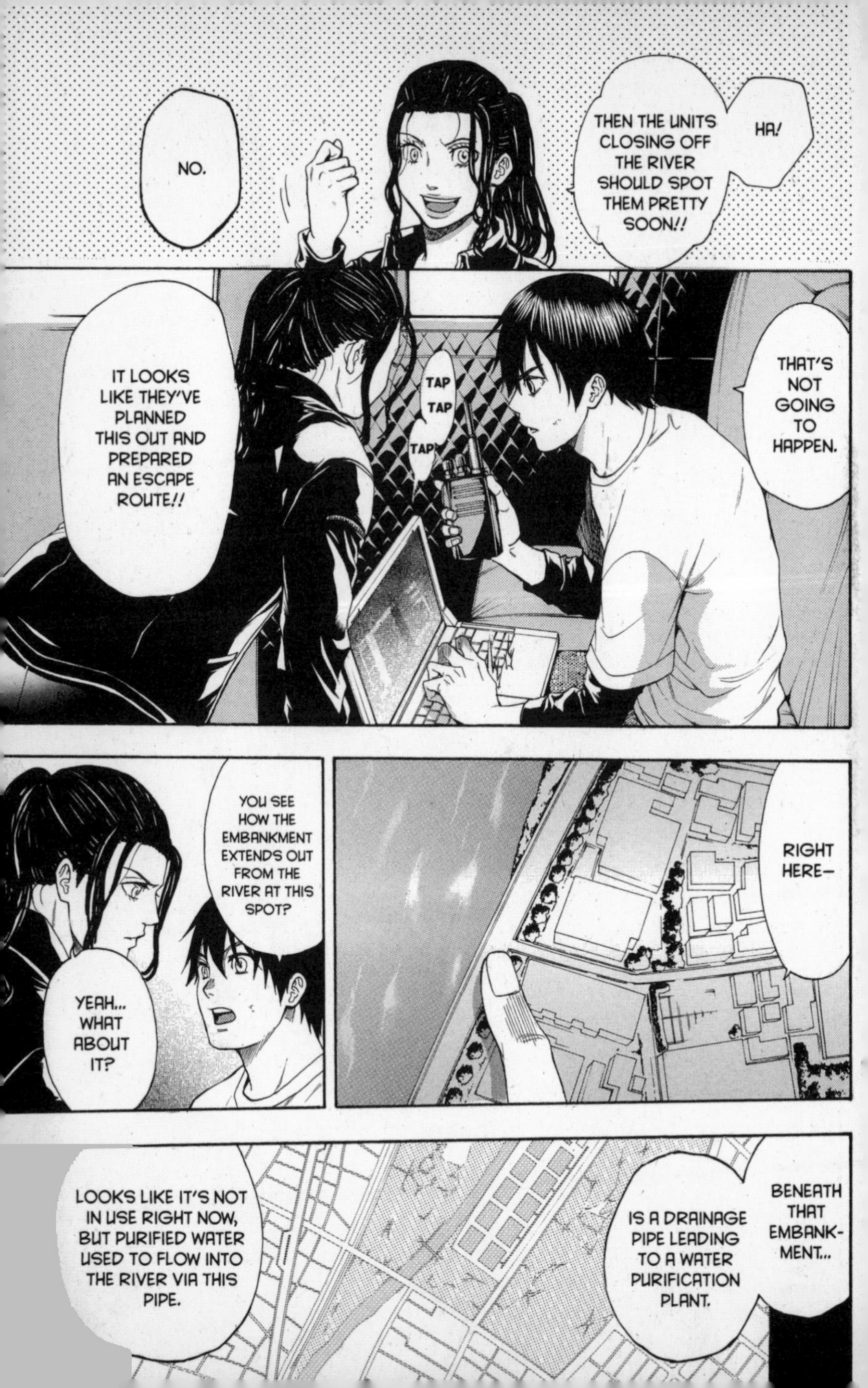
HA!
THEN THE UNITS CLOSING OFF THE RIVER SHOULD SPOT THEM PRETTY SOON!!
NO.
THAT'S NOT GOING TO HAPPEN.
TAP
TAP
TAP
IT LOOKS LIKE THEY'VE PLANNED THIS OUT AND PREPARED AN ESCAPE ROUTE!!
RIGHT HERE—
YOU SEE HOW THE EMBANKMENT EXTENDS OUT FROM THE RIVER AT THIS SPOT?
YEAH... WHAT ABOUT IT?
BENEATH THAT EMBANK-MENT...
IS A DRAINAGE PIPE LEADING TO A WATER PURIFICATION PLANT.
LOOKS LIKE IT'S NOT IN USE RIGHT NOW, BUT PURIFIED WATER USED TO FLOW INTO THE RIVER VIA THIS PIPE.

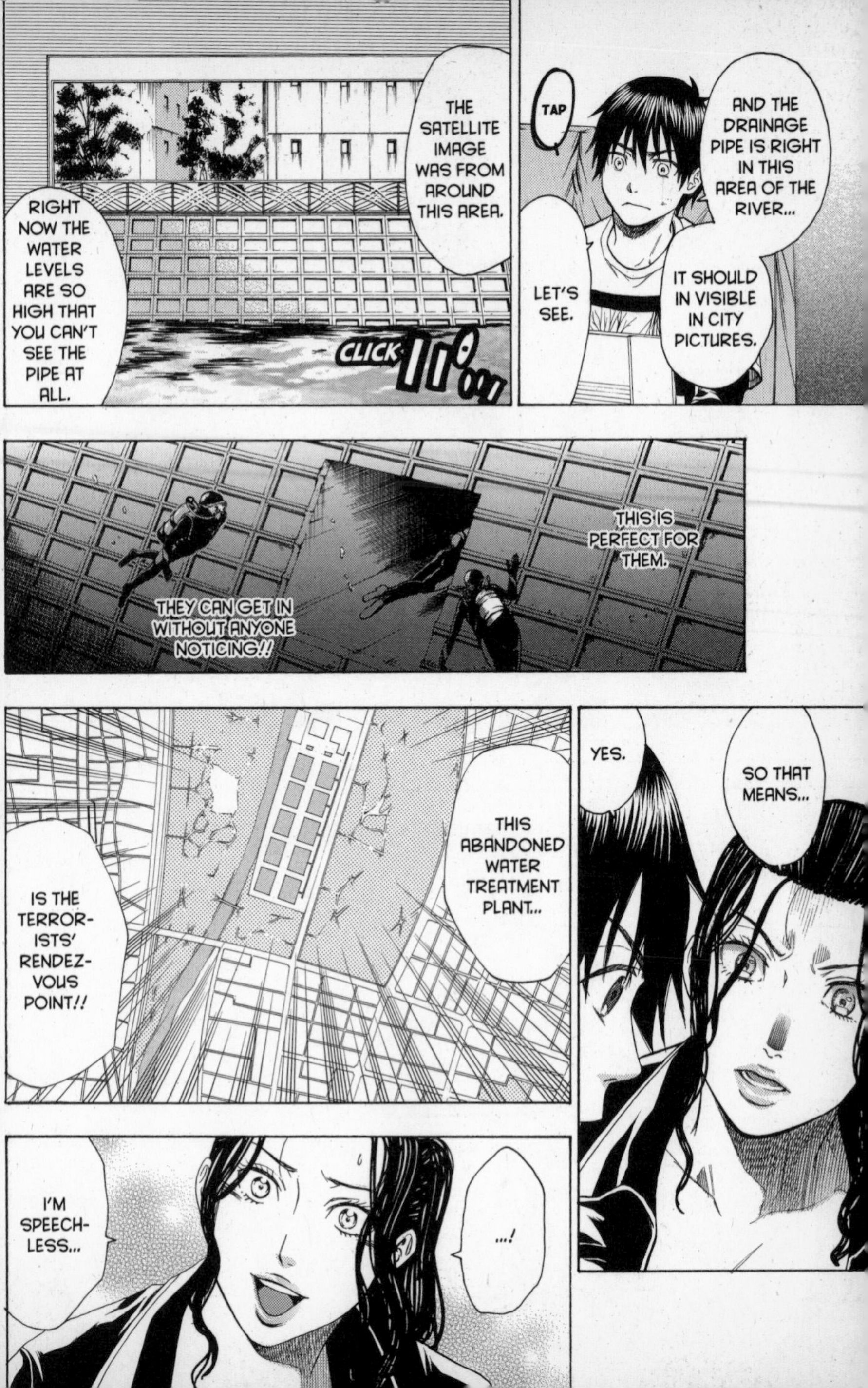
AND THE DRAINAGE PIPE IS RIGHT IN THIS AREA OF THE RIVER...
IT SHOULD IN VISIBLE IN CITY PICTURES.
TAP
LET'S SEE.
THE SATELLITE IMAGE WAS FROM AROUND THIS AREA.
CLICK
RIGHT NOW THE WATER LEVELS ARE SO HIGH THAT YOU CAN'T SEE THE PIPE AT ALL.
THIS IS PERFECT FOR THEM.
THEY CAN GET IN WITHOUT ANYONE NOTICING!!
SO THAT MEANS...
YES.
THIS ABANDONED WATER TREATMENT PLANT...
IS THE TERRORISTS' RENDEZVOUS POINT!!
...!
I'M SPEECHLESS...

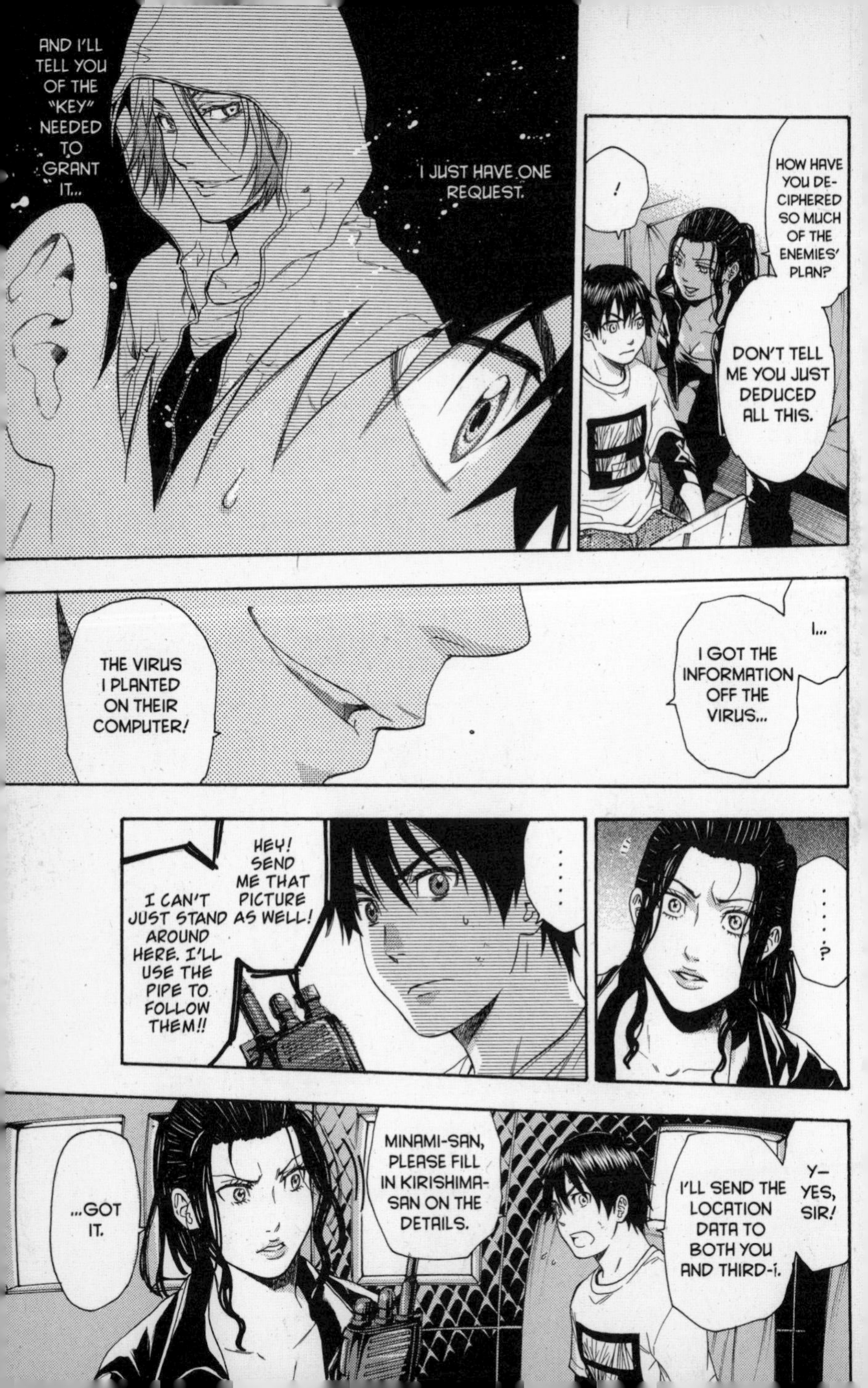
!
HOW HAVE YOU DECIPHERED SO MUCH OF THE ENEMIES' PLAN?
DON'T TELL ME YOU JUST DEDUCED ALL THIS.
I JUST HAVE ONE REQUEST.
AND I'LL TELL YOU OF THE "KEY" NEEDED TO GRANT IT...
I...
I GOT THE INFORMATION OFF THE VIRUS...
THE VIRUS I PLANTED ON THEIR COMPUTER!
......?
......
HEY! SEND ME THAT PICTURE AS WELL!
I CAN'T JUST STAND AROUND HERE. I'LL USE THE PIPE TO FOLLOW THEM!!
Y—YES, SIR!
I'LL SEND THE LOCATION DATA TO BOTH YOU AND THIRD-i.
MINAMI-SAN, PLEASE FILL IN KIRISHIMA-SAN ON THE DETAILS.
...GOT IT.

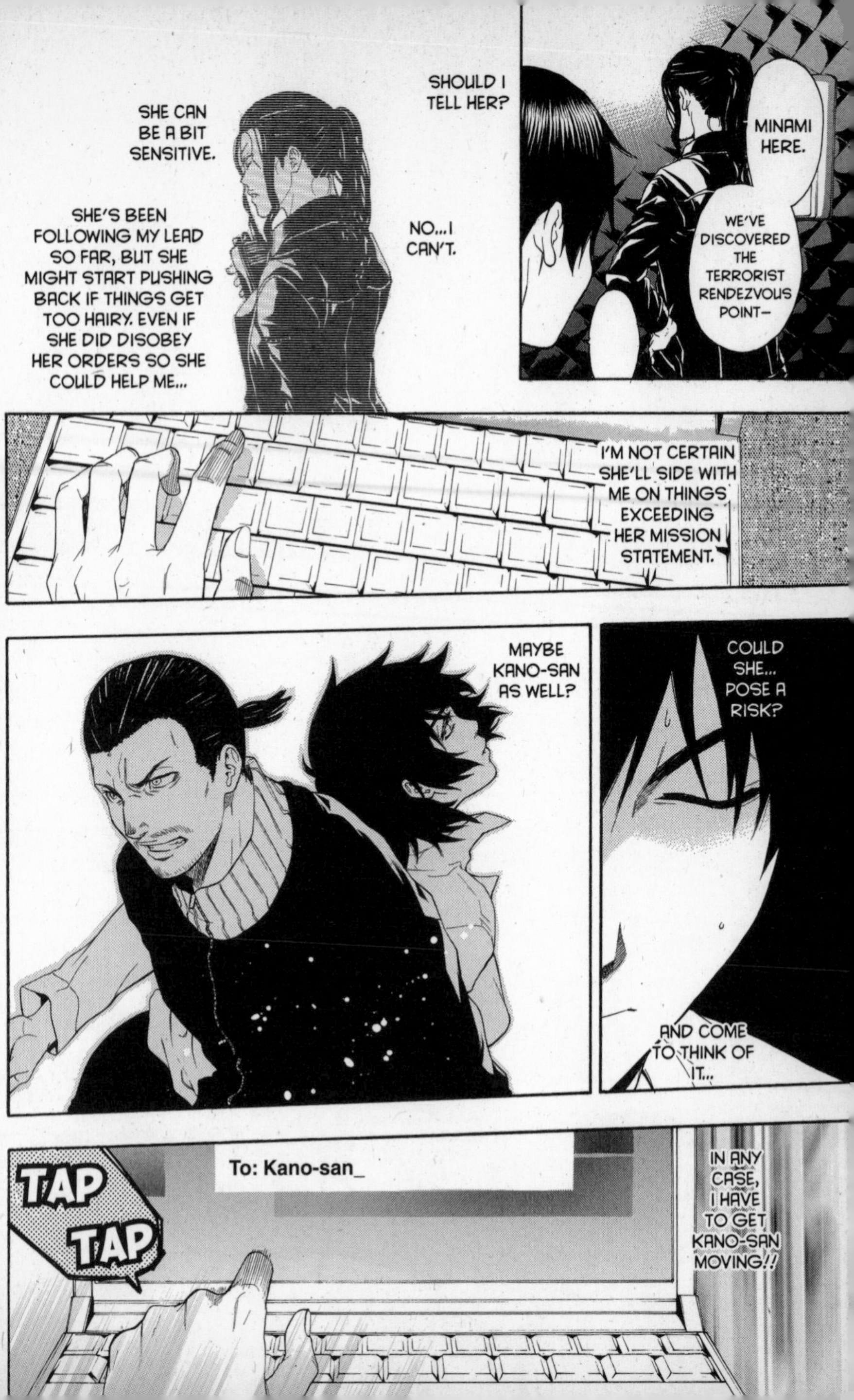
MINAMI HERE.
WE'VE DISCOVERED THE TERRORIST RENDEZVOUS POINT—
SHOULD I TELL HER?
NO...I CAN'T.
SHE CAN BE A BIT SENSITIVE.
SHE'S BEEN FOLLOWING MY LEAD SO FAR, BUT SHE MIGHT START PUSHING BACK IF THINGS GET TOO HAIRY. EVEN IF SHE DID DISOBEY HER ORDERS SO SHE COULD HELP ME...
I'M NOT CERTAIN SHE'LL SIDE WITH ME ON THINGS EXCEEDING HER MISSION STATEMENT.
COULD SHE... POSE A RISK?
AND COME TO THINK OF IT...
MAYBE KANO-SAN AS WELL?
IN ANY CASE, I HAVE TO GET KANO-SAN MOVING!!
To: Kano-san_
TAP
TAP

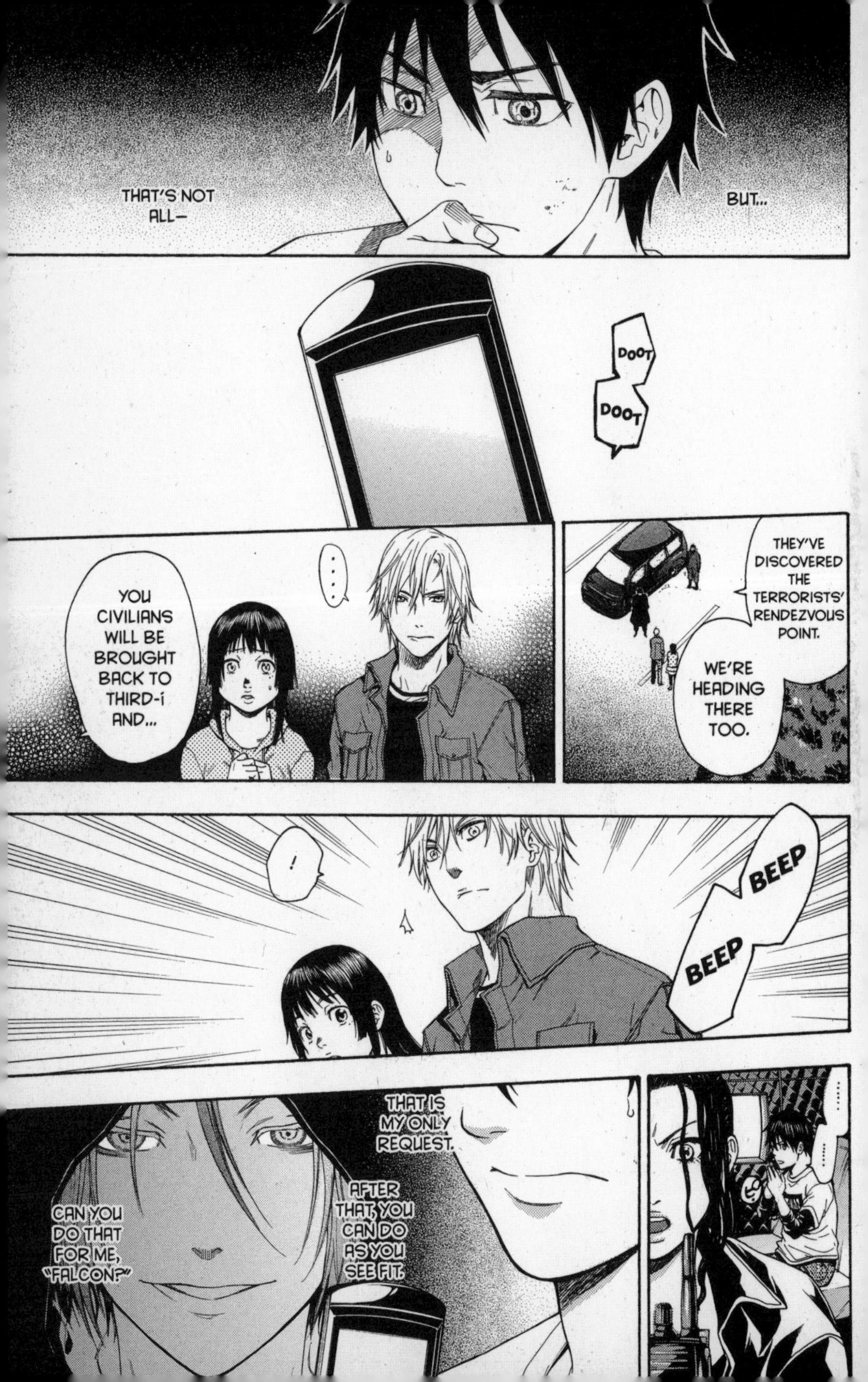
BUT...
THAT'S NOT ALL—
DOOT
DOOT
THEY'VE DISCOVERED THE TERRORISTS' RENDEZVOUS POINT.
WE'RE HEADING THERE TOO.
....
YOU CIVILIANS WILL BE BROUGHT BACK TO THIRD-i AND...
BEEP
BEEP
!
THAT IS MY ONLY REQUEST.
AFTER THAT, YOU CAN DO AS YOU SEE FIT.
CAN YOU DO THAT FOR ME, "FALCON?"

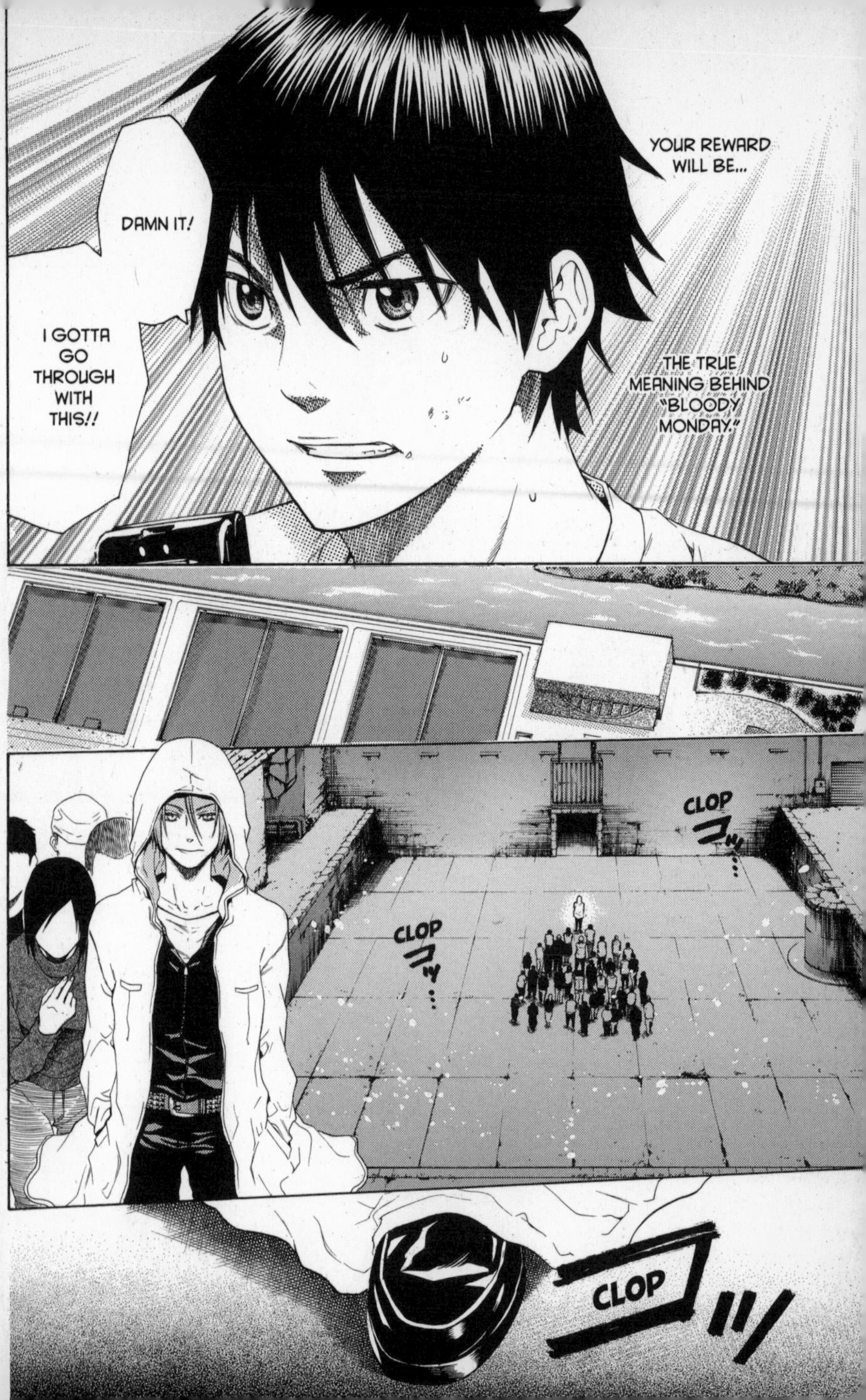
YOUR REWARD WILL BE...
THE TRUE MEANING BEHIND "BLOODY MONDAY."
DAMN IT!
I GOTTA GO THROUGH WITH THIS!!
CLOP
CLOP
CLOP

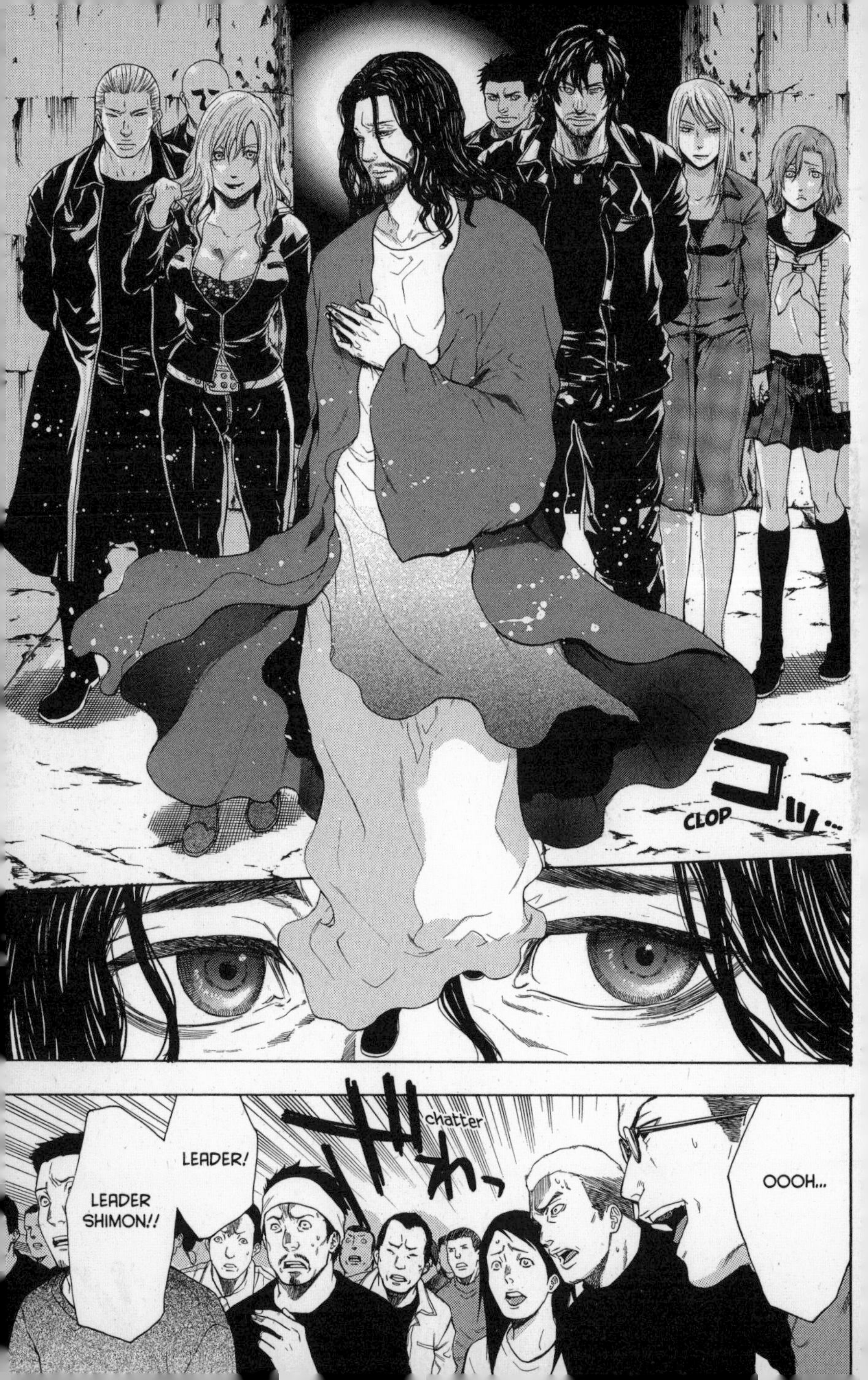
CLOP
OOOH...
chatter
LEADER!
LEADER SHIMON!!

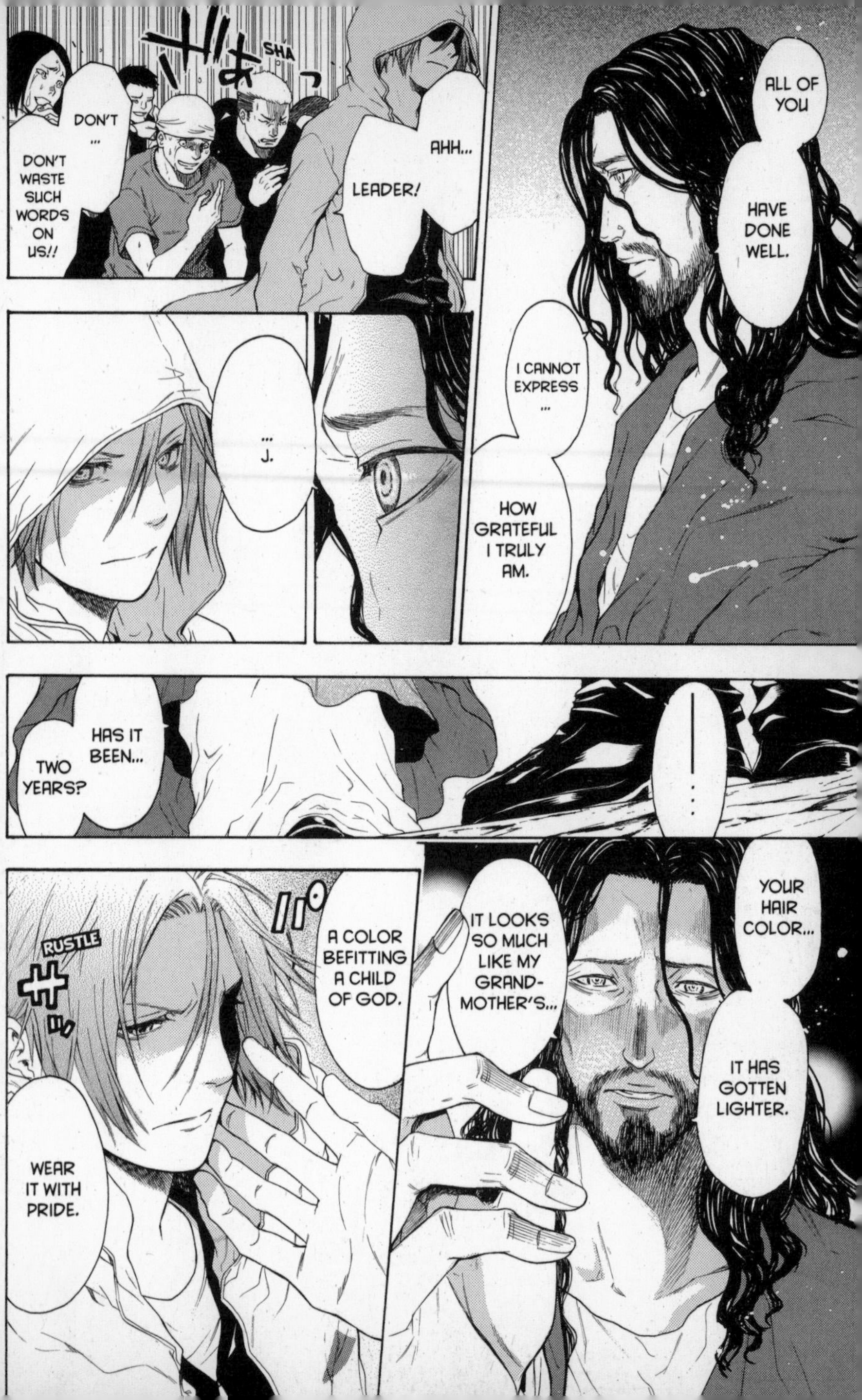
ALL OF YOU
HAVE DONE WELL.
I CANNOT EXPRESS ...
HOW GRATEFUL I TRULY AM.
SHA
AHH... LEADER!
DON'T ...
DON'T WASTE SUCH WORDS ON US!!
... J.
—— ...
HAS IT BEEN...
TWO YEARS?
YOUR HAIR COLOR...
IT HAS GOTTEN LIGHTER.
IT LOOKS SO MUCH LIKE MY GRAND-MOTHER'S...
A COLOR BEFITTING A CHILD OF GOD.
RUSTLE
WEAR IT WITH PRIDE.

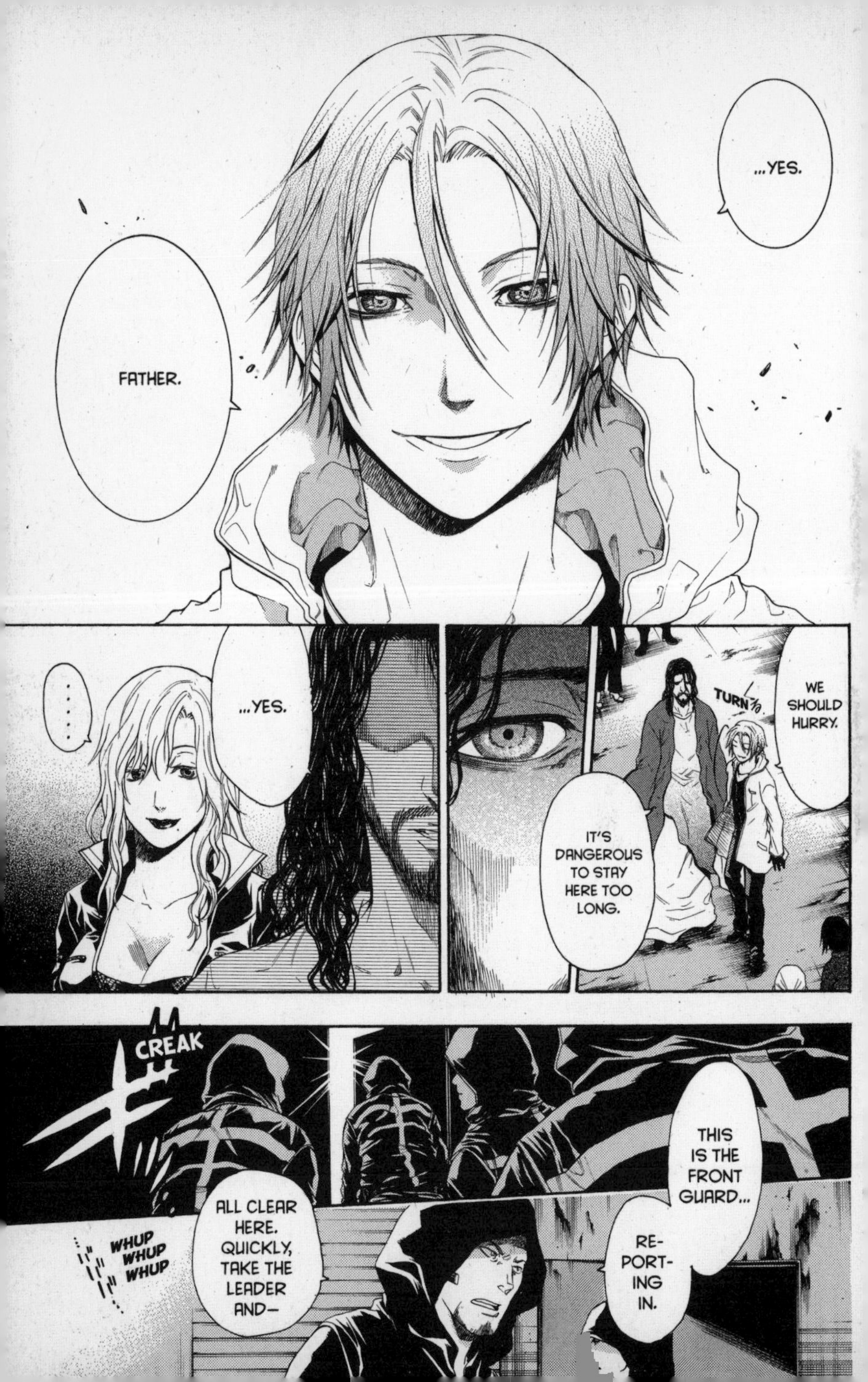
...YES.
FATHER.
WE SHOULD HURRY.
TURN
IT'S DANGEROUS TO STAY HERE TOO LONG.
...YES.
.....
THIS IS THE FRONT GUARD...
RE-PORT-ING IN.
CREAK
ALL CLEAR HERE. QUICKLY, TAKE THE LEADER AND—
WHUP WHUP WHUP

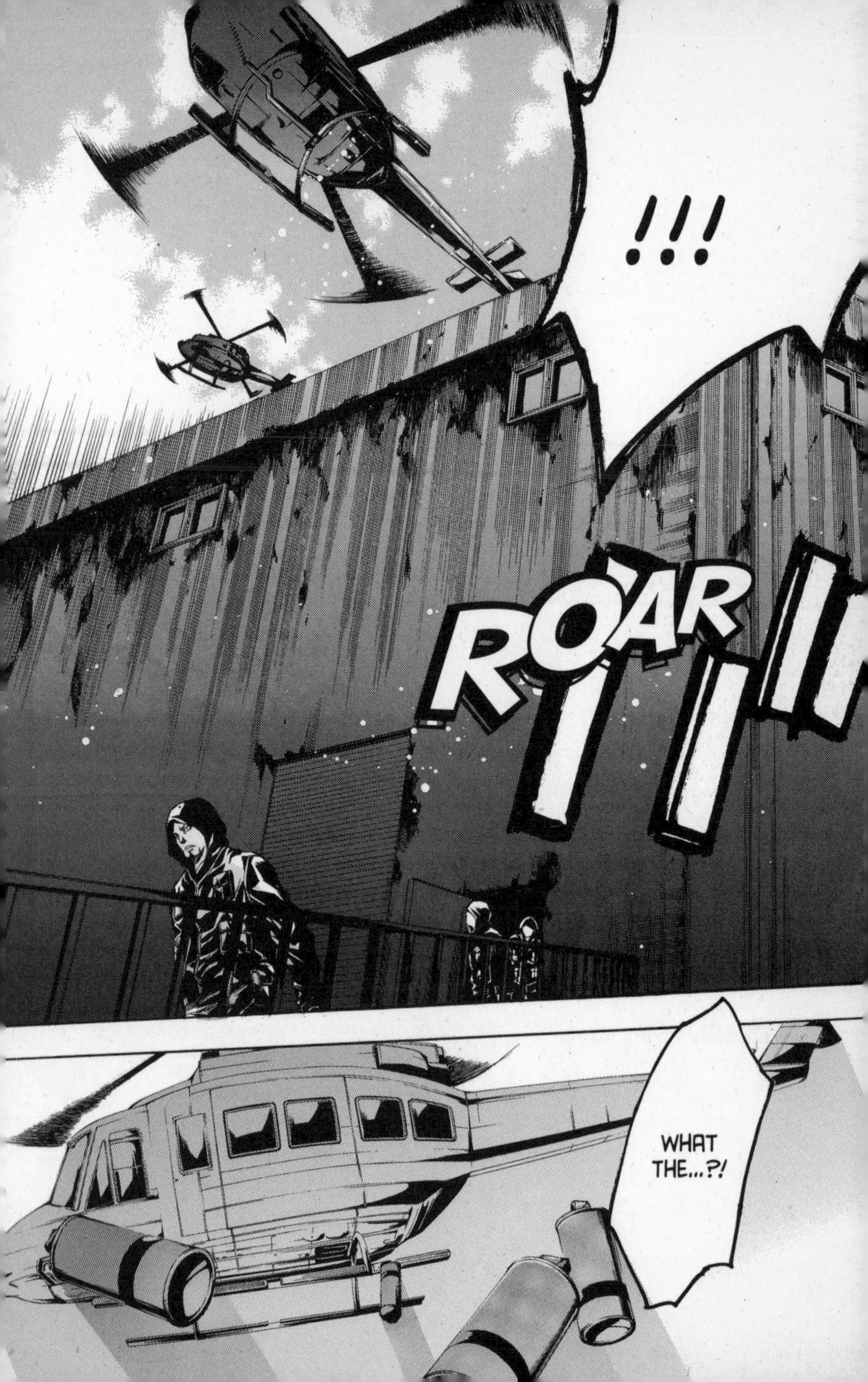
!!!
ROAR
WHAT THE...?!

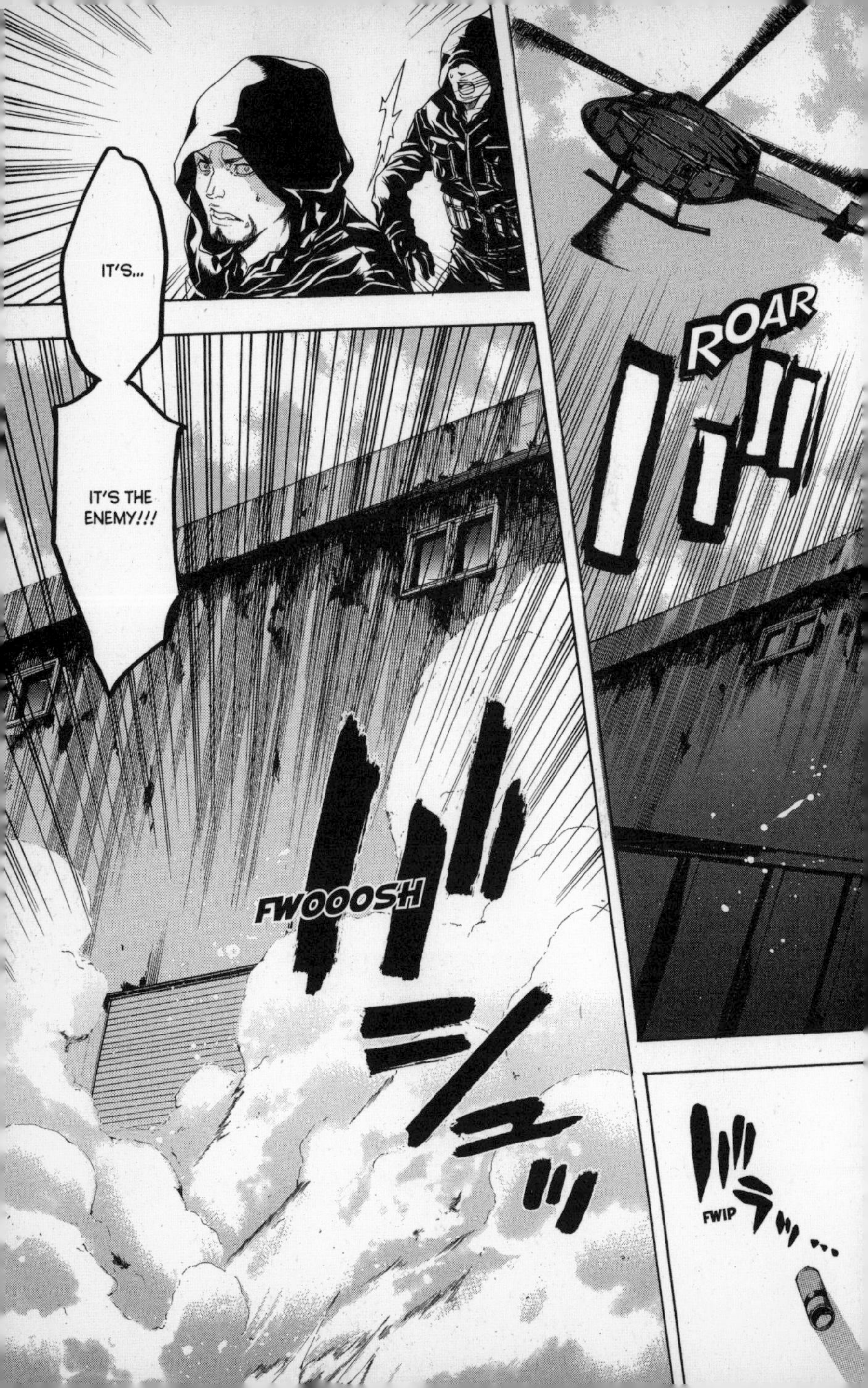
ROAR
IT'S...
IT'S THE ENEMY!!!
FWOOOSH
FWIP

Low-power radio transceiver
A form of short range, wireless radio communication that does not require special qualification, license or registry. The Ministry of Internal Affairs determines the equipment specs. There are no restrictions on who can use these transceivers.

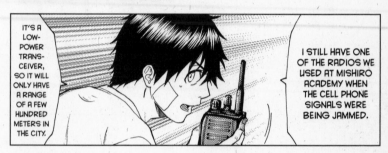

I STILL HAVE ONE OF THE RADIOS WE USED AT MISHIRO ACADEMY WHEN THE CELL PHONE SIGNALS WERE BEING JAMMED.
IT'S A LOW-POWER TRANS-CEIVER, SO IT WILL ONLY HAVE A RANGE OF A FEW HUNDRED METERS IN THE CITY.

Stealth Virus
A computer virus that operates secretly, avoiding detection by the user and antivirus software. A stealth virus operates by hiding in the memory of the computer and redirecting files to a storage area.

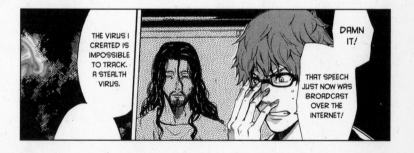

DAMN IT!
THAT SPEECH JUST NOW WAS BROADCAST OVER THE INTERNET!
THE VIRUS I CREATED IS IMPOSSIBLE TO TRACK. A STEALTH VIRUS.

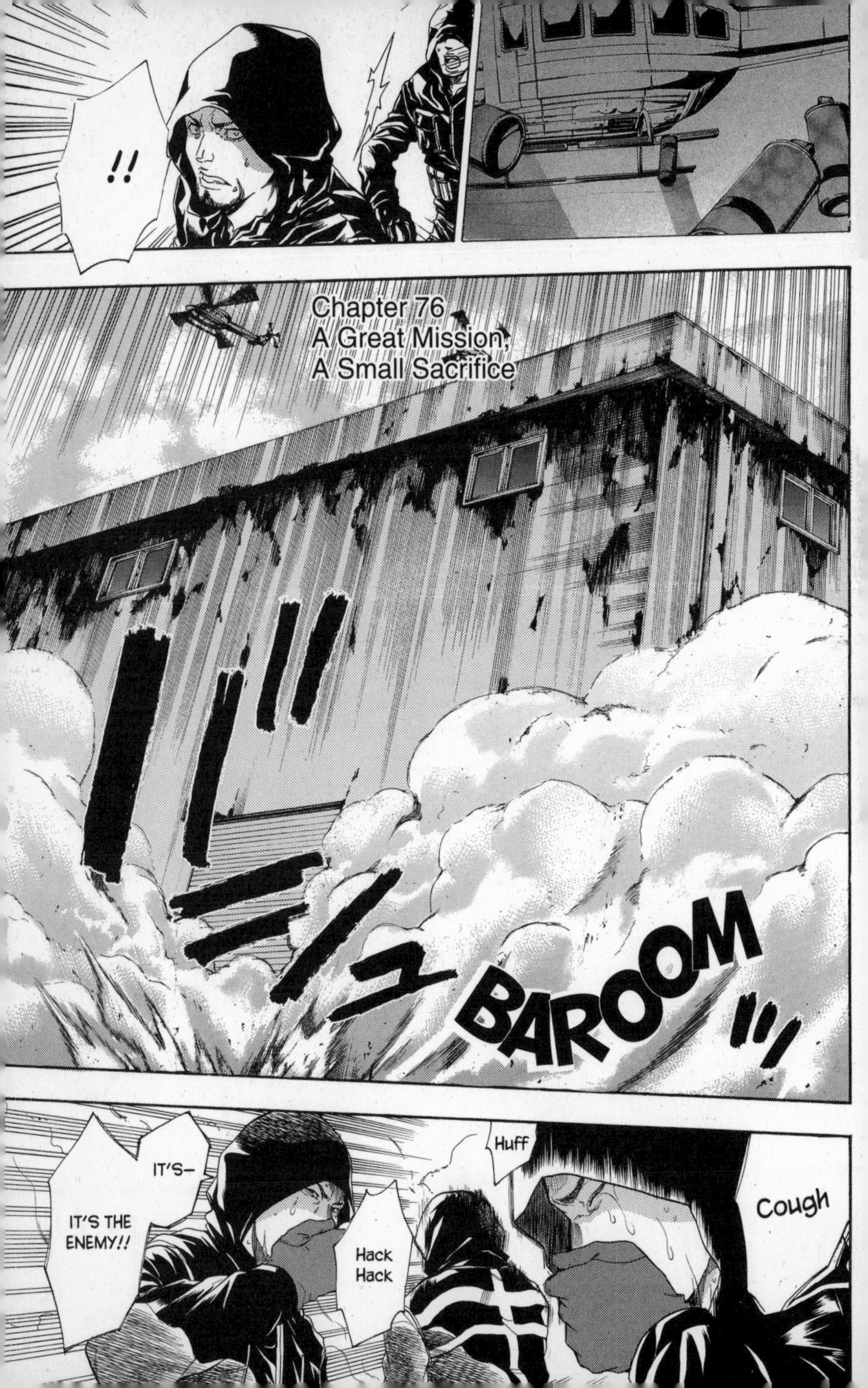
!!
Chapter 76
A Great Mission,
A Small Sacrifice
BAROOM
Cough
Huff
Hack
Hack
IT'S—
IT'S THE ENEMY!!

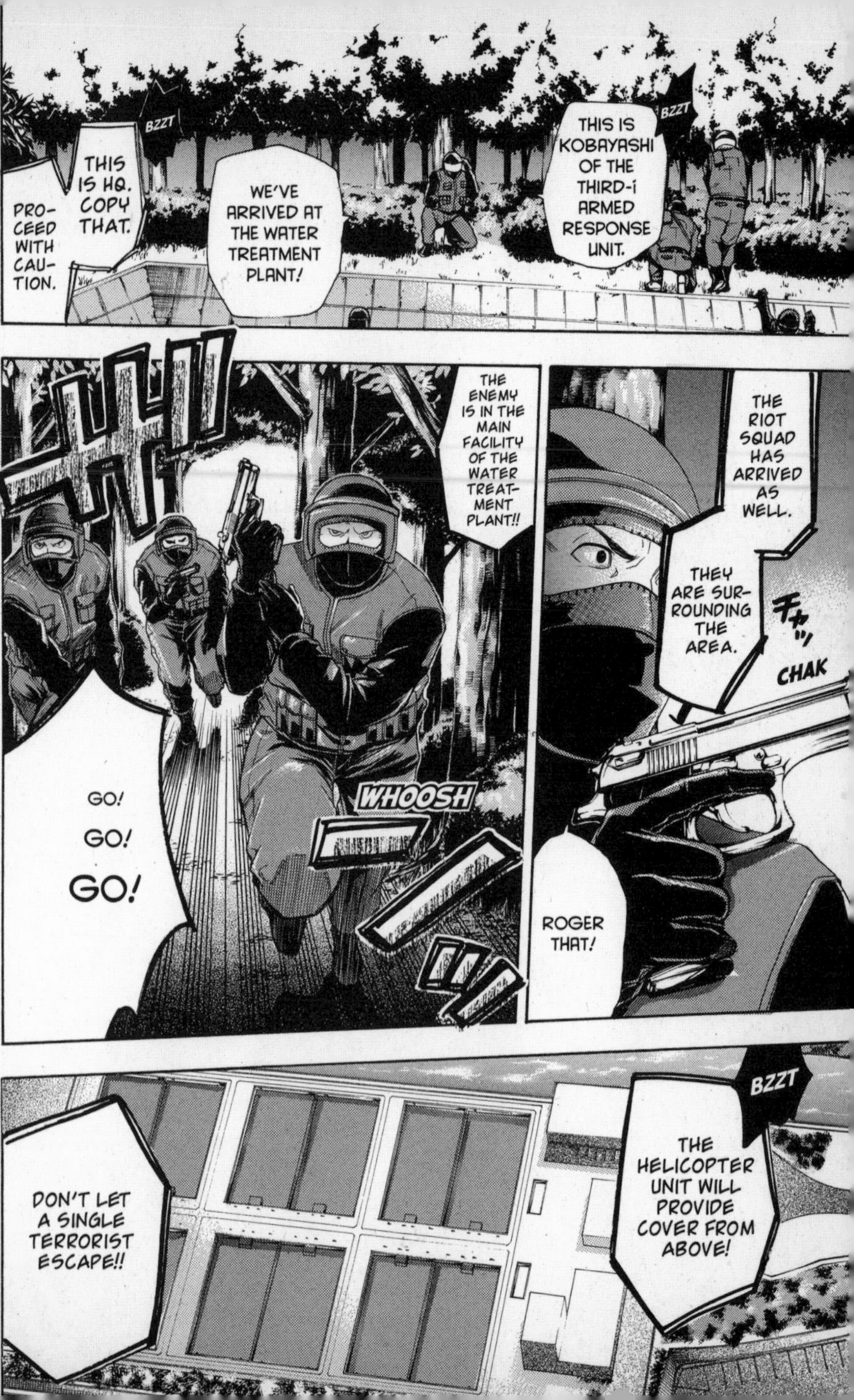
BZZT
THIS IS KOBAYASHI OF THE THIRD-i ARMED RESPONSE UNIT.
WE'VE ARRIVED AT THE WATER TREATMENT PLANT!
BZZT
THIS IS HQ. COPY THAT.
PROCEED WITH CAUTION.
THE RIOT SQUAD HAS ARRIVED AS WELL.
THEY ARE SURROUNDING THE AREA.
チャッ
CHAK
ROGER THAT!
THE ENEMY IS IN THE MAIN FACILITY OF THE WATER TREATMENT PLANT!!
WHOOSH
GO!
GO!
GO!
BZZT
THE HELICOPTER UNIT WILL PROVIDE COVER FROM ABOVE!
DON'T LET A SINGLE TERRORIST ESCAPE!!

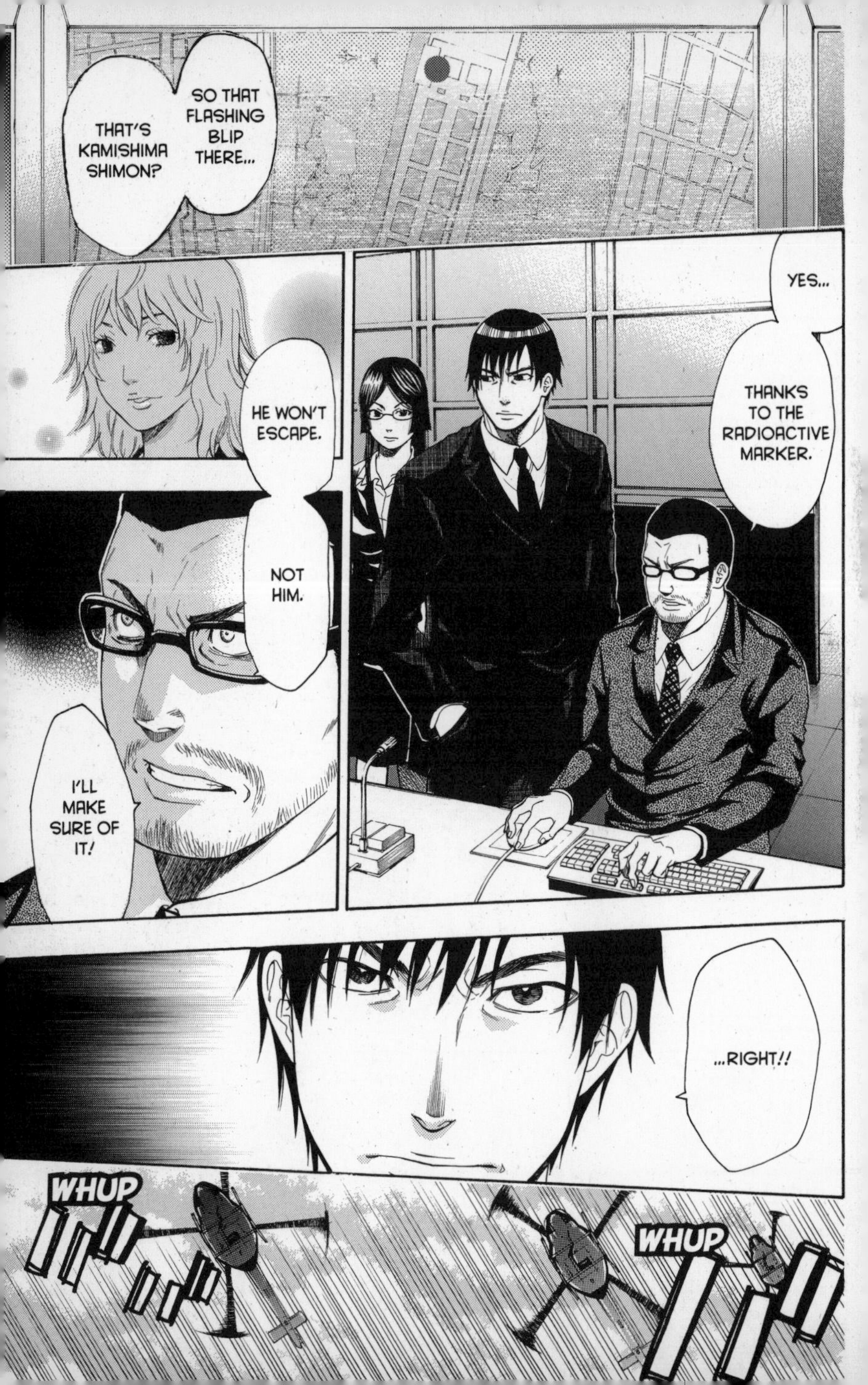
SO THAT FLASHING BLIP THERE...
THAT'S KAMISHIMA SHIMON?
YES...
THANKS TO THE RADIOACTIVE MARKER.
HE WON'T ESCAPE.
NOT HIM.
I'LL MAKE SURE OF IT!
...RIGHT!!
WHUP
WHUP

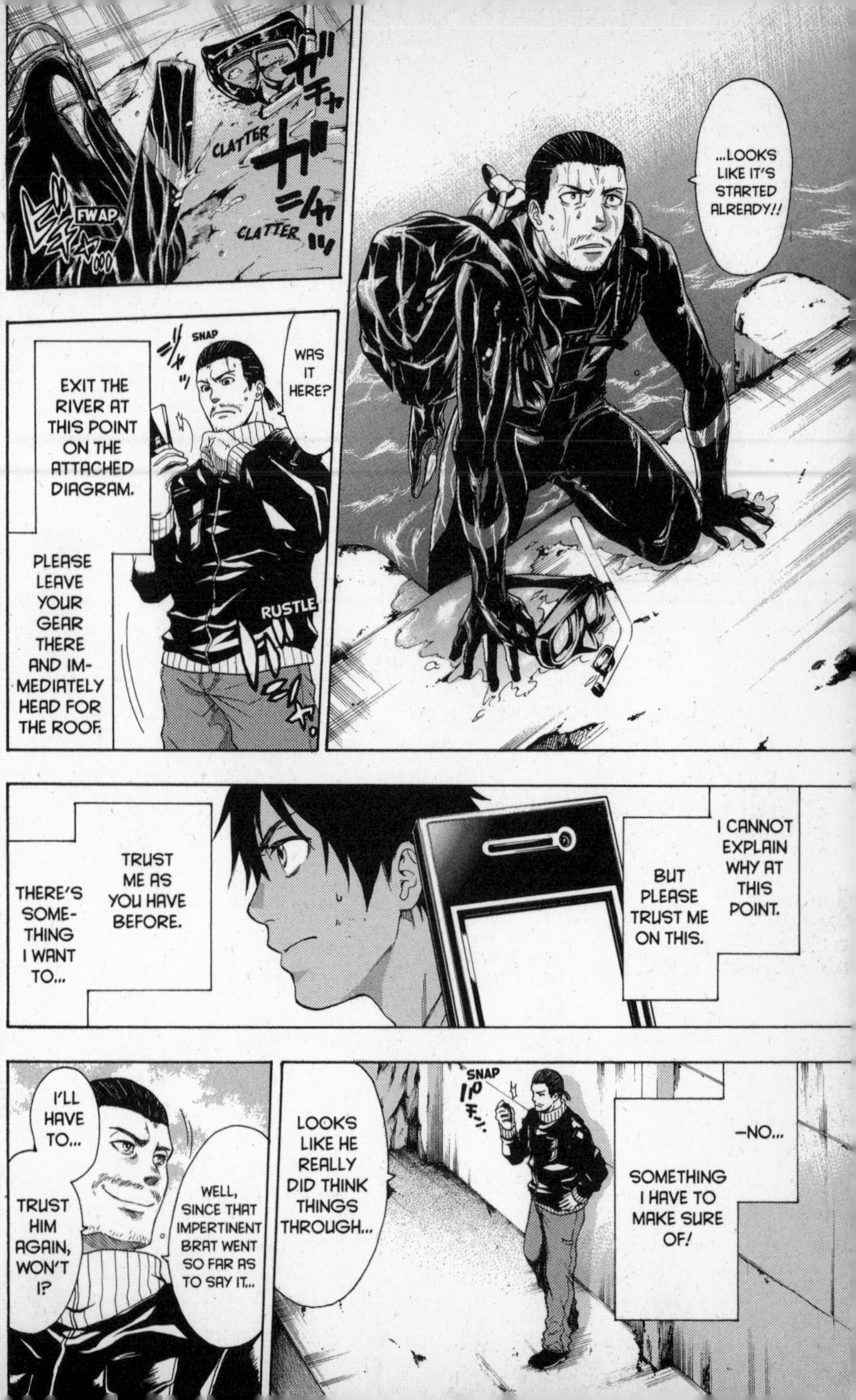
...LOOKS LIKE IT'S STARTED ALREADY!!
CLATTER
CLATTER
FWAP
SNAP
WAS IT HERE?
EXIT THE RIVER AT THIS POINT ON THE ATTACHED DIAGRAM.
PLEASE LEAVE YOUR GEAR THERE AND IM-MEDIATELY HEAD FOR THE ROOF.
RUSTLE
I CANNOT EXPLAIN WHY AT THIS POINT.
BUT PLEASE TRUST ME ON THIS.
TRUST ME AS YOU HAVE BEFORE.
THERE'S SOME-THING I WANT TO...
SNAP
—NO...
SOMETHING I HAVE TO MAKE SURE OF!
LOOKS LIKE HE REALLY DID THINK THINGS THROUGH...
WELL, SINCE THAT IMPERTINENT BRAT WENT SO FAR AS TO SAY IT...
I'LL HAVE TO...
TRUST HIM AGAIN, WON'T I?

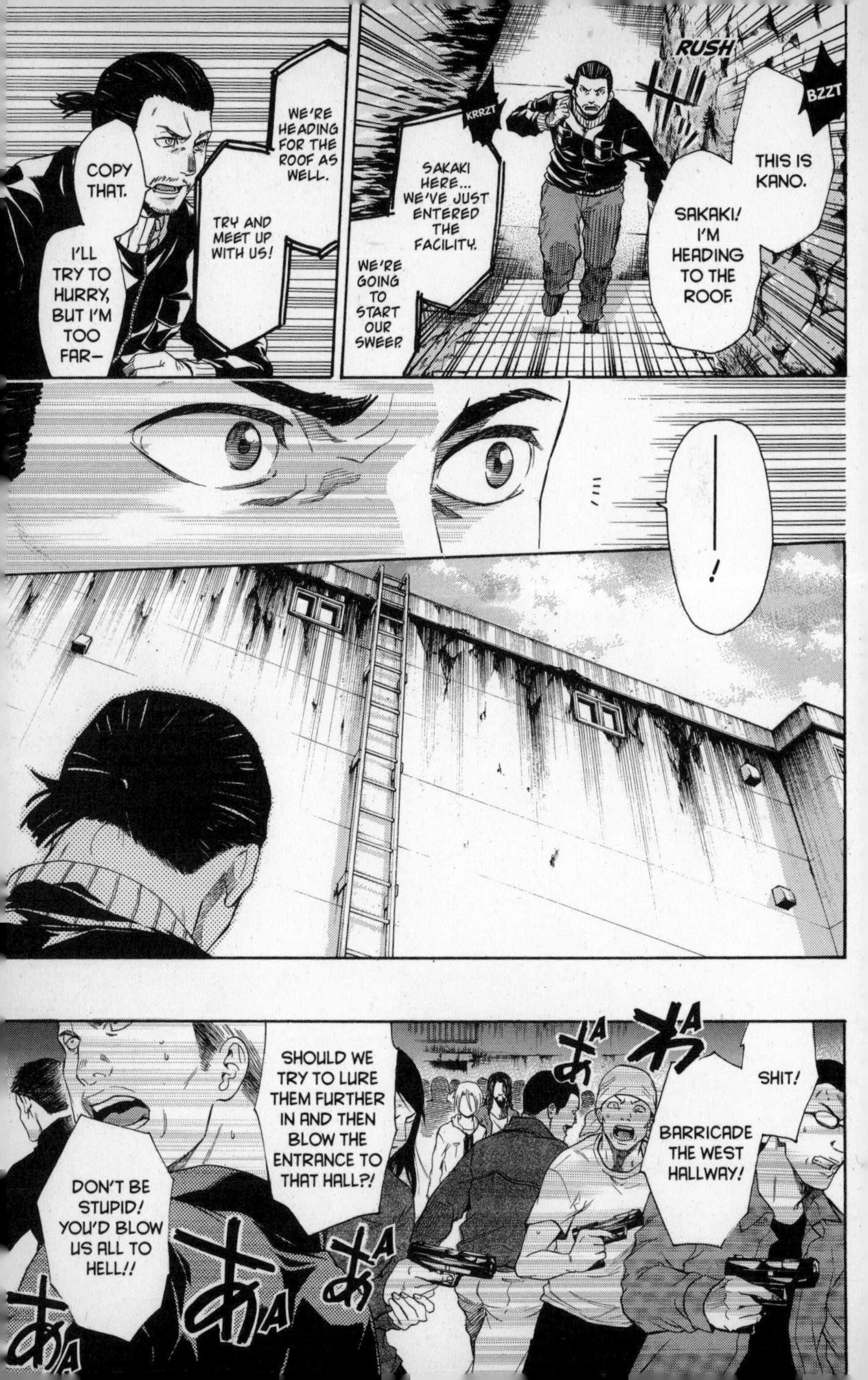
RUSH
BZZT
THIS IS KANO.
SAKAKI! I'M HEADING TO THE ROOF.
KRRZT
SAKAKI HERE... WE'VE JUST ENTERED THE FACILITY.
WE'RE GOING TO START OUR SWEEP.
WE'RE HEADING FOR THE ROOF AS WELL.
TRY AND MEET UP WITH US!
COPY THAT.
I'LL TRY TO HURRY, BUT I'M TOO FAR—
—!
あ A
あ A
SHIT!
BARRICADE THE WEST HALLWAY!
SHOULD WE TRY TO LURE THEM FURTHER IN AND THEN BLOW THE ENTRANCE TO THAT HALL?!
DON'T BE STUPID! YOU'D BLOW US ALL TO HELL!!
あ A
あ A
あ A
あ A

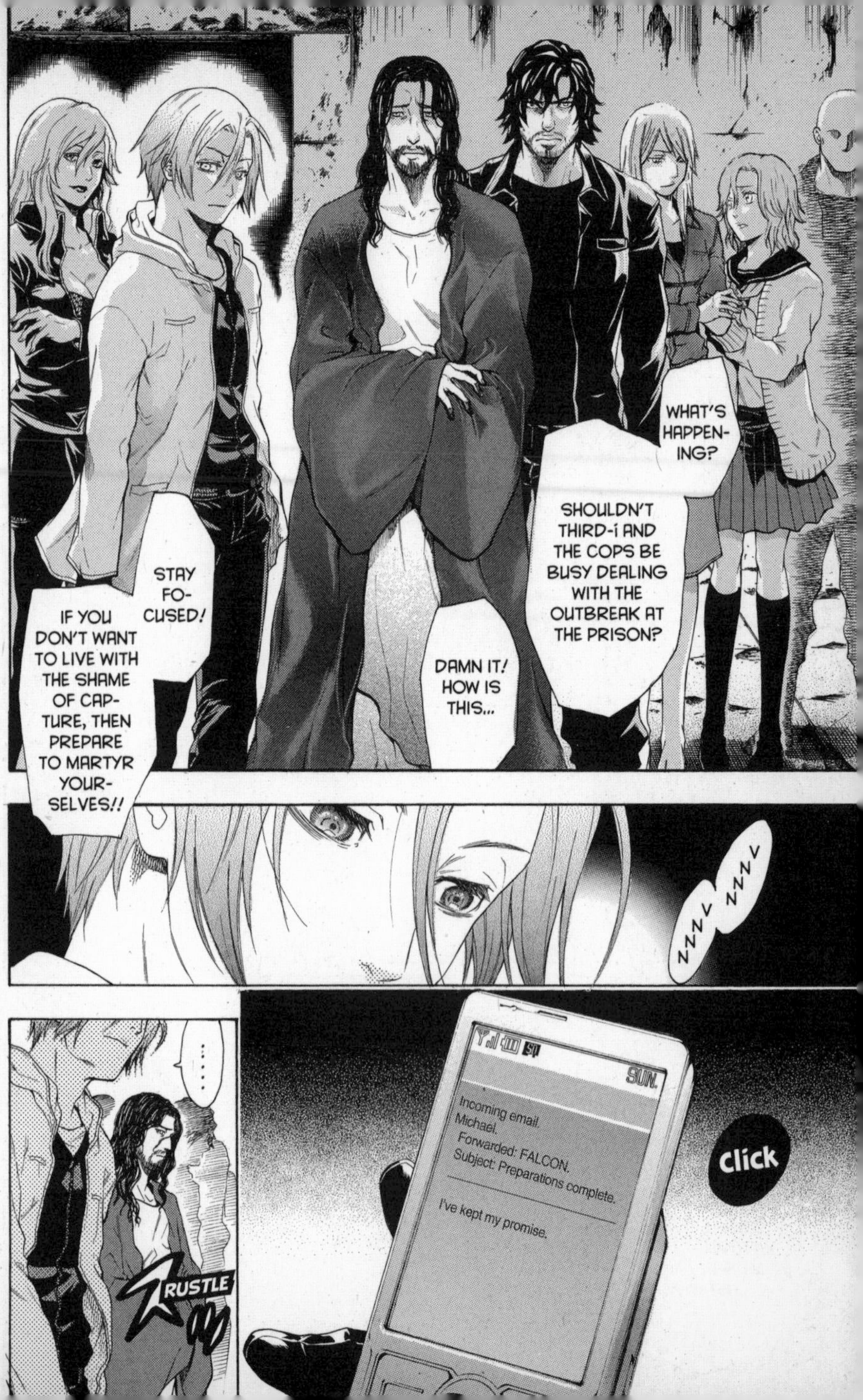
WHAT'S HAPPEN-ING?
SHOULDN'T THIRD-i AND THE COPS BE BUSY DEALING WITH THE OUTBREAK AT THE PRISON?
DAMN IT! HOW IS THIS...
STAY FO-CUSED!
IF YOU DON'T WANT TO LIVE WITH THE SHAME OF CAP-TURE, THEN PREPARE TO MARTYR YOUR-SELVES!!
NNNV
NNNV
SUN.
Incoming email.
Michael.
Forwarded: FALCON.
Subject: Preparations complete.
I've kept my promise.
Click
......
RUSTLE

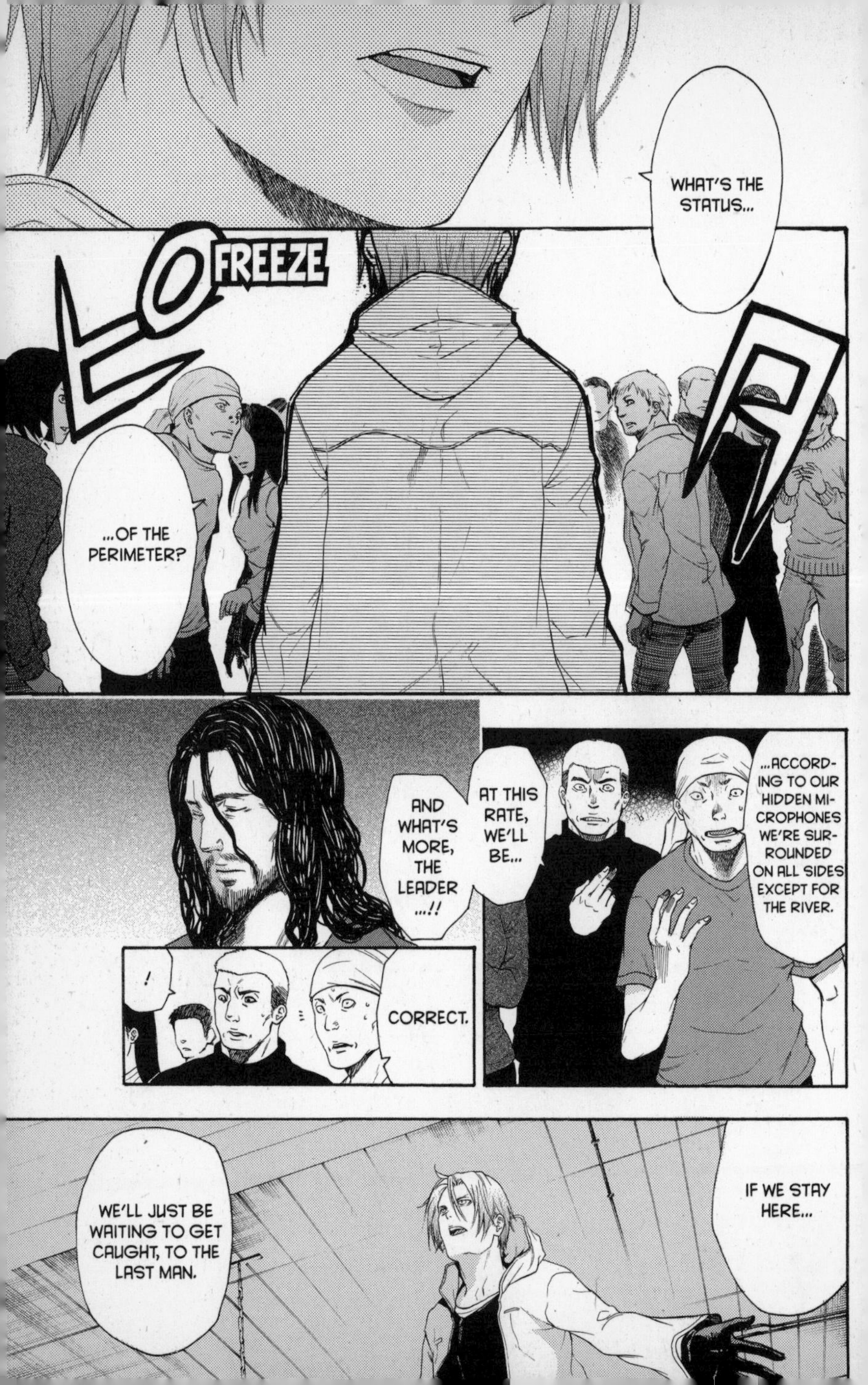
WHAT'S THE STATUS...
FREEZE
...OF THE PERIMETER?
...ACCORDING TO OUR HIDDEN MICROPHONES WE'RE SURROUNDED ON ALL SIDES EXCEPT FOR THE RIVER.
AT THIS RATE, WE'LL BE...
AND WHAT'S MORE, THE LEADER ...!!
CORRECT.
!
IF WE STAY HERE...
WE'LL JUST BE WAITING TO GET CAUGHT, TO THE LAST MAN.

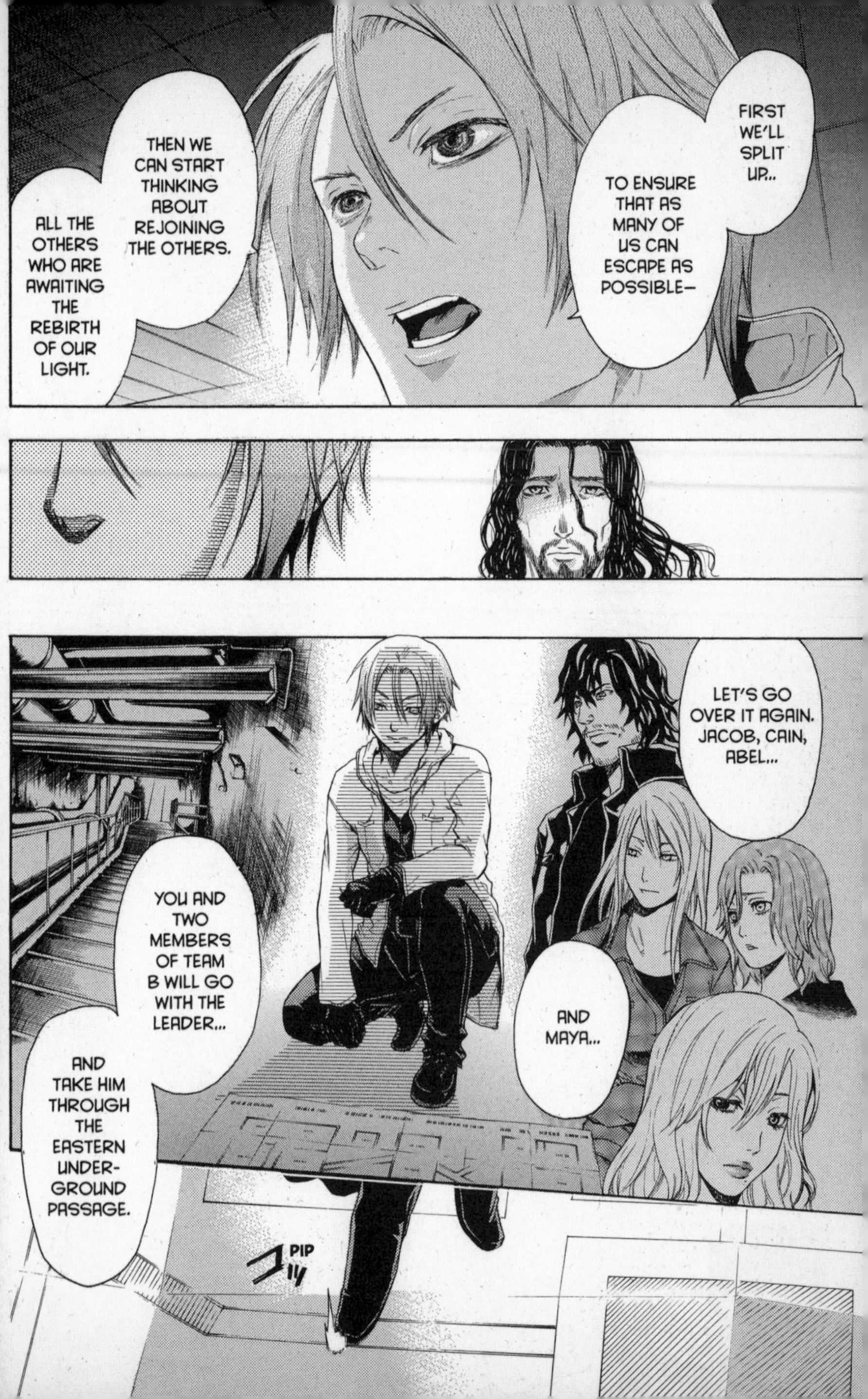
FIRST WE'LL SPLIT UP...
TO ENSURE THAT AS MANY OF US CAN ESCAPE AS POSSIBLE—
THEN WE CAN START THINKING ABOUT REJOINING THE OTHERS.
ALL THE OTHERS WHO ARE AWAITING THE REBIRTH OF OUR LIGHT.
LET'S GO OVER IT AGAIN. JACOB, CAIN, ABEL...
AND MAYA...
YOU AND TWO MEMBERS OF TEAM B WILL GO WITH THE LEADER...
AND TAKE HIM THROUGH THE EASTERN UNDER-GROUND PASSAGE.
PIP

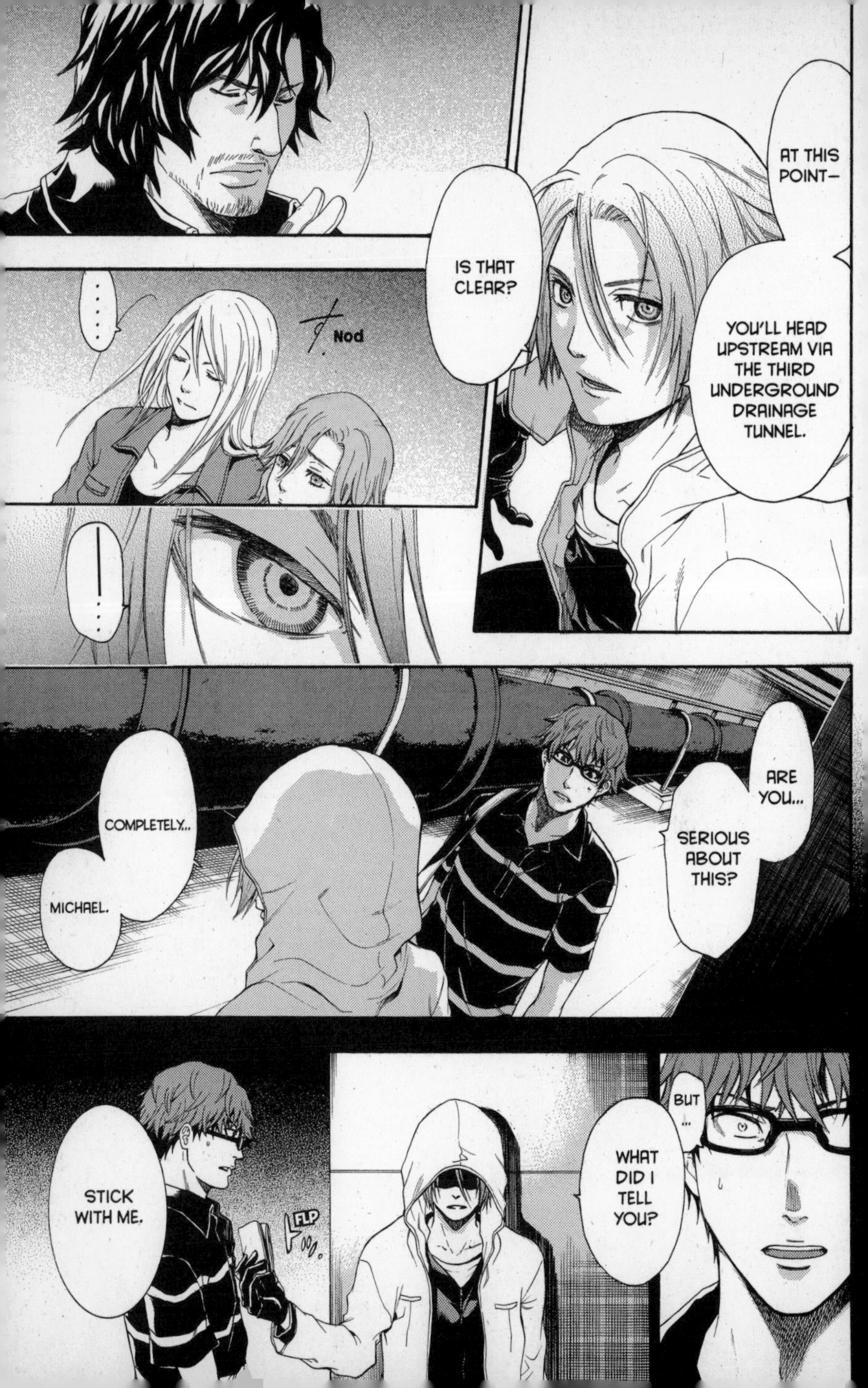
AT THIS POINT—
YOU'LL HEAD UPSTREAM VIA THE THIRD UNDERGROUND DRAINAGE TUNNEL.
IS THAT CLEAR?
......
Nod
!......
ARE YOU... SERIOUS ABOUT THIS?
COMPLETELY... MICHAEL.
BUT ...
WHAT DID I TELL YOU?
STICK WITH ME.
FLP

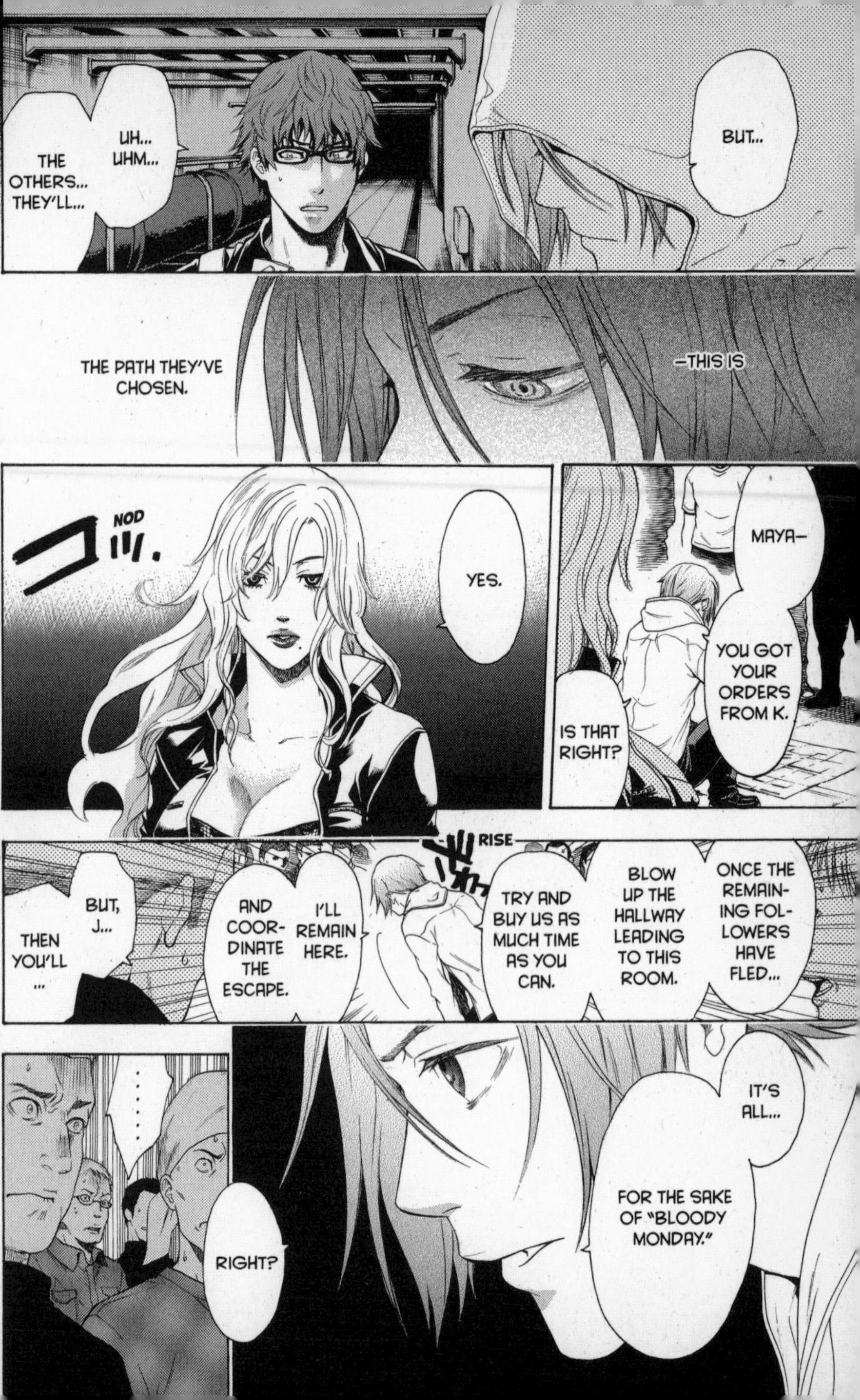
BUT...
UH... UHM...
THE OTHERS... THEY'LL...
—THIS IS
THE PATH THEY'VE CHOSEN.
MAYA—
YOU GOT YOUR ORDERS FROM K.
IS THAT RIGHT?
NOD
YES.
RISE
ONCE THE REMAIN-ING FOL-LOWERS HAVE FLED...
BLOW UP THE HALLWAY LEADING TO THIS ROOM.
TRY AND BUY US AS MUCH TIME AS YOU CAN.
I'LL REMAIN HERE.
AND COOR-DINATE THE ESCAPE.
BUT, J...
THEN YOU'LL ...
IT'S ALL...
FOR THE SAKE OF "BLOODY MONDAY."
RIGHT?
......

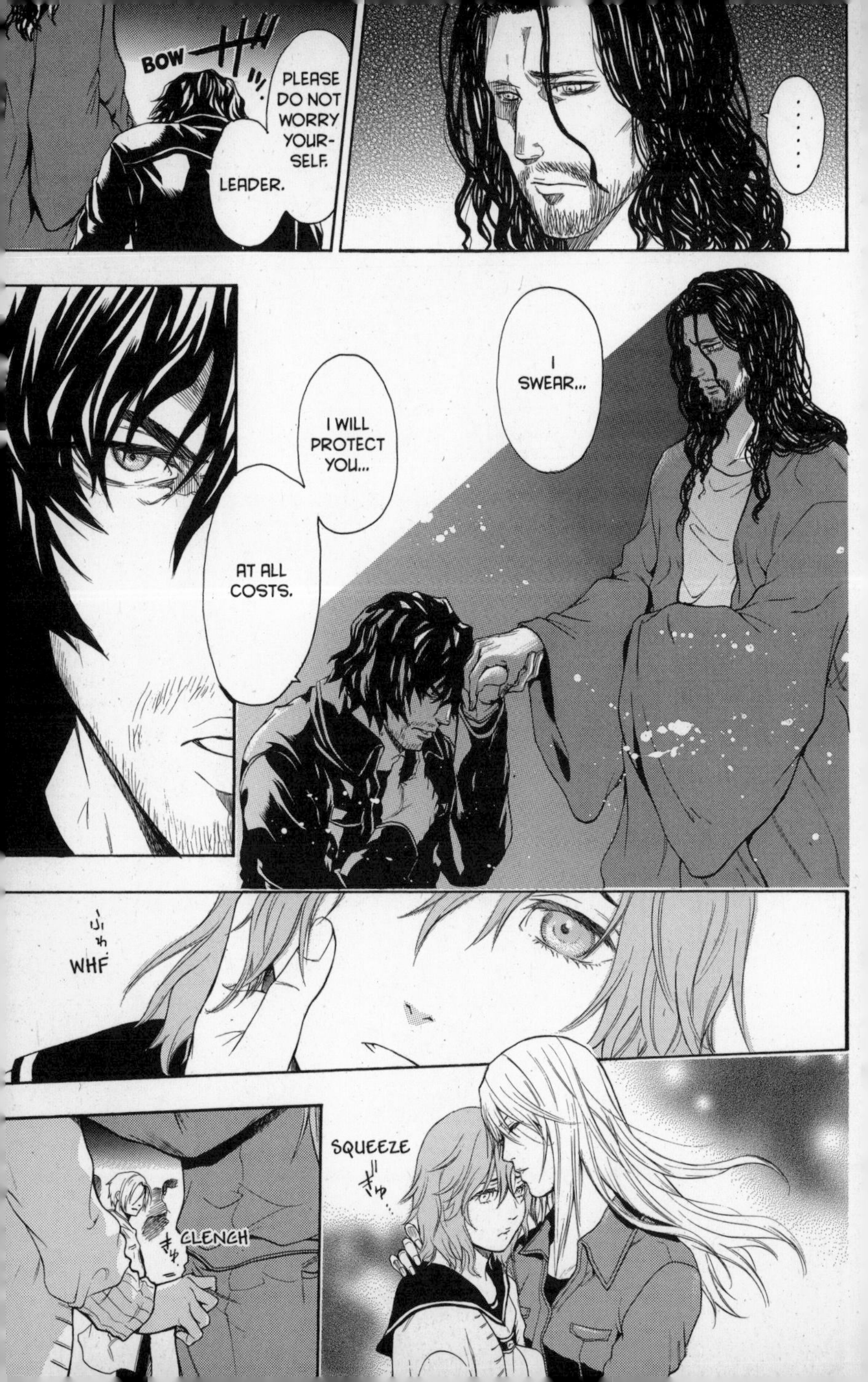
. . . . . .
BOW
PLEASE DO NOT WORRY YOURSELF.
LEADER.
I SWEAR...
I WILL PROTECT YOU...
AT ALL COSTS.
ふわ
WHF
SQUEEZE
ぎゅ...
CLENCH
ぎゅ

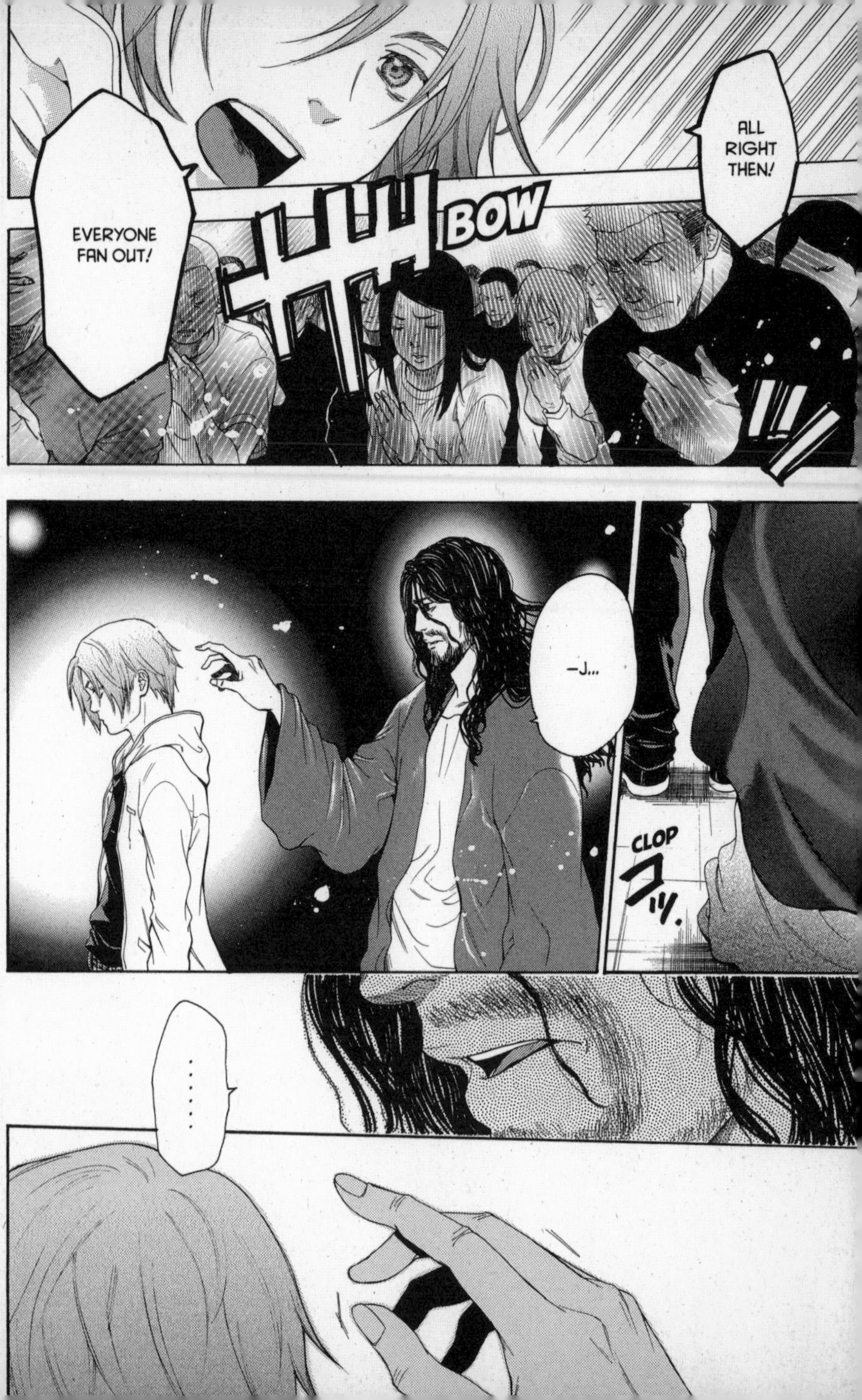
ALL RIGHT THEN!
BOW
EVERYONE FAN OUT!
CLOP
コッ
—J...
......

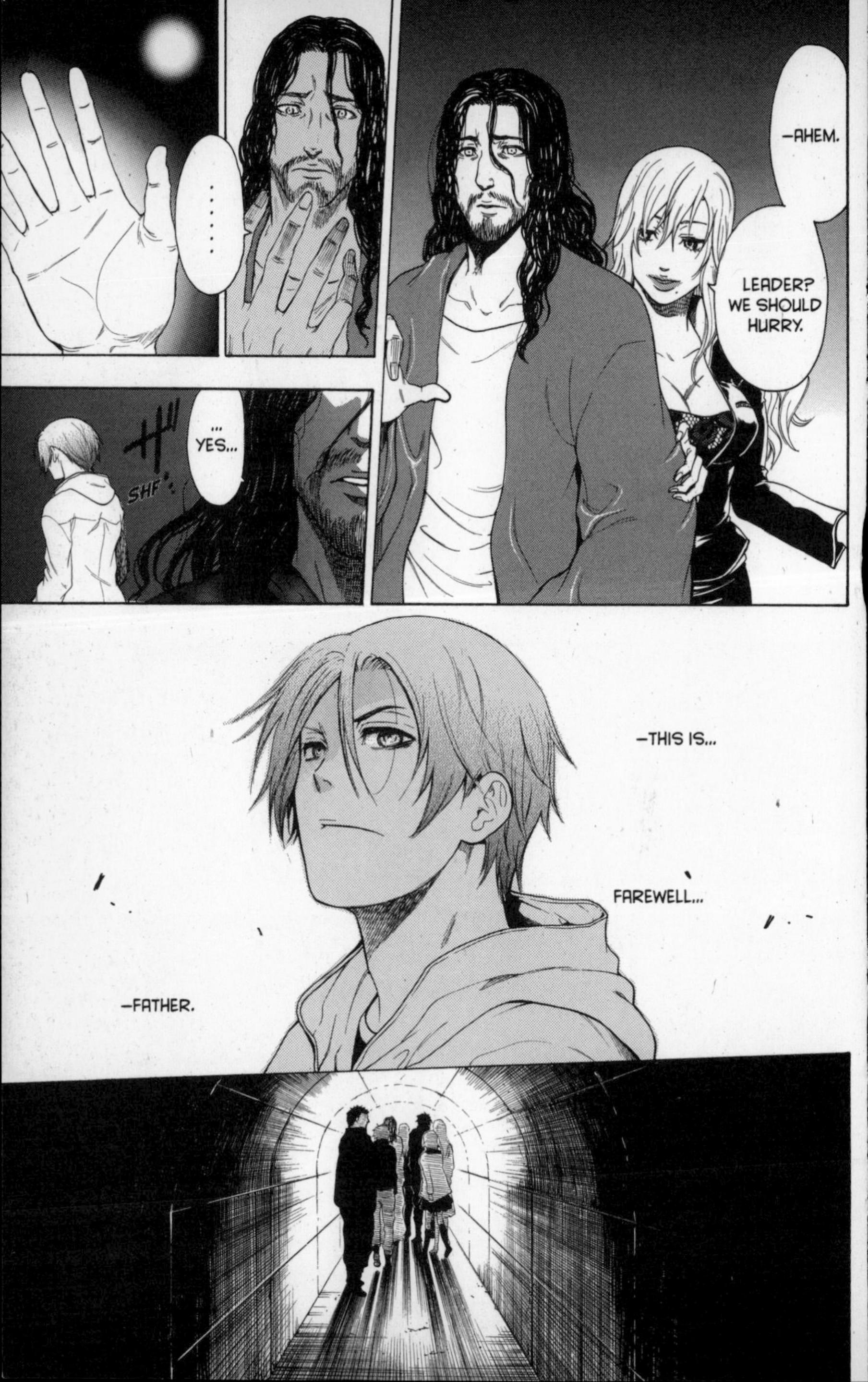
—AHEM.
LEADER? WE SHOULD HURRY.
……
... YES...
SHF
—THIS IS...
FAREWELL...
—FATHER.

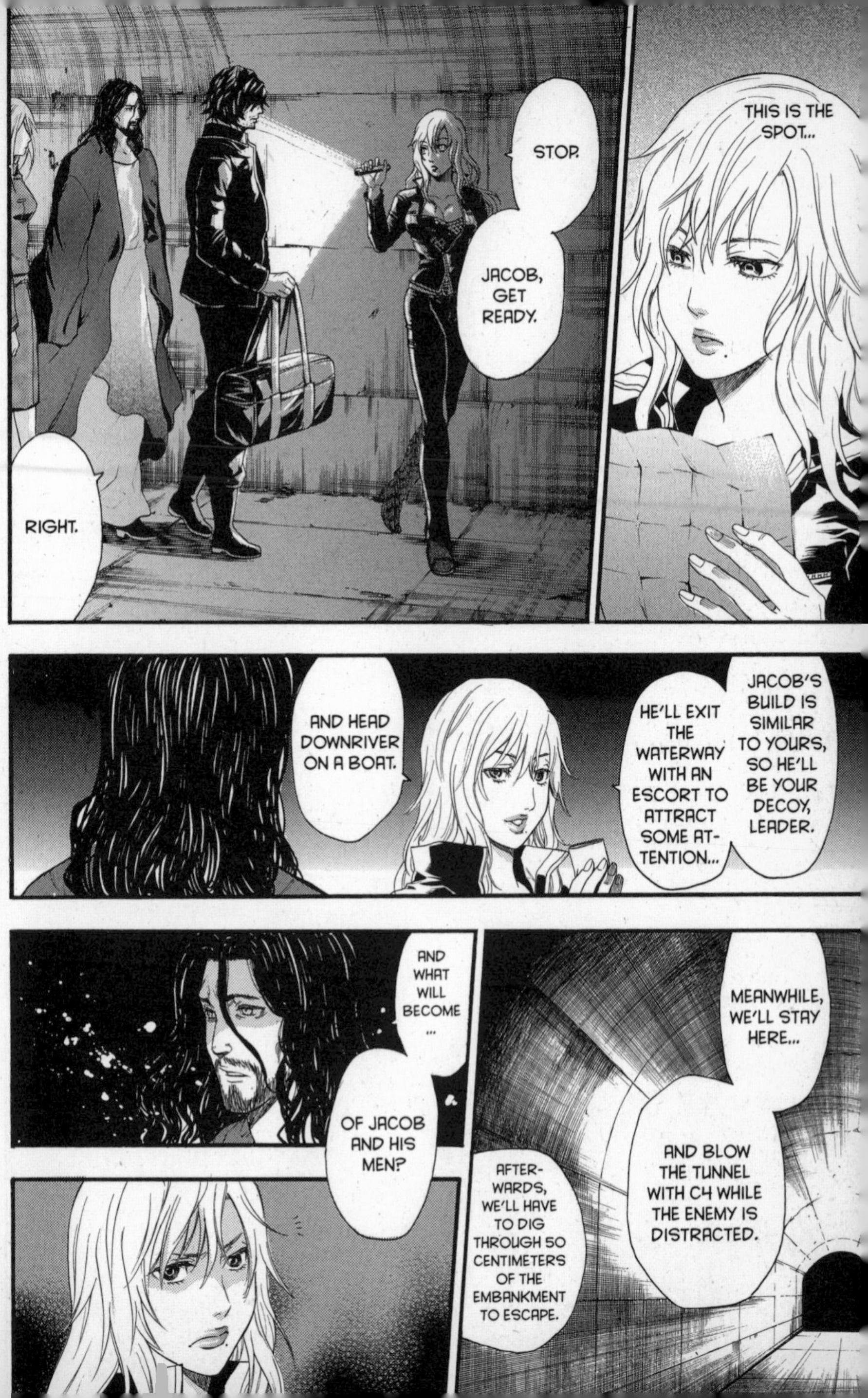
THIS IS THE SPOT...
STOP.
JACOB, GET READY.
RIGHT.
JACOB'S BUILD IS SIMILAR TO YOURS, SO HE'LL BE YOUR DECOY, LEADER.
HE'LL EXIT THE WATERWAY WITH AN ESCORT TO ATTRACT SOME AT-TENTION...
AND HEAD DOWNRIVER ON A BOAT.
MEANWHILE, WE'LL STAY HERE...
AND BLOW THE TUNNEL WITH C4 WHILE THE ENEMY IS DISTRACTED.
AFTER-WARDS, WE'LL HAVE TO DIG THROUGH 50 CENTIMETERS OF THE EMBANKMENT TO ESCAPE.
AND WHAT WILL BECOME ...
OF JACOB AND HIS MEN?

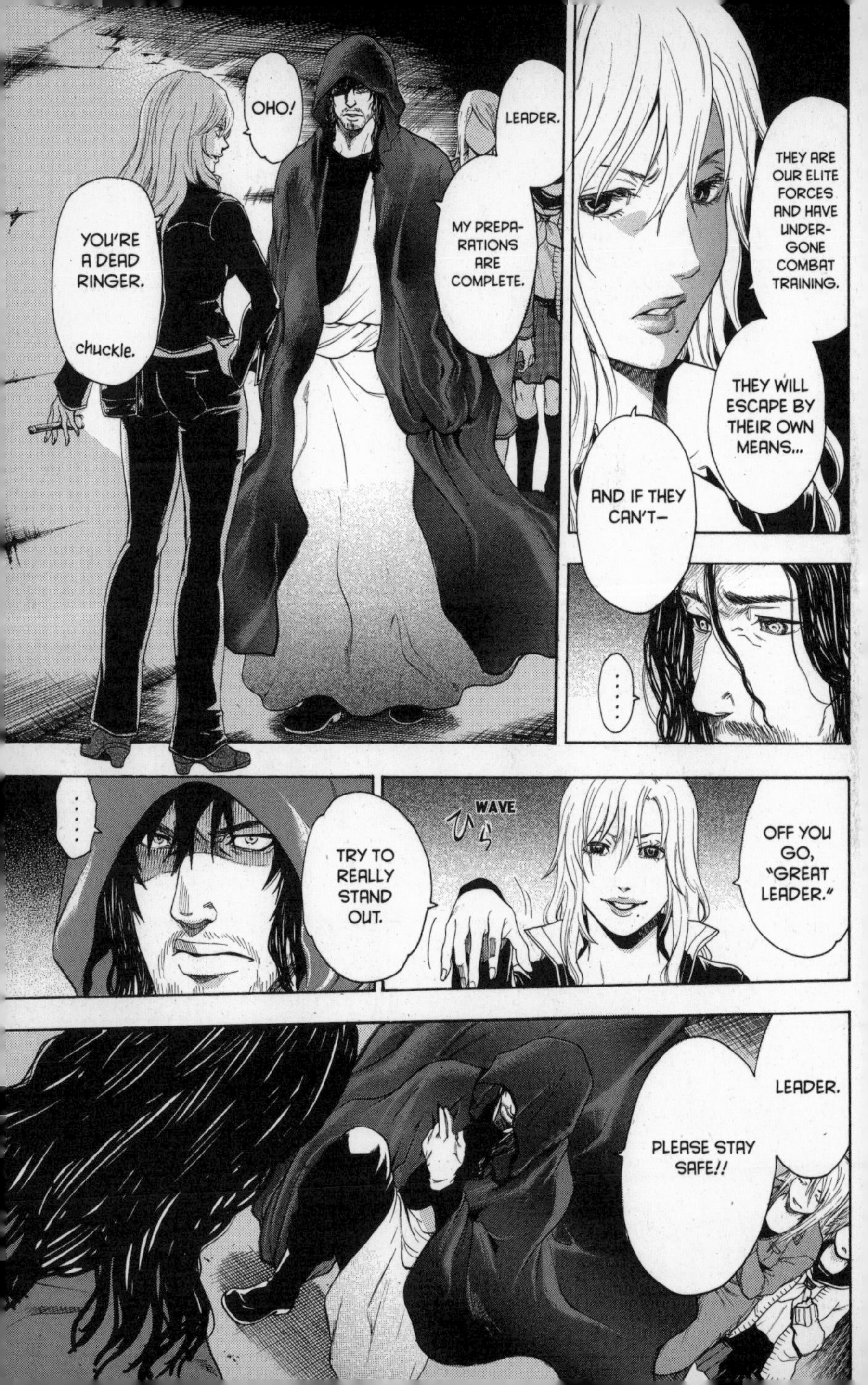
THEY ARE OUR ELITE FORCES AND HAVE UNDER-GONE COMBAT TRAINING.
THEY WILL ESCAPE BY THEIR OWN MEANS...
AND IF THEY CAN'T—
......
LEADER.
MY PREPA-RATIONS ARE COMPLETE.
OHO!
YOU'RE A DEAD RINGER.
chuckle.
OFF YOU GO, "GREAT LEADER."
WAVE
ひら
TRY TO REALLY STAND OUT.
......
LEADER.
PLEASE STAY SAFE!!

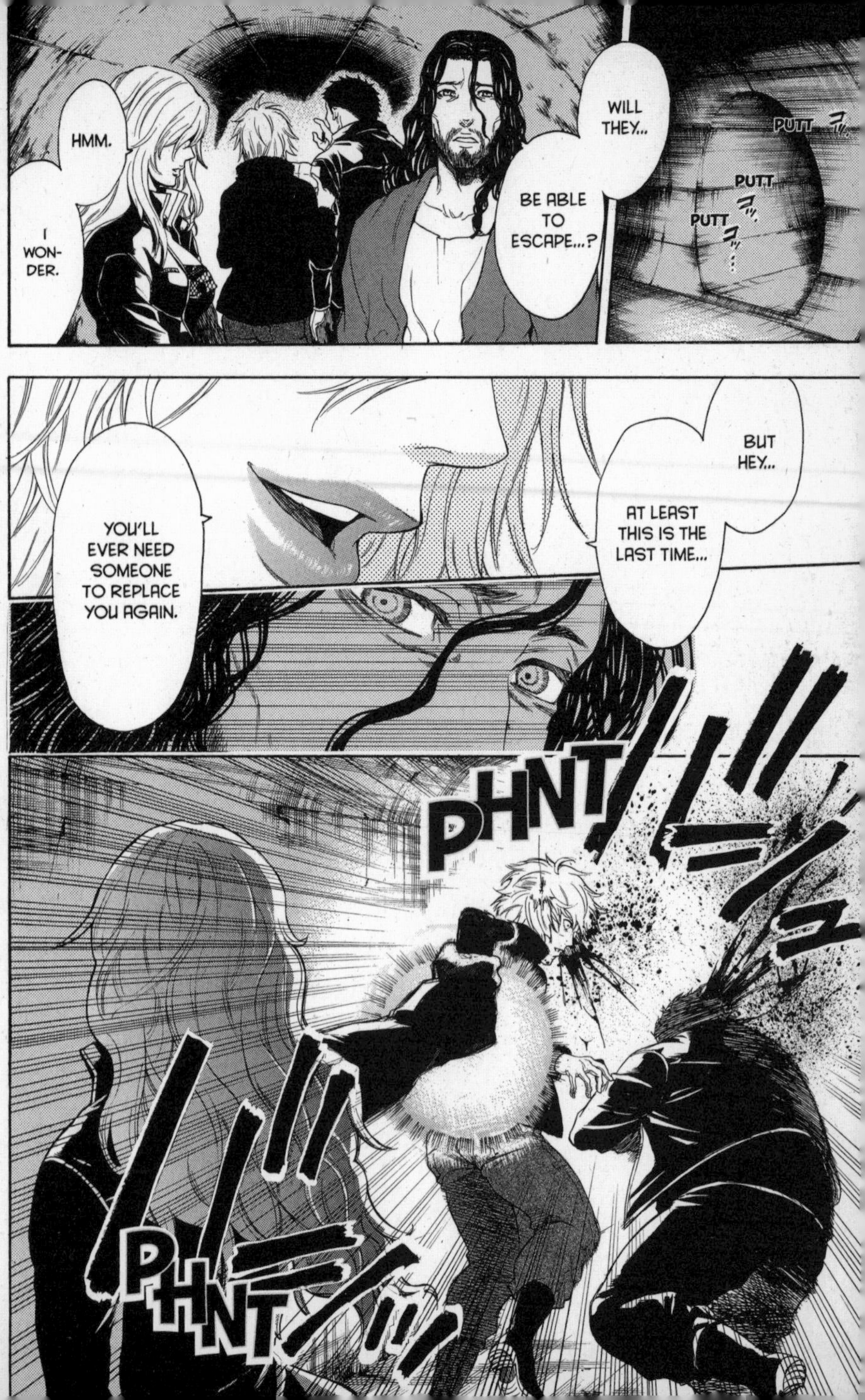
PUTT
PUTT
PUTT
WILL THEY...
BE ABLE TO ESCAPE...?
HMM.
I WON-DER.
BUT HEY...
AT LEAST THIS IS THE LAST TIME...
YOU'LL EVER NEED SOMEONE TO REPLACE YOU AGAIN.
PHNT
PHNT

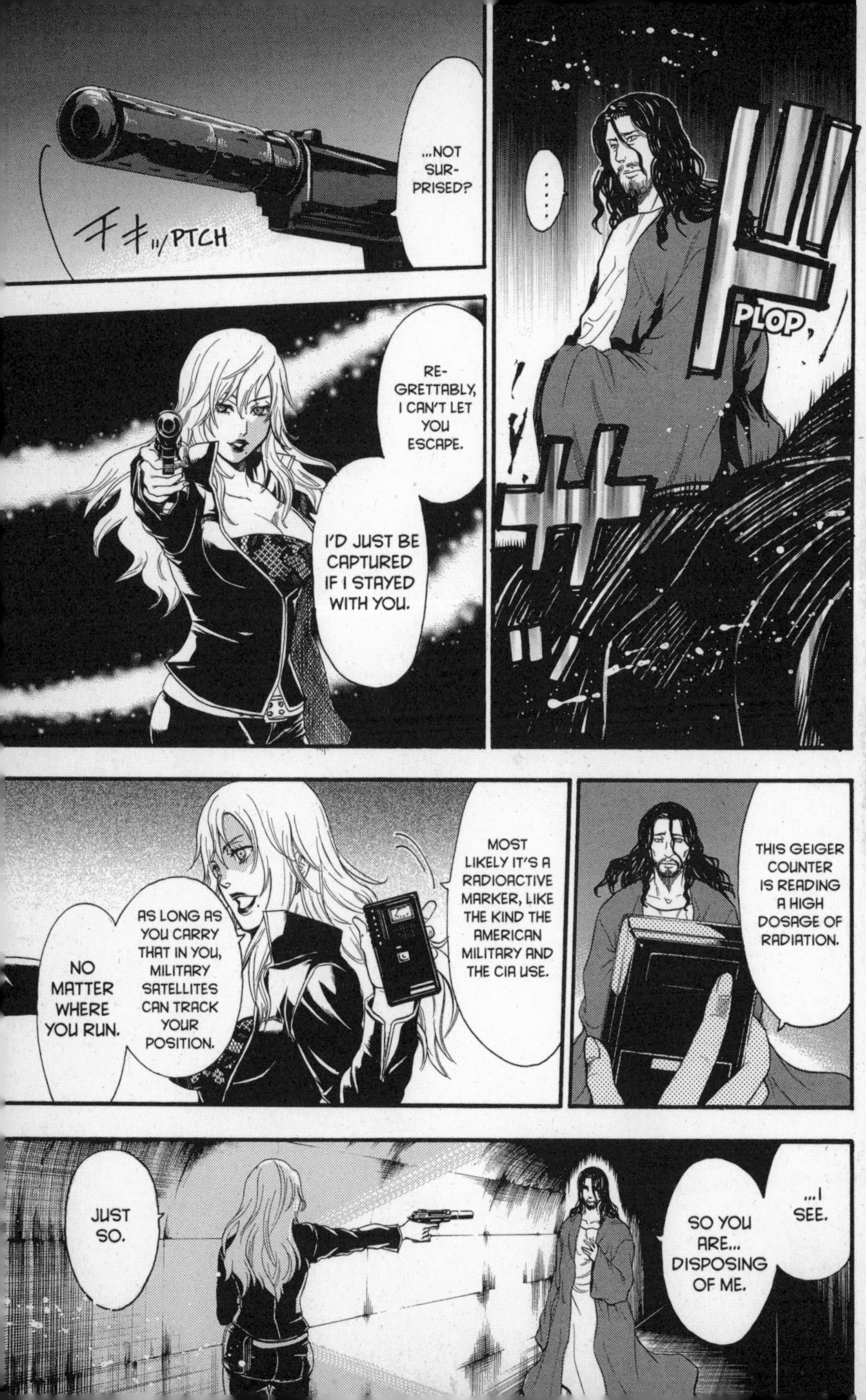
.....
PLOP
...NOT SUR-PRISED?
チキッ/PTCH
RE-GRETTABLY, I CAN'T LET YOU ESCAPE.
I'D JUST BE CAPTURED IF I STAYED WITH YOU.
THIS GEIGER COUNTER IS READING A HIGH DOSAGE OF RADIATION.
MOST LIKELY IT'S A RADIOACTIVE MARKER, LIKE THE KIND THE AMERICAN MILITARY AND THE CIA USE.
AS LONG AS YOU CARRY THAT IN YOU, MILITARY SATELLITES CAN TRACK YOUR POSITION.
NO MATTER WHERE YOU RUN.
...I SEE.
SO YOU ARE... DISPOSING OF ME.
JUST SO.

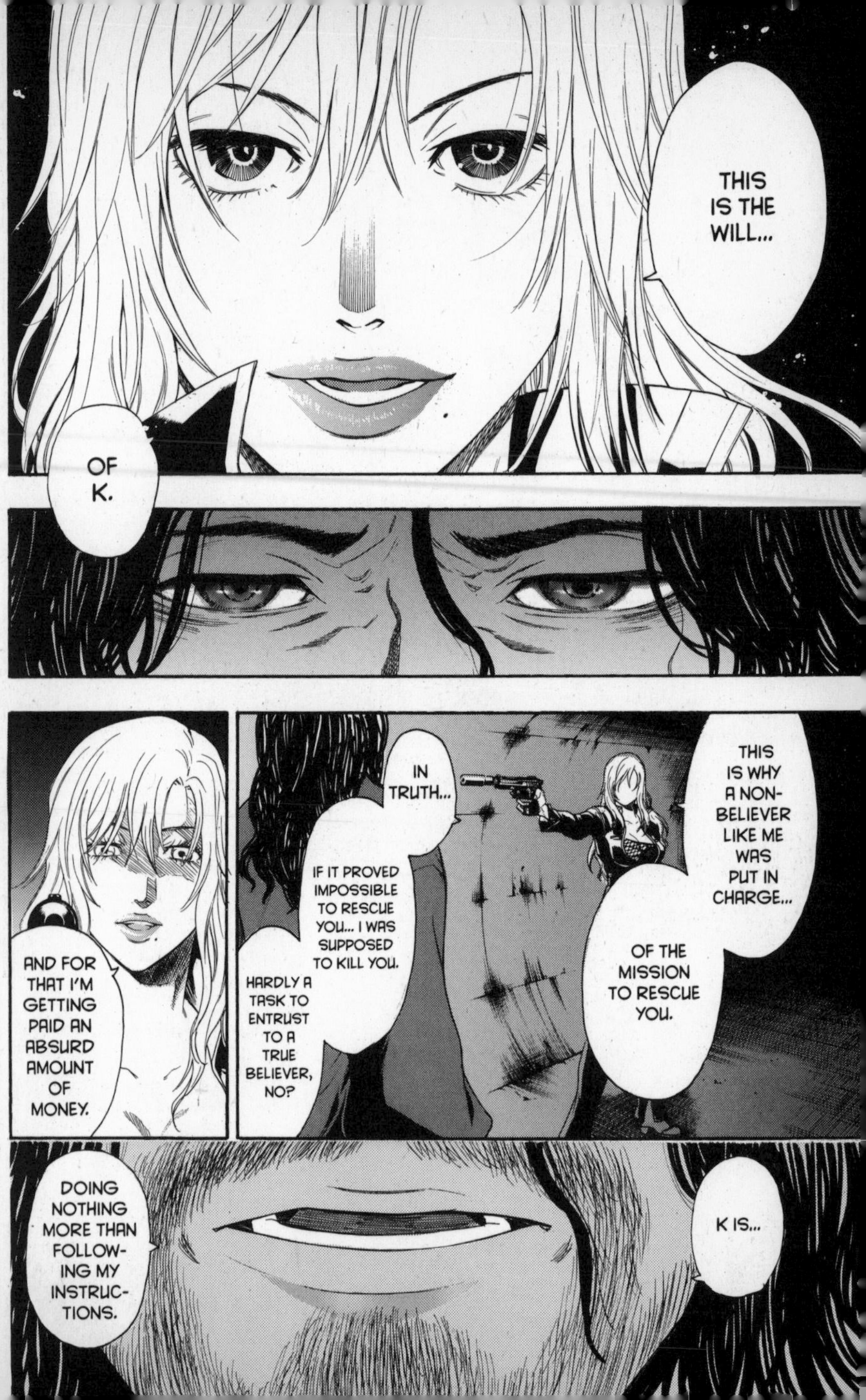
THIS IS THE WILL...
OF K.
THIS IS WHY A NON-BELIEVER LIKE ME WAS PUT IN CHARGE...
OF THE MISSION TO RESCUE YOU.
IN TRUTH...
IF IT PROVED IMPOSSIBLE TO RESCUE YOU... I WAS SUPPOSED TO KILL YOU.
HARDLY A TASK TO ENTRUST TO A TRUE BELIEVER, NO?
AND FOR THAT I'M GETTING PAID AN ABSURD AMOUNT OF MONEY.
K IS...
DOING NOTHING MORE THAN FOLLOWING MY INSTRUCTIONS.

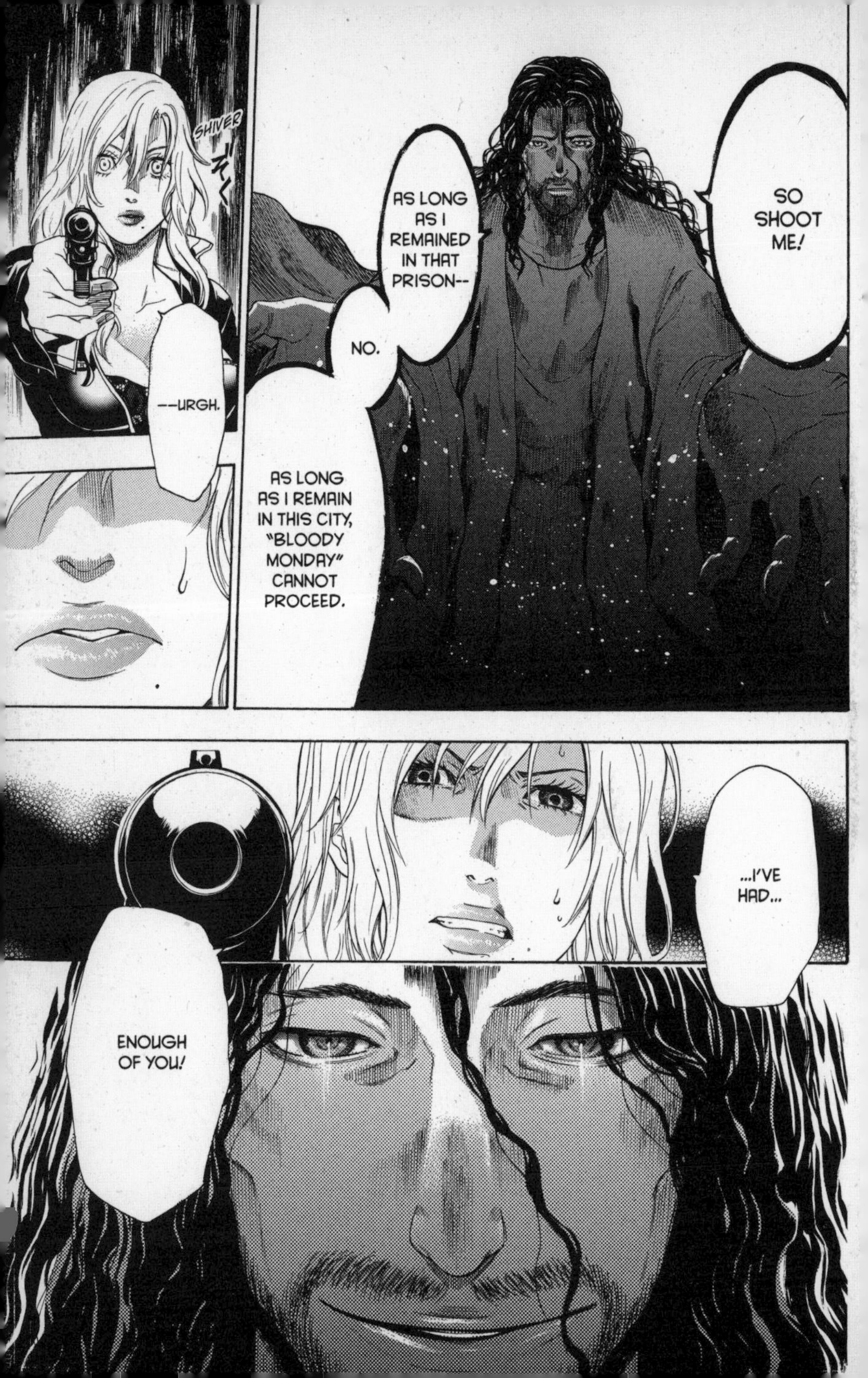
SO SHOOT ME!
AS LONG AS I REMAINED IN THAT PRISON--
NO.
AS LONG AS I REMAIN IN THIS CITY, "BLOODY MONDAY" CANNOT PROCEED.
SHIVER
--URGH.
...I'VE HAD...
ENOUGH OF YOU!

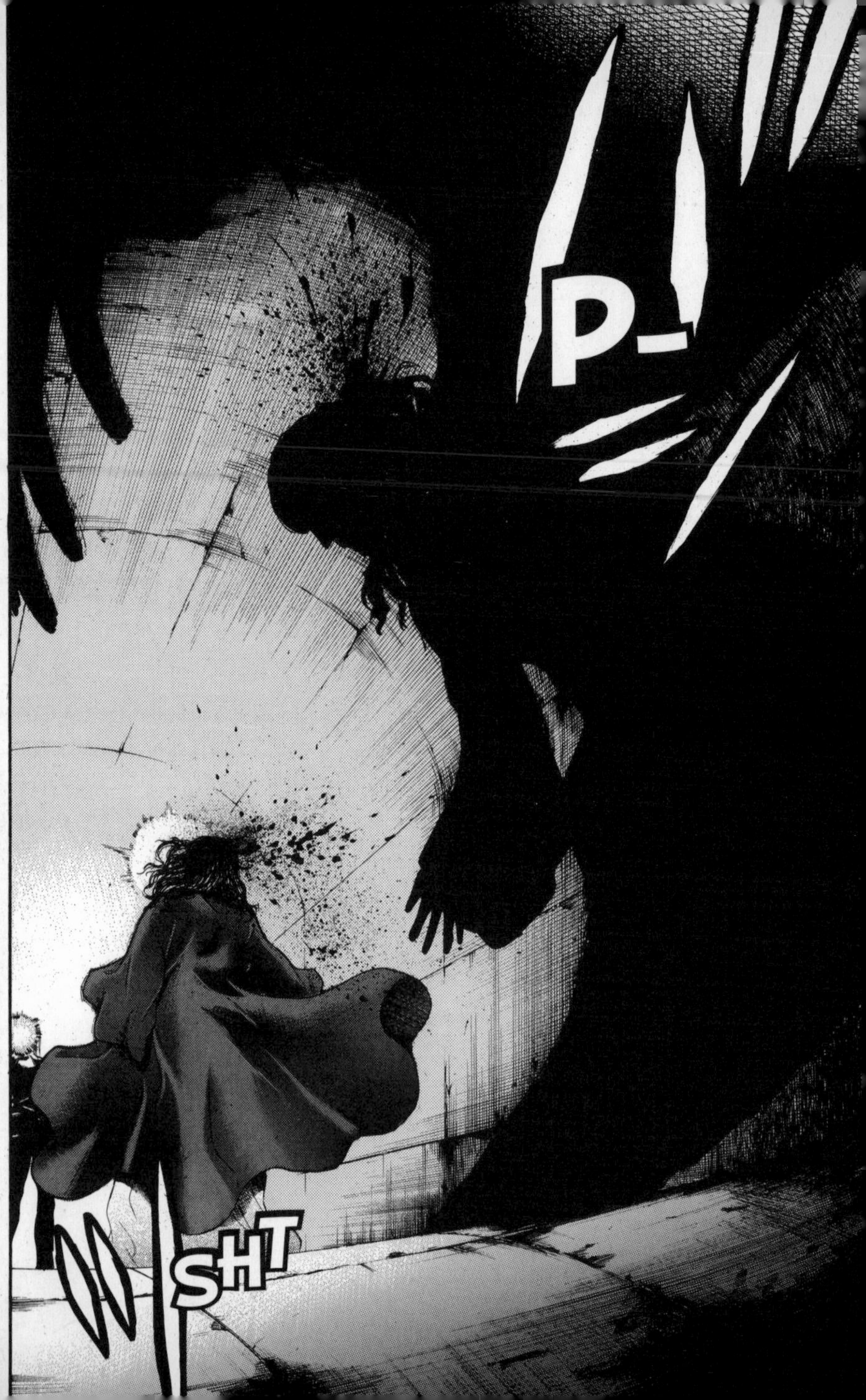
P-
SHT

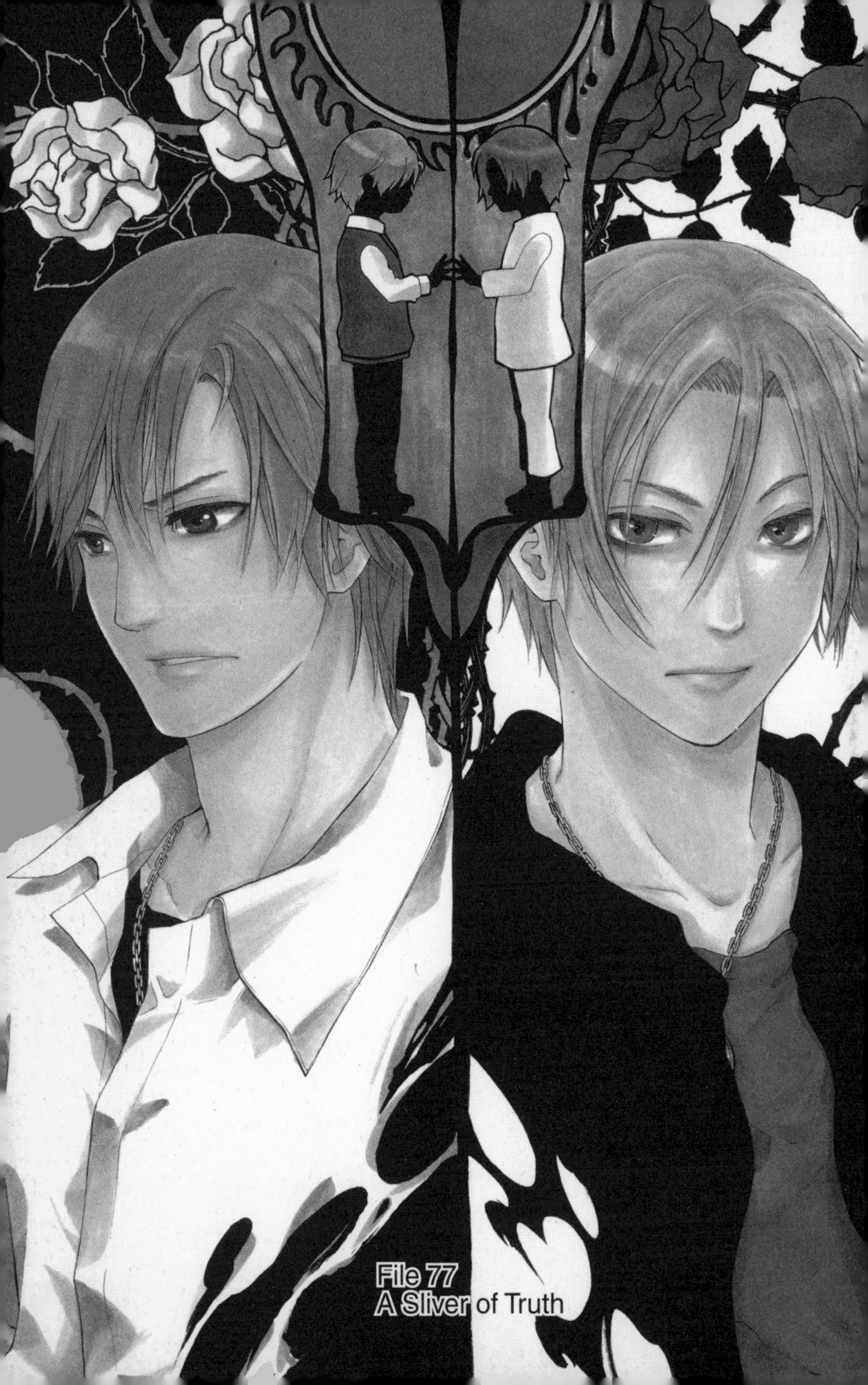
File 77
A Sliver of Truth

J: THE 10TH CHILD OF KAMISHIMA SHIMON AND THE 10TH TO INHERIT THE "BLOOD OF GOD," HE WAS NAMED AFTER THE 10TH LETTER OF THE ALPHABET, IN THE SAME MANNER AS HIS SIBLINGS. HIS REAL NAME IS KANZAKI JUN. TEN YEARS AGO, WHEN HIS SIBLINGS WERE ARRESTED FOLLOWING THE POISON GAS ATTACK ON THE POLICE STATION, HE ESCAPED BY MAKING EVERYONE BELIEVE HE HAD DIED IN A TRAIN ACCIDENT, WHEN IT FACT IT WAS THE CULT MEMBER WHO HAD RAISED HIM. AS FAR AS SOCIETY WAS CONCERNED, HE DIDN'T EXIST ANYMORE. HE BECAME LIKE THE BIBLICAL ABEL: CHOSEN, THEN KILLED BY GOD. HE DESPISES THE PIPE DREAM HIS FATHER, KAMISHIMA SHIMON, SELLS, AS HE DESPISES ALL THOSE WHO SPEAK OF JUSTICE. HE HATES PEOPLE WHO WOULD SHACKLE THEMSELVES TO SUCH FALSEHOODS. HE GREW FOND OF MICHAEL, WHO WAS HIMSELF AN UNBELIEVER, AND AFTER SPENDING TIME WITH JACOB, CAIN AND ABEL HE FOUND HIMSELF CARING FOR THEM AS WELL. WHEN STRESSED OUT, HE SUBCONSCIOUSLY BITES HIS NAILS. HE ALSO HAS A HABIT OF WATCHING PEOPLE. HE HAS AN UNBALANCED DIET.

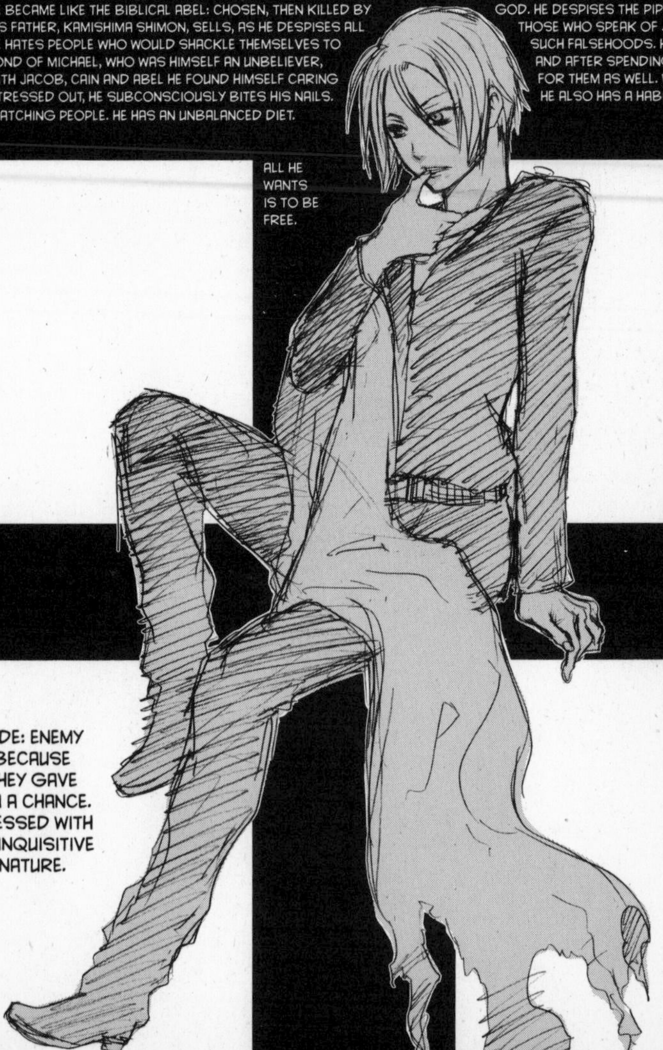

ALL HE WANTS IS TO BE FREE.

SIDE: ENEMY BECAUSE THEY GAVE HIM A CHANCE. BLESSED WITH AN INQUISITIVE NATURE.

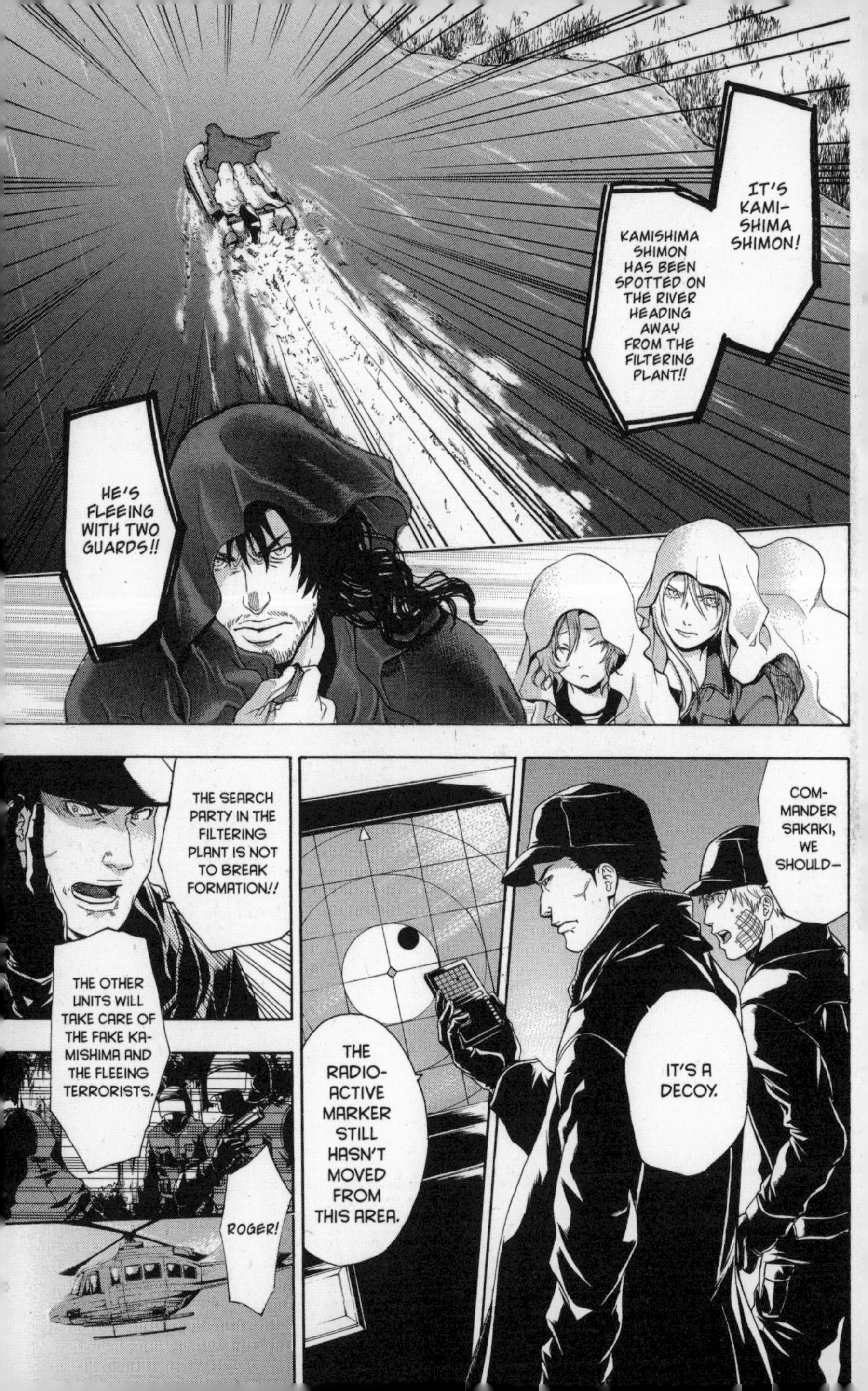
IT'S KAMISHIMA SHIMON!
KAMISHIMA SHIMON HAS BEEN SPOTTED ON THE RIVER HEADING AWAY FROM THE FILTERING PLANT!!
HE'S FLEEING WITH TWO GUARDS!!
COMMANDER SAKAKI, WE SHOULD—
IT'S A DECOY.
THE RADIOACTIVE MARKER STILL HASN'T MOVED FROM THIS AREA.
THE SEARCH PARTY IN THE FILTERING PLANT IS NOT TO BREAK FORMATION!!
THE OTHER UNITS WILL TAKE CARE OF THE FAKE KAMISHIMA AND THE FLEEING TERRORISTS.
ROGER!

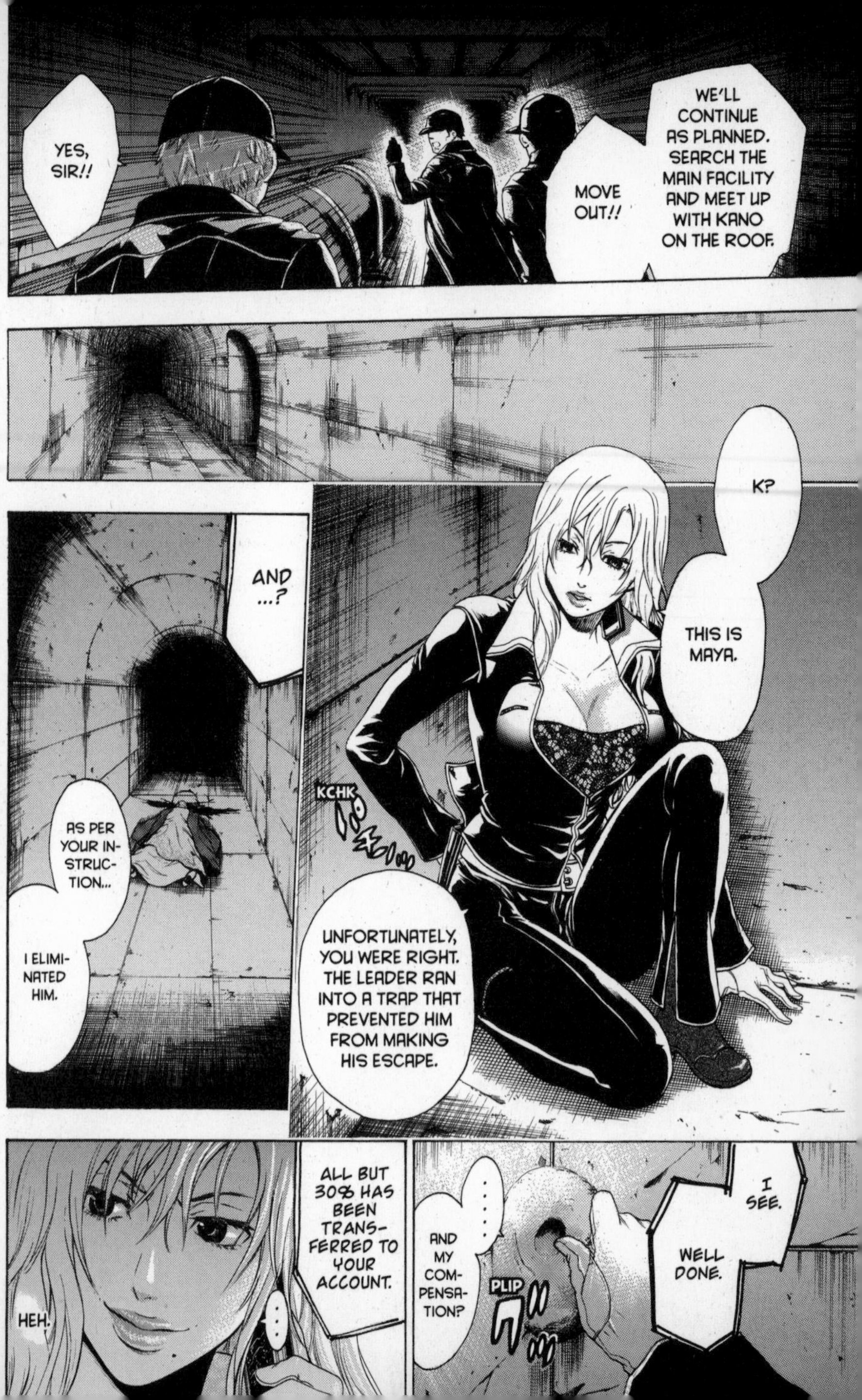

WE'LL CONTINUE AS PLANNED. SEARCH THE MAIN FACILITY AND MEET UP WITH KANO ON THE ROOF.
MOVE OUT!!
YES, SIR!!
K?
THIS IS MAYA.
KCHK
UNFORTUNATELY, YOU WERE RIGHT. THE LEADER RAN INTO A TRAP THAT PREVENTED HIM FROM MAKING HIS ESCAPE.
AND ...?
AS PER YOUR IN-STRUC-TION...
I ELIMI-NATED HIM.
I SEE.
WELL DONE.
.....
AND MY COM-PENSA-TION?
PLIP
ALL BUT 30% HAS BEEN TRANS-FERRED TO YOUR ACCOUNT.
...
HEH.

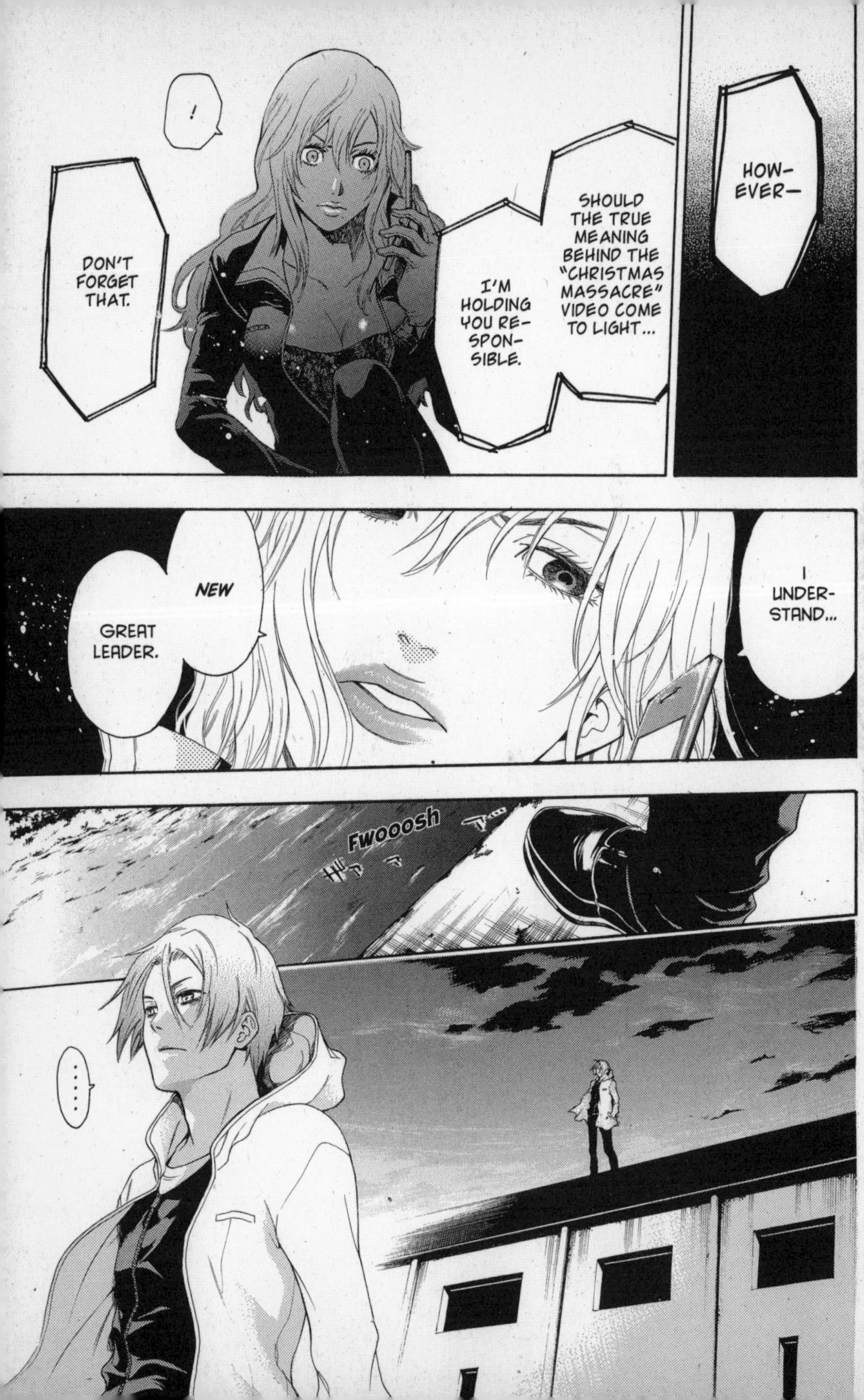
HOW-EVER—
SHOULD THE TRUE MEANING BEHIND THE "CHRISTMAS MASSACRE" VIDEO COME TO LIGHT...
I'M HOLDING YOU RE-SPON-SIBLE.
DON'T FORGET THAT.
!
I UNDER-STAND...
NEW GREAT LEADER.
Fwooosh
......

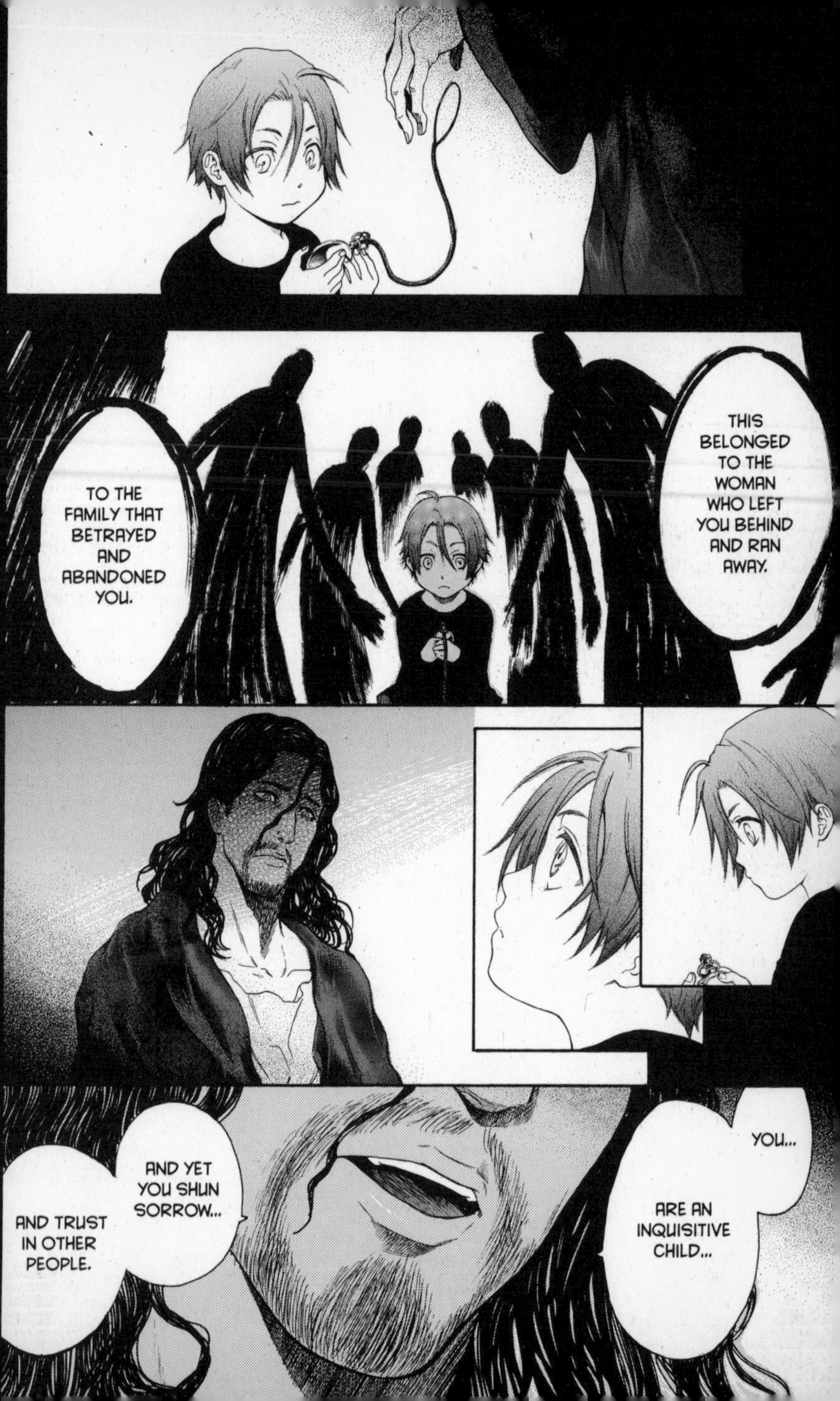
THIS BELONGED TO THE WOMAN WHO LEFT YOU BEHIND AND RAN AWAY.
TO THE FAMILY THAT BETRAYED AND ABANDONED YOU.
YOU...
ARE AN INQUISITIVE CHILD...
AND YET YOU SHUN SORROW...
AND TRUST IN OTHER PEOPLE.

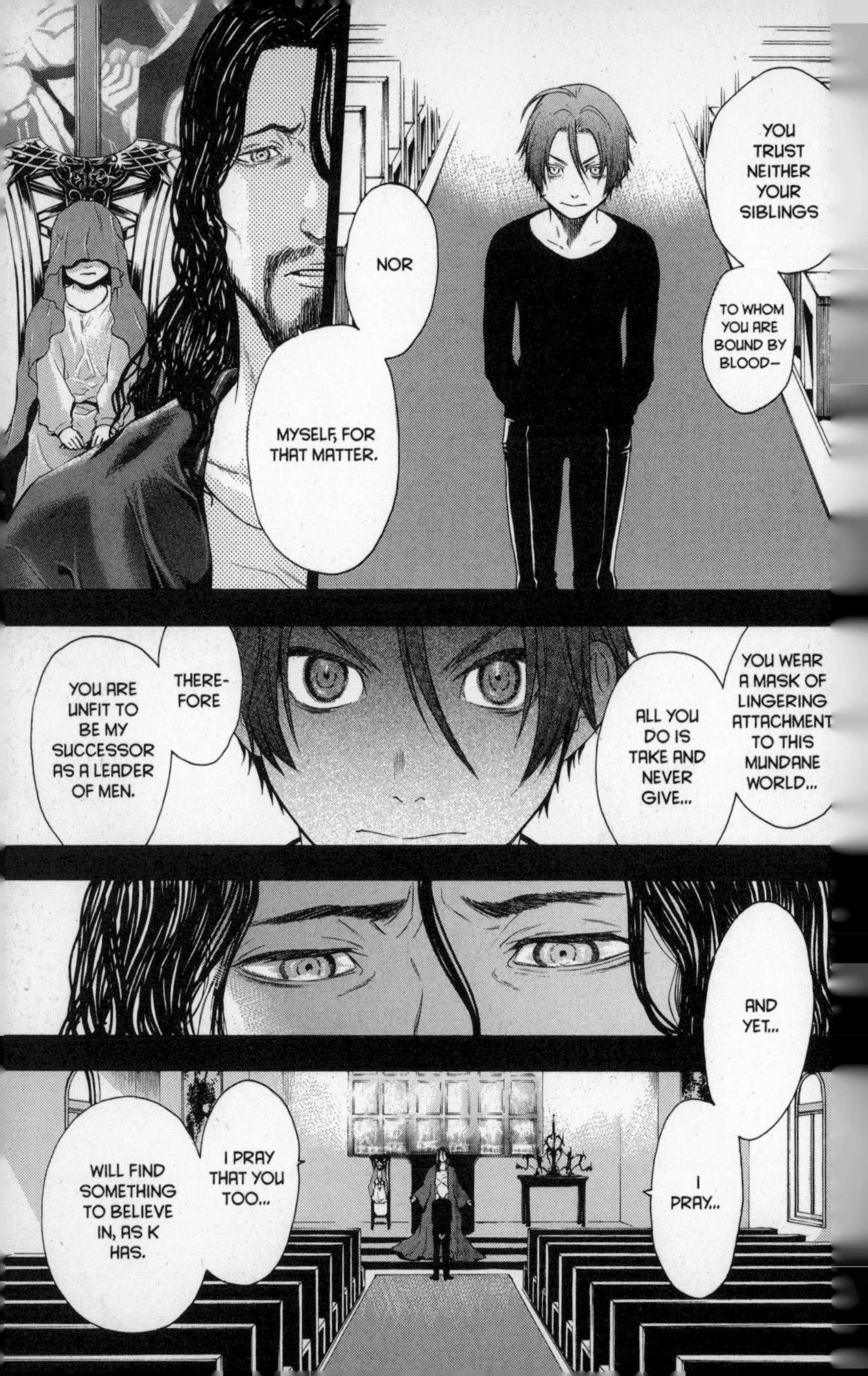
YOU TRUST NEITHER YOUR SIBLINGS
TO WHOM YOU ARE BOUND BY BLOOD—
NOR
MYSELF, FOR THAT MATTER.
YOU WEAR A MASK OF LINGERING ATTACHMENT TO THIS MUNDANE WORLD...
ALL YOU DO IS TAKE AND NEVER GIVE...
THERE-FORE
YOU ARE UNFIT TO BE MY SUCCESSOR AS A LEADER OF MEN.
AND YET...
I PRAY...
I PRAY THAT YOU TOO...
WILL FIND SOMETHING TO BELIEVE IN, AS K HAS.

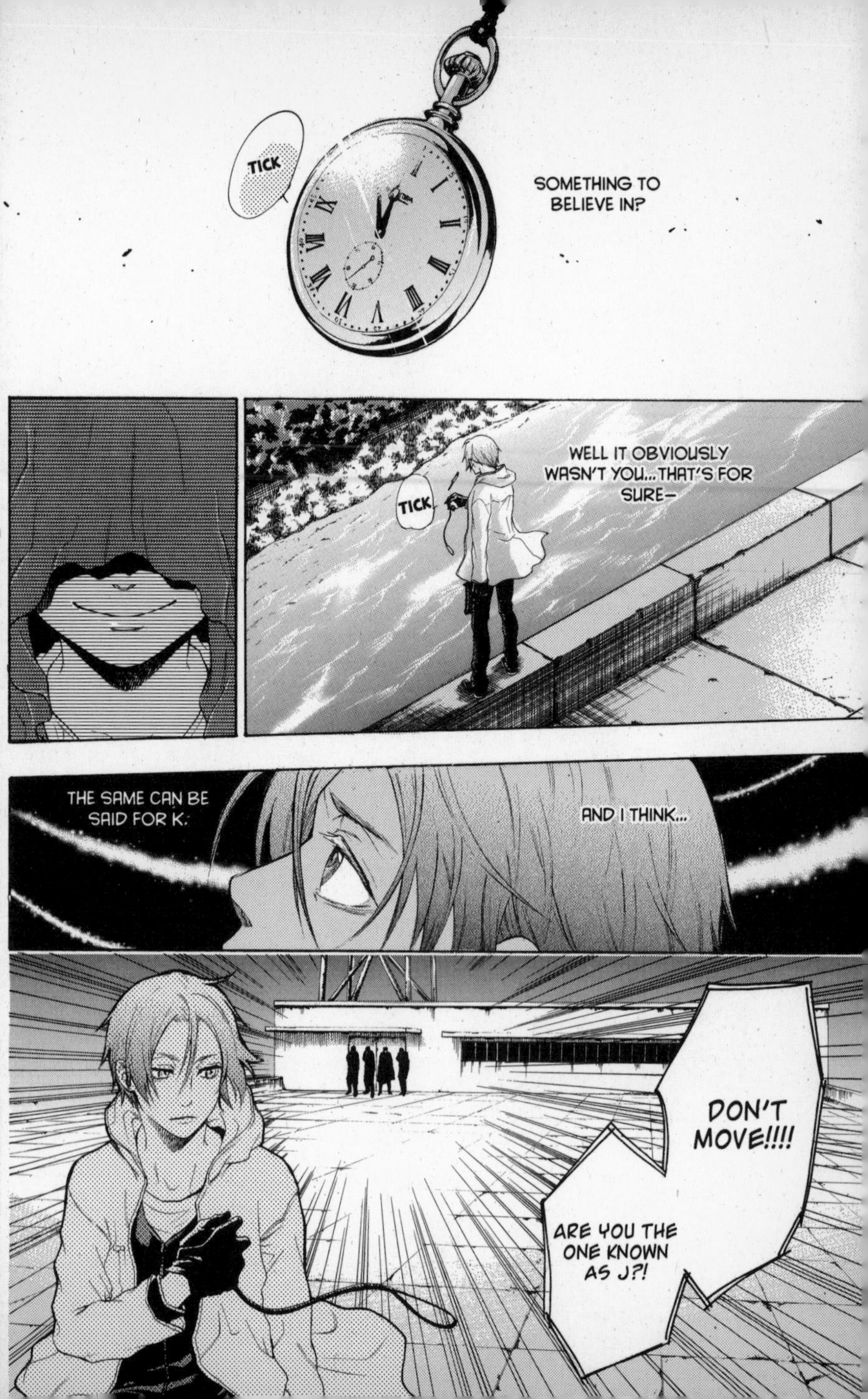
SOMETHING TO BELIEVE IN?
TICK
WELL IT OBVIOUSLY WASN'T YOU... THAT'S FOR SURE—
TICK
AND I THINK...
THE SAME CAN BE SAID FOR K.
DON'T MOVE!!!!
ARE YOU THE ONE KNOWN AS J?!

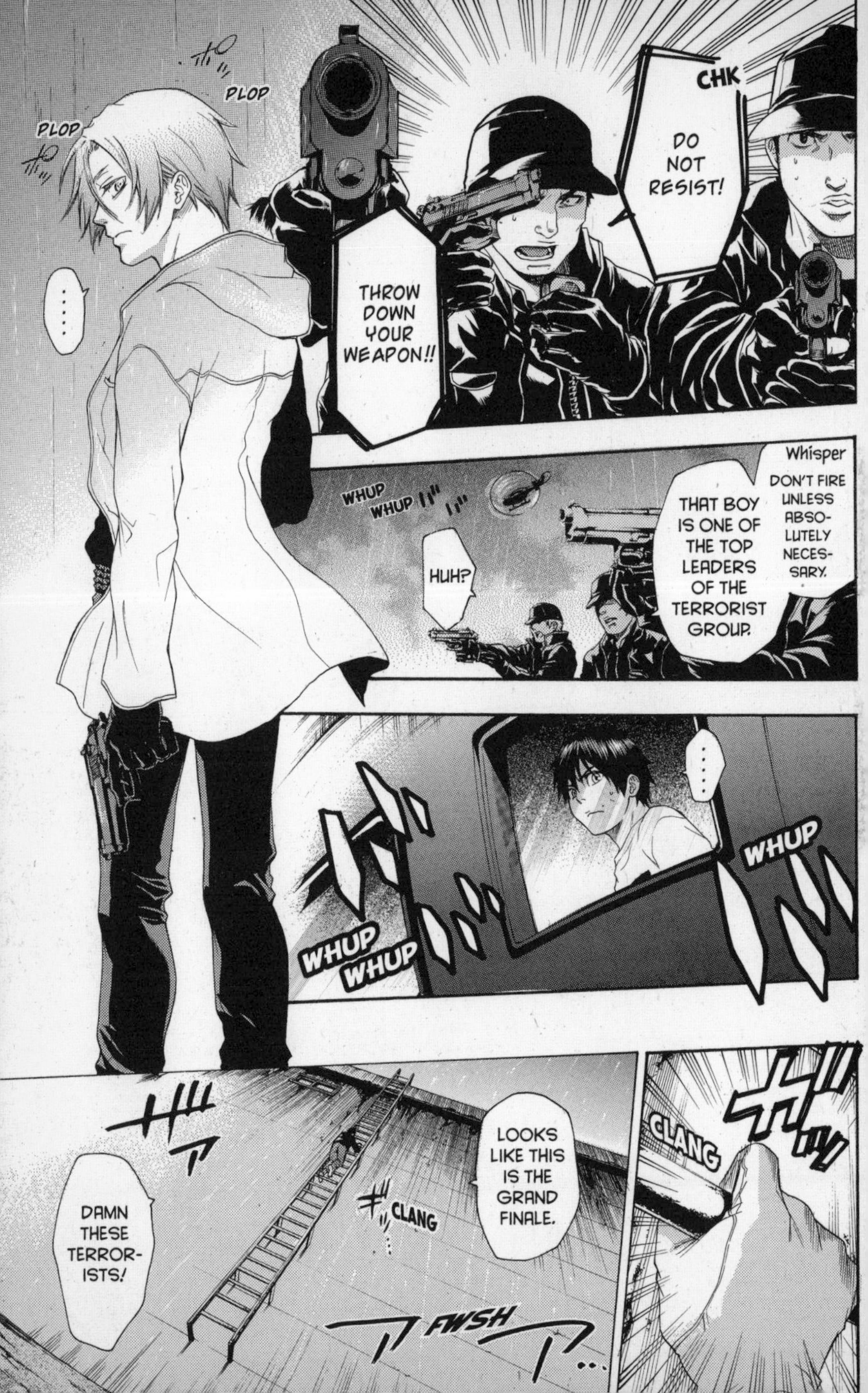
CHK
DO NOT RESIST!
THROW DOWN YOUR WEAPON!!
Whisper
DON'T FIRE UNLESS ABSOLUTELY NECESSARY.
THAT BOY IS ONE OF THE TOP LEADERS OF THE TERRORIST GROUP.
HUH?
WHUP WHUP
......
WHUP
WHUP WHUP
PLOP
PLOP
......
CLANG
LOOKS LIKE THIS IS THE GRAND FINALE.
CLANG
DAMN THESE TERRORISTS!
FWSH

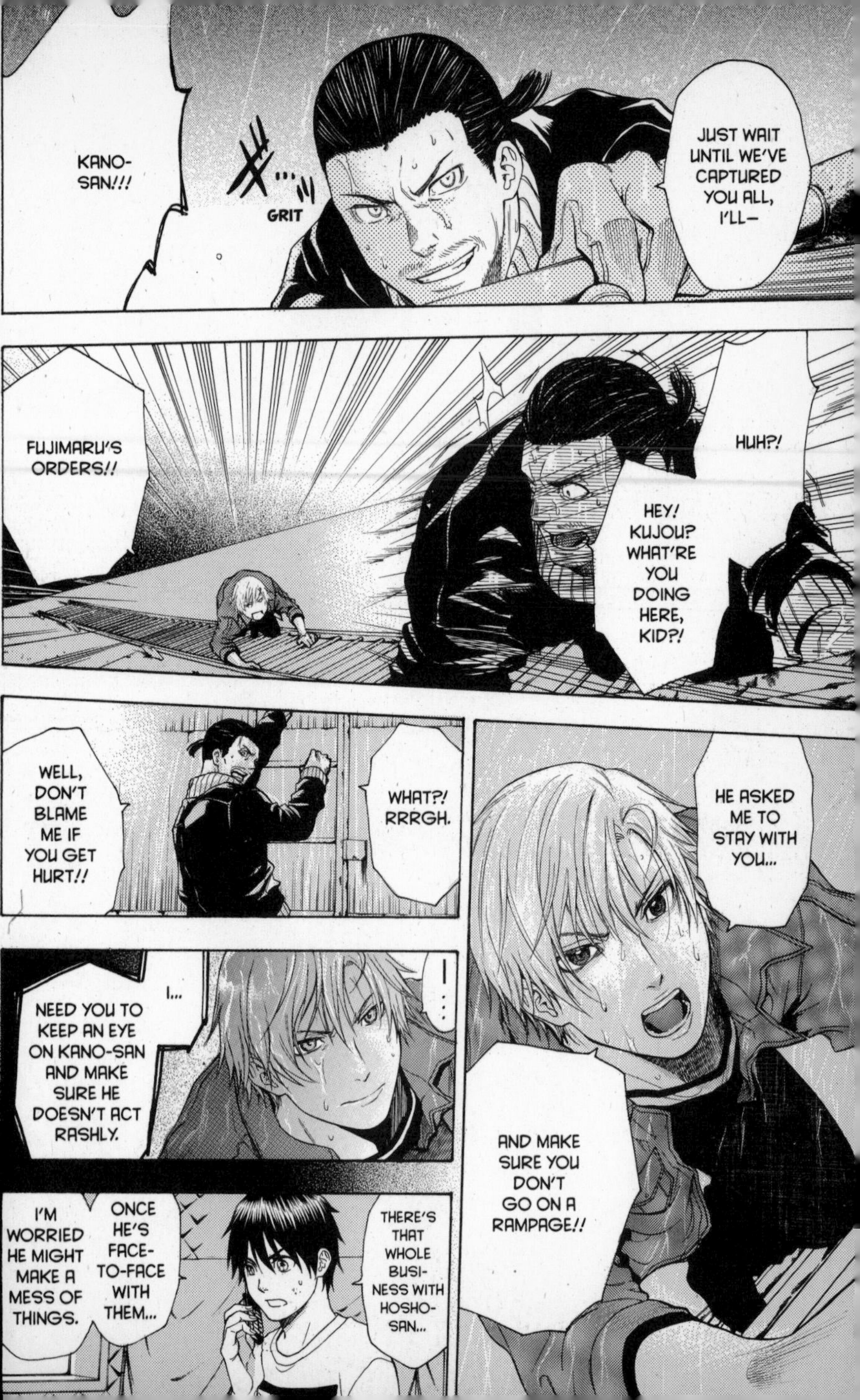
JUST WAIT UNTIL WE'VE CAPTURED YOU ALL, I'LL—
GRIT
KANO-SAN!!!
HUH?!
HEY! KUJOU? WHAT'RE YOU DOING HERE, KID?!
FUJIMARU'S ORDERS!!
HE ASKED ME TO STAY WITH YOU...
AND MAKE SURE YOU DON'T GO ON A RAMPAGE!!
WHAT?! RRRGH.
WELL, DON'T BLAME ME IF YOU GET HURT!!
I...
NEED YOU TO KEEP AN EYE ON KANO-SAN AND MAKE SURE HE DOESN'T ACT RASHLY.
THERE'S THAT WHOLE BUSINESS WITH HOSHO-SAN...
ONCE HE'S FACE-TO-FACE WITH THEM...
I'M WORRIED HE MIGHT MAKE A MESS OF THINGS.

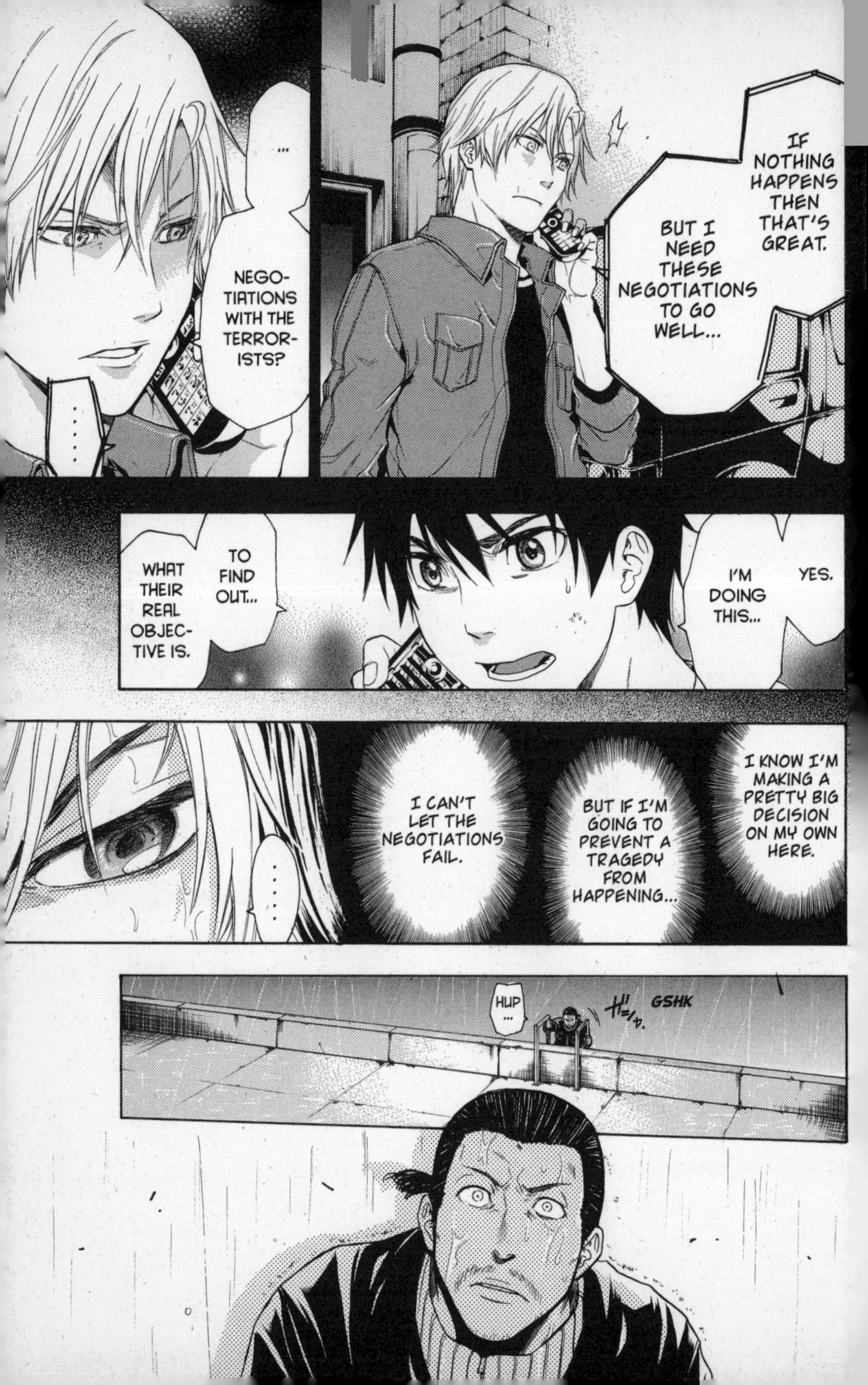
IF NOTHING HAPPENS THEN THAT'S GREAT.
BUT I NEED THESE NEGOTIATIONS TO GO WELL...
...
NEGO-TIATIONS WITH THE TERROR-ISTS?
......
YES.
I'M DOING THIS...
TO FIND OUT...
WHAT THEIR REAL OBJEC-TIVE IS.
I KNOW I'M MAKING A PRETTY BIG DECISION ON MY OWN HERE.
BUT IF I'M GOING TO PREVENT A TRAGEDY FROM HAPPENING...
I CAN'T LET THE NEGOTIATIONS FAIL.
.....
GSHK
HUP...

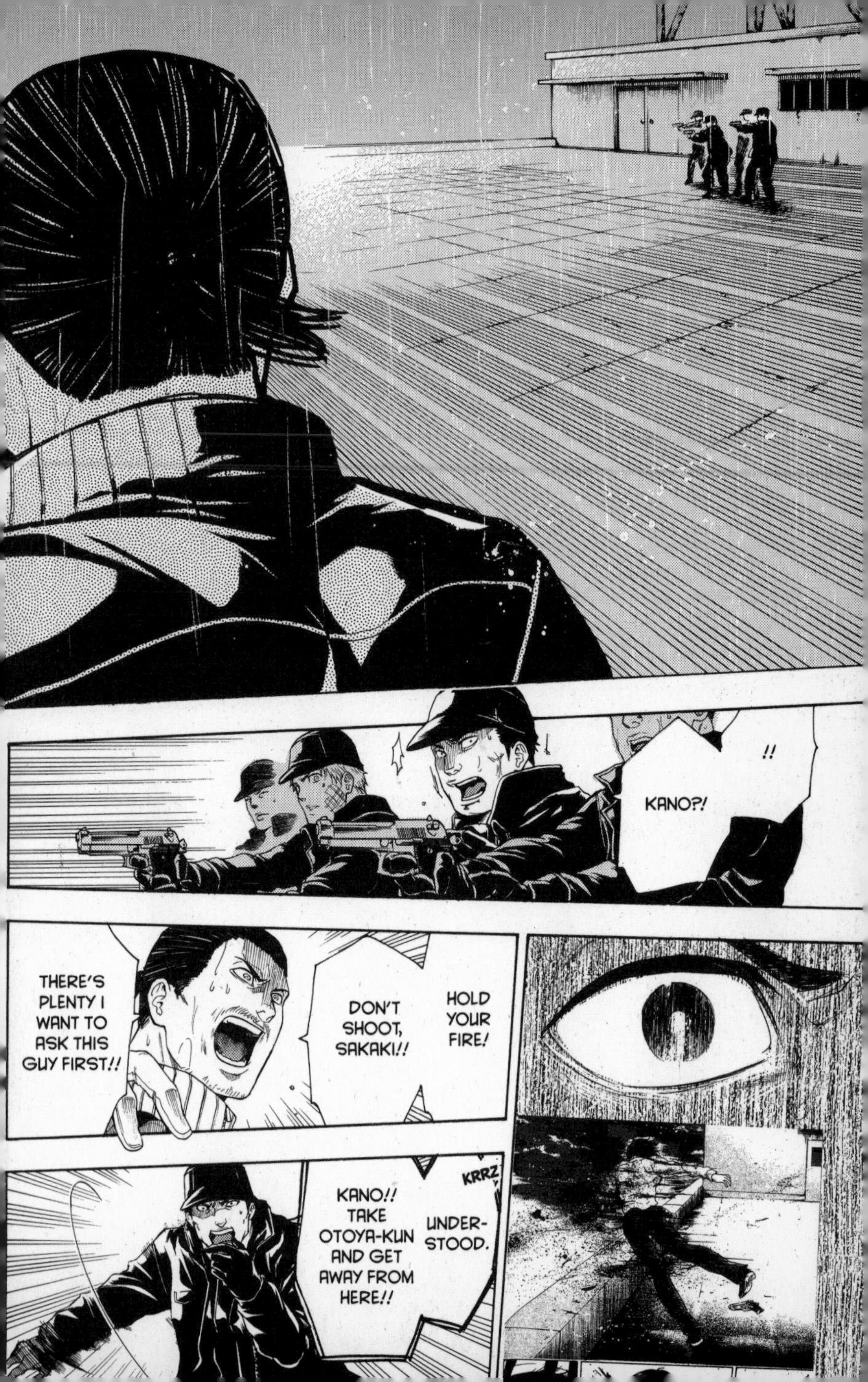
!!
KANO?!
HOLD YOUR FIRE!
DON'T SHOOT, SAKAKI!!
THERE'S PLENTY I WANT TO ASK THIS GUY FIRST!!
KRRZ
UNDER-STOOD.
KANO!! TAKE OTOYA-KUN AND GET AWAY FROM HERE!!

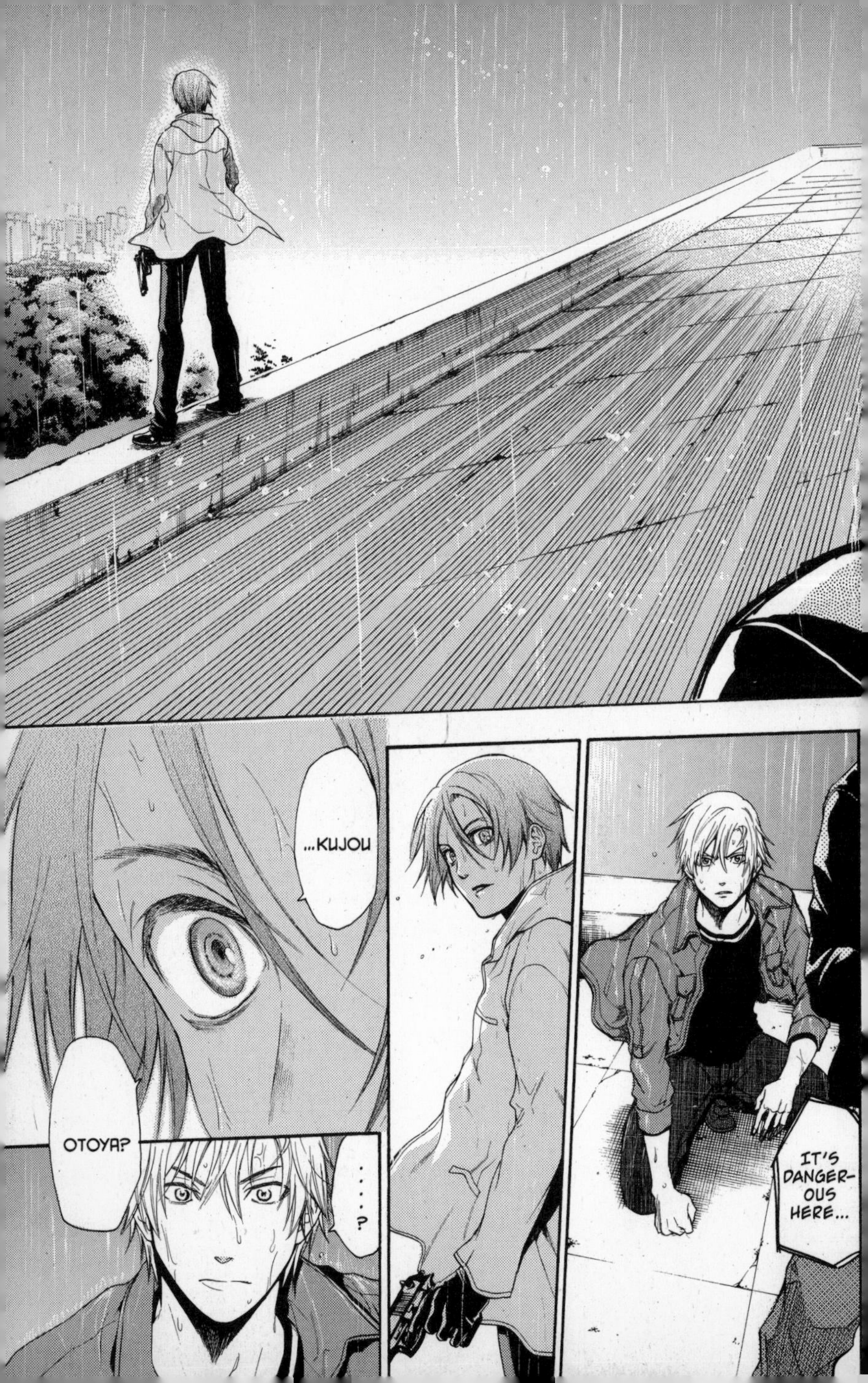
IT'S DANGER-OUS HERE...
...KUJOU
OTOYA?
....?

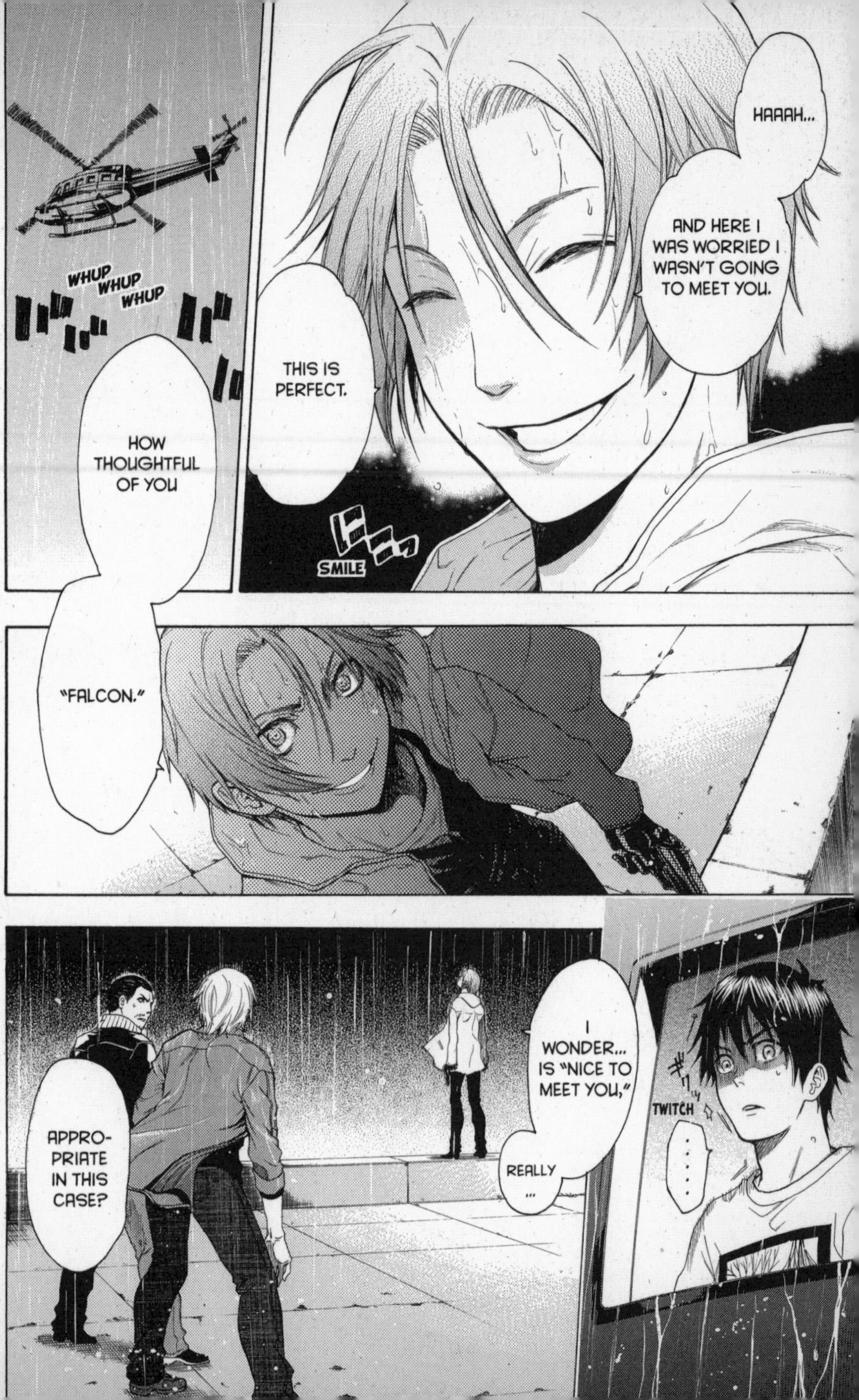
HAAAH...
AND HERE I WAS WORRIED I WASN'T GOING TO MEET YOU.
THIS IS PERFECT.
SMILE
WHUP WHUP WHUP
HOW THOUGHTFUL OF YOU
"FALCON."
TWITCH
......
I WONDER... IS "NICE TO MEET YOU,"
REALLY ...
APPRO-PRIATE IN THIS CASE?

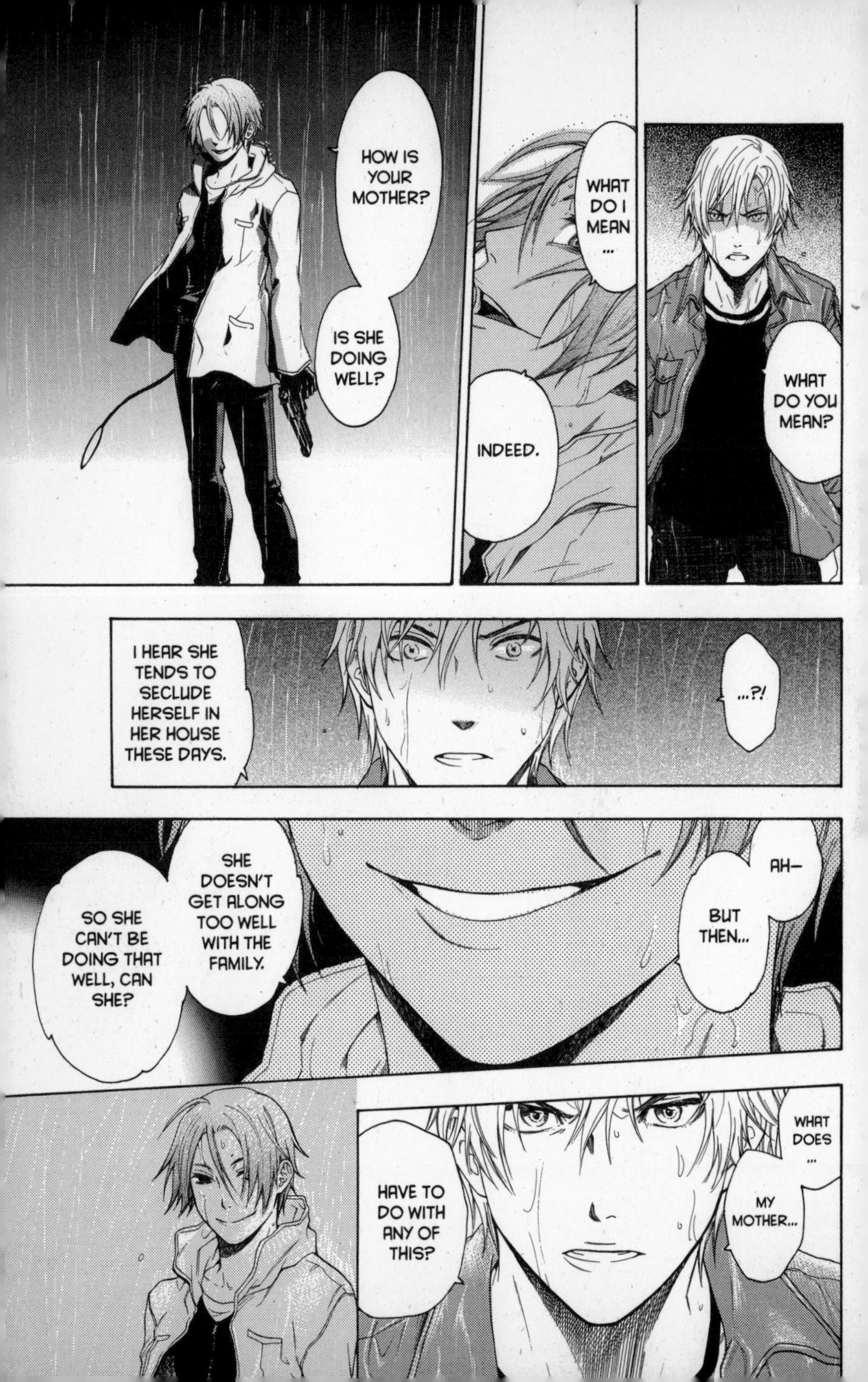
WHAT DO YOU MEAN?
WHAT DO I MEAN ...
INDEED.
HOW IS YOUR MOTHER?
IS SHE DOING WELL?
...?!
I HEAR SHE TENDS TO SECLUDE HERSELF IN HER HOUSE THESE DAYS.
AH—
BUT THEN...
SHE DOESN'T GET ALONG TOO WELL WITH THE FAMILY.
SO SHE CAN'T BE DOING THAT WELL, CAN SHE?
WHAT DOES ...
MY MOTHER...
HAVE TO DO WITH ANY OF THIS?

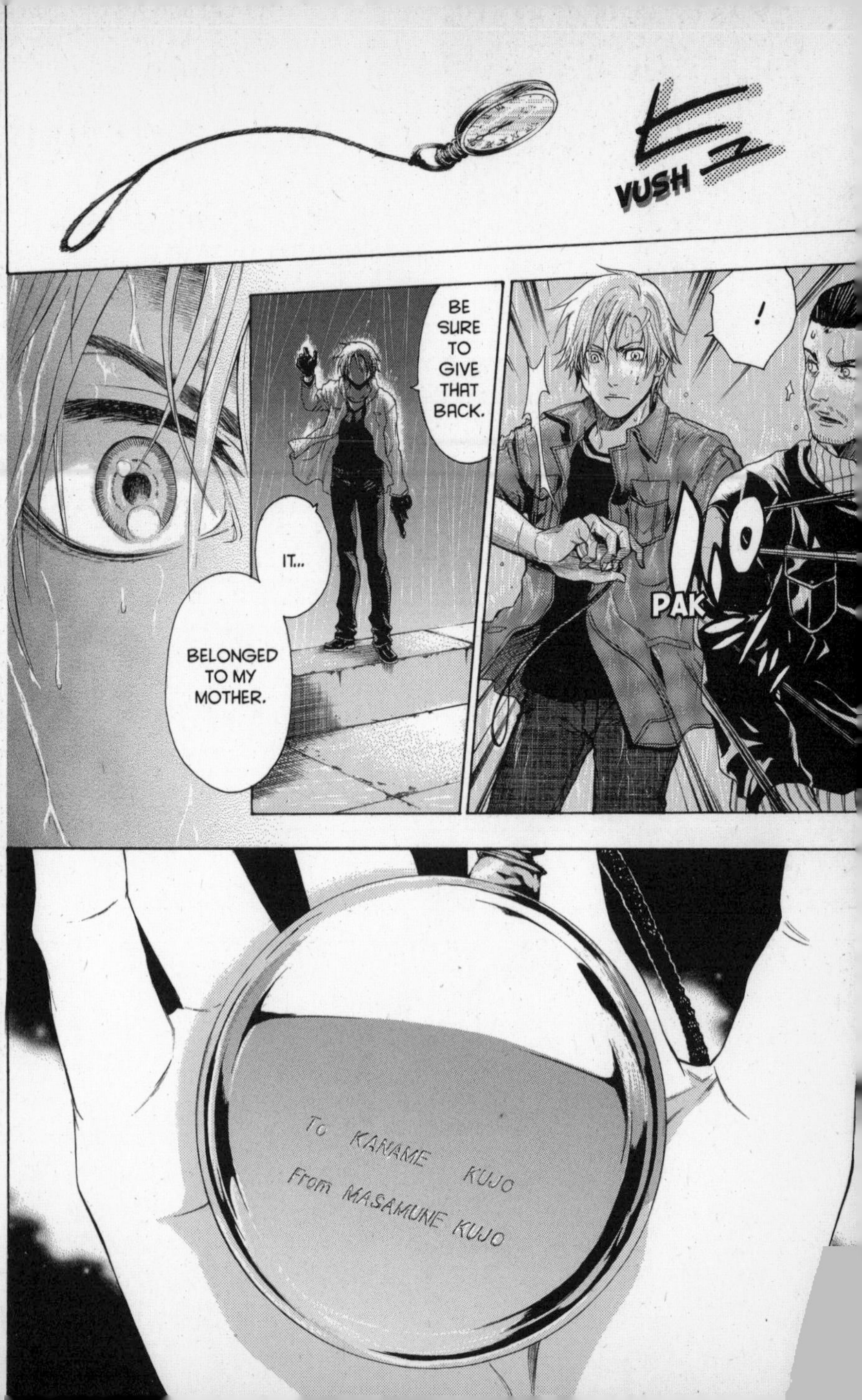
VUSH
!
PAK
BE SURE TO GIVE THAT BACK.
IT...
BELONGED TO MY MOTHER.
To KANAME KUJO
From MASAMUNE KUJO

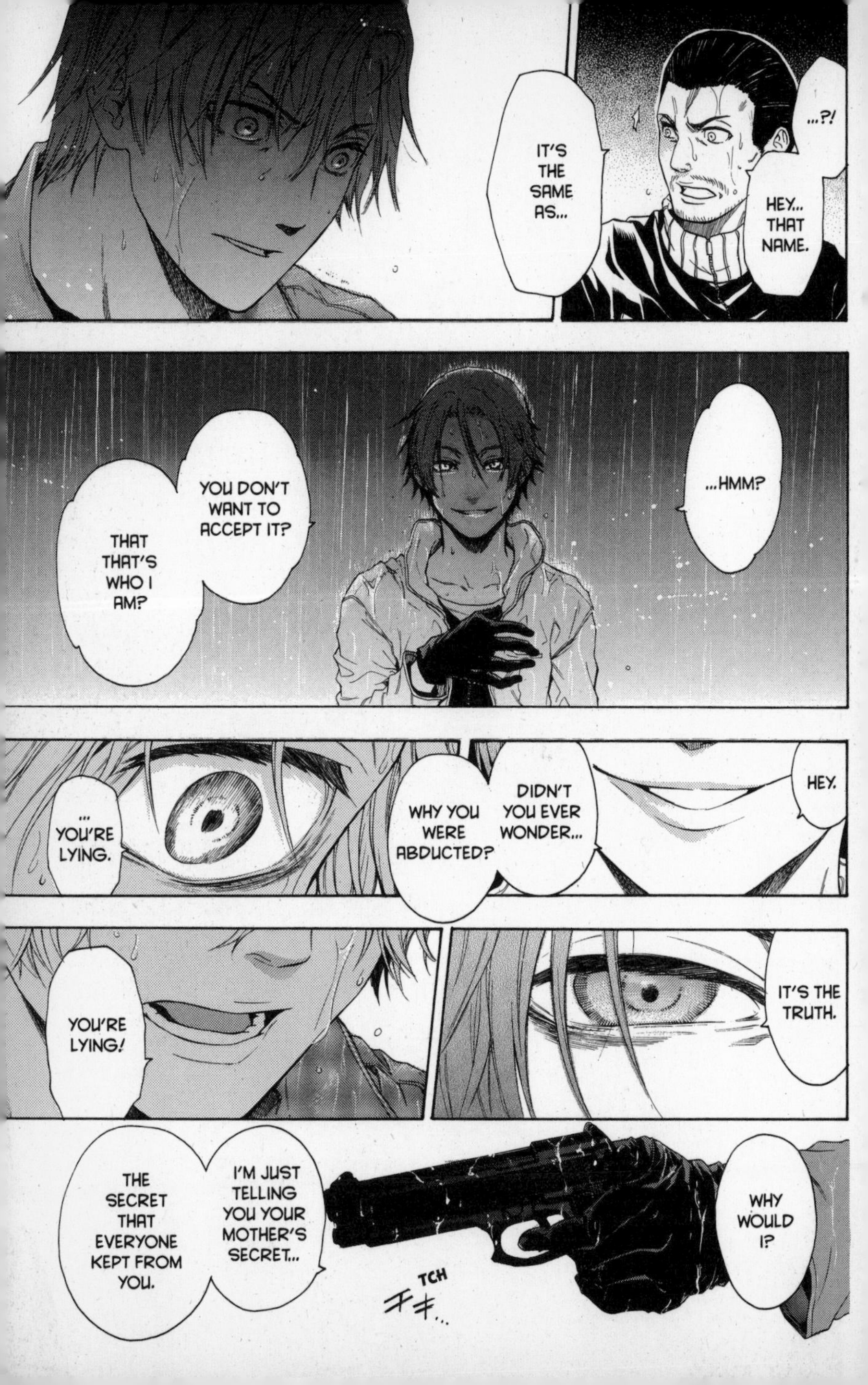

...?!
HEY... THAT NAME.
IT'S THE SAME AS...
...HMM?
YOU DON'T WANT TO ACCEPT IT?
THAT THAT'S WHO I AM?
HEY.
DIDN'T YOU EVER WONDER...
WHY YOU WERE ABDUCTED?
... YOU'RE LYING.
IT'S THE TRUTH.
YOU'RE LYING!
WHY WOULD I?
TCH
チキ...
I'M JUST TELLING YOU YOUR MOTHER'S SECRET...
THE SECRET THAT EVERYONE KEPT FROM YOU.

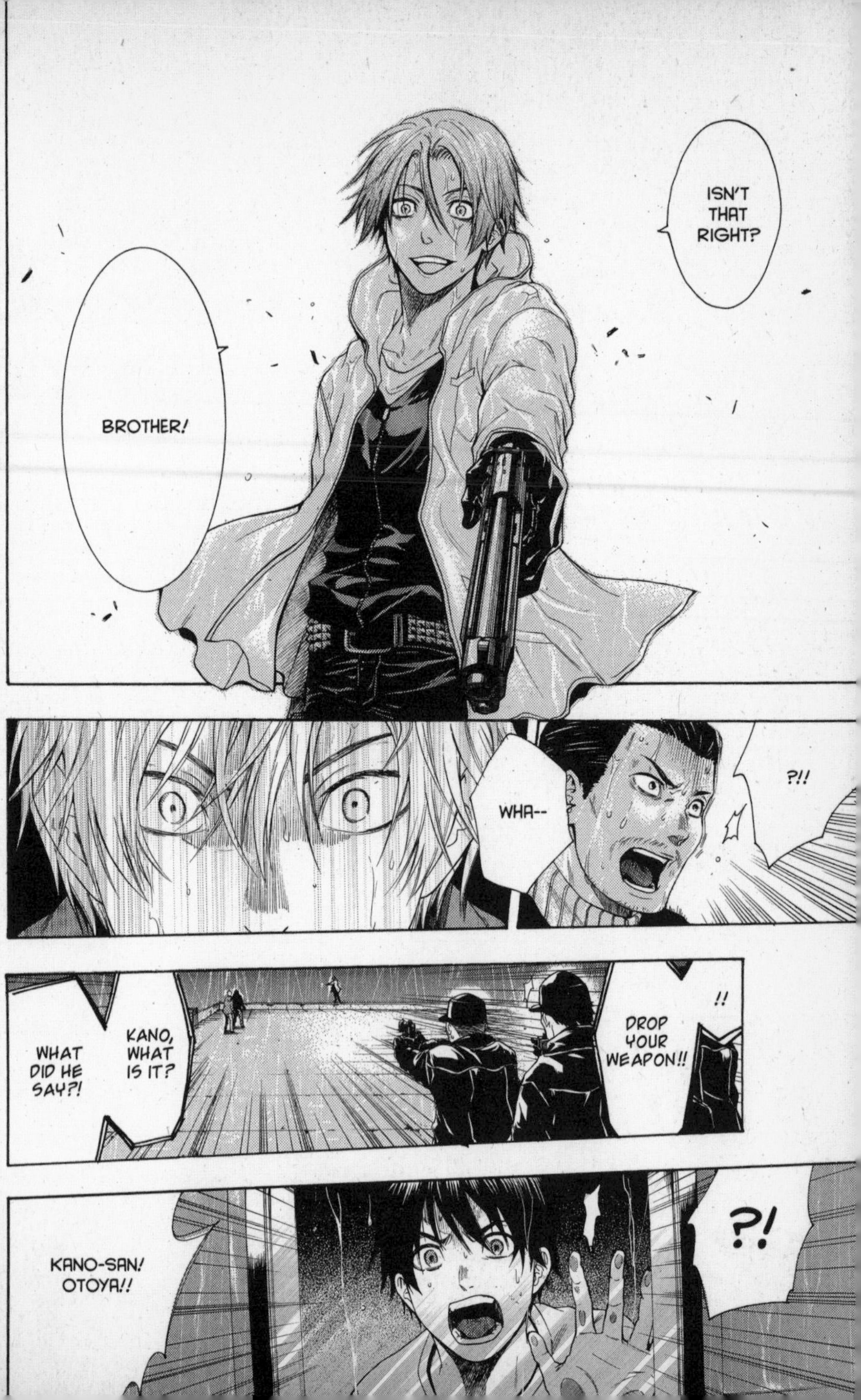
ISN'T THAT RIGHT?
BROTHER!
?!!
WHA--
!!
DROP YOUR WEAPON!!
KANO, WHAT IS IT?
WHAT DID HE SAY?!
?!
KANO-SAN! OTOYA!!

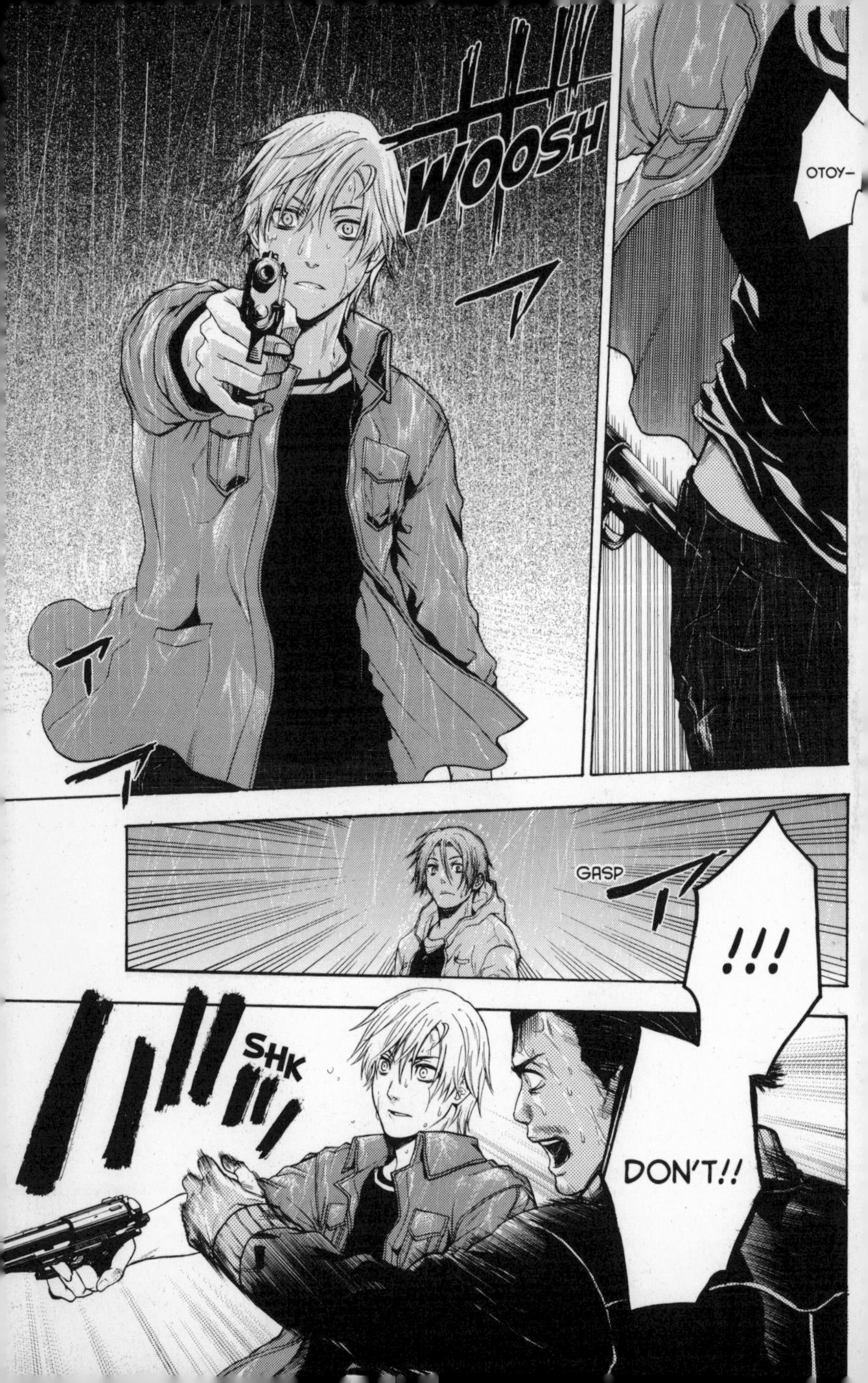
OTOY–
WOOSH
!!!
GASP
SHK
DON'T!!

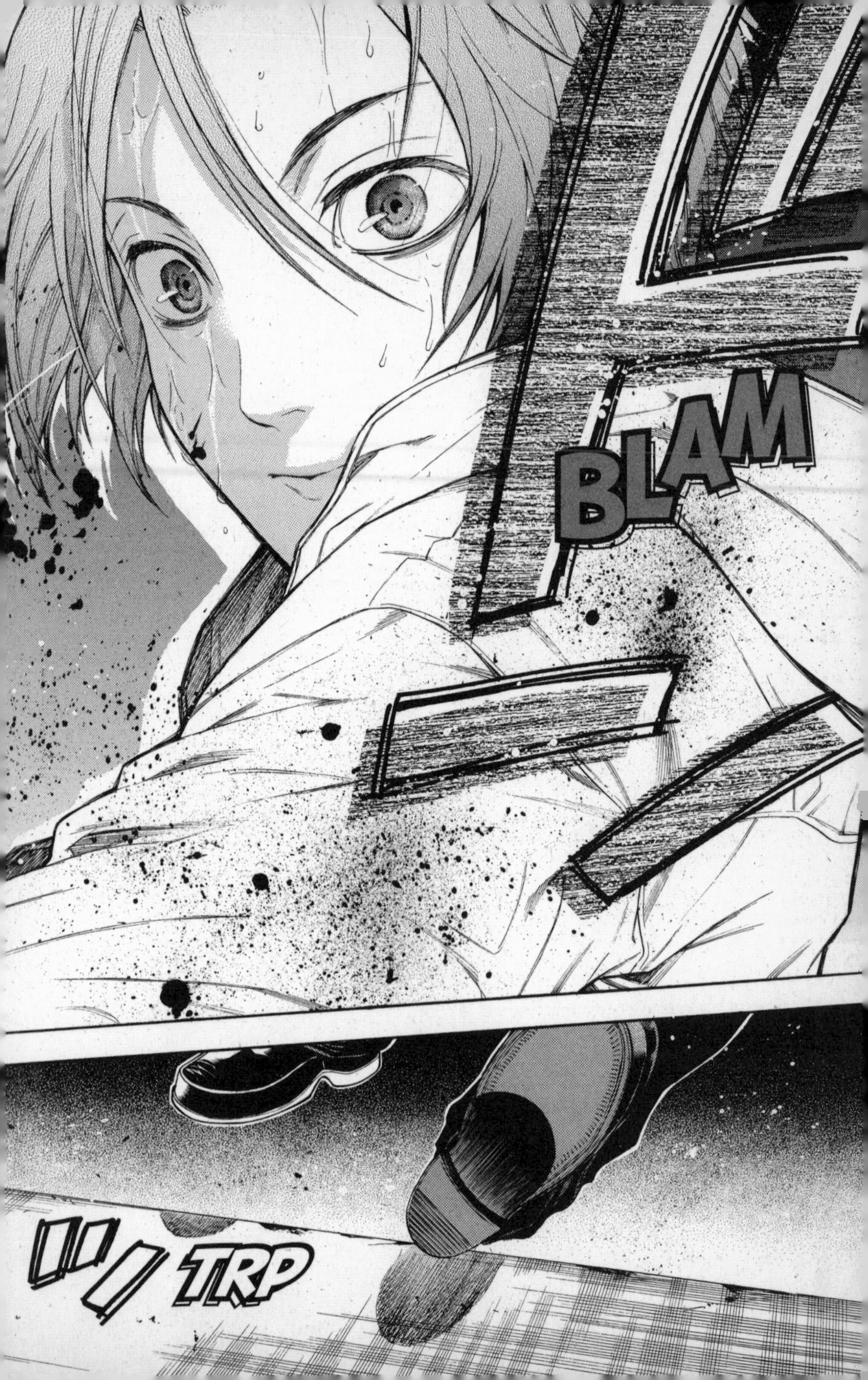
BLAM
TRP

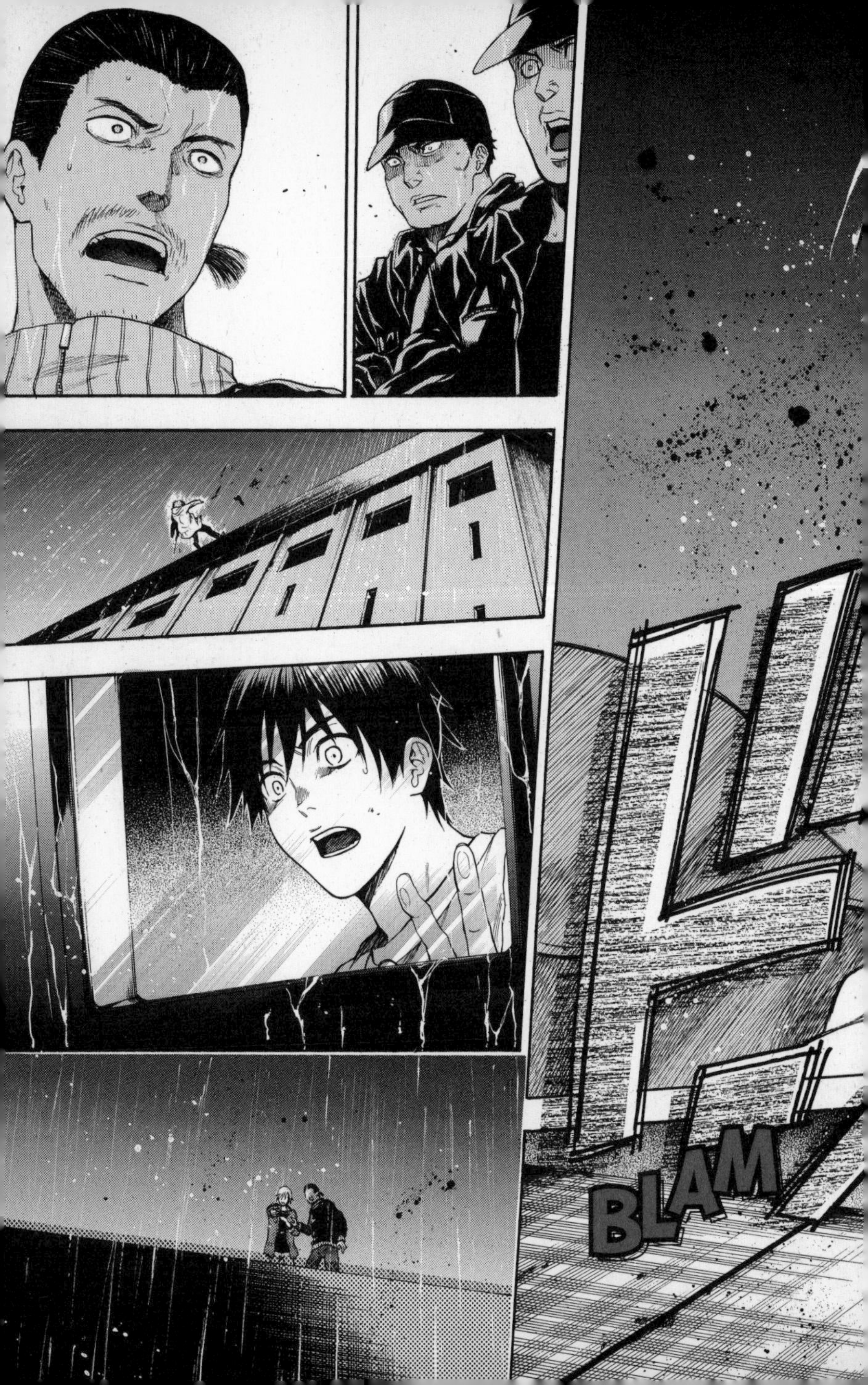
BLAM

THE NAMES...

CAIN AND ABEL...

NOW—

YOU SEE?

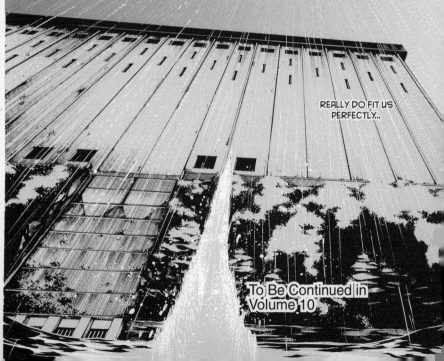

REALLY DO FIT US PERFECTLY...

To Be Continued in Volume 10

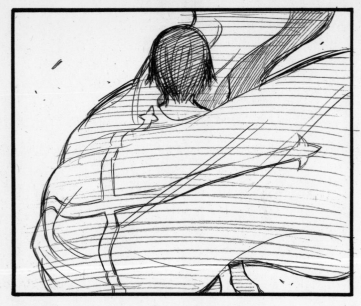

❦ BLOODY MONDAY 9 ❦

Many thanks.

Daiwa Mitsu   Kawabata Kunihiro   Chugun Kazushi
Sawai Takuji   Osaka Machiko   Kusunoki Rie

Editorial

Sato-san   Kawakubo-san

Manga

Ryumon Ryou X Megumi Kouji

THANK YOU FOR READING.

Comics! Bonus Terrorist

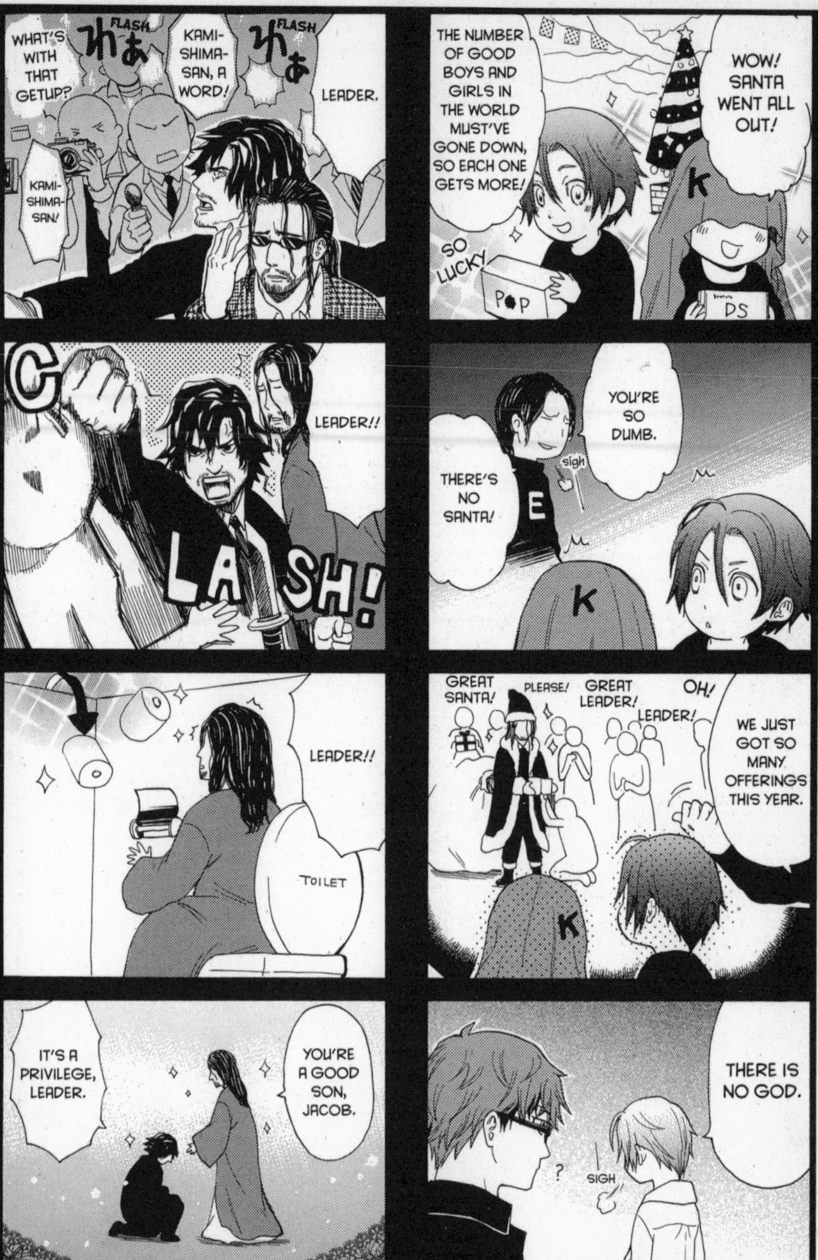
WOW! SANTA WENT ALL OUT!
THE NUMBER OF GOOD BOYS AND GIRLS IN THE WORLD MUST'VE GONE DOWN, SO EACH ONE GETS MORE!
SO LUCKY
YOU'RE SO DUMB.
sigh
THERE'S NO SANTA!
OH!
WE JUST GOT SO MANY OFFERINGS THIS YEAR.
LEADER!
GREAT LEADER!
PLEASE!
GREAT SANTA!
THERE IS NO GOD.
SIGH
?
LEADER.
FLASH
KAMI-SHIMA-SAN, A WORD!
FLASH
WHAT'S WITH THAT GETUP?
KAMI-SHIMA-SAN!
LEADER!!
CLASH!
LEADER!!
TOILET
YOU'RE A GOOD SON, JACOB.
IT'S A PRIVILEGE, LEADER.

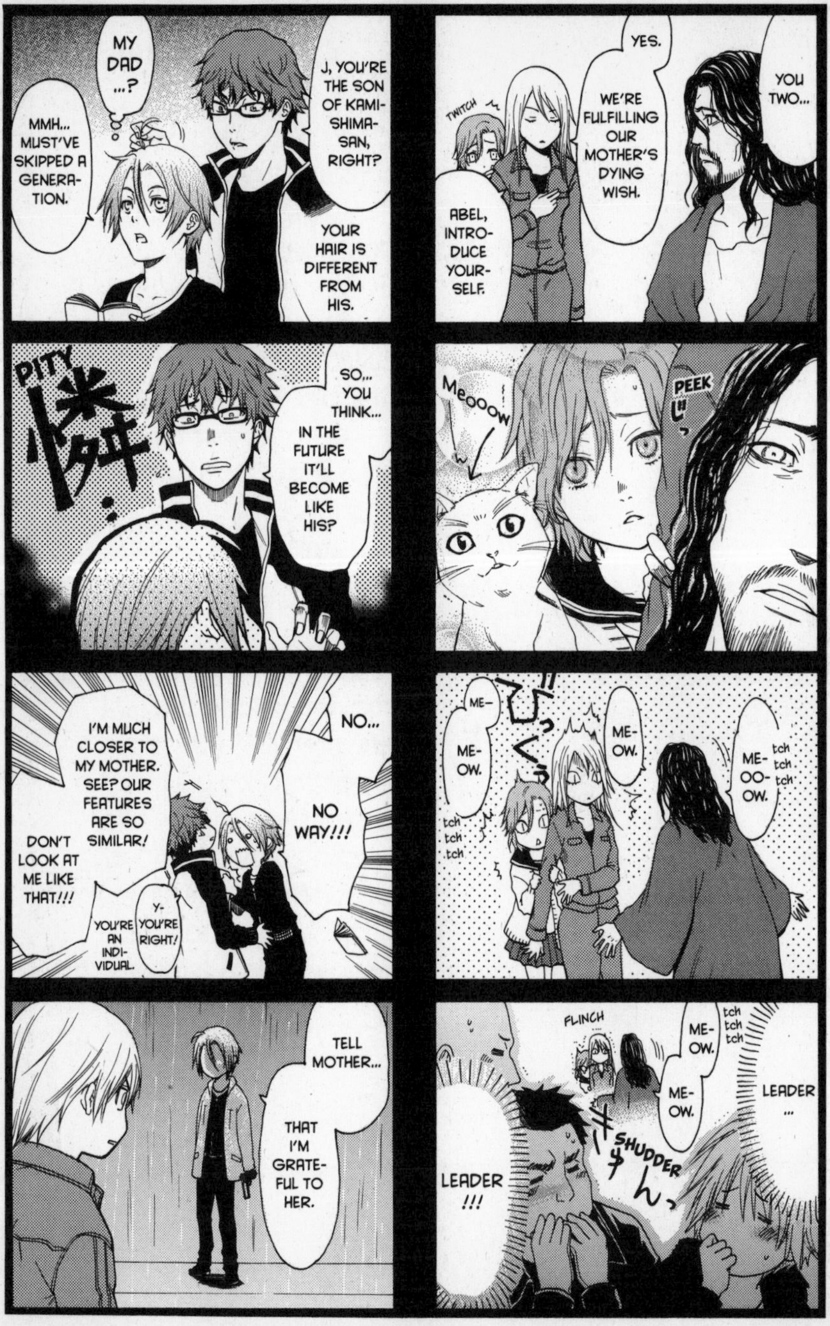
YOU TWO...
YES.
WE'RE FULFILLING OUR MOTHER'S DYING WISH.
TWITCH
ABEL, INTRODUCE YOURSELF.
J, YOU'RE THE SON OF KAMI-SHIMA-SAN, RIGHT?
YOUR HAIR IS DIFFERENT FROM HIS.
MY DAD ...?
MMH... MUST'VE SKIPPED A GENERA-TION.
PEEK
Meooow
SO... YOU THINK... IN THE FUTURE IT'LL BECOME LIKE HIS?
PITY
ME-OO-OW.
tch tch tch
ME-OW.
ME-
ME-OW.
tch tch tch
NO...
NO WAY!!!
I'M MUCH CLOSER TO MY MOTHER. SEE? OUR FEATURES ARE SO SIMILAR!
DON'T LOOK AT ME LIKE THAT!!!
Y- YOU'RE RIGHT!
YOU'RE AN INDI-VIDUAL.
LEADER ...
ME-OW.
tch tch tch
ME-OW.
FLINCH
SHUDDER
LEADER !!!
TELL MOTHER...
THAT I'M GRATE-FUL TO HER.

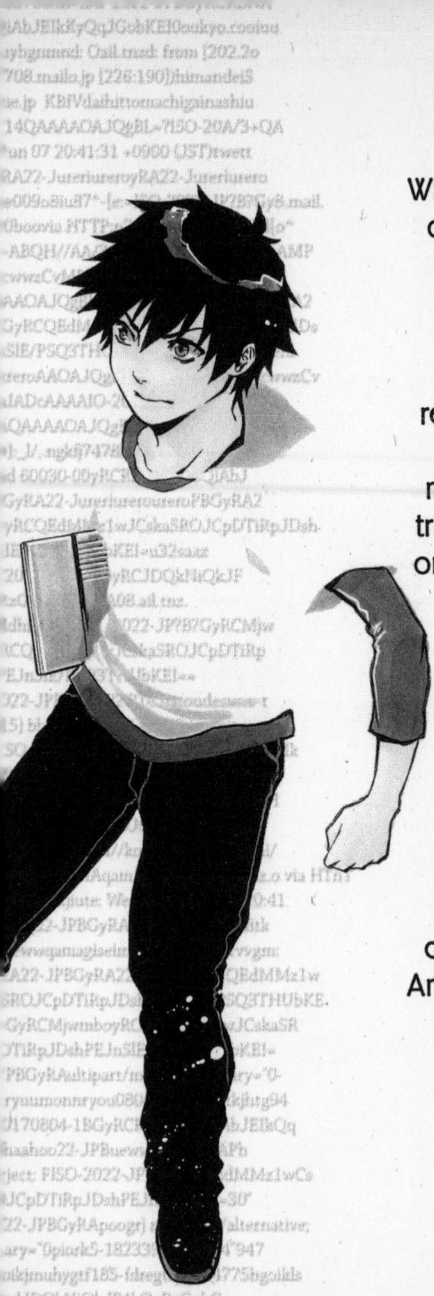

Author's Notes:

Windows' next generation operating system seems to be pretty simple compared to Vista. By sacrificing performance, they've managed to reduce both the size and the price of the trendy mini-laptops. But all this trimming of excess going on in the world is making me feel a bit sad.

-Ryumon.

So in this volume we make it rain in the last chapter. Rain is good. A gentle drizzle will set a somber mood while a raging downpour will convey strong emotions. And, I feel, somehow very showy. Rain is good.

-Megumi.

A Kodansha Comics Trade Paperback Original.

Bloody Monday volume 9 copyright © 2008 Ryou Ryumon & Kouji Megumi
English translation copyright © 2013 Ryou Ryumon & Kouji Megumi

Published in the United States by Kodansha Comics, an imprint of Kodansha USA Publishing, LLC, New York.

Publication rights for this English edition arranged through Kodansha Ltd., Tokyo.

First published in Japan in 2008 by Kodansha Ltd., Tokyo,,
ISBN 978-1-61262-045-9

Printed in the United States of America.

www.kodanshacomics.com

9 8 7 6 5 4 3 2 1

Translator: Sebastian Girner
Lettering: Christy Sawyer

TOMARE!
[STOP!]

You are going the wrong way!

Manga is a completely different type of reading experience.

To start at the *beginning*, go to the *end*!

That's right! Authentic manga is read the traditional Japanese way—from right to left, exactly the opposite of how American books are read. It's easy to follow: just go to the other end of the book, and read each page—and each panel—from the right side to the left side, starting at the top right. Now you're experiencing manga as it was meant to be.